Ethics and
the Elderly

Ethics and
the Elderly

Mark R. Wicclair

New York   Oxford
OXFORD UNIVERSITY PRESS
1993

Oxford University Press

Oxford   New York   Toronto
Delhi   Bombay   Calcutta   Madras   Karachi
Kuala Lumpur   Singapore   Hong Kong   Tokyo
Nairobi   Dar es Salaam   Cape Town
Melbourne   Auckland   Madrid

and associated companies in
Berlin   Ibadan

Published by Oxford University Press, Inc.,
200 Madison Avenue, New York, New York 10016

Oxford is a registered trademark of Oxford University Press

Library of Congress Cataloging-in-Publication Data
Wicclair, Mark R.
Ethics and the elderly / Mark R. Wicclair.
p. cm.   Includes bibliographical references and index.
ISBN 0-19-505315-X
1. Aged—Medical care—Moral and ethical aspects.
2. Aged—Care—Moral and ethical aspects.   I. Title.
[DNLM: 1. Decision Making—in old age. 2. Ethics, Medical.
3. Life Support Care—in old age. WT 104 W633e]
RA564.8.W49 1993
174'.2—dc20   DNLM/DLC
for Library of Congress   92–49054

2 4 6 8 9 7 5 3 1

Printed in the United States of America
on acid-free paper

To my Parents,
Germaine and Walter,
and my Son, David

Preface

Aging of the population is a universal phenomenon that affects both developed and developing countries.[1] In the United States, the number of elderly persons (i.e., persons 65 and older), the median age, and the proportion of the population that is elderly, are all increasing. In a twenty-eight-year interval from 1960 to 1988, the number of persons 65 years and over in the United States rose from 16,675,000 to 30,367,000, a growth of over 82 percent.[2] During the same period, the median age increased from 29.4 years to 32.3 years.[3] It is estimated that the median age in the United States will be 36 years by the year 2000 and 43 years by the year 2040.[4] In contrast, only 4 percent of the American population had reached 65 years of age by 1900.[5] By 1960, however, persons 65 years and older comprised 9.2 percent of the population; and by 1988, the percentage of the population that was 65 years or older had risen to 12.3 percent.[6] The projected percentage of the population that will be 65 years or older in 2050 is 22.9 percent, and the corresponding estimate for 2080 is 24.5 percent.[7]

The phenomenon of population aging is also affecting the subpopulation of elderly persons. Whereas 21.1 percent of persons 65 and over were at least 80 years old in 1985, it is projected that 37.4 percent of elderly persons will be 80 or older by 2080.[8] Moreover, whereas the median age of persons 65 and over was 71.9 years in 1960 and 73.1 years in 1987, it is projected to reach 76.4 years in 2080.[9]

The aging of the population in the United States is associated with significant changes in birth and mortality rates. Even if there are no changes in life expectancy, a population can age if the number of births decreases.[10] The number of births decreased from the time of the Great Depression to World

War II and again after the post-war baby boom.[11] The effect of these decreases in birth rates was heightened by an increase in the annual number of
births before 1920 and again after World War II during the baby boom
period.[12] Besides significant fluctuations in birth rates, there have also been
important changes in life expectancy. From 1900 to 1987, life expectancy at
birth grew from 47.3 years to 75 years.[13] Although much of this increase in
life expectancy at birth is attributable to improvements in survival during
infancy and early childhood, life expectancy has also increased for the elderly. The life expectancy of people who reached age 65 in 1900 was 11.9
years, but it had increased to 16.9 years by 1987.[14] The projection for 2080 is
18.8 years for men at 65 years and 23.9 years for women at 65 years.[15]

As the population continues to age, the frequency, urgency, and complexity of ethical questions about the elderly will continue to increase. Several
important ethical isues involve health care. As the well-known cases of
Karen Ann Quinlan, Nancy Cruzan, and "Baby Doe" demonstrate, the
question of forgoing life-sustaining treatment is not unique to elderly patients. Nevertheless, elderly persons are hospitalized more than three times
as often as younger persons, and the probability of suffering from a chronic
illness increases rapidly with age.[16] Accordingly, although it is not unique to
older patients, the issue of forgoing life-sustaining treatment is likely to arise
more frequently in relation to them.

Shared decision-making, the principle that decision-making should be a
collaborative activity between physicians and patients, is a recognized "first
principle" of health care decision-making generally, and there is no good
reason to exempt decisions about life-sustaining treatment for elderly patients. However, the shared decision-making model is directly applicable to
elderly patients only when they possess decision-making capacity. Accordingly, it is necessary to analyze the notion of this capacity. Since elderly
patients often have family (for example, spouses and adult children), it is
also important to consider the role of family members when elderly patients
possess decision-making capacity and when they do not. In addition, since
there is growing support for the position that physicians may *unilaterally*
decide that medical interventions are "futile" and withhold them without the
consent of patients or family, it is imperative to examine the notion of
"medical futility" and its relation to shared decision-making. These and
other issues related to elderly patients with decision-making capacity are
examined in Chapter 1.

Decision-making about life-sustaining treatment poses special ethical
problems when patients lack decision-making capacity. The three cases cited
above, Karen Ann Quinlan, Nancy Cruzan, and "Baby Doe," illustrate that
the problem of decision-making for patients who lack decision-making capacity is not unique to elderly patients. However, many of the diseases and

conditions that can make continued life contingent on life-prolonging measures can also destroy or substantially impair a person's decision-making capacity and are more likely to strike people in their later years. In addition, Alzheimer's disease and other dementing illnesses are more likely to be experienced by older persons. One estimate is that 5–7 percent of persons over 65, and 25 percent of those over 84, suffer from severe dementia.[17] Accordingly, the problem of decision-making for patients who lack decision-making capacity is likely to arise more frequently in relation to the elderly. Several ethical issues associated with decision-making about life-sustaining treatment for elderly patients who lack decision-making capacity are examined in Chapter 2. The proper scope and function of advance directives, standards for surrogate decision-making, and the propriety of continuing treatment for the sake of family members are among the topics discussed.

There is growing concern about the steadily rising cost of health care in the United States. One response, exemplified by the Oregon Health Plan, has been to propose the rationing of health care. While the average number of visits to a physician each year is five among the general population, elderly persons visit a physician an average of eight times a year.[18] In addition, elderly persons are hospitalized more than three times as often as younger people, stay 50 percent longer, and use twice as many prescription drugs.[19] Thus, it is to be expected that the demand for health care services will increase as the population ages, and it is not surprising that some advocates of health care rationing have proposed rationing *by age*. Several defenses of age-rationing are critically examined in Chapter 3. Particular attention is paid to two questions: (1) whether age-rationing comprises ageism or age bias, and (2) whether age-rationing is unjust.

Because people who either are, or are thought to be, cognitively impaired are more likely to be treated paternalistically, it is to be expected that elderly persons will be prime targets for paternalistic treatment. On the one hand, because of a variety of conditions that are more frequent in old age—among them, stroke, arteriosclerosis, and Alzheimer's disease—older adults are more likely to suffer some form of cognitive impairment than younger adults.[20] On the other hand, popular stereotypes encourage a presumption that elderly persons are mentally impaired or "senile."[21] In addition, because of the traditionally high social value ascribed to the medical profession, the current generation of the elderly may be especially inclined to expect and accept paternalistic treatment by professionals (e.g., physicians and social workers).[22] Accordingly, the aging of the population gives added urgency to an examination of paternalism toward the elderly, an issue that is explored in Chapter 4. The nature of paternalism, the distinction between "hard" and "soft" paternalism, and criteria for ethically evaluating paternalistic behavior toward elderly persons are discussed in Chapter 4.

The aging of the population also gives added urgency to an examination of research involving elderly subjects. As the number and proportion of elderly persons increases, there is likely to be more interest in conducting such research. Gerontological studies can have a variety of goals, from learning more about elderly persons and testing the effectiveness of programs designed to serve the elderly, to discovering ways to prevent or treat diseases and conditions that are more likely to strike elderly persons (e.g., Alzheimer's disease and hearing impairment). To achieve the goals of most such studies, *elderly* subjects are essential. However, even when the goals of research do not favor the use of elderly subjects, considerations of convenience may. For example, it may be more convenient to recruit residents of long-term care facilities, most of whom are elderly persons, than to recruit subjects living in the community. Research with elderly subjects is examined in Chapter 5. The chapter begins with an analysis of key concepts associated with research, including the distinction between research and practice and the distinction between "therapeutic" and "nontherapeutic" research. Then it explores ethical issues, focusing on informed consent in relation to the elderly and surrogate consent in relation to elderly persons without decision-making capacity.

It is a mistake to think of the elderly generally as sick and impaired. According to one study, 72.3 percent of non-institutionalized elderly persons described their health as "excellent," "very good," or "good," and only 27.6 percent described their health as "fair" or "poor."[23] Nevertheless, the same study indicated that in 1990, persons 65 and over experienced more than two and a half times the number of days of activity restriction due to acute and chronic conditions as persons between the ages of 25 and 44; and 37.5 percent of people 65 years and over experienced some activity limitation due to chronic conditions.[24] Another study showed that in 1990, 32 percent of people 65 and over who lived in the community had limitations in at least one of five activities of daily living.[25] Accordingly, as the population ages, more and more adult children will be confronted with difficult choices about their role in assisting impaired elderly parents. Chapter 6 examines the obligations of adult children to frail elderly parents.

This is a book in applied ethics, and its approach reflects a conviction that general ethical principles, such as the familiar principles of respect for autonomy, nonmaleficence, beneficence, and justice, provide a helpful framework for identifying and analyzing ethical problems.[26] However, it would be folly to suppose that answers to ethical questions can be "deduced" from abstract ethical principles or algorithms. To address the ethical issues dealt with in this book, it is essential to consider a variety of concrete situations and cases. This is one of the important insights of contemporary "casuistry."[27] To adapt a Kantian dictum, it might be said that cases without general principles are blind, and principles without cases are empty. Accordingly, although this book aims to provide general guidelines for addressing ethical questions involving the elderly, frequent use is made of examples, and each chapter ends with an extensive case analysis.

Notes

1. George C. Myers, "Demography of Aging," in Robert H. Binstock and Linda K. George, *Handbook of Aging and the Social Sciences,* 3rd ed. (San Diego: Academic Press, Inc., 1990), 19–44.

2. U.S. Department of Commerce, *Statistical Abstract of the United States 1990* (Washington, D.C.: U.S. Government Printing Office, 1990), 13.

3. *Statistical Abstract of the United States 1990,* 13.

4. U.S. Senate Special Committee on Aging, *Aging America: Trends and Projections,* 1991 Edition (Washington, D.C.: Department of Health and Human Services, Publication No. [FCoA] 91-28001, 1991), 6.

5. *Aging America,* 7.

6. *Statistical Abstract of the United States 1990,* 13.

7. U.S. Bureau of the Census, "Projections of the Population of the United States by Age, Sex, and Race: 1988 to 2080," *Current Population Reports,* Series P-25, No. 1018 (Washington, D.C.: U.S. Government Printing Office, 1989), 8. Three sets of projections are given: lowest series, middle series, and highest series. Each is based on different assumptions about future trends in fertility, mortality, and immigration. The figures cited here and below are from the middle series. These estimates are (much) too conservative according to researchers who deny that the current life span is close to a "natural limit." See "New Views on Life Spans Alter Forecasts on Elderly," *New York Times,* November 16, 1992, p. A1.

8. Myers, "Demography of Aging," 36.

9. "Projections of the Population of the United States by Age, Sex, and Race: 1988 to 2080," 9.

10. Christine K. Cassel and Jacob A. Brody, "Demography, Epidemiology, and Aging," in Christine K. Cassel et al., Eds., *Geriatric Medicine,* 2nd ed. (New York: Springer-Verlag, 1990), 16–27.

11. Dorothy P. Rice, "Demographic Realities and Projections of an Aging Population," in Spyros Andreopoulos and John R. Hogness, Eds., *Health Care for an Aging Society* (New York: Churchill Livingstone, 1989), 17–18; and *Statistical Abstract of the United States 1990,* 62.

12. *Aging America,* 4.

13. *Aging America,* 20.

14. *Aging America,* 20.

15. "Projections of the Population of the United States by Age, Sex, and Race: 1988 to 2080," 153.

16. *Aging America,* 123 and 112.

17. U.S. Congress, Office of Technology Assessment, *Losing a Million Minds: Confronting the Tragedy of Alzheimer's Disease and Other Dementias* (Washington, D.C.: U.S. Government Printing Office, April 1987), 15–16.

18. *Aging America,* 123.

19. *Aging America,* 123.

20. The Office of Technology Assessment report referred to above states that whereas only 1 percent of people between the ages of 65 to 74 experience severe dementia, 25 percent of people over the age of 85 suffer from it. *Losing a Million Minds*, 7.

21. See Mark H. Waymack and George A. Taler, *Medical Ethics and the Elderly: A Case Book* (Chicago: Pluribus Press, Inc., 1988), 29; and Thomas Halper, "The Double-Edged Sword: Paternalism as a Policy in the Problems of Aging," *Milbank Memorial Fund Quarterly/Health and Society* 58, no. 3 (1980): 473.

22. See Christine K. Cassel, "Research in Nursing Homes: Ethical Issues," *Journal of the American Geriatrics Society* 33, no. 11 (November 1985): 795–99.

23. U.S. Department of Health and Human Services, *Vital and Health Statistics: Current Estimates from the National Health Survey, 1990*, Series 10: Data from the National Health Survey, No. 181 (Hyattsville, MD: DHHS, Publication No. [PHS] 92-1509, December 1991), 112.

24. *Vital and Health Statistics*, 110 and 106.

25. Unpublished data cited in *Vital and Health Statistics*, 145.

26. For an in-depth discussion of these principles and their application to several issues in medical ethics, see Tom L. Beauchamp and James F. Childress, *Principles of Biomedical Ethics*, 3rd ed. (New York: Oxford University Press, 1989).

27. For an explanation and defense of casuistry, see Albert R. Jonsen and Stephen Toulmin, *The Abuse of Casuistry* (Berkeley: University of California Press, 1988).

Acknowledgments

In the fall of 1986, the Gerontology Center at West Virginia University invited me to present a two-day workshop on ethics and aging for professionals in social work and health care. The idea for this book grew out of that workshop. I am indebted to Lucille Nahemow and Rick Briggs, former Director and Acting Director, respectively, of the West Virginia University Gerontology Center, for helping me discover such fertile territory for philosophical exploration.

Work on this book was supported by three fellowships: a National Endowment for the Humanities Fellowship for College Teachers and Independent Scholars (grant FB-25521-88), a Humanities Foundation of West Virginia Fellowship, and a West Virginia University Research Fellowship. I am also thankful for support from the Department of Philosophy and College of Arts and Sciences at West Virginia University and the Center for Medical Ethics at the University of Pittsburgh.

I have benefited greatly from comments on earlier drafts of the book, and I would like to thank the following persons for reading and commenting on all or part of the manuscript: Robert Arnold, Dan Brock, Ralph W. Clark, Joel Frader, Thomas A. Mappes, Alvin H. Moss, Eric Rodriguez, Henry Ruf, Daniel Shapiro, and two anonymous reviewers for Oxford University Press.

I am very grateful to my wife, Lucy Fischer, for her encouragement, and to my son, David, for sharing his father with a computer. I also thank Jeffrey House at Oxford University Press for his helpful advice, patience, and support.

"Decision-Making Capacity" in Chapter 1 and part of Chapter 6 were previously published. The articles, respectively, are "Patient Decision-

Making Capacity and Risk,'' *Bioethics* 5, no. 2 (April 1991): 91–104; and "Caring for Frail Elderly Parents: Past Parental Sacrifices and the Obligations of Adult Children,'' *Social Theory and Practice* 16, no. 2 (Summer 1990): 163–89.

In an obvious respect, my parents have made this book possible. However, since they are both over 90 years old, they have also contributed to it directly by helping to make the issues discussed in it very real to me. This book grew in part out of my experience with my parents, and someday it may help my son David answer ethical questions about his elderly parents.

Contents

Abbreviations

ACP	American College of Physicians
AIDS	acquired immune deficiency syndrome
C_1	constant 1
C_2	constant 2
C_{ACP}	actually contrary to preferences condition
C_{BCP}	believed to be contrary to preferences condition
C_{DP}	disregarding preferences condition
CHF	congestive heart failure
C_{LA}	liberty of action condition
COPD	chronic obstructive pulmonary disease
CPR	cardiopulmonary resuscitation
DHHS	Department of Health and Human Services
DNR	do not resuscitate
DP	differential pull
DRG	Diagnostic Related Groups
EP	equal pull
FDA	Food and Drug Administration
GNP	gross national product

ICF	intermediate care nursing facility
ICU	intensive care unit
IRB	institutional review board
IV	intravenous
OTA	Office of Technology Assessment
PSDA	Patient Self-Determination Act
PVS	persistent vegetative state
RCT	randomized clinical trial
SNF	skilled care nursing facility

Ethics and
the Elderly

CHAPTER 1

Life-Sustaining Medical Care: Elderly Patients with Decision-Making Capacity

Efforts to find the legendary "fountain of youth" have proved fruitless. Over their lifetime, people age, and everyone will die some day. There has been a remarkable increase in life expectancy at birth in the United States since the beginning of this century: from 47.3 years in 1900 to 75 years in 1987, an increase of over 58 percent.[1] However, this increase is due largely to improvements in survival during infancy and early childhood. Whereas only two-fifths of babies born alive in 1900 reached the age of 65, a recent estimate is that more than three-fourths of babies born alive will live to age 65.[2] By contrast, life expectancy at age 65 has increased far less. Life expectancy at age 65 in 1900 was 11.9 years, and there was an increase of only 5 years over a period of 87 years.[3] Moreover, whereas tremendous progress has been made in preventing and curing a variety of life-threatening diseases and conditions, medical science has not conquered all of them. For example, no cure has been found for Alzheimer's disease, and cancer and cardiovascular disease are still leading causes of death. In addition, heretofore unknown fatal diseases, such as acquired immune deficiency syndrome (AIDS), continue to be discovered.

Nevertheless, as a result of advances in medicine and technology, the power to *prolong* the lives of seriously ill elderly persons has increased substantially. For elderly patients about whom it might have been said as recently as two or three decades ago that "nothing more can be done," now there is often much that can be done. For example, elderly persons who would have died of kidney failure not so long ago can now live with the aid of dialysis. Cardiopulmonary resuscitation (CPR), mechanical respirators, and tube and intravenous feeding, to name just a few advances in medical

3

technology, present substantial opportunities to extend the lives of elderly persons.

Unfortunately, this newly gained power to prolong life can be a two-edged sword. On the one hand, it offers what can be a valuable benefit: temporary escape from death. On the other hand, it can foster or facilitate increased suffering, denial, and senseless efforts to delay death. Since a return to an "age of innocence" without the technological capability to postpone death is neither desirable nor likely, decisions concerning life-sustaining medical interventions are inescapable.[4] Moreover, in view of the steady growth in the number of elderly persons, the frequency of such decisions can be expected to increase.

Because decisions concerning life-sustaining treatment for elderly patients are literally about life and death, it is essential to consider carefully the specific details of each case. It would be foolish to seek an algorithm for decision-making in all cases. However, general principles and concepts can facilitate ethically sound decision-making.

Shared Decision-Making

Shared decision-making is a recognized "first principle" of health care decision-making generally, and there is no good reason to exempt decisions about life-sustaining treatment for elderly patients.[5] According to this principle, when patients possess decision-making capacity, decision-making should be a collaborative activity between physicians and patients.[6] As experts in clinical matters (for example, diagnosis, prognosis, and treatment options and their expected outcomes), physicians should present the treatment alternatives (including nontreatment) to patients and provide information that will facilitate informed choices. However, the shared decision-making model incorporates the idea that it is the patient's prerogative to *evaluate* the options and to *choose* among them. Physicians are not required to present information in a "neutral" or "unbiased" manner, and they may recommend certain options over others.[7] However, in the final analysis, according to this model, the decision should be based on the patient's values, and patients have a right to accept or refuse options which physicians recommend.

Shared decision-making promotes two important ethical values: respect for autonomy and the patient's well-being.[8] There is an obvious connection between the shared decision-making model and respect for autonomy, an ethical principle that requires us to allow other persons to make important decisions concerning their lives for themselves. Decisions concerning one's own medical care clearly fall within the principle's scope, and it is hard to think of a decision more important and personal than whether to accept or forgo life-prolonging measures. Such a decision (for example, a decision to accept or refuse ventilator support or dialysis), can be both constitutive and expressive of who and what a person is.

The shared decision-making model also recognizes that it can take more than "medical expertise" (a physician's more or less scientific knowledge of means to prevent, diagnose, and treat diseases and illnesses) to determine what is best for a patient. A physician might know, say, that the probability of achieving result X (for example pain relief) is 80 percent with treatment option T^1 and only 60 percent with treatment option T^2. Which is better for the patient, T^1 or T^2? The answer depends on how the patient evaluates the benefits and burdens associated with each of the two treatment alternatives, and this in turn depends on the patient's values, goals, priorities, interests, and so forth. Accordingly, for one patient, the burdens associated with T^1 (say, nausea and drowsiness) may outweigh the increased likelihood of pain relief; for another patient, the increased likelihood of pain relief may outweigh the burdens associated with T^1.

To assess the benefits and burdens of a life-sustaining measure to a particular patient, the patient's values, goals, priorities, and interests are critical. For example, one elderly patient might savor life so much that any additional time that can be gained by means of dialysis or ventilator support offers sufficient benefit to outweigh corresponding burdens. By contrast, another elderly patient, one whose condition is medically indistinguishable from the first, might think that it is pointless to postpone death any longer and/or might value independence so much that the burdens of dialysis and ventilator support outweigh their benefits.[9] Shared decision-making recognizes that input from patients is important because the alternative that will best promote their good is in part a function of their values, goals, priorities, and interests.

Insofar as shared decision-making promotes the values of respect for patient autonomy and patient well-being, it exemplifies a patient-centered model of medicine. However, there are other important ethical values, including justice. Due to the cost and/or scarcity of medical resources, principles of distributive justice may warrant limits on the range of choices that are available to individual physicians and patients or their surrogates. Chapter 3 explores this issue in the context of a discussion of age-rationing of health care.

The notion of shared decision-making helps to identify several important issues associated with decisions about life-sustaining treatment for elderly patients. First, the shared decision-making model is directly applicable to elderly patients only when they possess decision-making capacity. Accordingly, it is necessary to analyze the notion of decision-making capacity.[10] Second, since elderly patients often have family (for example, spouses and adult children), it is also important to consider whether and how the preferences, opinions, and interests of family members may influence the decision-making process. Third, consistent with shared decision-making, there is a growing consensus that patients who possess decision-making capacity have an ethical and legal right to refuse life-sustaining treatment.[11] However, there is also increasing support for the position that physicians may *unilaterally* decide that a medical intervention is "futile" and withhold it even if patients or their surrogates want it. Accordingly, it is imperative to examine the notion of "medical futility" and its relation to shared decision-making. These three issues will be the primary focus of this chapter.

First, however, two important questions about life-sustaining treatment should be considered. First, is there an ethical difference between withholding and withdrawing life-sustaining treatment? Second, are decisions about tube and intravenous feeding (artificial nutrition and hydration) different *in principle* from decisions about CPR, mechanical ventilation, dialysis, antibiotics, and other life-extending measures? Answers to both of these questions are needed to prevent ethically flawed decision-making.

Withholding and Withdrawing Life-Sustaining Treatment

To clinicians, there may be an important *psychological* difference between withholding (not starting or initiating) and withdrawing (stopping or discontinuing) life-sustaining treatment.[12] For example, it might *feel* different to extubate a ventilator-dependent patient and to write a DNR (do not resuscitate) order in a patient's chart. Nevertheless, there is no significant *ethical* difference between withholding and withdrawing life-prolonging treatment.[13] Unless the patient's condition and prognosis have changed, it is ethically permissible to withdraw a life-extending treatment after it has been initiated if it would have been ethically acceptable to withhold it.

The primary reason for thinking that the distinction has ethical significance is based on the familiar distinction between acts of commission and acts of omission. It can be summarized as follows:[14]

If a physician withdraws treatment and the patient dies, then the physician's act of commission is the cause of the patient's death and the physician is morally responsible for that death. However, if treatment is not initiated and the patient dies, then the patient's death is the result of an omission. In this case, the patient's death is caused by no one, and no one is morally responsible for it.

This line of reasoning is seriously flawed. Suppose, for example, that a patient was not intubated because the attending physician, despite pleas by a resident and a nurse, failed to take appropriate action. If the physician's omission is a result of malice, negligence, or incompetence, then it will not take him off the hook ethically or legally to claim that he did nothing. Like acts of commission, acts of omission are subject to ethical assessment, and there is no reason to believe that different principles are required. Accordingly, if omitting treatment can be compatible with respect for autonomy and/or the patient's well-being, there is no reason to assume that acting to stop treatment cannot be compatible with those principles as well. The question, then, is not whether forgoing a life-extending measure in a particular case constitutes an act of commission or an act of omission, but whether forgoing treatment is supported by the values of patient autonomy and/or well-being.

Furthermore, the doctrine that there is an ethically significant difference between withholding and withdrawing life-extending treatment is incompatible with both of the primary values that underlie shared decision-making (patient autonomy and well-being). That doctrine would prevent physicians from respecting the wishes of elderly patients who want to discontinue mechanical ventilation after a time-limited trial. It could prevent withdrawing treatment in cases where continued treatment will not benefit patients or will pointlessly prolong pain and suffering. It could also deter trying measures that might benefit patients. For example, if there is only a slight chance that mechanical ventilation will benefit a patient, it might be withheld so as to prevent a situation in which the patient has to be kept alive indefinitely in a persistent vegetative state. From the perspective of the patient's well-being, it might be more reasonable to give the procedure a chance, and to withdraw it if it fails to produce any significant changes.

Artificial Nutrition and Hydration

A difficult and controversial decision about the care of elderly patients who have lost the capacity to eat and drink (for example, elderly patients who are permanently unconscious and some severely demented elderly patients) is whether to provide tube or intravenous feeding (artificial nutrition and hydration).[15] As upsetting and demanding as such decisions may be, ethically sound decision-making about artificial nutrition and hydration is no different in principle from ethically sound decision-making about CPR, mechanical ventilation, dialysis, antibiotics, and other life-sustaining measures. That is, decisions about artificial nutrition and hydration should be made according to the same ethical principles and standards as decisions about life-prolonging measures generally.[16]

Are there any good reasons for thinking that different principles and standards are needed for decisions about artificial nutrition and hydration? One reason that merits condideration is the symbolic significance of food and water. Callahan claims that "feeding of the hungry . . . is the most fundamental of all human relationships. It is the perfect symbol of the fact that human life is inescapably social and communal."[17] In a similar vein, Weisbard and Siegler assert that providing food and water "to those who hunger and thirst" is associated with "deep human responses of caring, of nurturing, of human connectedness, and of human community."[18] To be sure, providing food and water generally is a way of expressing care and concern, and it is hard to imagine an action more callous and inhumane than a refusal to give food and water to "those who hunger and thirst." However, depending on their clinical conditions, patients who cannot eat and drink may not *experience* hunger and thirst.[19] In addition, tube or intravenous feeding does not express care and concern for a particular patient if it is contrary to the patient's wishes or if the burdens outweigh the benefits to the patient. In this crucial respect, artificial nutrition and hydration are no different from mechanical ventilation or any other life-sustaining interventions. To provide a medical intervention against a patient's wishes or when the benefits do not outweigh the burdens to the patient is not an expression of care and concern for *that patient* (*person*). To insist that patients must receive artificial nutrition and hydration because of the *symbolic* significance of food and water is to treat patients as abstractions ("people who cannot eat or drink") rather than as concrete persons with distinctive preferences, values, medical histories, and prognoses.

The claim that food and water have symbolic significance can also have a *social* dimension. It is sometimes claimed that due to the symbolic significance of food and water, forgoing nutrition and hydration will have serious negative social consequences. In particular, it is argued that even if forgoing nutrition and hydration is compatible with the preferences and interests of some patients, social acceptance of the practice, even in those limited cases, will result in a serious deterioration in compassion, care, and concern. As Callahan argues: "It is a most dangerous business to tamper with, or adulterate, so enduring and central a moral emotion, one in which the repugnance against starving people to death could be, on occasion, greater than that which a more straitened rationality would call for."[20] This line of argument is a variation on the standard "heart" versus "mind" dichotomy, according to which each has its own "logic." In this case, it is assumed that the acceptance of moral rules has an "emotional basis," and that once the mind interferes by making fine distinctions, this emotional basis will erode. In particular, although the mind may be able to identify legitimate exceptions to the general rule, "the needy and the helpless must be fed," if the practice of allowing exceptions to the general rule is accepted, the rule's emotional

support will be undermined.[21] Thus, in view of the emotional and psychological limitations of human beings, it is said to be necessary to discourage
people from making exceptions—even legitimate exceptions—to the general
rule that "the needy and the helpless must be fed."

This is not the place to evaluate the moral psychology that underlies the
foregoing line of argument. Without doing so, however, it is still possible to
cast considerable doubt on that argument. It is unlikely that the specific rule,
"the needy and the helpless must be fed," is a basic or fundamental rule.
Instead, it is plausible to construe it as a derivative rule. Since the provision
of food and water is often linked to care, compassion, and concern, let us
suppose that the rule that the needy and the helpless must be fed is derived
from moral rules that require care, compassion, and concern. Insofar as the
rule that "the needy and the helpless must be fed" is based on moral rules
requiring care, compassion, and concern, it can be thought of as a "rule of
thumb." That is, generally, to exhibit care, compassion, and concern, people should feed the needy and the helpless.

For the sake of argument, let us assume that the practice of recognizing
legitimate exceptions to *moral rules* will tend to undermine their emotional
support. It does not follow that recognizing legitimate exceptions to *rules of
thumb* will undermine the emotional support of the corresponding moral
rules. Suppose that tube and intravenous feeding are incompatible with a
patient's preferences and/or well-being. In this case, artificial nutrition and
hydration are incompatible with care, compassion, and concern. Accordingly, it is implausible to hold that forgoing artificial nutrition and hydration
will undermine the "emotional basis" of care, compassion, and concern.
Since care, compassion, and concern require that we pay attention to the
wishes and interests of *individual persons,* these values are not promoted by
inflexible rules that require us to disregard individual circumstances. Furthermore, one can continue to show care, compassion, and concern for
patients even afer a decision has been made to withhold or withdraw nutrition and hydration. As Carson observes, care can take alternative forms,
such as "liquids for sipping, ice chips for dry mouth, analgesics, anti-
emetics, and backrubs."[22]

There is another reason to discourage efforts to identify legitimate exceptions to the rule of thumb that the needy and the helpless must be fed. It
might be claimed that if people are allowed to exercise their judgment in
deciding when this rule of thumb actually applies, many mistakes will be
made. Callahan offers an argument along these lines, referring to what he
calls the "klutz factor." He concedes that "the first pioneers" might well
decide to forgo nutrition and hydration "carefully and thoughtfully after due
deliberation." But he worries about what might happen over time as more
and more health care professionals and family members disregard the rule of

thumb that favors nutrition and hydration and attempt to make judgments on a case-by-case basis: "What happens when you turn something that was a minority movement into a mass movement? In this case, what if caregivers withhold food and water thoughtlessly, carelessly, and incorrectly, thereby causing much suffering and debasing a loyalty and duty to a large number of seriously ill people?"[23]

The obvious answer to Callahan's (rhetorical) question is that *if* decisions to forgo artificial nutrition and hydration were generally made "thoughtlessly, carelessly, and incorrectly," it would be a tragedy. *If* there were good reason to believe that such decisions would generally be made thoughtlessly, carelessly, and incorrectly, then it might be better to encourage health care professionals to treat the rule of thumb in favor of providing nutrition and hydration as an exceptionless principle. But the mere *possibility* of careless and faulty judgments does not warrant such a policy, especially in view of the potential ethical costs (for example, failing to respect the patient's wishes and harming the patient).[24] In addition, decisions about CPR, mechanical ventilation, and other life-sustaining measures would also be tragic if they were made thoughtlessly, carelessly, and incorrectly. Thus, the "klutz factor" fails to provide a good reason for singling out decisions about artificial nutrition and hydration.[25]

Some commentators have expressed the concern that if forgoing nutrition and hydration becomes an accepted practice, more and more frail elderly persons will be abandoned and allowed to die because it is felt that they are a burden and/or their care is too costly.[26] To forgo tube or intravenous feeding contrary to an elderly patient's preferences and interests for such reasons is surely incompatible with care and concern and—with the possible exception of conditions of extreme resource scarcity—is ethically intolerable. But a similar point applies to CPR, dialysis, mechanical ventilation, and other life-prolonging measures. It is no less incompatible with care and concern to forgo these measures contrary to an elderly patient's preferences or interests because it is thought that the patient is a "burden" to others or that his or her care is "too costly." The *possibility* of unethical practices does not provide an ethical warrant for CPR, dialysis, and ventilator support when none can be derived from a consideration of the specific circumstances in a particular case. Similarly, there is no good reason to think that the *possibility* of unethical practices provides an ethical warrant for nutritional support and hydration when none can be derived from consideration of the specific circumstances in a particular case. Rather than adopting a general rule against forgoing nutritional support and hydration, it is more appropriate to adopt a case-by-case approach, applying the same general principles and criteria that apply to other life-extending measures.[27]

Decision-Making Capacity

Shared decision-making implies that elderly patients with decision-making capacity have a right to accept or refuse life-sustaining medical interventions. But what does it mean to say that patients possess decision-making capacity?[28] According to the standard analysis, decision-making capacity requires (1) a capacity to understand and communicate, (2) a capacity to reason and deliberate, and (3) possession of a set of values and goals.[29]

The first requirement encompasses a broad range of skills and capacities, including linguistic, conceptual, and cognitive abilities that enable people to receive, process, store, and retrieve information. However, understanding is not limited to cognitive or intellectual capacities; it also includes an ability to imagine what life would be like in certain states and conditions. Understanding in this sense requires, among other things, imagination and relevant life experience. The first requirement also includes the capacity to communicate to others. People who can understand information, but who cannot communicate to others by means of spoken or written language, gestures, or other behavioral means, lack (effective) decision-making capacity.

The second requirement, a capacity to reason and deliberate, includes an ability to evaluate and compare or weigh alternatives and their expected consequences. An ability to engage in elementary probabilistic reasoning may also be necessary, especially when there are significant differences in the likelihoods of outcomes. Finally, to satisfy this requirement, people must have the ability to give due consideration to possible future consequences of their choices.

The third requirement, possession of a set of values or goals, is related to the second requirement. If the third requirement were not satisfied, people would lack a basis for evaluating and comparing options. These values need not comprise a fully developed, systematic, and detailed conception of the good, but they cannot totally lack coherence or stability.

There may be general agreement about the foregoing three requirements, but there is no single, universally accepted standard of decision-making capacity.[30] There is at least one good reason for thinking that it would be misguided to aim for a single standard; namely, decision-making capacity is a *task*-related concept. The requisite skills and abilities vary according to the specific decision, and a standard of decision-making capacity therefore should be decision- or task-related. It is likely, for example, that there are significant differences between the cognitive skills and capacities that are required to make a reasoned decision concerning life-extending medical treatment, on the one hand, and the cognitive skills and capacities that are required to make sound financial investments, on the other hand. Accordingly, decision-making capacity is not an all-or-nothing concept, and people can have the capacity to make some decisions, and not others. For example, a mildly demented 76-year-old man can have the capacity to decide whether to accept antibiotics to treat a pneumonia and lack the capacity to decide whether to buy long-term health insurance. Lack of decision-making capacity with respect to certain matters also may not be permanent. Temporary loss of decision-making capacity with respect to certain decisions can be triggered by diseases, depression, drugs, and a variety of environmental factors, for example, being moved from a familiar setting, such as home or a nursing home, to an unfamiliar setting, such as a hospital.

Another reason is often given for rejecting the idea of a determinate and invariable standard of decision-making capacity. It is said that the relevant criteria should vary according to the *risk* to a patient. A detailed analysis and defense of such a "risk-related" standard is provided by Buchanan and Brock. They hold that "the standard of competence ought to vary in part with the expected harms or benefits to the patient of acting in accordance with the patient's choice."[31] A strong standard of decision-making capacity is said to be appropriate when the expected benefit to expected harm ratio is (substantially) worse than that of other options (a "high-risk" choice from the perspective of the patient's well-being); and a weak standard of decision-making capacity is said to be appropriate when the net balance of expected benefits and harms is better than that of other options (a "low-risk" choice from the perspective of the patient's well-being).

If a risk-related standard of decision-making capacity is accepted, then low risk can offset deficits in patients' decision-making skills and abilities. For example, if it is thought that refusal of a life-extending intervention will not be harmful on balance to a patient, then the decision-making standard will be weak and a low level of understanding, reasoning skills, and the like will be required. By contrast, if it is thought that refusal of a life-extending intervention has a high net balance of expected harm, the decision-making standard will be strong and patients will have to possess a high level of understanding, reasoning skills, and so forth.

Buchanan and Brock advance several reasons in support of a risk-related standard, including the following:[32] (1) it "better coheres with our basic legal framework"; (2) a risk-related standard "receives indirect support from the doctrine of informed consent"; (3) a risk-related standard is said to be "more consonant with the way people actually make informal competence determinations in areas of judgment in which they have the greatest confidence and on which there is the most consensus"; and (4) a risk-related standard is said to strike an appropriate balance between respect for autonomy and concern for patient well-being.

Buchanan and Brock claim that the first is "perhaps the most important reason."[33] Although its importance is clear if the aim is an explication of the *legal* notion of competence, the relevance of the first reason is less clear if the aim is an explication of the notion of decision-making capacity within the framework of the standard triconditional analysis (capacity to understand and communicate, capacity to reason and deliberate, and possession of a set of values and goals). In addition, the following observation by Buchanan and Brock about the legal notion of competence presents a problem for their analysis: "[T]he law in this country has in general steadfastly refused to recognize a right to interfere with a *competent* patient's voluntary choice on purely paternalistic grounds. . . . Instead, the law makes a finding of in-competence a necessary condition for justified paternalistic interference with the patient's choice."[34] The statement that a finding of incompetence is a *necessary condition* of justified paternalism implies that it is justified to set aside a patient's treatment preferences for the patient's own good only if there is an independent finding of incompetence; such a requirement ex-presses a strong commitment to an autonomous patient's right of self-determination. However, in Buchanan and Brock's analysis, risk/benefit assessments enter into competency determinations, and a finding of incom-petence (or competence) is not independent of the judgment that paternalism is (or is not) justified. In their view, a physician must find that a patient is incompetent if the physician decides to set aside the patient's treatment preferences for the patient's own good because (a) patients "whose volun-tary decisions . . . must be respected by others and accepted as binding" are to be *classified as competent,* and (b) patients "whose decisions, even if uncoerced, will be set aside and for whom others will act as surrogate decision-makers" are to be *classified as incompetent.*[35] In effect, it is true by definition that the treatment preferences of competent patients are not to be set aside for their own good. If a patient is classified as competent, it is *logically contradictory* (not ethically mistaken) to hold that the patient's treatment choice can be overridden for her own good.

With respect to the second reason, since decision-making capacity is one of the components of informed consent, it is hard to see how that doctrine can provide support for a particular standard of decision-making capacity. If the claim is that informed consent as currently practiced makes use of a risk-related standard, then the second reason is similar to the first and third reasons.

By their third reason, Buchanan and Brock claim that the use of a risk-related standard to assess the decision-making capacities of patients is stan-dard practice within the medical profession. However, the third reason is not restricted to medical contexts. Indeed, the example that Buchanan and Brock cite has to do with parents' judgments about the decision-making capacities of children. They observe that whereas a parent is likely to believe that a five-year-old child has the capacity to decide whether to have a hamburger or a hot dog for lunch, the parent is not likely to believe that the child has the capacity to make investment decisions involving large sums of money. The reason, they claim, "is because the risk in the latter case is greater, and the information required for reasoning about the relevant consequences of the options is much more complex."[36] The following modification of their example appears to support the claimed significance of risk. Suppose the five-year-old is allergic to hot dogs and may, after eating a hot dog, suffer convulsions and without immediate medical treatment, perhaps lapse into a coma and die. Under these circumstances a parent is unlikely to hold that the child has the capacity to decide whether to eat a hot dog or a hamburger for lunch. What has changed from the original example? It may appear that the risk of substantial harm is the primary difference between the two cases, a conclusion that appears to support the claim that it is common (sense) to tie the standard of decision-making capacity to the (perceived) risk to the agent.

It is premature, however, to conclude that the most important difference between the original example and the modified example is the potential harm to the child in the latter case. The nature and complexity of the choice has also changed markedly. Originally the choice was between two common lunchtime foods, a choice that is widely perceived to be essentially a matter of taste.[37] Since such a choice requires so little by way of cognitive skills, it seems plausible to hold that it is one that even a five-year-old can make. In the modified example, however, the choice requires understanding of allergic reactions and their consequences, a comprehension of the meaning of serious illness and death, the ability to give due consideration to future consequences, and so forth. Such capacities and abilities are beyond the maturity level of most five-year-olds. This example shows that even if standards of decision-making capacity vary with the expected risk to the agent, it does not follow that greater expected risk is the primary *reason* for a stricter standard. As in the foregoing example, there may also be a correlation between greater risk and increased complexity of requisite decision-making skills and abilities; and it is arguable that from the perspective of the standard triconditional analysis of decision-making capacity, the latter is the primary reason for adopting a stricter criterion. That is, risk may be relevant, but *not* because (1) the perceived risk in the original example is so low that the standard of decision-making capacity can be lowered to a point at which it is satisfied by a five-year-old, and (2) the perceived risk in the modified example is so high that the standard of decision-making capacity has to be raised so much that it cannot be satisfied by a five-year-old. Rather, risk may be relevant because it is only in the modified example that a *capacity to appreciate significant risks* is required, and such a capacity is beyond the cognitive abilities of most five-year-olds. Moreover, even if there are high-risk decisions that do not require complex decision-making skills and abilities, and even if it is accepted practice to utilize a strong criterion of decision-making capacity in such cases, the mere fact that the use of a strong criterion is accepted practice under such circumstances does not show that it is warranted—or compatible with the standard analysis—to do so.

It remains to consider the fourth reason, the claim that a risk-related standard strikes an appropriate balance between respect for autonomy and concern for patient well-being. The reasoning for this conclusion is as follows. Respect for autonomy requires that patients with decision-making capacity be allowed to decide for themselves whether to accept or forgo treatment. On the other hand, from an ethical perspective, it is also imperative to consider patient welfare or well-being. Accordingly, a standard of decision-making capacity should strike an appropriate balance between two potential errors: (1) failing to allow patients with decision-making capacity to make decisions for themselves and (2) failing to protect patients from the harmful consequences of decisions that are the result of deficits in decision-making capacity. A risk-related standard of decision-making capacity strikes an appropriate balance between these two errors. On the one hand, if the risk to patients is low, then the balance tips in the direction of avoiding the first kind of error, and a weaker standard of decision-making capacity is appropriate. On the other hand, if the risk to patients is high, then the balance tips in the direction of avoiding the second type of error, and a stronger standard is appropriate.

As plausible as this line of reasoning may appear, it is doubtful that it is appropriate to assign to a standard of decision-making capacity the crucial and difficult task of striking a proper balance between respect for autonomy and concern for patient welfare. To strike such a balance, Buchanan and Brock divide patients into two categories: (1) patients who are competent (patients with decision-making capacity) and whose treatment choices should be respected; and (2) patients who are not competent (patients without decision-making capacity), whose treatment choices should be set aside, and for whom surrogate decision-makers are required.[38] This twofold classification conflates two distinct questions: First, within the framework of the standard triconditional analysis, does a patient have the capacity to make a particular decision? Second, is there sufficient reason to disregard a patient's expressed preferences and for a surrogate to make decisions for the patient?

Suppose, say, that an otherwise healthy 71-year-old patient refuses an appendectomy. The substantial expected benefits appear to far outweigh the minor expected burdens, but from the perspective of the standard analysis of decision-making capacity, there do not seem to be any relevant deficits in the patient's decision-making abilities or in the decision-making process. No deficits in understanding or reasoning can be identified, and the values and weights that the patient assigns to the various outcomes are consistent with *his* system of values.[39] Someone who accepts this assessment of the patient's decision-making capacity can nevertheless claim that it is justified to override the patient's refusal in order to prevent a serious and irreversible harm to him.[40] However, the twofold classification implies that if no deficits can be identified in the patient's decision-making abilities or in the decision-making process, then it cannot be claimed that overriding the patient's decision is justified. Anyone who holds that overriding the patient's choice is justified is precluded from offering the direct defense that it should be overridden to prevent a substantial and irreversible harm to the patient. Rather, it would have to be claimed that there was a significant deficit in understanding, reasoning, and so forth, and the standard of decision-making capacity would have to be raised accordingly. Thus, if the twofold classification is accepted, what are at root ethical disagreements about whether it is permissible to override an autonomous patient's wishes for the patient's own good may be transformed into disagreements about whether individual patients satisfy decision-making criteria within the framework of the standard analysis. As a result, there is a danger that standards of understanding, reasoning, and so forth will be set arbitrarily and unattainably high by those who believe that paternalism is justified when perceived risks are great.

There is the opposite danger as well. It may well be that if the perceived risk to a patient of a treatment preference is low enough, then even if she does not have the capacity to make a particular decision, there is no need to disregard her preferences and to set aside her choice. The twofold classification of patients precludes this position. It requires that patients be classified as having decision-making capacity if their treatment preferences are not set aside. As a result, there is the danger that decision-making standards will be set so low when patients concur with the recommendations of health care professionals that they will be classified as having the capacity to make health care decisions, regardless of their mental status.

An example of an overly weak standard is provided by Drane's detailed proposal for a risk-related standard of decision-making capacity. Drane formulates three standards of decision-making capacity, the weakest of which is *"awareness* in the sense of orientation or being conscious of the general situation."[41] This standard is said to be appropriate for "those medical decisions that are not dangerous and objectively are in the patient's best interest."[42] It also applies to a refusal "by a patient dying of a chronic illness of treatments that are useless and only prolong the dying [process]."[43] Infants, people who are unconscious, the severely retarded, and "patients who use psychotic defenses that severely compromise reality testing" are cited as the only categories of people who fail to satisfy the weakest standard.[44] On the other hand, it is said that this standard can be satisfied by children who are six or older, and by people who are senile, mildly retarded, or intoxicated.

It may be helpful to apply this weak standard to an example. Suppose Ms. O., an 81-year-old nursing home resident, is hospitalized for tests to determine the cause of rectal bleeding, and it is discovered that she has colon cancer with widespread metastases. Chemotherapy might prolong Ms. O.'s life a little, but it will cause her considerable discomfort and pain. She is disoriented and does not appear to understand the nature and seriousness of her condition, and she is unable to comprehend explanations of her prognosis, treatment options, and so forth. However, she adamantly and repeatedly states that she does not want any additional medical treatment, and she appears to favor returning to the more familiar surroundings of the nursing home. The attending physician, the nursing staff, and Ms. O.'s family all agree that chemotherapy would be pointless and would only prolong the dying process. Consequently, the weakest standard of decision-making capacity would apply, and despite her significant mental deficits, Ms. O. appears to satisfy that standard.

Since Ms. O. does not seem to want chemotherapy, and since all parties agree that chemotherapy would not be in her best interests, a formal assessment of her decision-making capacity and the appointment of a formal guardian or surrogate may be unnecessary (and a waste of time and resources).[45] Nevertheless, there are four reasons to resist the use of a risk-related standard to conclude that patients like Ms. O. have health care decision-making capacity.

First, from the perspective of the standard analysis, Ms. O. would have the capacity to decide whether to forgo chemotherapy only if she is able to understand and evaluate the options and their consequences, make a reasoned choice between the alternatives, and the like. Insofar as Ms. O. lacks these abilities, then even if her immediate preferences are not incompatible with her future welfare, it seems inappropriate to conclude that she has the capacity to decide whether to forgo chemotherapy. Rejecting a course of action that is not in her best interests fails to demonstrate that Ms. O. possesses the capacity to make the decision. If a two-year-old child does not want to play in the street or pet a strange dog, it does not follow that she has the capacity to decide whether to play in the street or to pet strange dogs. Assent to the correct option from the perspective of one's welfare no more suffices to establish decision-making capacity than a lucky guess suffices to establish knowledge. Indeed, in view of Ms. O.'s mental status, it even may be misleading to say that she *decided* to forgo treatment.

Second, even when forgoing life-extending measures will not be harmful on balance to a patient, substantial cognitive ability is required to decide whether to forgo those measures. It may be clear to health care professionals and family members that life-extending measures would not be beneficial on balance to a patient, but reasoning to that conclusion requires a capacity to identify, understand, and weigh the relevant harms and benefits. Among other things, it requires a capacity to understand that extended life by medical means in the circumstances would not be beneficial on balance and that a "natural" death in the circumstances would not be harmful on balance. It is doubtful that patients who only satisfy a weak standard would have the requisite decision-making capacity.

Third, if it is concluded that Ms. O. has the capacity to decide whether to forgo chemotherapy, it would follow that she had *authorized* withholding chemotherapy, and that she is in part *responsible* for that decision. However, given her severely compromised mental status, these conclusions seem unwarranted. To justify withholding chemotherapy, there is no need to insist on the fiction that despite Ms. O.'s obvious mental impairment, she has the capacity to decide whether to forgo chemotherapy. Withholding chemotherapy is ethically justified insofar as it would not promote her welfare and there is no basis for concluding that she either wants or would want chemotherapy, but *not* because she has authorized withholding it.

Fourth, if it is concluded that Ms. O. has the capacity to decide whether to forgo chemotherapy, it would follow that her expressed wish to withhold chemotherapy is a good reason to believe that chemotherapy is contrary to her best interests. However, given her severely compromised mental status, this conclusion is also unwarranted.[46]

If appropriate *minimum* levels of decision-making capacity (that is, minimums corresponding to the cognitive demands of specific decision-making tasks) were incorporated into a risk-related standard, patients such as Ms. O. who have significant mental impairments would not be classifiable as patients with decision-making capacity. However, Buchanan and Brock reject the idea of setting such a minimum.[47] Moreover, setting plausible minimums would significantly limit the range of variation of a risk-related standard, and the other difficulties discussed previously would still remain.

There is one additional problem that merits attention. Although proponents of a risk-related standard generally hold that judgments of decision-making capacity should be independent of the *content* of a person's choice, a risk-related standard can call for a consideration of that content.[48] The following example illustrates this point. Ms. A. and Mr. B. are two 78-year-old patients with identical decision-making skills and abilities and identical medical conditions, and they are faced with deciding whether to accept or forgo dialysis. If it appears that refusal will result in substantial harm to Ms. A. and Mr. B., then according to a risk-related criterion, refusal would call for a stronger standard of decision-making capacity than acceptance. Accordingly, if Ms. A. refuses dialysis, and Mr. B. accepts dialysis, it is consistent with a risk-related standard to conclude that Ms. A. lacks, and Mr. B. possesses, decision-making capacity—despite their identical decision-making skills and abilities. Moreover, the same patient can be classified as having or lacking decision-making capacity, depending on which choice she makes. Suppose, say, a strong standard of decision-making capacity is deemed appropriate because of the high perceived risk, and Ms. A., the patient who refused dialysis, is said to lack decision-making capacity. If she had decided to accept dialysis, a weaker standard would have been deemed appropriate, and it could have been concluded that she had decision-making capacity. However, no matter what Ms. A. finally decided, the decision she faced was to accept or forgo dialysis. Insofar as a choice between these options requires an ability to comprehend and to weigh the consequences of *both*, it seems odd to maintain that accepting dialysis calls for significantly less decision-making ability than refusing dialysis.[49]

Finally, it is important to recognize that a stronger reason for making sure that a patient has the capacity to make a particular decision should not be confused with a stronger standard of decision-making capacity. When it appears that a patient's decision is likely to result in substantial harm to her, there may well be more reason to determine whether she has the capacity to make that decision than when her decision is not likely to result in substantial harm to her. If, say, an 81-year-old patient does not want life-prolonging measures, and those measures clearly offer no reasonable prospect of benefit to her, there is no compelling reason to make sure that she has the capacity to decide to forgo treatment before it is withheld. By contrast, if it appears that life-extending measures would promote the patient's welfare, it would be essential to ascertain with reasonable certainty that she is capable of making that decision before treatment is withheld.[50] Compared to the first situation, there may be more reason in the second situation to make sure that the patient has the capacity to decide to forgo treatment before withholding it. But it does not follow that the latter calls for a stronger standard of decision-making capacity than the former. Consequently, although there may be more reason to determine whether elderly patients who refuse life-sustaining measures have the capacity to decide to forgo treatment when such refusals appear to be contrary to their own well-being, it does not follow that the standard of decision-making capacity should vary according to the perceived risk to them.

It is beyond the scope of this book to present specific guidelines for clinical assessments of the decision-making capacity of elderly patients.[51] However, the standard triconditional analysis (possession of a set of values and goals, and a capacity to understand, communicate, reason, and deliberate) functions as an appropriate general framework for determinations of decision-making capacity. Whereas task-related criteria of decision-making capacity are consistent with the standard analysis, the foregoing discussion suggests that risk-related criteria may not be.

The Preferences and Interests of Family Members

Shared decision-making requires physicians to give elderly patients with decision-making capacity an opportunity to accept or refuse medical treatment. But family members may favor a particular decision and/or may be significantly affected by the outcome of a decision. As Waymack and Taler observe, "it is often the case that health care professionals find themselves in an ethical triad involving the patient and family. This is particularly true in the case of elderly patients where, because of the nature of chronic care, families often ask or are asked to play a significant role."[52] Thus, it is important to consider whether and how the preferences, opinions, and interests of the family of elderly patients with decision-making capacity may affect the decision-making process.

When elderly patients decide to accept or refuse life-sustaining treatment, respect for the opinions of family members, or a concern for their psychological, physical, and/or financial well-being, may tip the balance one way or the other. It is perfectly appropriate for elderly patients to consider the preferences of loved ones, and they should not automatically be encouraged to make decisions concerning life-extending treatment for exclusively self-regarding or purely selfish reasons.[53] Moreover, although undue pressure and influence are clearly improper, it is mistaken to assume that any advice and counsel from family members constitutes undue pressure or influence.

When elderly patients possess decision-making capacity, generally they and only they have the moral authority to decide how much weight to give the preferences and interests of family members.[54] Suppose, say, Ms. K. asks the attending physician to withhold further aggressive treatment from her father, an 82-year-old man with terminal prostate cancer. In support of her request, she states that her father would be better off if aggressive treatment were discontinued and only comfort care were provided. Ms. K.'s father has the capacity to decide whether or not to forgo aggressive treatment, and he prefers to receive it. The attending should not honor Ms. K.'s request and disregard her father's wishes. He might hold a conference with Ms. K. and her father. If the attending agrees with Ms. K.'s assessment, it would be appropriate for him to attempt to persuade her father to change his mind,[55] though not, of course, to use undue pressure or influence.

If Ms. K.'s father possesses decision-making capacity but has not expressed any treatment preference, his daughter may decide on his behalf if he has authorized her to do so. If he has not authorized his daughter to decide on his behalf, her opposition to aggressive therapy does not provide a sufficient reason for denying him an opportunity to accept or refuse treatment.

Alternatively, suppose Ms. K.'s father tells the attending that he does not want aggressive treatment. Out of a concern for her mother, Ms. K. asks the attending to "do everything possible" to keep her father alive. If Ms. K.'s father possesses decision-making capacity, it would be inappropriate for the attending to order aggressive therapy for the sake of Ms. K.'s mother unless Ms. K.'s father agrees to accept further treatment. He might hold a conference with Ms. K., her father, and other family members, possibly including Ms. K.'s mother. If the attending shares Ms. K.'s concern about her mother, he may attempt to persuade her father to accept aggressive therapy.[56] However, he should avoid undue pressure and influence, and he should also be careful not to misrepresent the situation. Thus, for example, even if it is proper for the physician to discuss the expected impact on Ms. K.'s mother, he should not attempt to persuade Ms. K.'s father to accept aggressive therapy by exaggerating the direct health-related benefits to him, or by understating the burdens. More important, a concern for Ms. K.'s mother does not give the attending physician sufficient reason to deny Ms. K.'s father an opportunity to accept or refuse treatment.[57]

If elderly patients are not estranged from family members, it is arguable that they ought to consider the family's wishes and interests when they decide whether to accept or refuse life-sustaining measures. Moreover, if a particular decision would require little, if any, sacrifice on the part of an elderly patient and would prevent substantial harm or produce substantial benefit to one or more family members, it is arguable that the patient ought to make that decision. Although Ms. K.'s father may have an obligation to consider his wife's interests, accepting unwanted aggressive therapy appears to require a substantial sacrifice on his part. Thus, it is doubtful that he has an obligation to accept aggressive therapy for the sake of his wife if he prefers to forgo it.

However, there may be cases in which no significant sacrifice is required. Suppose that Ms. P. is a 77-year-old patient with end-stage chronic obstructive pulmonary disease (COPD). She has just developed pneumonia, and if she refuses antibiotics, it is expected that she will die in a few days. She would prefer to forgo antibiotics, but her son's wife is scheduled for surgery for ovarian cancer in three days, and Ms. P. realizes that her death would add a substantial burden to her son and daughter-in-law at this time. If accepting antibiotics is not a substantial burden to Ms. P. it is arguable that she has a good reason to accept them for the sake of her son and daughter-in-law.

Even if there are situations in which elderly patients ought to select a particular treatment option for the sake of family members, it would be a mistake for physicians to deny elderly patients with decision-making capacity an opportunity to accept or refuse treatment when physicians believe that patients ought to choose one of the two options. For one thing, patients may well be more knowledgeable than physicians about the likely impact of decisions concerning life-prolonging treatment on family members. Second, as in the example of Ms. P., the claim that an elderly patient should select a particular option for the sake of family members may be controversial, and it is beyond the scope of the expertise of health care professionals to identify patients' ethical obligations to family members. Even ethics consultants and members of institutional ethics committees or other health care professionals with training in ethics may be unable to provide an authoritative answer. Moreover, even if there appears to be no room for reasonable people to disagree in a particular case, it is inappropriate for physicians or other health care professionals to force unwilling and/or unwitting patients to honor obligations toward family members. It may be proper to encourage elderly patients to consider the wishes and interests of family members and possible obligations to them. But it is not appropriate for health care professionals to act as "ethical police" or enforcers of morality in relation to such private and personal matters. Consequently, even when physicians believe that elderly patients with decision-making capacity ought to either accept or forgo life-prolonging treatment for the sake of family members, generally it is not justified to deny them an opportunity to accept or refuse treatment.

Elderly Patients and "Medical Futility"

Consistent with the principle of shared decision-making, elderly patients with decision-making capacity should be given an opportunity to accept or refuse life-sustaining medical interventions. As observed earlier, there is a growing consensus that patients who possess decision-making capacity have an ethical and legal right to refuse life-extending treatment. However, there is also increasing support for the position that physicians may *unilaterally* decide that a medical intervention is "futile" and withhold such interventions even if patients want them.[58] The notion of medical futility is of particular relevance to a discussion of decision-making for elderly patients because it has been claimed that advanced age can be an indicator of the futility of life-sustaining procedures, such as cardiopulmonary resuscitation (CPR).[59]

The following is a sample of statements about medical futility. (1) Physicians are not required to provide or discuss useless (futile) therapy with patients.[60] (2) If a medical intervention is futile, then the physician may unilaterally decide to withhold it.[61] (3) If a medical intervention is futile, then the physician has no duty to ascertain the patient's preferences.[62] (4) It is justified to exclude patients from the process of determining whether a medical intervention is futile.[63] (5) If a medical intervention is futile, then the physician may withhold it without the consent of the patient.[64] (6) Physicians are not obligated to offer futile medical interventions to patients.[65] (7) Physicians should discuss their decisions to withhold futile treatment with patients.[66] Taken together, these statements hardly provide a clear and coherent account of medical futility and its relation to shared decision-making. However, proponents of unilateral futility judgments by physicians appear to agree on at least one point: A physician can justifiably decide that a medical intervention is futile and withhold it for that reason even if a patient wants it.

If shared decision-making limits patients' choices to "medically acceptable treatment options," and futile medical interventions are "medically unacceptable," then the concept of medical futility is not incompatible with shared decision-making.[67] However, even if unilateral futility decisions are compatible with the accepted model of shared decision-making, it is important to explore their basis. If futility judgments are based on expertise that physicians possess and patients lack, there is a good reason for concluding that unilateral decisions by physicians to withhold futile treatment are justified. On the other hand, if futility judgments are not based on the special expertise of physicians, there appear to be grounds for questioning the legitimacy of unilateral decisions by physicians to withhold futile treatment.

To determine whether futility decisions are based on expertise that physicians possess and patients lack, it is necessary to distinguish four senses of "futility."[68] First, *general physiological futility;* that is, a medical intervention is futile if there is no reasonable chance that it will have *any* physiological effect. Second, *specific physiological futility;* that is, a medical intervention is futile if there is no reasonable chance that it will achieve its direct physiological (medical) objective. For example, CPR is futile in this sense if there is no reasonable chance that it will succeed in restoring cardiopulmonary function; dialysis is futile if there is no reasonable chance that it will succeed in cleansing the patient's blood of toxins; and tube feeding is futile if there is no reasonable chance that it will succeed in providing the patient with life-sustaining nutrition. Third, *futile in relation to the patient's goals and objectives;* that is, a medical intervention is futile if there is no reasonable chance that it will achieve the patient's goals and objectives. For example, if the patient's goal is to survive to leave the hospital, CPR is futile in this sense if there is no reasonable chance that it will achieve the patient's goal. Fourth, *futile in relation to goals and means compatible with standards of professional integrity;* that is, a medical intervention is futile if there is no reasonable chance that it will achieve any goals compatible with norms of professional integrity and by means compatible with those norms.[69]

Judgments of futility in the first sense, "general physiological futility," appear to be based on expertise that physicians possess and patients lack. Physicians have scientific and clinical expertise that enables them to ascertain the likely physiological effects of medical interventions, and most patients lack this expertise. Consequently, if anyone is capable of determining that a medical intervention (say, CPR or intubation) is unlikely to have any physiological effect in a particular case, it is the physician and not the patient.

However, it is rarely, if ever, the case that a medical intervention is unlikely to have *any* physiological effect. For example, although a blood transfusion or chemotherapy may not extend a patient's life, each is likely to produce some physiological changes (for example, an alteration in blood count); and even if CPR fails to restore cardiopulmonary function, it is likely to produce some physiological changes. Consequently, if a medical intervention is futile only when there is no reasonable chance that it will have *any* physiological effect, there would be few, if any, situations in which physicians could conclude that a particular medical intervention is futile.

To turn to the second sense of futility, "specific physiological futility," it has already been observed that physicians have scientific and clinical expertise that enables them to ascertain the likely physiological effects of medical interventions, and this expertise is essential for judgments of specific physiological futility. However, there are still two reasons for doubting that the scientific and clinical expertise of physicians uniquely qualifies them to make futility judgments in this sense.

First, although the scientific and clinical expertise of physicians enables them to determine whether, in relation to a particular standard of reasonableness, a specified physiological outcome is reasonable; setting the standard involves a value judgment that goes beyond that expertise. Suppose, say, a 79-year-old patient wants CPR in the event that he suffers cardiopulmonary arrest because he believes that *any* chance that CPR will restore cardiopulmonary function is worthwhile. The scientific and clinical expertise of the physician uniquely qualifies her to determine whether the chance of restoring cardiopulmonary function in the particular circumstances is greater than x percent. However, unless $x = 0$, that expertise does not uniquely qualify her to determine whether the chance of restoring cardiopulmonary function is reasonable or worthwhile only if it is greater than x percent.

Second, although physicians' expertise enables them to determine whether a medical intervention is likely to achieve a specified outcome, determining whether an outcome is an appropriate objective for a medical intervention involves value judgments that go beyond that expertise. Suppose a physician concludes that it would be futile to amputate the leg of a terminally ill cancer patient because an amputation would neither prevent the spread of the cancer nor significantly reduce pain. But the patient wants an amputation because he is disgusted by the thought of having a cancerous leg. Insofar as an amputation would achieve the patient's objective of removing a source of disgust and extreme displeasure, it would not be futile to the patient. The scientific and clinical expertise of the physician uniquely qualifies her to determine whether an amputation will prevent the spread of the cancer or significantly reduce pain. However, that expertise does not uniquely qualify her to evaluate the patient's goal and to determine that the amputation is futile even if there is a reasonable chance of achieving the patient's goal.

If a patient wants a medical intervention that the physician deems to be futile because she concludes that there is no reasonable chance that the intervention will achieve its direct physiological (medical) objective, the physician can attempt to justify withholding it by citing standards of professional integrity. For example, the physician can claim that it is incompatible with those norms: (1) to attempt resuscitation when there is less than an x percent chance that it will restore cardiopulmonary function or (2) to amputate a limb because it disgusts a patient. However, the physician's unilateral decision to withhold treatment would then involve a judgment of futility in the fourth sense.

A medical intervention is futile in the third sense if there is no reasonable chance that it will achieve the patient's goals and objectives. Since medical interventions are futile in relation to the *patient's* goals, the third sense of futility provides a very limited basis for unilateral decisions to withhold medical interventions that patients want. A patient might want a treatment a physician deems futile in this sense for one of two reasons.

First, the patient might want treatment because he refuses to accept the physician's estimation of the probability of achieving his goals. For example, the patient's primary goal is to survive to leave the hospital, and the physician concludes that the chance of achieving this goal by means of CPR if the patient were to experience cardiac arrest is close to nil. The patient agrees that CPR would be futile if the physician were right, but the patient refuses to accept the physician's conclusion. Instead, he insists that there is a very good chance that he would survive to leave the hospital if he were to receive CPR after experiencing cardiac arrest. In cases of this type, the disputed judgments call for scientific and clinical expertise that physicians have and patients lack. Consequently, in situations of this type the expertise of physicians appears to support unilateral decisions to withhold medical interventions.

Second, even if the patient accepts the physician's estimation of the probability of achieving his goals, he might want treatment a physician deems futile in the third sense because he believes that despite the very poor odds, it is still worthwhile to give it a try. As it is sometimes put, "there is always a chance for a miracle," and the patient may not want to foreclose whatever slim chance there is. This disagreement between the physician and the patient concerns the standard for determining whether the probability of achieving a specified outcome is "reasonable." To recall what was said in relation to the second sense of futility, although physicians' expertise enables them to determine whether, in relation to a particular standard of reasonableness, a chance of producing a specified outcome is reasonable; setting that standard involves a value judgment that goes beyond that expertise. Again, the physician can attempt to justify a particular standard of reasonableness by citing standards of professional integrity. However, the physician's unilateral decision to withhold treatment would then involve a judgment of futility in the fourth sense.

The reasoning for unilateral judgments of futility in the fourth sense is as follows. As the principle of shared decision-making rightly recognizes, since the best treatment choice for a patient is a function of the patient's preferences and values, physicians' expertise ordinarily does not qualify them to make unilateral treatment decisions for patients. However, as practitioners of medicine, physicians have a special responsibility to uphold standards of professional integrity. These are standards for the medical profession, and not merely personal standards of individual physicians. For example, performing abortions or withdrawing life support might be contrary to the personal standards of a particular physician, but she might not hold that it is improper for *any* physician to perform an abortion or withdraw life support. That is, she need not believe that it is wrong to do either *as a physician*.

Among other things, standards of professional integrity identify the proper goals of medicine and the appropriate objectives and uses of medical interventions. These standards provide a basis for claiming, say, that whereas certain surgical procedures (for example, surgically altering the size and shape of a person's nose) are properly used for cosmetic purposes, others (for example, an amputation of a healthy leg or arm) are not. Accordingly, standards of professional integrity can be used to justify statements such as the following: Whereas it would be proper for a surgeon to alter the shape and size of a patient's nose in order to satisfy the patient's desire to "look better," it would not be appropriate to amputate a healthy limb for the same reason.

Of more relevance to futility decisions, standards of professional integrity provide a basis for the following rule: A medical intervention is futile and may be withheld by a physician even though a patient wants it if the probability of achieving the patient's treatment goals is too low and/or those goals or the means to achieve them are inappropriate. Suppose a physician informs an elderly patient with liver cancer that it is now time to consider measures to make her as comfortable as possible because further aggressive treatment is futile. The patient responds that she *wants* CPR if she suffers cardiopulmonary arrest. The physician carefully explains the burdens of CPR and states that it is futile because the patient is within a group which has less than a 1 percent chance of surviving to leave the hospital. The patient responds that any chance of extending her life, even if it will be spent in the hospital, is worthwhile to her, and clearly outweighs the burdens of CPR. The physician can still maintain that CPR is futile because resuscitative efforts would be incompatible with norms of professional integrity. In effect, the physician would be claiming that the use of CPR in this case would comprise a *misuse* of that medical procedure. However, standards of professional integrity might recognize compelling reasons that can justify otherwise futile or inappropriate medical interventions, for example, the patient's desire to stay alive until her daughter returns from an African safari.[70]

It is important to recognize that this account of futility decisions is not based on the presumed special expertise of physicians. Rather, it is based on the presumed special responsibility of physicians to maintain standards of professional integrity. The term "standards of professional integrity" is ambiguous. It can be used descriptively or prescriptively (in an evaluative sense). Descriptively, standards of professional integrity can refer either to (1) an individual physician's standards of professional integrity (that is, the physician's conception of the proper goals of medicine, the appropriate objectives and uses of medical interventions, and so forth) or (2) customary or currently accepted standards relating to the proper goals of medicine, the appropriate objectives and uses of medical interventions, and so forth. On some questions (for example, whether laetrile is an appropriate treatment for cancer) there may be enough agreement among members of the medical profession to warrant referring to "customary or currently accepted standards." However, on other questions (for example, whether tube feeding is appropriate for patients in a persistent vegetative state), there may be insufficient agreement. Prescriptively, standards of professional integrity refer to *valid* or *legitimate* standards. Validity can be a function of procedural or substantive criteria. As an example of the former, it might be said standards are valid if and only if (1) they were adopted through a democratic process open to physicians and the general public or (2) they would be adopted if such a process were followed. From the perspective of a substantive criterion, standards are valid if and only if their content is *worthy* of being adopted and maintained by members of the medical profession.

There is a consensus that physicians are not obligated to honor requests that violate their conscience or their professional standards (for example, requests for abortions or withdrawal of life support).[71] However, it is unclear that a physician's beliefs and standards—even when they correspond to customary standards—can justify a decision to withhold requested life-sustaining treatment if a transfer of the patient to a physician who will provide it is infeasible. In such circumstances, the justification of unilateral decisions to withhold life-prolonging treatment appears to require *valid* standards of professional integrity. Suppose Ms. F. is a 74-year-old patient with lung cancer. She suffers renal failure and tells her physician, Dr. D., that she wants dialysis. Providing dialysis under these circumstances is contrary to Dr. D.'s conception of the appropriate objectives and uses of dialysis. It is not feasible to transfer Ms. F. to another physician, and she is expected to die within a few days without dialysis. If it is not contrary to valid standards of professional integrity to provide dialysis, it is doubtful that Dr. D. can justifiably refuse to provide it on the grounds that doing so violates *his* and/or *customary* standards of professional integrity. In any event, only valid standards of professional integrity can justify the claim that dialysis in these circumstances is contrary to *reasonable* (and not merely customary) medical practice and inappropriate for *any* physician to offer or provide.

It is beyond the scope of this chapter to provide criteria for identifying valid standards of professional integrity. By way of a modest conclusion about futility, however, I suggest the following. The statement that a medical intervention is futile communicates a sense of scientific objectivity and finality and tends to suggest that clinical data alone can decisively demonstrate that it is justified to withhold treatment even if the patient should want it. However, standards of professional integrity can be an essential component of judgments of futility in every sense (with the possible exception of general physiological futility), and these standards are evaluative. Whereas a medical intervention may be futile in relation to one conception of the proper goals of medicine and the appropriate objectives and uses of that intervention, it may not be futile in relation to another conception. For example, according to one conception of the proper objectives and uses of tube feeding, it may be futile for patients in a persistent vegetative state (PVS); and according to another conception, tube feeding may not be futile for such patients. Similarly, according to one conception of the proper objectives and uses of CPR, resuscitative efforts can be futile if the probability of survival until discharge is less than 2 percent; and according to another conception, resuscitative efforts may not be futile in the same circumstances. A key issue, then, is whether the medical intervention is *appropriate* from the perspective of valid standards of professional integrity.

Since the term "futility" tends to communicate a false sense of scientific objectivity and finality and to obscure the evaluative nature of the corresponding judgments, it is recommended that physicians avoid using it to justify unilateral decisions to withhold life-sustaining treatment.[72] Instead of saying, "life-extending treatment is unwarranted because it is futile," it is recommended that physicians explain the specific grounds for concluding that life support generally, or a particular life-sustaining measure, is inappropriate in the circumstances. Whereas the statement that life-sustaining treatment is futile tends to discourage discussion, explaining the grounds for concluding that (some or all) life-extending interventions are inappropriate in the circumstances tends to invite discussion and point it in the right direction.[73]

Case Study: Leaving an Elderly Patient "Out of the Loop"

Some of the most difficult decisions concerning life-sustaining medical treatment for elderly patients arise when they are no longer capable of participating in those decisions. However, it is important not to neglect decision-making when elderly patients possess decision-making capacity. The following case description presents a fairly common situation, namely, a failure to involve an elderly patient in the decision-making process.

Case Description

Mr. H., a 79-year-old widower, lives alone in the house he shared with his wife for more than forty years. He has developed minor short-term memory loss, but has no significant cognitive impairment. Mr. H. smoked two to three packs of cigarettes a day until he stopped smoking after his wife died of lung cancer about ten years ago. For quite some time, Mr. H. has experienced shortness of breath, and it has been getting more and more difficult for him to move around. However, he has steadfastly refused to see a doctor.

A few days ago, Mr. H. experienced severe respiratory distress. He called his daughter, Ms. T., who immediately drove her father to the emergency department of the nearest hospital. Mr. H. was given oxygen, and he was admitted to the medical floor. He is conscious and alert.

Dr. K., Mr. H.'s attending physician, explained the results of the medical evaluation to Ms. T. He told her that her father has chronic obstructive pulmonary disease (COPD) and congestive heart failure (CHF). Dr. K. explained that Ms. T.'s father is very sick and could not be cured. However, he indicated that it would be possible to extend Mr. H.'s life by placing him on a mechanical ventilator when he was no longer able to breathe on his own.

"When will that decision have to be made?" asked Ms. T.

"Fairly soon, I think," responded Dr. K. "Your father's lung and heart disease is very advanced. I'm surprised that he was able to manage for so long in his condition."

"Well, I've been trying to get him to see a doctor for quite a while, but he always refused. What will happen if he isn't put on the breathing machine?" asked Ms. T.

"If he can't breathe on his own, and he isn't given ventilator support, he will die. However, we can make him comfortable if you decide that you don't want him to receive mechanical ventilation. Why don't you think about it for a day or so, and let me know what you decide."

"It's a tough decision, but I'll do my best," responded Ms. T.

Case Analysis

From an ethical perspective, there are several problems with the decision-making process described in the foregoing case description. The most important are the exclusion of the patient from the process and the failure to respect his autonomy and privacy.[74]

If Mr. H. had been unconscious or severely demented, he would have lacked the capacity to participate in decisions about his care. However, Mr. H. was conscious and alert, and there appears to be no reason to think that he lacks the capacity to participate in the process of choosing treatment goals and a treatment plan. To respect Mr. H.'s autonomy and privacy, he should have been given an opportunity to participate in that decision-making process and to decide how much to involve his daughter.

Before discussing Mr. H.'s condition with his daughter, Dr. K. should have talked to the patient to ascertain whether he had the capacity and the desire to participate in the decision-making process. Dr. K. could have spoken to Mr. H.'s daughter, but to determine whether she had any information pertaining to her father's capacity to participate in the decision-making process, and not to determine whether Mr. H. should be intubated.

Assuming that Mr. H. had the capacity to participate in the process of choosing a treatment plan, Dr. K. should have attempted to solicit from his patient how much involvement he wanted. If Mr. H. were to state that he does not want to be involved in the decision-making process, Dr. K. might try to explore Mr. K.'s reasons, and he might even try to persuade his patient to change his mind. However, if Mr. H. remains firm in his refusal to participate, it would be ethically unacceptable to force him to do so against his will. Nevertheless, it also would be ethically unacceptable for Dr. K. to turn to Mr. H.'s daughter without first ascertaining whether doing so would be compatible with his patient's wishes. Mr. H. may not want his daughter to represent him, and/or there may be someone else (for example, another family member or a close friend) whom he prefers to represent him.

If Mr. H. expresses an interest in participating in the process of working out a treatment plan, Dr. K. may ask him if he would like his daughter to be present. Dr. K. should not assume that Mr. H. wants his daughter to be an active participant in the decision-making process. To be sure, Mr. H. may want his daughter to participate in the discussion of his condition, prognosis, treatment alternatives, and so forth. However, he may prefer to tell his daughter himself after he has been informed, or he may not want her to find out now that he is dying. Alternatively, Mr. H. might not want his daughter to participate in the process of deciding on a treatment plan. He might fear, say, that she will press for aggressive treatment that he doesn't want, or that she will disregard his wishes and interfere with his ability to decide for himself.

If Mr. H. wants to exclude his daughter from the decision-making process, and Dr. K. believes that it would be better for his patient to include her, Dr. K. may try to persuade Mr. H. to change his mind. Ideally, it might be preferable not to exclude father or daughter from the decision-making process. However, if Mr. H. continues to insist that his daughter be excluded, Dr. K. should respect his patient's autonomy and privacy and honor Mr. H.'s wishes.

Notes

1. U.S. Senate Special Committee on Aging, *Aging America: Trends and Projections,* 1991 Edition (Washington, D.C.: Department of Health and Human Services, Publication No. [FCoA] 91-28001, 1991), 20.

2. U.S. Congress, Office of Technology Assessment, *Losing a Million Minds: Confronting the Tragedy of Alzheimer's Disease and Other Dementias* (Washington, D.C.: U.S. Government Printing Office, April 1987), 77.

3. *Aging America,* 20.

4. There are both broad and narrow senses of the term "life-sustaining" treatment. A broad definition is utilized by the President's Commission in its report on forgoing life-sustaining treatment: "life-sustaining treatment . . . encompasses all health care interventions that have the effect of increasing the life span of the patient." The President's Commission for the Study of Ethical Problems in Medicine and Biomedical and Behavioral Research, *Deciding to Forego Life-Sustaining Treatment* (Washington, D.C.: U.S. Government Printing Office, 1983), 3. The Office of Technology Assessment (OTA) report, *Life-Sustaining Technologies and the Elderly,* adopts a similar usage: "Life-sustaining technologies are drugs, medical devices, or procedures that can keep individuals alive who would otherwise die within a foreseeable, but usually uncertain, time period" (4). Guidelines published by the Hastings Center also use a broad definition of the term: "Life-sustaining treatment is any medical intervention, technology, procedure, or medication that is administered to a patient in

order to forestall the moment of death, *whether or not* the treatment is intended to affect the underlying life-threatening diseases(s) or biologic processes." The Hastings Center, *Guidelines on the Termination of Life-Sustaining Treatment and the Care of the Dying* (Briarcliff Manor, N.Y.: Hastings Center, 1987), 4 (emphasis added).

A significantly narrower definition of "life-sustaining" treatment can be found in many living will or natural death statutes in which life-sustaining procedures are limited to interventions that "serve only to prolong the dying process." In addition, it is sometimes stipulated that "death will occur whether or not such procedures are utilized," or "death is imminent whether or not such procedures are utilized." Society for the Right to Die, *1991 Refusal of Treatment Legislation* (New York: Society for the Right to Die, 1991). In contrast to the definition offered by the Hastings Center Guidelines, life-sustaining measures in natural death statutes are often limited to treatment that is *not* intended or expected to affect the "underlying life-threatening disease(s) or biologic processes."

According to the broader definition, for example, dialysis generally is a life-sustaining procedure. However, according to the narrower definition, if dialysis is expected to affect the underlying life-threatening disease(s) or biologic processes, or if it is expected that dialysis will succeed in keeping a patient alive and functional for a considerable period of time, it cannot be termed a "life-sustaining" procedure.

Meisel distinguishes between "life-sustaining" and "life-saving" treatment. The former term is reserved for patients who are "terminally ill or hopelessly ill," and the latter term applies to patients "who are critically ill or injured but have a reasonably good prognosis for recovery if treatment is administered." Alan Meisel, *The Right To Die* (New York: John Wiley and Sons, 1989), 6.

To facilitate a more comprehensive discussion of medical decision-making for critically ill elderly patients, the broader definition of "life-sustaining measures" will be adopted: that is, life-sustaining treatment includes any medical intervention that has the potential effect of increasing the life span of patients. The following are life-sustaining measures: cardiopulmonary resuscitation (CPR), ventilator support, dialysis, antibiotics, nutritional support and hydration, and all of the other interventions and technologies of modern intensive care medicine. Life-sustaining medical interventions in the broad sense will also be referred to as "life-extending" and "life-prolonging" interventions.

5. *Deciding to Forego Life-Sustaining Treatment* and the President's Commission for the Study of Ethical Problems in Medicine and Biomedical Research, *Making Health Care Decisions, Volume One: Report* (Washington, D.C.: U.S. Government Printing Office, 1982).

6. The concept of decision-making capacity will be discussed in the following section.

7. Lynn observes that physician recommendations can be helpful to patients who are conflicted about choices. See Joanne Lynn, "Conflicts of Interest in Medical Decision-Making," *Journal of the American Geriatrics Society* 36, no. 10 (October 1988): 945–50.

8. For an extensive discussion of the principle of respect for autonomy, see Tom L. Beauchamp and James F. Childress, *Principles of Biomedical Ethics,* 3d ed. (New York: Oxford University Press, 1989).

9. For a discussion of how the treatment preferences of elderly patients can vary, see Christine K. Cassel, "The Meaning of Health Care in Old Age" in Thomas R. Cole and Sally A. Gadow, eds., *What Does It Mean to Grow Old? Reflections from the Humanities* (Durham: Duke University Press, 1986), 179–98.

10. Decision-making for elderly patients who lack decision-making capacity will be examined in Chapter 2.

11. See the President's Commission report, *Deciding to Forego Life-Sustaining Treatment;* D. Joanne Lynn, "Deciding About Life-Sustaining Therapy" in Christine K. Cassel

and John R. Walsh, eds., *Geriatric Medicine,* vol. 2, *Fundamentals of Geriatric Care* (New York: Springer-Verlag, 1984), 325–31; the OTA report, *Life-Sustaining Technologies and the Elderly;* Robert F. Weir, *Abating Treatment With Critically Ill Patients: Ethical and Legal Limits to the Medical Prolongation of Life* (New York: Oxford University Press, 1989); and Meisel, *The Right to Die.*

12. See the Hastings Center *Guidelines,* 130; Meisel, *The Right to Die,* 80; and Weir, *Abating Treatment with Critically Ill Patients,* 401.

13. See the President's Commission report, *Deciding to Forego Life-Sustaining Treatment,* 73–77; Lynn, "Deciding About Life-Sustaining Therapy"; and The Hastings Center *Guidelines on the Termination of Life-Sustaining Treatment and the Care of the Dying,* 130–31. As Weir aptly observes, there is "a widespread consensus among philosophers, religious ethicists, legal scholars, judges, and many physicians . . . that there is *no morally significant or legally significant difference* between withholding and withdrawing life-sustaining treatment" (*Abating Treatment,* 401; emphasis in original). For a discussion of the legal perspective, see Meisel, *The Right to Die* and the book's "1992 Cumulative Supplement No. 2."

14. For a critical discussion of additional reasons, see the President's Commission report, *Deciding to Forego Life-Sustaining Treatment,* 73–77.

15. Weir refers to a "continuing controversy" and the existence of "fundamental disagreements" about the ethical permissibility of forgoing nutritional support and hydration (*Abating Treatment,* 409). Nevertheless, he refers to a "mainstream position that has emerged in this controversy," namely, the position that artificial nutrition and hydration are "morally equivalent to mechanical ventilation and other life-sustaining technologies" (409). Meisel observes that "[b]etween 1982 and 1987, virtually every reported case held that artificial nutrition and hydration is a medical procedure, that it may be forgone under appropriate circumstances as may any other procedure, and that the fact that it involves basic sustenance is not relevant to whether it must be administered or may be forgone" (*The Right to Die, 1992 Cumulative Supplement No. 2,* 88). Several states (e.g., Florida, Maine, Oklahoma, Virginia, and Wyoming) have amended their living will legislation to authorize people to refuse artificial nutrition and hydration and several states have enacted durable power of attorney for health care legislation that authorizes surrogates to refuse nutrition and hydration. This information is from the Society for the Right to Die, "News from Society for the Right to Die: Significant Legal Developments," March 1990–August 1990 and September 1990–April 1991.

16. See Joanne Lynn and James F. Childress, "Must Patients Always be Given Food and Water?" in Joanne Lynn, ed. *By No Extraordinary Means: The Choice to Forgo Life-Sustaining Food and Water,* expanded ed. (Bloomington: Indiana University Press, 1989), 47–60; and Roberta M. Myers and Michael A. Grodin, "Decisionmaking Regarding the Initiation of Tube Feedings in the Severely Demented Elderly: A Review," *Journal of the American Geriatrics Society* 39, no. 5 (May 1991): 526–31.

17. Daniel Callahan, "On Feeding the Dying," *The Hastings Center Report* 13, no. 5 (October 1983): 22. In a subsequent book, Callahan accepts withholding artificial nutrition and hydration in some cases, but he continues to express strong reservations about that practice. He warns against "tampering with traditions such as continuance of food and water . . . [that] were cultivated to provide as solid a fortress as morality can offer against a human propensity—seen time and again with the elderly—to neglect, abuse, or kill the powerless, the burdensome, and the inconvenient." *Setting Limits: Medical Goals in an Aging Society* (New York: Simon and Schuster, 1987), 188. In this book, Callahan also defends age-rationing of medical care. However, if he is concerned about maintaining tradi-

tions to protect elderly persons from being neglected, abused, and even killed, it is surprising that Callahan does not give more consideration to the possible negative impact on those traditions of the age-rationing policies that he recommends. Age-rationing is discussed in Chapter 3.

18. Alan J. Weisbard and Mark Siegler, "On Killing Patients with Kindness: An Appeal for Caution," in Lynn, ed., *By No Extraordinary Means*, 112.

19. See the OTA report, *Life-Sustaining Technologies and the Elderly*, chapter 8 ("Nutritional Support and Hydration").

20. Callahan, "On Feeding the Dying," 22.

21. According to Callahan, "one of the most important [rules] in all cultures, save the most debased, is that the needy and the helpless must be fed." Daniel Callahan, "Public Policy and the Cessation of Nutrition" in Lynn, ed. *By No Extraordinary Means*, 61.

22. Ronald A. Carson,"The Symbolic Significance of Giving to Eat and Drink," in Lynn, ed., *By No Extraordinary Means*, 87.

23. "Public Policy and the Cessation of Nutrition," 63.

24. See Meyers and Grodin, "Decisionmaking Regarding the Initiation of Tube Feeding in the Severely Demented Elderly." According to Lynn and Childress: "Patients who are allowed to die without artificial hydration and nutrition may well die more comfortably than patients who receive conventional amounts of intravenous hydration. Terminal pulmonary edema, nausea, and mental confusion are more likely when patients have been treated to maintain fluid and nutrition until close to the time of death" ("Must Patients Always Be Given Food and Water?" 52–53). See also Phyllis Schmitz and Merry O'Brien, "Observations on Nutrition and Hydration in Dying Cancer Patients" in Lynn, ed., *By No Extraordinary Means*, 29–38; and Louise A. Printz, "Terminal Dehydration, a Compassionate Treatment," *Archives of Internal Medicine* 152 (April 1992): 697–700. For a discussion of various means of tube and intravenous feeding, and the advantages and disadvantages of each, see chapter 8 of the OTA report, *Life-Sustaining Technologies and the Elderly*.

25. In *Setting Limits*, Callahan concedes that it is permissible to withhold or withdraw artificial nutrition and hydration from elderly patients in two situations: (1) the patient is "imminently dying;" and (2) the patient is "irreversibly comatose." In such cases, he claims, artificial nutrition and hydration are of no "genuine benefit" to patients. Callahan draws the line here, excluding elderly patients who are "wholly and most likely irreversibly demented." His reason for drawing the line here is that we cannot "speak with any certainty about what benefits such a person, much less confidently judge that life itself is a burden" (191). Consistency would seem to preclude assessments of benefits and burdens in relation to CPR, dialysis, and other life-sustaining measures for such patients as well, a position that Callahan does not endorse.

26. See Callahan, "Public Policy and the Cessation of Nutrition;" and Weisbard and Siegler, "On Killing Patients With Kindness: An Appeal for Caution."

27. For an analysis of a case involving nutritional support, see David T. Watts and Christine K. Cassel, "Extraordinary Nutritional Support: A Case Study and Ethical Analysis," *Journal of the American Geriatrics Society* 32, no. 3 (March 1984): 237–42.

28. The President's Commission recommends the term "decisionmaking capacity" rather than "competence" to "avoid the sometimes confounding legal overtones associated with the terms competence and incompetence" (*Making Health Care Decisions*, 56). "Incapacitated person," the President's Commission's substitute for "incompetent person," is problematical because it includes a broad range of physical and mental disabilities that need not be associated with an inability to make certain health care decisions.

29. See the President's Commission reports, *Making Health Care Decisions* and *Decid-

ing to Forego Life-Sustaining Treatment, and Allen E. Buchanan and Dan W. Brock, *Deciding for Others: The Ethics of Surrogate Decision Making* (Cambridge: Cambridge University Press, 1989).

30. It has been claimed that "the search for a single test of competency is a search for a Holy Grail." Loren H. Roth, Alan Meisel, and Charles W. Lidz, "Tests of Competency to Consent to Treatment," *American Journal of Psychiatry* 134 (1977): 283. The President's Commission and Buchanan and Brock also rule out the possibility of a single test of decision-making capacity.

31. *Deciding for Others,* 51. Buchanan and Brock provide an analysis of "competence," which they claim "is to be understood as *decision-making capacity*" (18).

32. *Deciding for Others,* 60–65. Buchanan and Brock defend a "decision-relative" standard, one that is risk-related and task-related. Some of their arguments for a decision-relative standard support a *task*-related criterion and others support a *risk*-related criterion.

33. *Deciding for Others,* 61. Brock reiterates this claim and responds to my criticisms in Dan W. Brock, "Decisionmaking Competence and Risk," *Bioethics* 5, no. 2 (April 1991): 105–12. For my response, see "A Response to Brock and Skene," *Bioethics* 5, no. 2 (April 1991): 118–22.

34. *Deciding for Others,* 61–62.

35. *Deciding for Others,* 27. Buchanan and Brock maintain that "there are not two distinct questions of whether the patient is competent and then whether, even if competent, paternalistic setting aside of the patient's choice about treatment is justified. Instead, there is the one question of whether the patient's exercise of decision-making capacities on this occasion has been sufficiently defective and has yielded a decision sufficiently contrary to the patient's good to warrant setting aside the patient's choice by deeming him or her incompetent" (*Deciding for Others,* 63).

36. *Deciding for Others,* 60.

37. Differences, such as fat content and additives, will be disregarded for the purpose of this example.

38. *Deciding for Others,* 27.

39. Refusals of life-saving medical treatment on religious grounds are a classic example of this type of situation.

40. I am *not* suggesting that it would be ethically permissible to override the patient's refusal, and I am also not suggesting that it would be permitted by law. I am only claiming that it is not *inconsistent* to hold that (1) within the framework of the standard analysis, there are no identifiable deficits in the patient's decision-making capacity and (2) it is ethically permissible to override the patient's refusal to prevent his death. Paternalism is discussed in Chapter 4.

41. James F. Drane, "Competency to Give an Informed Consent: A Model for Making Clinical Assessments," *Journal of the American Medical Association* 252, no. 7 (August 17, 1984): 926.

42. "Competency to Give an Informed Consent," 926.

43. "Competency to Give an Informed Consent," 926.

44. "Competency to Give an Informed Consent," 926.

45. The President's Commission observed that it generally is pointless to undertake a formal examination of a patient's decision-making capacity when patients, physicians, and family favor the same option (*Making Health Care Decisions,* 61–62).

46. Buchanan and Brock acknowledge that when patients satisfy only a weak standard of decision-making capacity, "the benefit/risk assessment *made by others*" is the primary basis for believing that the patient's choice best promotes her own well-being (*Deciding for Others,*

53; emphasis added). However, they fail to recognize the anomaly between saying, on the one hand, that a patient has the capacity to make a particular decision, and saying, on the other hand, that her choice has little if any evidential value in relation to identifying the course of action that will best promote her welfare.

47. Buchanan and Brock defend their analysis against an alternative they call a "fixed minimal capacity" view (*Deciding for Others*, 59ff.). The latter view sets a *general* minimum or threshold, one that holds for *all* decisions, with no allowance for the complexity of the decision, the specific cognitive skills and abilities required, and so forth. Such a view appears to rule out even a *task*-related standard. The following passage rules out setting minimum levels of decision-making capacity for *specific* decisions: "It might seem that there are very low-risk but also very complex decisions that we rightly let people make, despite their inability to understand them, because nothing significant for their well-being rides on the outcome of their decision. This might seem a case in which the person is incompetent to decide but is still given the authority to decide. Instead, we consider this a case in which the lowest standard for competence applies since only the person's self-determination and not well-being is at stake in his choice between options" (*Deciding for Others*, 61).

48. Buchanan and Brock state that an "adequate standard of competence will focus primarily not on the content of the patient's decision but on the *process* of the reasoning that leads up to that decision" (*Deciding for Others*, 50). They refer to their standard as a "process standard." A similar position is taken by the President's Commission in its report, *Making Health Care Decisions*.

49. Consistent with their construal of the *function* of competency assessments, Buchanan and Brock claim that "just because a patient is competent to consent to a treatment, it does *not* follow that the patient is competent to refuse it, and vice versa" (*Deciding for Others*, 51–52). However, if there are no relevant differences in the corresponding *processes of reasoning*, this claim appears to be at odds with the statement cited above that an "adequate standard of competence will focus primarily not on the content of the patient's decision but on the *process* of the reasoning that leads up to that decision."

50. As the President's Commission observed, "when the consequences for well-being are substantial, there is a greater need to be *certain* that the patient possesses the necessary level of capacity" (*Making Health Care Decisions*, 60; emphasis added). See also *Deciding for Others*, 51.

51. For a general discussion of clinical assessments of decision-making capacity, see Charles M. Culver, "The Clinical Determination of Competence" in Marshall B. Kapp, Harvey E. Pies, and A. Edward Doudera, eds., *Legal and Ethical Aspects of Health Care for the Elderly* (Ann Arbor: Health Administration Press, 1985), 277–85; Thomas Grisso, *Evaluating Competencies: Forensic Assessments and Instruments* (New York: Plenum, 1986); and Paul S. Apelbaum and Thomas Grisso, "Assessing Patients' Capacities to Consent to Treatment," *New England Journal of Medicine* 319, no. 25 (December 22, 1988): 1635–38. For a discussion of clinical assessments of elderly patients' decision-making capacity, see L. Jaime Fitten, Richard Lusky, and Claus Hamann, "Assessing Treatment Decision-Making Capacity in Elderly Nursing Home Residents," *Journal of the American Geriatrics Society* 38, no. 10 (October 1990): 1097–1104.

52. Mark H. Waymack and Geroge A. Taler, *Medical Ethics and the Elderly: A Case Book* (Chicago: Pluribus, 1988), 53.

53. See Lynn, "Conflicts of Interest in Medical Decision-Making."

54. Waymack and Taler state that "the family's moral authority is negligible when the patient is competent" (*Medical Ethics and the Elderly*, 57). Elderly patients can have ethical obligations toward family members that have a bearing on treatment decisions. Accordingly,

as Hardwig observes, the interests of family members can be ''[ethically] relevant *whether or not* the patient is inclined to consider them.'' John Hardwig, ''What About the Family?'' *Hastings Center Report* 20, no. 2 (March/April 1990): 8. For reasons to be discussed below, however, elderly patients generally should retain decision-making authority even if physicians believe that they are failing to give due consideration to the interests of family members. Accordingly, Hardwig appears to overstate the ethical significance of the interests of family members when he claims that ''it is sometimes the moral thing to do for a physician to sacrifice the interests of her patient to those of nonpatients—specifically, to those of the other members of the patient's family'' (5). For a perceptive discussion of families and medical decision-making, see James Lindemann Nelson, ''Taking Families Seriously,'' *Hastings Center Report* 22, no. 4 (July–August 1992): 6–12.

55. If the attending concludes that aggressive therapy would be ''futile,'' it might be argued that he has no obligation to give Ms. K.'s father an opportunity to accept or reject aggressive therapy. Medical futility will be discussed below.

56. According to the traditional notion of fidelity to the *patient's* interests, a physician should recommend treatment to a patient only if the physician believes that it will benefit that particular patient. By contrast, a central principle of family medicine is that the concern of the physician should extend beyond the individual patient to members of his or her family. The apparent gap between these two conceptions is narrowed when it is recognized that patients can and often do take an interest in the wishes and interests of family members. For an explanation and defense of the basic principles of family medicine, see Ronald J. Christie and C. Barry Hoffmaster, *Ethical Issues in Family Medicine* (New York: Oxford University Press, 1986). The traditional notion of fidelity to the patient's interests is also challenged by Hardwig and Nelson in the articles cited above.

57. Although Christie and Hoffmaster maintain that the interests of family members are ethically relevant, they do not call for family physicians to deny individual patients an opportunity to accept or refuse treatment. For example, when they discuss a case in which they claim that a physician should consider the interests of the granddaughters of an elderly woman who initially refused an amputation of a gangrenous leg, Christie and Hoffmaster cite with approval the physician's efforts to persuade the woman to agree to the amputation (*Ethical Issues in Family Medicine,* 79–82).

58. Recent articles defending futility judgments include: Leslie J. Blackhall, ''Must We Always Use CPR?'' *New England Journal of Medicine* 317, no. 20 (November 12, 1987): 1281–85; Donald J. Murphy, ''Do-Not-Resuscitate Orders: Time for Reappraisal in Long-term–Care Institutions,'' *Journal of the American Medical Association* 260, no. 14 (October 14, 1988): 2098–2101; Tom Tomlinson and Howard Brody, ''Ethics and Communication in Do-Not-Resuscitate Orders,'' *New England Journal of Medicine* 318, no. 1 (January 7, 1988): 43–46; Tom Tomlinson and Howard Brody, ''Futility and the Ethics of Resuscitation,'' *Journal of the American Medical Association* 264, no. 10 (September 12, 1990): 1276–80; and Lawrence J. Schneiderman, Nancy S. Jecker, and Albert R. Jonsen, ''Medical Futility: Its Meaning and Ethical Implications,'' *Annals of Internal Medicine* 112, no. 12 (June 15, 1990): 949–54. Dissenters include Stuart J. Youngner, ''Who Defines Futility?'' *Journal of the American Medical Association* 260, no. 14 (October 14, 1988): 2094–95; John D. Lantos, et al., ''The Illusion of Futility in Clinical Practice,'' *American Journal of Medicine* 87 (July 1989): 81–84; and Giles R. Scofield, ''Is Consent Useful When Resuscitation Isn't?'' *Hastings Center Report* 21, no. 6 (November–December 1991): 28–36.

59. See Geroge E. Taffet, Thomas A. Teasdale, and Robert J. Luchi, ''In-Hospital Cardiopulmonary Resuscitation,'' *Journal of the American Medical Association* 260, no. 14 (October 14, 1988): 2069–72. For a different view, see Michael Gordon and Eric Hurowitz,

"Cardiopulmonary Resuscitation of the Elderly," *Journal of the American Geriatrics Society* 32, no. 12 (December 1984): 930–34; and the OTA report, *Life-Sustaining Technologies and the Elderly*.

60. Murphy, "Do-Not-Resuscitate Orders," 2098.

61. Murphy, "Do-Not-Resuscitate Orders," 2098.

62. Tomlinson and Brody state that when the rationale for a DNR decision is that "resuscitation would be of no medical benefit, . . . the physician has no duty to ascertain the patient's preferences" ("Ethics and Communication in Do-Not-Resuscitate Orders," 45). Earlier in the article they state that "when resuscitation offers no medical benefit, the physician can make a reasoned determination that a DNR order should be written without any knowledge of the patient's values in the matter" (44).

63. Schneiderman, Jecker, and Jonsen, "Medical Futility: Its Meaning and Ethical Implications," 953.

64. Schneiderman, Jecker, and Jonsen claim that "futility is a professional judgment that takes precedence over patient autonomy and permits physicians to withhold or withdraw care deemed to be inappropriate without subjecting such a decision to patient approval" ("Medical Futility: Its Meaning and Ethical Implications," 953).

65. Blackhall, "Must We Always Use CPR?"; and Schneiderman, Jecker, and Jonsen, "Medical Futility: Its Meaning and Ethical Implications."

66. Tomlinson and Brody, "Futility and the Ethics of Resuscitation;" and Stuart J. Youngner, "Futility in Context," *Journal of the American Medical Association* 264, no. 10 (September 12, 1990): 1295–96.

67. In its report, *Deciding to Forego Life-Sustaining Treatment*, the President's Commission stated: "Although competent patients thus have the legal and ethical authority to forego some or all care, this does not mean that patients may insist on particular treatments. The care available from health care professionals is generally limited to what is consistent with role-related professional standards and conscientiously held personal beliefs. A health care professional has an obligation to allow a patient to choose from among medically acceptable treatment options . . . or to reject all options. No one, however, has an obligation to provide interventions that would, in his or her judgment, be countertherapeutic" (44).

68. "Futility" decisions can also serve as a smokescreen for cost-containment by means of rationing. Rationing of health care by age is discussed in Chapter 3.

69. See Tomlinson and Brody, "Futility and the Ethics of Resuscitation;" and Howard Brody, Robert M. Arnold, and Tom Tomlinson, "Futility and Refusing to Provide Treatment: Important Distinctions" (unpublished paper). Although the authors discuss norms of professional integrity in the context of an examination of futility, they recommend against using the term *futility* in this context. I shall make a similar recommendation below.

70. Schneiderman et al., cite the example of a "patient with terminal metastatic cancer who requests resuscitation in the event of cardiac arrest to survive long enough to see a son or daughter who has not yet arrived from afar to pay last respects" ("Medical Futility: Its Meaning and Ethical Implications," 953).

71. See the President's Commission report, *Deciding to Forego Life-Sustaining Treatment*, 44.

72. In "Futility and Refusing to Provide Treatment: Important Distinctions," Brody, Arnold, and Tomlinson maintain that only judgments of "probabilistic futility" should be referred to as judgments of *futility*. A medical intervention is futile in this sense if and only if no reasonable physician would expect it to achieve the patient's goals (which can include "psychological" and "social" as well as "biomedical" goals). Even if the only judgments

that could be designated futility judgments were judgments of probabilistic futility, the term "futility" still tends to mask the evaluative character of the "reasonable physician" standard.

73. See Scofield, "Is Consent Useful When Resuscitation Isn't?" In relation to "futile resuscitation attempts," Youngner writes, "Don't offer, perhaps, but please discuss" ("Futility in Context," 1296).

74. Another problem is the inadequacy of the information given to the patient's daughter. Informed consent is discussed in Chapter 5.

CHAPTER 2

Life-Sustaining Medical Care: Elderly Patients without Decision-Making Capacity

Unfortunately, by the time elderly persons become "candidates" for life-sustaining treatment, it may no longer be possible for physicians to give them an opportunity to decide whether to accept or reject it because they have lost their decision-making capacity.[1] One obvious example is cardio-pulmonary resuscitation (CPR). Clearly, elderly persons whose hearts have stopped are in no position to decide whether to accept or reject CPR. But this situation is not limited to CPR. Many of the diseases and conditions that can make continued life contingent on life-prolonging measures can also destroy or substantially impair a person's decision-making capacity and are more likely to strike people in their later years. In addition, dementing illnesses are more likely to be experienced by older persons.[2] Accordingly, it is not an overstatement to maintain that "decision making under circumstances of mental incapacity is a particularly relevant issue in the care of elderly persons."[3] Decision-making for elderly patients who lack decision-making capacity can be difficult, and it has been remarked that "few problem areas in medicine are more complex . . . ."[4]

When elderly patients lack decision-making capacity, it is obviously impossible for them to participate directly in decision-making about life-sustaining treatment. However, people can plan for such a contingency by making their wishes known when their decision-making capacity is still unimpaired.[5] There are several obvious advantages to advance planning. First, it is more likely that the decision will reflect the patient's own values, a central objective of shared decision-making. Accordingly, advance planning can facilitate a close approximation to shared decision-making for elderly patients without decision-making capacity. Second, if family members are asked to decide whether treatment should be withheld or withdrawn and the patient herself has failed to engage in any advance planning, family members may experience strong feelings of guilt, anxiety, resentment, self-doubt, and so forth. Third, in the absence of advance planning by patients, there is a greater potential for conflict among family members, among health care professionals, and between family members and health care professionals. Such conflicts can impede sound decision-making, require a considerable expenditure of resources, and increase the likelihood of lawsuits and other legal action. Consequently, it is desirable, and in the interests of everyone concerned, to plan ahead and, while one is still able to do so, to determine and express one's preferences about life-extending treatment.

Advance Directives

An advance directive is a means by which people with decision-making capacity give directions pertaining to future health care decision-making in the event that they lose their ability to choose for themselves.[6] There are three types of advance directives. First, *instruction directives,* which give substantive guidelines or instructions pertaining to wanted and/or unwanted medical interventions. Living wills or natural death directives are instruction directives. Second, *proxy directives,* which designate a representative or surrogate to make health care decisions. A durable power of attorney for health care is a proxy directive. Third, *combination directives,* or two-part advance directives that give instructions and designate a surrogate. Advance directives may be either statutory or nonstatutory and oral (including messages that have been audiotaped or videotaped) or written.

Instruction Directives and Living Wills

Instruction directives can request life-saving interventions and/or they can instruct treatment to be forgone or limited in certain circumstances. Instruction directives are subject to the same constraints applying to requests by patients with decision-making capacity. Accordingly, health care professionals may refuse to comply with instruction directives incompatible with conscientiously held convictions or standards of professional integrity.[7]

As I will use the terms, a "living will" or a "natural death directive" refers to a written instruction that includes a statement directing life-saving treatment to be forgone or limited in certain circumstances.[8] As of October 1992, the District of Columbia and all but three states (Massachusetts, Michigan, and New York) had legislation authorizing living wills.[9] The first statutory living will, the California Natural Death Act, was enacted in

1976.[10] Its passage was fueled in part by reaction to the case of Karen Ann Quinlan, a young New Jersey woman in a persistent vegetative state whose parents sought court permission to withdraw ventilatory support.[11] Ironically, however, the California directive would not have applied to Karen Quinlan. That directive applies only to patients who have a "terminal condition" and who are being kept alive by narrowly defined "life-sustaining" procedures. The California Natural Death Act defines a "terminal condition" as:

> an incurable condition caused by injury, disease, or illness, which, regardless of the application of life-sustaining procedures, would, within reasonable medical judgment, produce death, and where the application of life-sustaining procedures serve only to postpone the moment of death of the patient.[12]

A "life-sustaining procedure" is defined as:

> any medical procedure or intervention which utilizes mechanical or other artificial means to sustain, restore, or supplant a vital function, which, when applied to a qualified patient, would serve only to artificially prolong the moment of death and where, in the judgment of the attending physician, death is imminent whether or not such procedures are utilized.[13]

Thus, the California Natural Death Act applies only to patients who are near death (that is, expected to die within a relatively short period of time with or without medical treatment).[14] This restriction will be referred to as the "terminal condition/illness" requirement. Since Karen Quinlan lived for more than nine years with the help of tube feeding after the ventilator was withdrawn, she did not satisfy this requirement and therefore was not a "qualified patient" under the legislation that her plight helped to enact.

The terminal condition requirement was a typical feature of earlier living will laws. For example, in 1983, eleven out of fifteen natural death statutes imposed that requirement.[15] However, living will legislation currently is in a state of considerable flux with respect to this and other provisions.[16] For example, in the seven-month period from September 1990 to April 1991, three states (Louisiana, Virginia, and West Virginia) amended their natural death legislation to include some form of permanent unconsciousness within its scope; and one state (South Dakota) enacted legislation stipulating that "terminal condition" includes "a coma or other condition of permanent unconsciousness."[17]

The inclusion of permanent unconsciousness may satisfy the concern of elderly persons who want to avoid a Karen Quinlan situation, but it fails to provide an opportunity to limit life-extending treatment in the event of other irreversible and severely debilitating conditions (for example, Alzheimer's-related dementia or severe mental and physical impairment as a result of massive strokes).[18] People can suffer severely disabling injuries and illnesses at any age. However, elderly persons are particularly at risk of developing disabling and/or dementing illnesses.[19] For elderly persons who are troubled by the prospect of being maintained by life-sustaining procedures if and when they become severely impaired physically and/or mentally, statutory living wills offer only a limited remedy.[20] To be sure, such persons can execute nonstatutory instruction directives by drafting personal statements or using one of many prepared forms.[21] For example, a Society for the Right to Die Living Will Declaration states: ''If I should be in an incurable or irreversible mental or physical condition with no reasonable expectation of recovery, I direct my attending physician to withhold or withdraw treatment that merely prolongs my dying.'' A Concern for Dying living will states: ''If at such a time the situation should arise in which there is no reasonable expectation of my recovery from extreme physical or mental disability, I direct that I be allowed to die and not be kept alive by medications, artificial means or 'heroic measures.'''[22] And the Emanuels' Medical Directive provides an opportunity to express a desire to forgo up to twelve medical interventions if one were to become severely impaired cognitively.[23] Still, in view of the statutory restrictions, it is imperative to ask whether there are good reasons from an ethical perspective for implementing living wills only when patients are terminally ill or permanently unconsciousness.

A natural place to begin is by considering the situation of patients with decision-making capacity. Obviously patients who are permanently unconscious do not possess decision-making capacity, but for patients with that capacity, the right to refuse medical interventions is not contingent upon their having a terminal condition. There is no requirement, say, that a patient's refusal of dialysis or a tracheostomy should be honored only if the patient is terminally ill. Are there any differences between contemporaneous treatment refusals by patients with decision-making capacity and prospective treatment refusals expressed in instruction directives that justify restrictions for the latter but not the former?

Buchanan and Brock identify four purported ''morally significant asymmetries.''[24] First, when patients with decision-making capacity decide whether to accept or refuse treatment, they can be given up-to-date information about available therapeutic options. However, there can be significant developments in medicine and medical technology between the time a person executes an advance directive and the time of its implementation. Consequently, the information on which the instruction directive was based may be outdated and no longer accurate. Suppose, say, that after a year of comprehensive testing, doctors conclude that Ms. Q. has Alzheimer's disease. Ms. Q. is told that she has Alzheimer's, the disease is explained to her, and she is informed that there is no cure or effective treatment. After much reflection and discussion with her family, Ms. Q. writes a living will stating that when her mental condition deteriorates to the point that she is unable to make decisions concerning her health care, she does not want treatment for any life-threatening illnesses, even if they are curable. All she wants is comfort care. Five years later, when Ms. Q. lacks decision-making capacity, she develops pneumonia. If the pneumonia is successfully treated, she will live to participate in a trial of a promising experimental drug for Alzheimer's, but treatment of the pneumonia appears to be incompatible with her living will.

A second claimed asymmetry is associated with advance directives that rule out specified types of medical interventions.[25] When patients with decision-making capacity decide whether to accept or refuse a medical intervention (for example, mechanical respiration), they can tailor their decision to the particular circumstances. For example, someone who would decide to refuse intubation for end-stage COPD might decide to accept it for acute and reversible respiratory failure. However, if a living will includes a blanket objection to "mechanical ventilators," it undermines the distinction between intubation for acute and chronic respiratory failure.

A third purported asymmetry pertains to informal safeguards that reduce the risk of imprudent or unreasonable choices. When patients with decision-making capacity decide whether to accept or refuse life-sustaining treatment, health care professionals, family members, and friends can, and sometimes do, attempt to persuade them to accept those measures. If physicians, family members and/or friends favor life-sustaining treatment, talking to patients can help prevent them from making literally fatal mistakes. By contrast since withholding or withdrawing life-sustaining treatment is a remote and abstract possibility at the time when many people enact advance directives, the decision to execute one is not likely to be subject to so much careful scrutiny by physicians and loved ones.

The last of Buchanan and Brock's four claimed asymmetries between contemporaneous and prospective treatment refusals relates to an assumption underlying the principle of shared decision-making: people with decision-making capacity generally are the best judges of their own interests or good. The reasoning for this purported asymmetry is as follows: One reason for thinking that people with decision-making capacity are the best judges of their own interests or good is that they are generally best acquainted with their own capacities and limitations (i.e., what they can and cannot do, what does and does not give them satisfaction and make them happy, and so forth). However, a loss of decision-making capacity as a result of illness or injury is often correlated with significant changes in other capacities as well. Thus, people may derive satisfaction from substantially different activities after a loss of decision-making capacity, and it is doubtful that their advance decisions will accurately reflect their best interests if and when they should suffer a loss of decision-making capacity.

A fifth possible morally significant difference between contemporaneous and advance refusals is related to the possibility that people will change their minds after deciding to forgo life-sustaining treatment. Since many years can elapse between the execution and implementation of advance directives, people may undergo a change of mind that their directives fail to reflect and that they are unable to communicate due to cognitive impairment. By contrast, there is much less time for patients with decision-making capacity who have decided to forgo life-sustaining measures to change their minds, and if they do, they are able to communicate such changes to health care professionals.

When health care professionals honor advance directives that call for life-extending treatment to be forgone, patients die. The five alleged differences between contemporaneous and advance refusals of life-prolonging treatment suggest that if the advance refusals of elderly patients are honored, there is the danger that some elderly persons will be allowed to die when this result does not reflect their current wishes and/or best interests. Accordingly, the terminal condition or permanent unconsciousness requirement might be defended as a reasonable effort to "play it safe": if living wills are honored only when patients are terminally ill or permanently unconscious, there is little danger that withholding or withdrawing life-sustaining measures will be a serious mistake from the perspective of patients' wishes and interests.

However, it is misleading to claim that physicians would be playing it safe if they adopted a policy of implementing advance refusals of life-extending treatment only if patients are terminally ill or permanently unconsciousness. This claim fails to consider the important patient interests that are promoted by advance refusals and that would not be served if such a policy were adopted. These interests include (1) an autonomy or self-determination interest; (2) an interest in avoiding pointless, burdensome, and demeaning medical manipulations; and (3) an interest in protecting others (for example, family and friends) from emotional and financial costs.[26] In addition, when people are thwarted from executing living wills to promote these interests they may experience anger, resentment, frustration, anxiety, and so forth. Consequently, it is necessary to consider whether the only adequate safeguard for patients is the principle that advance refusals of life-extending treatment should be implemented only if patients are terminally ill or permanently unconscious.

Corresponding to the claimed asymmetries identified above—with the possible exception of the fourth, which will be discussed shortly—there are important differences between advance and contemporaneous refusals. However, the ethical significance of these differences can be mitigated significantly by the following procedures. First, physicians should engage in a process of advance planning with their patients; written instruction directives should record and summarize, rather than supplant, discussions between physicians and patients.[27] Second, advance planning between physicians and patients should include a discussion of *goals,* and not be restricted to specific interventions.[28] Third, physicians should periodically review instruction directives with patients, and not treat written directives as pieces of paper to be considered only when decisions have to be made. Periodic discussions of patients' health care preferences can (1) provide patients with up-to-date medical information; (2) ascertain patients' intentions when they express a blanket objection to certain medical interventions (for example, what a 73-year-old patient means when she says "I never want to be put on machines"); (c) provide some of the same informal safeguards that tend to prevent or reduce imprudent contemporaneous refusals; and (d) identify significant changes over time in the patient's preferences and goals. In view of the important interests that can be served by advance refusals, it is preferable that physicians protect patients by engaging in periodic discussions with them about their health care preferences and goals rather than by a policy of implementing living wills only if patients are terminally ill or permanently unconscious.

Even in the absence of such discussions, written advance directives can provide important guidance, but it would be a serious mistake to adopt a literal reading of them. Such a reading would take the language of the living will literally and would not think it necessary to determine the intent of the person who executed it. Consider the living will executed by Ms. Q., the Alzheimer's patient, which states that she does not want medical treatment for any life-threatening condition. A literal reading of Ms. Q.'s living will would support a decision to withhold antibiotics when she develops pneumonia shortly before she is scheduled to receive a promising experimental Alzheimer's drug. Similarly, a literal reading of an advance directive that states "I do not want to be kept alive by any machines" would support a decision not to temporarily intubate a patient with reversible respiratory failure.

A general rule that advance refusals should be implemented only if patients are terminally ill or permanently unconscious is one means of protecting them from literal readings of their advance directives. However, that rule may also thwart patients' wishes and well-being. Suppose Mr. H., a 76-year-old retired postal worker, executed a living will that states in part that he does not want to be "maintained by machines." His intent, let us suppose, was to prevent his being kept alive if he should become permanently dependent on a respirator. If Mr. H. develops reversible respiratory failure, the terminal illness or permanent unconsciousness requirement is not satisfied, and it protects him from the consequences of a literal interpretation of his living will. However, that requirement is also not satisfied if Mr. H. suffers a massive stroke that leaves him permanently ventilator-dependent and mentally devastated with no chance of significant recovery. In this situation, then, the terminal condition or permanent unconsciousness requirement thwarts his wishes. As in the case of Mr. H., a general rule stating that advance refusals will be implemented only if patients are terminally ill or permanently unconscious can protect them from unwarranted literal readings of their living wills. However, there is an alternative, namely, attempting to ascertain patients' intentions on a case-by-case basis. This alternative, in contrast to the terminal illness or permanent unconsciousness requirement, does not undermine the use of living wills to forestall unwanted health care, and is therefore preferable.[29]

A claim associated with the fourth alleged asymmetry cited above can generate another argument for the terminal illness or permanent unconsciousness requirement. This is the claim that a person's ability to determine what is in her current best interests does not translate into an ability to determine what will be in her best interests when her physical and/or mental capacities have deteriorated significantly due to illness or injury. Thus, it is claimed, there will be conflicts between advance best interests judgments by people who execute living wills (for example, Ms. A.'s judgment that life-extending medical care will not be in her best interests if, at some time in the future, she were to experience a substantial and irreversible loss of physical and/or mental capacity) and patients' contemporaneous best interests (for example, Ms. A.'s best interests when she is severely demented).[30]

The terminal illness or permanent unconsciousness requirement might be defended along the following lines. It is doubtful that forgoing life-sustaining treatment for terminally ill or permanently unconscious patients who have executed living wills is harmful to them. By contrast, whether or not mentally impaired patients have executed living wills, it is generally incompatible with their contemporaneous best interests to forgo life-extending treatment if they are not terminally ill or permanently unconscious. Whenever there are clear conflicts between advance best interests judgments recorded in living wills and a patient's contemporaneous best interests, the latter should prevail.[31] Thus, to protect the contemporaneous best interests of mentally impaired patients, living wills that direct life prolonging treatment to be withheld or withdrawn generally should be implemented only when patients are terminally ill or permanently unconscious.

One problem with this line of argument is that the terminal condition or permanent unconsciousness requirement is too narrow to serve as a plausible standard for deciding whether implementing a living will is compatible with the contemporaneous best interests of patients who lack decision-making capacity. If there is a net balance of burdens over benefits, then even if a patient is neither terminally ill nor permanently unconscious, treatment is not in the patient's best interests. Suppose Mr. H., the 76-year-old retired postal worker, suffers a massive stroke that leaves him permanently ventilator-dependent and mentally devastated with no chance of meaningful recovery. Mr. H. has developed decubitus ulcers (bedsores), is restrained to prevent him from withdrawing his feeding tube, and moans constantly. Whether or not Mr. H. executed a living will, it is arguable that the benefits of continued life support do not outweigh the burdens to him.

A deeper problem with the foregoing line of argument is associated with the claim that a person's ability to determine what is currently in her best interests does not translate into an ability to determine what will be in her best interests if and when she lacks decision-making capacity. The primary basis for this claim, it will be recalled, is the alleged correlation between a person's capacities and what gives her pleasure and enjoyment.[32]

This reasoning can be illustrated as follows. I now have the capacity to read and write, to teach, to run 7 miles, to play baseball with my son, to interact with my wife and friends, and so forth. I derive great pleasure and enjoyment from such activities, and it is hard to think of anything less satisfying to me than to be demented, confined to a nursing home, and limited to activities such as playing bingo, attending programs performed by amateurs, and watching mindless television programs. However, when I am demented and frail, a wide array of my capacities will have changed. As a result, I may derive pleasure and satisfaction from activities that I now dislike and find boring. Thus, although I may be the best judge of my current interests, I am not uniquely qualified to determine what will promote my well-being if and when I become demented in the future.

An important flaw in using this line of argument to challenge the moral authority of advance directives is the underlying assumption that when people execute living wills, their decision is based exclusively on a desire to prevent lives that they will *experience* as bad or unpleasant.[33] When people execute living wills, their primary or exclusive concern need not be about how they will experience their lives when their cognitive abilities deteriorate. That is, their intent may not be to promote and protect their "experiential interests."[34] A person can recognize, say, that if she were to become severely demented, she might not be unhappy if she were incontinent, disoriented, unable to recognize loved ones, unable to read and write, and so forth. However, that kind of life, as well as the disturbing recognition that it might not be experienced as bad or unpleasant by her, can be highly repugnant to her and can prompt a decision to execute a living will. Thus, a living will can be executed out of a desire to not become, or continue existing as, a person of a type whom one finds repugnant. A living will can also be executed out of a desire to not end one's life in a condition that one perceives as demeaning, undignified, and/or dehumanizing. Metaphorically, people might desire to make sure that the last chapter of their biographies does not include a description of themselves in such a state. Less metaphorically, people might wish to not be remembered by their loved ones and friends in a debilitated and undignified state. A nonexperiential interest along any of the foregoing lines constitutes what I will refer to as a "dignity interest."[35] Another nonexperiential interest that can motivate the execution of a living will is an interest in the emotional and financial well-being of loved ones.[36]

Insofar as the execution of living wills is motivated by nonexperiential interests, such as dignity interests and an interest in the well-being of others, the fourth alleged asymmetry between contemporaneous and advance refusals does not appear to undermine their moral authority. However, Dresser challenges the moral authority of living wills by maintaining that patients who are severely impaired mentally do not have dignity and other nonexperiential interests because the values that underlie those interests (for example, dignity, autonomy, altruism, and love) no longer matter to them.[37] To be sure, such values may no longer matter to elderly patients who are severely impaired cognitively. However, the import of this point is unclear, for the recognition that dignity, autonomy, altruism, love and other important human values will no longer matter to an individual if and when she is severely impaired mentally can be one of her primary reasons for executing a living will.

The position that dignity and other nonexperiential interests reflected in living wills have no moral authority when the corresponding values no longer matter to cognitively impaired patients might be defended along the following lines. Patients who have become severely impaired mentally due to illness or injury have two distinct selves: a past self with nonexperiential interests and a current self without nonexperiential interests. One shows respect for the patient's current self by disregarding the nonexperiential interests of her past self and by promoting and protecting her current experiential interests. The aim is to "discover how these patients actually experience their lives" and health care decisions for them should "accord with what rational maximizers of self-interest would want: the outcome that is most beneficial and least burdensome to them in their current situations."[38]

This conception of respect for mentally impaired elderly patients is particularly problematical from the perspective of family members and friends who, along with physicians, have to decide whether to honor or disregard advance directives. It is problematical because it artificially fragments the patient's life and overlooks the importance of her history.[39] With the possible exception of physical characteristics and medical conditions, there is not much that distinguishes my mother as she is now from the other residents of the nursing home in which she lives. On what grounds, then, do I distinguish her from those other residents? The primary basis is my familiarity with my mother's history (for example, her experiences and the stories she would tell about them, her personality, her likes and dislikes, her outlook on life, and her values) and the history of my relationship with her. To disregard that history, including my mother's nonexperiential interests while she was mentally alert, and to reduce her to nothing more than her current experiential interests is tantamount to reducing her to a young child. In effect, I would be treating my mother as her parents treated her more than eighty-five years ago. Sadly, my mother's current mental capacity may be similar to what it was when she was two or three years old, but her history distinguishes her from the young child that she was in 1904 and 1905.

In 1975, one year before the California Natural Death Act was enacted and before my mother's mental status began to decline, she executed a living will that states: "If there is no reasonable expectation of my recovery from physical or mental disability, I, Germaine Wicclair, request that I be allowed to die and not be kept alive by artificial means or heroic measures." It also includes the following statement: "I do not fear death as much as I fear the indignity of deterioration, dependence and hopeless pain." My mother and I discussed her living will and her reasons for executing it, and I was persuaded that her desire to avoid "the indignity of deterioration, dependence and hopeless pain" was genuine, intense, and consistent with her personality and enduring values. If my mother's physician were to ask me to participate in the decision-making process about my mother's medical care and I were to recommend that her living will be disregarded because she no longer has any dignity interests, I would not be respecting *my mother.*[40]

To be sure, to respect my mother, I should also consider her current experiential interests. For example, if my mother develops a life-threatening illness, I should consider whether treatment will increase or decrease pain and suffering and whether it will make her more or less comfortable. However, in addition to considering whether extended life is likely to offer my mother more pleasant than unpleasant sensations, respect for my mother requires that I consider her living will. I shall sketch two scenarios, one in which a decision to forgo life-sustaining treatment best expresses respect for my mother (scenario 1), and another in which it does not (scenario 2).

Scenario 1. My mother's mental condition has deteriorated to the point where she appears to be oblivious to other people and her surroundings. She has stopped communicating with others by means of words or gestures. Although my visits used to bring her pleasure, there is no noticeable response when I visit or when anyone talks to her. She is dependent on others for activities of daily living (eating, dressing, bathing, and personal hygiene). Nevertheless, she does not appear to be in any pain or discomfort, and she gives no indication of a wish to die (for example, by refusing to eat). My mother develops acute respiratory failure, and ventilator support for a few weeks could restore her to her current baseline. Since she does not appear to experience her life as unpleasant, a consideration of my mother's current experiential interests alone cannot justify a decision to provide comfort care only. However, her living will, or rather the strong dignity interest it documents, does support such a decision.[41] Although extended life is likely to offer my mother more pleasant than unpleasant sensations, a decision to forgo ventilator support best expresses respect for her.

Scenario 2. My mother has substantial mental deficits, such as short-term memory loss, disorientation, and impaired ability to communicate. She is dependent on others for activities of daily living, but she does not appear to be unhappy. Quite the contrary, she has adjusted to life in a nursing home, participates in activities, smiles often, never complains, and generally seems to have a positive outlook. As an example of her positive outlook, when we go out on the patio on nice days, she frequently comments on the "beautiful weather." Extended conversations with her are impossible, but she recognizes and seems to enjoy being with me, my wife, and my five-year-old son, with whom she sings children's songs. My mother develops acute respiratory failure, and ventilator support for a few weeks could restore her to her current baseline. I could not justify a decision to withhold ventilator support by citing her living will and claiming that I am respecting my mother.

The conclusion in scenario 2 is not based on a belief that since extended life is likely to offer my mother more pleasant than unpleasant sensations, I should disregard her living will and the dignity interests it expresses. Rather, in view of the capacities my mother retains, it seems reasonable to require convincing evidence that a life of that sort is incompatible with her considered conception of a dignified existence. Since my mother's living will is vague, I am uncertain that her life is incompatible with her considered conception of an undignified existence. This uncertainty would be eliminated if it turned out to be impossible to wean her from the respirator. If she were to become ventilator dependent, I would have no doubt that her quality of life would be incompatible with her considered conception of a dignified existence, and respect for her would require withdrawing ventilator support. However, a decision for a time-limited ventilator trial is compatible with respect for the person my mother was and, in part, still is in scenario 2. Her adjustment to the nursing home and her generally positive attitude are consistent with the type of person my mother was before her mental status deteriorated. She was an active, creative person with a zest for life and the will and ability to persevere in hard times. She continues to display these traits in scenario 2 despite the many changes she has undergone. Thus, even if I were to conclude that my mother's life is incompatible with her conception of a dignified existence when she executed her living will, it still would be unclear that a time-limited ventilator trial would be inconsistent with respect for her as a person.

In sum, living wills should never be blindly implemented; neither should they be disregarded unless patients are terminally ill or permanently unconscious. Indeed, intelligently used, living wills can facilitate respect for the patient as a person, including her dignity and other nonexperiential interests as well as her current best interests.[42]

Proxy and Combination Directives

All states and the District of Columbia have durable power of attorney statutes, whereby individuals ("principals") can empower a representative to make decisions on their behalf.[43] Whereas the standard power of attorney loses its legal force if the principal becomes incompetent, *durable* powers of attorney retain their validity. As of June 1992, forty-six states and the District of Columbia had statutes specifically authorizing representatives to make medical decisions, including decisions to withhold or withdraw life support; two states (Maryland and Washington) had statutes interpreted by court decisions, attorney general opinions, or other statutes to permit agents to make medical decisions, including decisions to withhold or withdraw life support; one state (Alaska) had a statute authorizing consent to medical treatment, but barring representatives from consenting to withhold or withdraw life support; and one state (Alabama) had no statutory means of appointing a proxy to make medical decisions.[44]

Statutory proxy directives can promote several important objectives. First, they can prevent or reduce conflicts among family members and health care professionals. Such conflicts can stymie or impede effective decision-making and can result in lawsuits and other legal action. If an elderly patient who lacks decision-making capacity has one legally designated representative, then others (for example, relatives other than the representative) may be less likely to impede the decision-making process. In any event, other persons would have no authority to obstruct the decision-making process by, say, second-guessing or vetoing the representative's decisions. Moreover, the physician could disregard differences of opinion among family members without the fear of legal liability. Second, since statutory proxy directives in many states lack the restrictions of the state's living will or natural death legislation, they can promote autonomy by giving elderly persons a means to exercise more control over medical decisions that may have to be made when they lack decision-making capacity. However, treatment requests by proxies are subject to the same constraints that apply to requests by patients with decision-making capacity. Accordingly, health care professionals may refuse to comply with any requests of designated representatives that are incompatible with conscientiously held convictions or standards of professional integrity. Third, proxy directives have the virtue of flexibility.[45] That is, representatives can make decisions that are tailored to the specific circumstances at the time decisions have to be made.

Nevertheless, by themselves, proxy directives do not offer a panacea for effective and ethically sound decision-making for elderly patients without decision-making capacity. If elderly patients fail to determine and communicate their health care preferences in advance by means of oral or written instruction directives, a representative's decision may not reflect the patient's own preferences.[46] Representatives who lack adequate guidance may experience feelings of guilt, anxiety, resentment, and self-doubt.

Combination directives promote autonomy without sacrificing flexibility. Instruction directives enable people to communicate their wishes in advance, and proxy directives enable representatives to fill in gaps that can result when patients' statements are either so general or so specific that they fail to generate an unambiguous decision in the specific circumstances at hand. In addition, proxy directives designate representatives to help facilitate and supervise implementation of instruction directives. Consequently, the various objectives of advance planning appear to be best served by executing combination directives.[47]

Instruction or combination directives can facilitate a close approximation to shared decision-making for elderly patients without decision-making capacity. However, several studies indicate that only a small percentage of elderly persons have executed such advance directives.[48] The Patient Self-Determination Act (PSDA), legislation passed by the U.S. Congress in 1990 which went into effect in December 1991, may promote an increased use of advance directives.[49] Among other provisions, the PSDA requires institutional health care providers receiving Medicare or Medicaid funds (hospitals, skilled nursing facilities, home health agencies, hospices, and health maintenance organizations) to (1) ascertain whether patients have advance directives, (2) provide patients with information about their rights under state law to execute advance directives, and (3) provide education to the staff and community about advance directives. In addition, the PSDA requires the Department of Health and Human Services to develop a program for educating the public about advance directives. For now, however, it is unrealistic to think that most elderly patients without decision-making capacity have executed advance directives that can guide decisions about life-sustaining treatment for them.

The Substituted Judgment Standard

The substituted judgment standard directs surrogates to choose as the patient who lacks decision-making capacity would choose if she were fully informed and able to decide.[50] This standard can function in one of two contexts. First, when elderly patients have executed advance directives, the substituted judgment standard can guide their interpretation and implementation. Second, it can facilitate an approximation of shared decision-making in the case of elderly patients who lack decision-making capacity and who have not executed advance directives.

When elderly patients execute proxy directives only, the substituted judg-ment standard is an appropriate substantive decision-making criterion for representatives. If an instruction directive is either so general or specific that it fails to support one decision in the current circumstances unambiguously, the substituted judgment standard is an appropriate substantive decision-making criterion for a surrogate. In such circumstances, instruction direc-tives can provide important evidence for inferences about the choices a patient would make if she had the capacity to decide.

It is mistaken, however, to think that the exclusive function of instruction directives is to provide evidence for substituted judgments. When a living will gives unambiguous instructions to forgo or limit treatment in the current circumstances, it does not provide evidence for inferring that the patient would refuse treatment if he had the capacity to decide. Rather, it records the patient's prior decision to refuse treatment in circumstances that currently obtain.[51] For example, suppose Mr. W. executes a living will that gives specific instructions to forgo tube feeding if he were to become permanently unconscious. If he is permanently unconscious, no inference about how he would choose is needed because he already made the decision to forgo tube feeding in the current circumstances when he executed his living will.

In this respect, living wills might be compared to standard wills. The latter do not provide evidence concerning the testator's wishes. Rather, they docu-ment the testator's decisions, and the executor's primary function is to im-plement those decisions. However, recalling the dangers of literal readings of advance directives and the importance of considering the patient's intent, it is misleading generally to interpret living wills along the lines of standard wills. Indeed, Mr. W.'s living will, which includes an unequivocal directive that unambiguously applies in the current circumstances, may be more the exception than the rule.

Substituted judgment offers the possibility of extending shared decision-making to elderly patients who lack decision-making capacity and who have not executed advance directives. However, this objective can be achieved in a particular case only if there is a qualified surrogate for the patient. For the purposes of substituted judgment, a qualified surrogate is someone who has sufficient knowledge about the patient and who will put aside her own interests and sincerely attempt to decide as the patient would. Generally, if there is a qualified surrogate, it is likely to be a member of the patient's "family," broadly construed to include a spouse, biological relations, and close friends.[52] Accordingly, it seems reasonable to presume that members of the patient's family are the most qualified to apply the substituted judg-ment standard. There are unlikely to be any qualified surrogates for elderly patients who have no known relatives or friends, have been abandoned by their families, or do not have a functional family.[53] The likelihood is highest that there will be a qualified surrogate if, before losing their decision-making capacity, elderly patients communicated their treatment preferences to someone. Unfortunately, several studies suggest that most elderly patients do *not* discuss their treatment preferences with family members or their physicians.[54]

When elderly persons do talk to family about their future care, family members should be wary of misinterpreting or attaching too much evidential value to ambiguous, general, vague, and/or offhand comments.[55] Suppose, say, Ms. M., an 81-year-old woman who lives in her own home and who currently requires no assistance from others, says to her son, "I would rather die than have to live in a nursing home or depend on others for care." Ms. M.'s statement might express a preference that life-extending procedures be withheld unless their temporary use would allow her to regain her ability to live alone at home. However, it might instead express her anxiety about the aging process and a fear of increased dependence on others. Alternatively, and without knowing it herself, Ms. M. may have been looking for an expression of care and concern from her son. Then again, Ms. M. may have uttered the statement while in a state of depression, and it may not express her considered views about future medical care. Consequently, Ms. M.'s statement hardly provides unambiguous evidence for her views about life-prolonging treatment.

When people make statements that do reflect their attitudes about life-sustaining measures, family members should be wary of interpreting them too broadly. For example, last year when Mr. A. was talking to his wife about their 75-year-old friend who was kept alive in a comatose state for over a year, he said: "I never want to be kept alive by heroic means." If Mr. A. currently is permanently unconscious and ventilator-dependent, his prior statement provides substantial evidential support for the inference that he would refuse ventilation if he had the capacity to decide. However, if he is mildly demented and experiences reversible respiratory failure, Mr. A.'s statement provides little, if any, evidential support for a similar inference.

When elderly patients without decision-making capacity did not discuss their treatment preferences while they were still able to do so, the exercise of substituted judgment is based on general knowledge of the patient (patient's preferences, interests, values, and personality). Even when there are concerned and caring family members to serve as surrogates, if elderly patients failed to communicate their treatment preferences, there are several obstacles to reliable inferences about whether the patient would accept or refuse treatment if she had the capacity to decide. For one thing, despite their care and concern, family members may not know the elderly person that well. This can be a particular problem if there is a wide age gap between the elderly patient and relatives. For example, although "Grandma" may occupy a special place within the family, members of the family may not take her seriously *as a person,* and there may be very little communication with the individual behind the label. In addition, even if one does know someone well as a person, there may be insufficient grounds for a reliable inference about whether the person would accept or refuse life-prolonging medical treatment in the current situation. Two people with quite similar general values and preferences might make opposite decisions with respect to life-sustaining measures. For example, suppose Ms. C. and Mr. D. enjoy similar activities, and both are strong-willed and generally have a positive attitude toward life. Ms. C. might choose to forgo life-prolonging treatment in a specified situation, and Mr. D. might choose to accept it in a similar situation. Neither choice is necessarily "out of character" for Ms. C. or Mr. D.

In view of the apparent infrequency with which elderly persons discuss their future care with family or physicians and the uncertainty of substituted judgment when patients without decision-making capacity have not done so, it is not surprising that recent studies raise doubts about the ability of family members and physicians to accurately identify the treatment preferences of elderly patients. In one study, Uhlmann, Pearlman, and Cain conclude that "the resuscitation preferences of elderly outpatients often are not understood even by their primary care physicians and spouses of long duration."[56] A similar result for family members generally is reported by Seckler et al.[57] And a study by Zweibel and Cassel reports a corresponding conclusion for physicians and younger family members (adult children, daughters-in-law, sons-in-law, nieces, and nephews) in relation to ventilation, resuscitation, chemotherapy, amputation, and tube feeding.[58] Moreover, even when family members are familiar with the treatment preferences of elderly patients who lack decision-making capacity, conflicts of interest can bias substituted judgment. Substituted judgment can be biased, say, when the death of an elderly patient will result in the termination of Social Security payments, the elimination of severe emotional and/or financial stress, or the acquisition of a substantial inheritance.

Despite serious questions about the reliability of family substituted judgment, it would be foolish to conclude that family decisions based on the substituted judgment standard are without moral authority. It would be equally foolish to discourage health care professionals from asking family members whether or not their loved ones would want treatment in the current situation if they had the capacity to decide. For one thing, although family substituted judgment is not always reliable, it can best approximate shared decision-making for patients who lack decision-making capacity and have not executed advance directives.[59] In addition, even when elderly patients who lack decision-making capacity have not formally designated family members as surrogates, they may have expected family members to perform this function.[60] In both of these respects, family substituted judgment can facilitate patient self-determination. In addition, honoring the decisions of family members expresses respect for the family, a valued social unit. Respect for the family requires recognizing a zone of privacy and autonomy, and judgments about life-sustaining treatment for family members who lack decision-making capacity fall within its scope.[61]

However, due to the questionable accuracy of family claims about what elderly patients without decision-making capacity would choose if they had the capacity to decide, those claims should be carefully scrutinized, and physicians and other health care professionals should be prepared to challenge them when they appear to pose a serious threat to the patient's good. More scrutiny is appropriate when there is a known or suspected conflict of interest. Standards of professional integrity provide another possible basis for challenging family substituted judgment. The task for health care professionals is to navigate between the Scylla of uncritically accepting the claims of family, and the Charybdis of adopting an overly stringent standard to assess those claims. The following guidelines are informed by this objective.

When family members exercise substituted judgment, health care professionals should encourage them to discuss their reasons and evidence. If, in the health care professional's judgment, the evidence presented does not warrant the family's inference about what the patient would choose if she had the capacity to decide, the family should be encouraged to reconsider its conclusion. The family should also be encouraged to reconsider, if, in the health care professional's judgment, implementing the decision that the family says the patient would make will result in harm or loss of benefit to the patient. If disagreement persists, review by an institutional ethics committee or ethics consultation service may be helpful. However, the family's recommendation generally is decisive unless (a) the family's inference about the patient's choice is not reasonable in relation to the evidence they present, and the expected result of implementing the inferred patient choice is significant harm or loss of benefit to the patient; (b) the family's inference about the patient's choice is reasonable in relation to the evidence presented, but that evidence is indirect and ambiguous, and the expected result of implementing the inferred choice is severe harm to the patient; or (c) implementing the inferred choice is incompatible with conscientiously held convictions or standards of professional integrity.[62]

Honoring family recommendations based on substituted judgment unless one of the three conditions is satisfied gives discretion to family members and places the burden on health care professionals to show that the family's choices should not be implemented.[63] The requirement that a family's inference about the patient's choice be a reasonable inference from the evidence they present is considerably weaker than a requirement that it be the only reasonable inference from the evidence presented. It is also weaker than a "preponderance of the evidence" standard, which would require the family to show that it is more probable than not that the patient would have made that particular choice. The stronger standards would substantially restrict the exercise of family substituted judgment and would fail to give due consideration to patient self-determination and family privacy and autonomy. A rule that family substituted judgment can be overridden whenever the expected result of implementing the inferred patient choice is *any* harm or loss of benefit to the patient also fails to give due consideration to patient self-determination and family privacy and autonomy. Accordingly, a policy of honoring family recommendations based on substituted judgment unless the conditions in (a), (b), or (c) are satisfied (1) facilitates the goal of approximating shared decision-making for elderly patients who lack decision-making capacity without exposing them to unreasonable risks and (2) offers a reasonable balance among the values of patient self-determination and well-being and family privacy and autonomy.

The Best Interests Standard and the No Benefit Principle

The substituted judgment standard is inapplicable when it is not possible to determine whether an elderly patient without decision-making capacity would accept or refuse life-sustaining treatment had he the capacity to decide. Such inferences cannot be made when there is insufficient information about a patient's goals and values, or when a patient's cognitive capacities have been substantially impaired since birth or childhood. When the substituted judgment standard is inapplicable and when no advance directive has been executed, decision-making cannot be based on respect for patient autonomy. However, the patient's good, the primary ethical value of the best interests standard, can still be utilized as a decision-making criterion.

The best interests standard directs surrogates to consider the expected benefits and harms (burdens) to patients of each treatment option, including nontreatment, and to select the option with the greatest expected net benefit or the least expected net harm.[64] That is, the best interests standard instructs surrogates to select the best option from the perspective of a patient's interests.[65] Insofar as there is insufficient knowledge of a patient's values to apply the substituted judgment standard, the criterion of benefits and harms associated with the best interests standard cannot be subjective. A common objective standard is the "reasonable person" standard.[66] To apply this standard, surrogates should assess the expected benefits and harms to patients of life-extending measures from the perspective of a "reasonable" or "average" person. From this perspective, for example, pain, suffering, and discomfort are harms; and reduction or elimination of pain, suffering, and discomfort and restoration or preservation of mental and physical capacities are benefits.[67]

Since the best interests standard instructs surrogates to select the treatment option that is *best* for the patient, that standard justifies a decision to forgo a life-sustaining treatment only if withholding or withdrawing that treatment is expected to promote the patient's interests better than providing it. This condition is satisfied when the expected harms or burdens of receiving a treatment (for example, pain and suffering) outweigh the expected benefits of receiving it (for example, extended life and associated benefits).[68] There are situations in which this condition is satisfied. It appears to be satisfied if life-sustaining treatment is expected to result in two additional months of life with the patient in a semi-comatose state, lying in a fetal position, restrained, and experiencing pain and discomfort. In addition, intrusive medical procedures can be burdensome, and life-sustaining measures are no exception. CPR can cause significant injury, and mechanical ventilation can cause significant discomfort, inhibit verbal communication, require the use of physical restraints, and trigger infection. It therefore cannot be assumed that the burdens of receiving life-prolonging measures never outweigh the benefits of treatment.

However, even when the expected harms do not outweigh the expected benefits, patients have no interest in receiving life-extending medical interventions that will not benefit them. From the perspective of a patient's interests, there is no reason to provide life-sustaining treatment that will not benefit the patient. On the contrary, if a patient's preferences are unknown, it seems reasonable to forgo life-sustaining treatment when treatment is of no expected benefit to the patient.[69] But when a life-prolonging treatment is of no expected benefit to a patient, unless it is expected to *harm* the patient, the best interests standard fails to justify forgoing treatment.[70] In the absence of expected harm to the patient, there appears to be no basis for claiming that forgoing treatment promotes the patient's interests better than providing treatment. Consequently, the best interests standard should be supplemented with a "no benefit" principle, which states that it is justified to forgo a medical intervention when it is of no expected benefit to the patient. According to the combined standard, the "best interests/no benefit standard," it is justified to forgo a life-sustaining medical intervention when (1) the expected harms or burdens to the patient outweigh the expected benefits, or (2) the intervention is of no expected benefit to the patient. The best interests/no benefit standard is an appropriate decision-making standard for elderly patients without decision-making capacity when they have not executed a living will that unambiguously supports one decision, and when the substituted judgment standard is inapplicable due to insufficient information about a patient's values.

The claim that a life-extending intervention is not expected to extend the life of a patient appears to be the least controversial basis for concluding that the intervention is of no expected benefit to the patient. If, say, clinical evidence warrants a conclusion that restoring cardiopulmonary function would be unprecedented in the circumstances, it is clear that CPR will not benefit the patient. However, matters are more controversial when prolonging life is improbable, but not unprecedented. In such cases, it is necessary to answer the following question: What criterion would a reasonable person use to determine that a medical intervention is not expected to extend a patient's life?

When there is a reasonable expectation that life-sustaining measures will prolong an elderly patient's life, it still can be questioned whether extended life will benefit the patient. If there is any situation in which extended life is of no benefit to elderly patients, it is when they are in a persistent vegetative state (PVS). Such patients experience neither pain nor pleasure.[71] The patient's body may still be alive, but the person the patient used to be is no more. Since PVS patients cannot experience pain or suffering, they no longer have any experiential interests and in this respect will neither be harmed nor benefited by life-extending interventions. However, PVS patients can have nonexperiential interests. For example, they may have a dignity interest in not being kept alive by mechanical ventilation, especially if they have executed living wills directing that they not be so maintained. Despite the absence of experiential interests, such patients can be harmed if they are sustained by mechanical ventilation. Although vitalists might wish to be sustained while in a PVS, the best interests standard applies when the patient's values are unknown. It is implausible to claim that a reasonable or average person would want to be maintained if she should become permanently unconscious.[72]

The severely demented elderly constitute another category of patients about whom it might be claimed that they will receive no benefit from life-prolonging measures. Although they are not unconscious, it is nevertheless arguable that their quality of life is so low that extended life is of no benefit to them. However, on the continuum from PVS to cognitively unimpaired, the further an elderly patient's condition moves away from PVS, the more controversial is the claim that a reasonable person would not consider extended life to be a benefit.[73]

When applying the best interests/no benefit standard, it is important to distinguish between the elderly patient's perspective and the perspective of observers. Serious mistakes can result if one attempts to imagine oneself in another's place. Elderly patients themelves may be more or less unaware of

their situation: it would therefore be wrong to attribute burdens to them that derive from an *awareness* of dependence, mental and physical deterioration, being subject to invasive medical interventions, and so forth.[74] Extreme caution is required when applying the best interests/no benefit standard.

Bearing in mind this need for caution, we may still presume, for several reasons, that family should serve as surrogates when decisions are made by applying the best interests/no benefit standard. First, family members are most likely to be concerned about the patient's well-being and to want to protect the patient's interests. Second, even when elderly patients who lack decision-making capacity have not formally designated family members as surrogates, they may have expected family members to perform this function. Third, respect for the family, a valued social unit, requires a protected zone of privacy and autonomy, and decisions concerning life-sustaining treatment are properly included within the scope of this protected zone.[75] Fourth, familiarity with the patient may be relevant when the reasonable person standard fails to provide a basis for deciding among two or more acceptable options. When that standard fails to provide a decisive answer, one of the options may be more in character with the patient, and the family might be the best qualified to identify that option.[76]

For these reasons, family members should be given latitude in applying the best interests/no benefit standard. However, just as the interests of family members can bias the exercise of substituted judgment, their self-regarding interests can also bias the application of the best interests/no benefit standard. In addition, even the most concerned and selfless family members can make innocent, yet serious, misjudgments. Consequently, health care professionals would be well advised to determine independently whether the expected benefits of life-sustaining treatment outweigh the expected burdens. If a family's conclusion is significantly different, further discussion with the family is essential. If the health care professional is convinced that family members are mistaken and disagreement persists, review by an institutional ethics committee or ethics consultation service may be helpful. However, the family's decision generally should be decisive unless its implementation is incompatible with conscientiously held convictions or standards of professional integrity, or the expected result of its implementation is significant harm or loss of benefit to the patient.[77] The stipulation that the harm or loss of benefit must be "significant" indicates a need to strike a reasonable balance between the objectives of benefiting patients, protecting patients from harm, and respecting family privacy and autonomy. Unfortunately, there is no perfect formula for striking such a balance.

Insofar as it is incompatible with standards of professional integrity to provide life-extending treatment when it is of no expected benefit to a patient, a physician is not ethically obligated to comply with a family's request to "do everything possible" to keep a patient alive if the physician is confident that those measures will not benefit the patient. However, respect for family privacy and autonomy, concern for the well-being of family members, compassion, and prudence may support continued negotiation with family members and *temporary* provision of life support to give them an opportunity to accept the loss of a loved one.

Yarborough argues that if life support is not burdensome to patients who are "beyond help" medically, it sometimes is morally permissible to provide life-sustaining treatment "for the emotional and psychological benefit of a third party such as a spouse or child."[78] To defend this position against the charge that it is impermissible to treat patients exclusively for the benefit of others, Yarborough argues that patients can have an interest in the well-being of family members. Accordingly, even if a patient's self-regarding interests are not served by life-sustaining measures, the patient's other-regarding interests, in particular an interest in the well-being of family members, may be served.

Suppose, say, Mrs. C.'s 72-year-old husband has been in a PVS for several months. She visits her husband for many hours daily, and her life seems to revolve around him, as it has for more than forty years. Dr. H. recommends discontinuing ventilator support on the grounds that the diagnosis of PVS is now beyond doubt and further life support will not benefit Mr. C. Mrs. C. dismisses Dr. H.'s recommendation, tearfully stating that life would not be worth living without her husband. "Please, doctor," she pleads, "do everything you can to keep my husband alive as long as possible." For the sake of Mrs. C.'s well-being, Dr. H. decides to continue ventilator support.

In addition to concerns about justice and resource allocation and standards of professional integrity, there are several reasons to question Dr. H.'s decision to continue treating Mr. C. First, even if it is assumed that Mr. C. has an interest in his wife's well-being, it does not follow that he would be willing to undergo life-extending measures that would not benefit him for the sake of his wife's well-being. Such a practice might have seemed offensive, undignified, ghoulish, and/or counterproductive to him. Second, although Mrs. C.'s insistence that her husband continue to receive life support may be the result of a variety of psychological factors, including guilt, denial, and fear of loneliness, she probably believes that she is acting to help and protect *him*. Accordingly, by treating Mr. C. to protect Mrs. C., Dr. H. may be an accomplice to Mrs. C.'s self-deception. Third, if Mrs. C. would not want aggressive treatment for her husband if she understood that its function was to help her and not her husband, Dr. H. would be treating her paternalistically.[79] Fourth, ordering treatment sends a mixed message to Mrs. C.

While Dr. H. may *say* that treatment is of no benefit to Mrs. C.'s husband, he continues to provide it. In such cases, actions may well speak louder than words. Fifth, although Dr. H. may intend to promote Mrs. C.'s well-being, indefinitely postponing Mr. C.'s death may not be the best way to accomplish that objective.[80] From the perspective of Mrs. C.'s good, it might be better for her to come to terms with her guilt, denial, fear of loneliness, and so forth sooner rather than later. Moreover, by devoting her time and energy to her husband, she may be neglecting her other interests and the interests of other family members. In any event, Dr. H. cannot simply assume that the best way to promote Mrs. C.'s well-being is to comply with her request for continued life support for her husband.

For all these reasons, treatment beyond the point of expected therapeutic benefit to the patient is not an acceptable substitute for sincere efforts to help people like Mrs. C. come to grips with reality. Accordingly, rather than trying to help Mrs. C. by indefinitely providing treatment that is not expected to benefit her husband, Dr. H. should attempt to help her understand the true nature of Mr. C.'s condition, accept his death, deal with guilt, and so forth. Psychiatric referral and discussions with a hospital social worker and/or chaplain can supplement the efforts of attending physicians and nurses, and additional guidance can be provided by a hospital ethics committee or consultation service.

It may take family members several days or even longer to accept the loss of a loved one, and patience on the part of health care professionals who have concluded that further treatment is inappropriate may be a virtue. Temporarily continuing such treatment may be appropriate as a means to give family members an opportunity to understand and accept the situation. Nevertheless, postponing death will only delay grief and emotional trauma; it will not prevent them. Postponing death may also be counterproductive by unnecessarily delaying psychological and emotional adjustment. Sooner or later, family members will have to come to terms with the loss of a loved one, and delay can have significant costs. Consequently, indefinitely providing life support that is not expected to benefit elderly patients generally is neither the most effective nor the ethically preferred means to promote the well-being of their families.

Case Study: Deciding Whether to Forgo Tube Feeding

When elderly patients are not able to decide for themselves, deciding whether to forgo life-sustaining measures like CPR, dialysis, and mechanical ventilation can be extremely difficult. As challenging as such decisions can be, it is sometimes thought that decisions concerning nutrition and hydration are particularly demanding and troublesome.[81] It is therefore appropriate to consider a case that presents the problem of deciding whether to provide tube feeding.

If elderly patients without decision-making capacity have executed advance directives, decision-making is quite different from what it would be had they not. Consequently, two scenarios will be considered, one in which the patient executed a living will (scenario 1), and a second in which the patient did not execute an advance directive (scenario 2).

Case Description

Ms. E. is eighty-five years old and has lived in a nursing home in Seattle, Washington, for about five years. She has been divorced for more than thirty-five years and has lived alone in a house in a Seattle suburb for almost thirty years after the divorce. She shunned social contact with co-workers prior to her retirement at the age of sixty-two, and consistently resisted attempts by neighbors to become more friendly. She has had little contact with the only relative who lives in Seattle, her 78-year-old brother, who is divorced and lives alone. The only person with whom Ms. E. has maintained a close personal relationship is her son, who has lived in several distant cities for more than twenty-five years.

Despite her self-imposed isolation, Ms. E. was a very pleasant person. People generally found her to be charming and congenial, and they were therefore surprised by her tendency to keep them at arm's length and to shun friendships. Whereas some older people might have become depressed living alone, Ms. E. was generally cheerful, and she had a very positive attitude toward life. She avoided boredom by reading, walking, painting, and by working on a wide range of arts and crafts projects.

Prior to moving into the nursing home, Ms. E.'s mental condition deteriorated significantly. It began with frequent instances of forgetfulness and disorientation. As Ms. E. was increasingly unable to engage in her normal routine of activities, she also began to experience episodes of depression. During a visit, Ms. E.'s son urged his mother to seek medical attention, but she had always displayed a reluctance to go to the doctor, and she adamantly refused. However, she later began to experience hallucinations, and when her son arrived, he was able to persuade her to see a psychiatrist. At the urging of the psychiatrist and her son, Ms. E. was admitted to a psychiatric hospital on a voluntary basis. Tests failed to reveal a stroke or any identifiable neurological disorder, and no specific cause of Ms. E.'s condition was discovered. Haloperidol (Haldol) was prescribed, and soon after she began taking the drug, the hallucinations stopped.

After consulting with the psychiatrist, Ms. E.'s son and brother concluded that she was no longer able to live by herself. At the urging of her son and brother, Ms. E. agreed to move from her house into a retirement apartment (congregate care facility). Ms. E. had her own room, but meals were provided in a dining room, and other services (hair care, transportation, social activities, and so forth) were available.

Ms. E. did not do well at the congregate care facility. She was depressed, and spent most of the time in her room lying on her bed. When she began to develop bedsores, the director of the facility told Ms. E.'s son and brother that she would have to be moved. He suggested an intermediate care nursing facility (ICF), and within a week, Ms. E. was transferred to the ICF unit of a nearby nursing home.

Upon Ms. E.'s admission to the nursing home, her Haldol prescription was discontinued. After an initial period of adjustment, Ms. E. seemed to be quite comfortable and content. Her disorientation continued, and her short-term memory was extremely poor. But the hallucinations did not recur, and she showed no signs of depression. She participated in activities, such as field trips and bingo, and she regularly attended special events. She still displayed a reluctance to form friendships, but she was very well liked by the staff.

A little over a year ago, Ms. E. fell and fractured her shoulder. Soon after she recovered, she experienced a minor stroke. After the stroke, her disorientation increased, and she required more assistance with personal care and hygiene. About six months ago, it was discovered that Ms. E. had colon cancer. Surgery was performed, and tests revealed that the cancer had not metastasized.

When Ms. E. was released from the hospital, she was admitted to the skilled care section (SNF) of the nursing home. When her condition was reevaluated a few weeks later, it was decided to keep her in the SNF indefinitely. The decision was based on her increased disorientation and incontinence and on her greater need for assistance with personal care and hygiene.

Five days ago, Ms. E. suddenly lost consciousness. She was rushed to a hospital, and it was determined that she had suffered a massive stroke. She is semi-comatose and unable to communicate or to eat or drink, and she is receiving intravenous (IV) fluids. After numerous tests and consultations, a medical consensus is reached that there is no reasonable chance that Ms. E. will regain meaningful cognitive function. Without tube feeding, she will probably die within a week. However, with tube feeding, there is no telling how long she can continue to live.

Scenario 1. Several years ago Ms. E. executed a Washington Natural Death Act directive. She sent copies to her physician, brother, and son, but did not discuss her specific wishes with anyone. The directive states:

If at any time I should have an incurable injury, disease or illness certified to be a terminal condition by two physicians, and where the application of life-sustaining procedures would serve only to artificially prolong the moment of my death and where my physician determines that my death is imminent whether or not life-sustaining procedures are utilized, I direct that such procedures be withheld or withdrawn, and that I be permitted to die naturally.[82]

When Dr. J., the attending physician, meets with Ms. E.'s son and brother, she carefully explains Ms. E.'s condition and bleak prognosis. She states that in view of Ms. E.'s living will, the appropriate medical goal at this point is to keep Ms. E. comfortable, and this objective can be attained without tube feeding. Ms. E.'s son responds that the directive does not apply to the current situation because his mother is not dying, and he insists that everything be done to keep her alive as long as possible.

Scenario 2. Ms. E. did not execute an advance directive, and she did not discuss her health care preferences with anyone. When Dr. J., the attending physician, meets with Ms. E.'s son and brother, she carefully explains Ms. E.'s condition and bleak prognosis. She states that the appropriate medical goal at this point is to keep Ms. E. comfortable, and this objective can be attained without tube feeding. Ms. E.'s son responds that he has not given up hope and cannot agree to let his mother die. When Dr. J. asks him whether he thinks his mother would want to be kept alive medically in her condition, Ms. E.'s son responds that he does not know what his mother would want, but he does know that it would be wrong to let her starve to death.

Analysis of Scenario 1

Strictly speaking, Ms. E.'s son is correct to claim that his mother's advance directive does not apply to her current condition. Since she can live for an indefinite period of time with tube feeding, her condition is *not* terminal; and her death is imminent only if she does not receive tube feeding. Moreover, although some recently enacted or revised natural death acts (living will laws) specify that "qualified patients" can be either terminally ill or permanently unconscious, Ms. E. is neither.

However, it does not follow that Ms. E.'s living will is without moral authority in the current situation. Her living will clearly indicates that she rejected the vitalist view that people should be kept alive as long as medically possible under any conditions. Indeed, the fact that Ms. E. executed the living will indicates that she felt very strongly about not being given unwanted life-extending medical treatment. What remains unclear is precisely where she drew the line between wanted and unwanted life-sustaining measures. Did she draw the line where Washington legislators drew it, at a terminal condition when death is imminent, or did she include her current condition? Ethically, this is the important question, and not whether a literal reading of the advance directive can justify a decision to forgo tube feeding.

This question would be much easier to answer if Ms. E. had discussed her specific treatment preferences with her son, brother, and/or physician. Indeed, this case demonstrates the problems that can arise when people execute standard living will forms, especially those that do not give them an opportunity to identify their specific preferences, without also discussing various contingencies and their wishes with family members, friends, and/or physicians. However, despite the lack of additional information from such discussions, it still is possible to make an educated inference about Ms. E.'s preferences.

When Ms. E. executed the living will, she may not have realized that it applied only to terminally ill patients who are near death. But even if she did, she may not have endorsed that limitation. The specter of being sustained indefinitely with no meaningful cognitive function can be just as terrifying and repugnant, if not more so, as the thought of being kept alive a few more days or weeks after the loss of decision-making capacity due to a terminal illness. This observation would seem to apply especially to a person such as Ms. E. who valued independence and avoided going to doctors. If Ms. E. was so strongly opposed to being kept alive for a relatively short time in a debilitating condition that she executed a living will, it seems reasonable to presume that she also would not want to be kept alive indefinitely in a severely debilitating condition. This presumption is supported by a recent study in which a group of outpatients and members of the general public were asked whether they would want specified life-sustaining measures in four different scenarios (coma with a small chance of full recovery, persistent vegetative state, dementia with no other life-threatening illness, and dementia with a terminal illness). The subjects' responses for the last two scenarios were not substantially different for several categories of life-sustaining treatment, including artificial nutrition.[83] Thus, Ms. E.'s living will supports the presumption that she did not want to be kept alive indefinitely after suffering a devastating and irreversible loss of cognitive function. Accordingly, since there is no reasonable chance that Ms. E. will regain meaningful cognitive function, unless someone who knew her (most likely, her son, brother, or physician) can provide credible evidence to rebut this presumption, her living will justifies forgoing life-sustaining treatment. Moreover, unless someone who knew Ms. E. can provide credible evidence to show that she intended to refuse mechanical ventilation, dialysis, and all other life-sustaining measures except tube feeding, it is reasonable to conclude that her living will justifies withholding tube feeding as long as no additional suffering would result.[84]

Since there is no reasonable chance that Ms. E. will regain meaningful cognitive function, it is implausible to challenge the moral authority of her living will by claiming that withholding life-sustaining treatment would result in significant harm or loss of benefit to her. Moreover, since effective comfort measures can be provided so that withholding tube feeding does not cause Ms. E. to suffer, the same conclusion also applies to tube feeding. Thus, there is no significant risk of harm to Ms. E. by acting on the reasonable assumption that when she enacted the living will, she did not intend to exclude withholding tube feeding in the current circumstances. By contrast, by not acting on this assumption, there is a significant risk of failing to honor her wishes. If Ms. E.'s son and brother continue to insist that she be kept alive as long as medically possible, her living will has greater moral authority than their preferences and wishes. As a practical matter, since Ms. E. is not a qualified patient under the Washington Natural Death Act, Dr. J. and the hospital may not have legal immunity if tube feeding is withheld. But it is nonetheless ethically justified to do so.

Analysis of Scenario 2

Although Ms. E. neither executed an advance directive nor discussed her health care preferences with her son or anyone else, there are certain signs that she would not want to be kept alive indefinitely in her current condition. These signs include her independence and her aversion to doctors. However, this information is an insufficient basis for claiming that the substituted judgment standard can justify withholding tube feeding.[85] In addition, Ms. E.'s son, the obvious surrogate decision-maker, indicated that he does not know whether his mother would accept or refuse tube feeding if she had the capacity to decide. Consequently, it is appropriate to apply the best interests/ no benefit principle.

In view of Ms. E.'s cognitive status, it is arguable that extended life is of no significant benefit to her. She would be unable to interact with others, and although she might be able to experience some pleasant sensations, there are a number of possible harms or burdens, including physical restraints, infection, and decubitus ulcers. Several studies suggest that most people (elderly and nonelderly alike) reject the view that the benefits of extended life by means of life-sustaining treatment always outweigh the corresponding burdens, and some of these studies report that most respondents would elect to forgo tube feeding and/or other life-sustaining measures if they should suffer devastating and irreversible loss of cognitive function.[86] Accordingly, since there is a medical consensus that Ms. E.'s condition is irreversible, it is warranted to conclude that a "reasonable" or "average" person would not want her life extended indefinitely by life-sustaining measures in a condition similar to Ms. E.'s.[87] If effective comfort measures can be provided so that withholding tube feeding does not increase Ms. E's suffering, it seems reasonable to conclude that the expected benefits to Ms. E. of tube feeding are so low that they do not outweigh the expected burdens to her.

If, after further discussion with Dr. J. or after meeting with the hospital's ethics committee/consultation service, Ms. E.'s son agrees to withhold tube feeding, it is ethically justified to do so. If Ms. E.'s son agrees that it would be pointless to keep his mother alive indefinitely in her current condition, but he continues to favor tube feeding because he still believes that there is a chance that his mother will regain significant cognitive function, a limited trial might be proposed. A reasonable proposal would be to provide tube feeding for a specified period of time, and if there is no improvement in Ms. E.'s cognitive status, life-sustaining treatment, including tube feeding, will be discontinued.

If Ms. E.'s son continues to insist that his mother be given tube feeding because he believes that it will benefit her, or protect her from harm ("starving to death"), his wishes are not without moral authority. Although it is reasonable to conclude that the expected benefits of tube feeding to Ms. E. are so low that they do not outweigh the expected burdens to her, two reasons might be given for thinking that it is not ethically justified to withhold tube feeding if her son disagrees. First, reasonable people can disagree about whether the expected benefits of tube feeding to Ms. E. are so low that they do not outweigh the expected burdens to her. Second, out of respect for family privacy and autonomy, Ms. E.'s son should be given some discretion in applying the best interests/no benefit standard. It is arguable that the second reason is more plausible than the first.

In any event, the son's discretion does not extend to treatment decisions that are incompatible with Ms. E.'s preferences and values, incompatible with standards of professional integrity, or likely to result in significant harm or loss of benefit to Ms. E. It is doubtful, however, that a decision to administer tube feeding runs afoul of any of these three constraints. First, there is insufficient evidence to reasonably conclude that tube feeding is contrary to Ms. E.'s preferences and values. Second, it is doubtful that tube feeding would be incompatible with standards of professional integrity. Third, it is doubtful that the expected harm to Ms. E. is so great that her son's request for tube feeding disqualifies him as a competent surrogate.[88]

Notes

1. As noted in Chapter 1, life-sustaining treatment includes any medical intervention that has the potential effect of increasing the life span of patients, and life-sustaining medical interventions will also be referred to as "life-extending" and "life-prolonging" interventions.

2. According to an Office of Technology Assessment (OTA) report, 5 percent to 7 percent of persons over sixty-five, and 25 percent of those over eighty-four, suffer from severe dementia. U.S. Congress, Office of Technology Assessment, *Losing a Million Minds: Confronting the Tragedy of Alzheimer's Disease and Other Dementias* (Washington, D.C.:

U.S. Government Printing Office, April 1987), 15–16. See also Jeffrey L. Cummings and Lissy F. Jarvik, "Dementia," in Christine K. Cassel et al., eds., *Geriatric Medicine,* 2d ed. (New York: Springer-Verlag, 1990), 428–48.

3. Richard F. Uhlmann, Robert A. Pearlman, and Kevin C. Cain, "Physicians' and Spouses' Predictions of Elderly Patients' Resuscitation Preferences," *Journal of Gerontology: Medical Sciences* 43, no. 5 (1988): M115. According to High, "the decisionally incapacitated elderly" are "one of the most rapidly growing groups of special patients." Dallas M. High, "Caring for Decisionally Incapacitated Elderly," *Theoretical Medicine* 10 (1989): 83–96. Janofsky states that in geriatrics "there is a high risk of true cognitive impairment, and a correspondingly high risk that patients may truly lack the . . . capacity to make decisions regarding their own health care." Jeffrey S. Janofsky, "Assessing Competency in the Elderly," *Geriatrics* 45, no. 10 (October 1990): 46.

4. David W. Molloy et al., "Decision Making in the Incompetent Elderly: 'The Daughter from California Syndrome'," *Journal of the American Geriatrics Society* 39, no. 4 (April 1991): 397.

5. Obviously, advance planning is a feasible option only when individuals have decision-making capacity. The best interests standard is an appropriate decision-making standard for elderly patients who never had decision-making capacity. The best interests standard will be discussed below.

6. For an extensive discussion of advance directives, see Alan Meisel, *The Right to Die* and *1992 Cumulative Supplement No. 2* (New York: John Wiley & Sons, 1989 and 1992).

7. Standards of professional integrity are discussed in Chapter 1 in the context of an analysis of "medical futility."

8. Meisel distinguishes between living wills and natural death act directives, reserving the latter term for statutory instruction directives (*The Right to Die,* 318–19). However, as Meisel himself observes, the distinction is blurred by the fact that some states refer to the statutory directive as a "living will." Statutory instruction directives (living wills or natural death directives) and prepared living will forms distributed by organizations, such as Choice In Dying (an organization created by the merger of Concern for Dying and the Society for the Right to Die) and the American Association of Retired Persons, include a provision to forgo treatment in certain circumstances. Emanuel and Emanuel distinguish between "advance care documents," which are "general statements of a patient's preferences regarding the medical interventions to be implemented if he or she becomes incompetent," and "living wills," which are "restricted to rejecting life-sustaining medical interventions." Ezekiel J. Emanuel and Linda L. Emanuel, "Living Wills: Past, Present, and Future," *Journal of Clinical Ethics* 1, no. 1 (Spring 1990): 9.

9. This information is from an October 12, 1992, Choice In Dying fact sheet entitled "State Law Governing Living Wills/Declarations and Appointment of a Health Care Agent." Massachusetts, Michigan, and New York have legislation that authorizes the appointment of a health care agent (proxy).

10. The California Natural Death Act is reprinted in the President's Commission for the Study of Ethical Problems in Medicine and Biomedical and Behavioral Research, *Deciding to Forego Life-Sustaining Treatment* (Washington, D.C.: U.S. Government Printing Office, 1983), 324–29. It is also reprinted in Society for the Right to Die, *1991 Refusal of Treatment Legislation* and *Update for 1991* (New York: Society for the Right to Die, 1991), CA-1–CA-6.

11. *In re Quinlan* 70 N.J. 10, 355 A.2d 647. Both Meisel and Weir cite a connection between the Quinlan case and passage of the California Natural Death Act. See Meisel, *The*

Right to Die, 357; and Robert F. Weir, *Abating Treatment with Critically Ill Patients* (New York: Oxford University Press, 1989), 171.

12. Society for the Right to Die, *1991 Refusal of Treatment Legislation,* CA-2.

13. *1991 Refusal of Treatment Legislation,* CA-2. As noted in Chapter 1, the President's Commission in its report, *Deciding to Forego Life-Sustaining Treatment,* adopted a much broader definition: "life-sustaining treatment . . . encompasses all health care interventions that have the effect of increasing the life span of the patient" (3).

14. The California legislation also states that a natural death directive "shall be conclusively presumed, unless revoked, to be the directions of the patient" *if* the patient "was a qualified patient at least 14 days prior to executing or reexecuting the directive." Otherwise, "physicians *may give weight* to the directive as evidence of the patient's directions" (*1991 Refusal of Treatment Legislation,* CA-5 and CA-6; emphasis added).

15. *Deciding to Forego Life-Sustaining Treatment,* 310–11.

16. The status of tube feeding is also in considerable flux.

17. Society for the Right to Die, "Significant Legal Developments (September 1990–April 1991)." This update does not include information about the amended West Virginia Natural Death Act which was passed March 9, 1991, and became effective June 7, 1991 (W. Va. Code 16-30-1 to 16-30-13). The revised West Virginia Natural Death Act is reprinted in *1991 Refusal of Treatment Legislation, Update for 1991,* WV-1–WV-6. Pennsylvania, one state that enacted living will legislation subsequent to publication of the *Update for 1991,* requires a "terminal condition" or a "state of permanent unconsciousness" for a statutory living will to go into effect.

18. One study found that most patients would not want life-sustaining treatment if they were severely demented. See Bernard Lo, Gary A. McLeod, and Glenn Saika, "Patient Attitudes to Discussing Life-Sustaining Treatment," *Archives of Internal Medicine* 146 (August 1986): 1613–15. In another study, a group of outpatients and members of the general public were asked whether they would want specified life-sustaining measures in four different scenarios (coma with a small chance of full recovery, persistent vegetative state, dementia with no other life-threatening illness, and dementia with a terminal illness). The subjects' responses for the last three scenarios were not substantially different for several categories of life-sustaining treatment. For example, for dementia with a terminal illness, 9 percent said they would want artificial nutrition and 8 percent would want mechanical respiration; 82 percent would not want artificial nutrition and 84 percent would not want mechanical respiration. For persistent vegetative state, 8 percent would want artificial nutrition and 7 percent would want mechanical respiration; 80 percent would not want artificial nutrition and 80 percent would not want mechanical respiration. For dementia with no other life-threatening illness, 11 percent would want artificial nutrition and 10 percent would want mechanical respiration; 76 percent would not want artificial nutrition and 75 percent would not want mechanical respiration. See Linda L. Emanuel et al., "Advance Directives for Medical Care—A Case for Greater Use," *New England Journal of Medicine* 324, no. 13 (March 28, 1991): 889–95.

19. See Christine K. Cassel and Jacob A. Brody, "Demography, Epidemiology, and Aging," in Christine K. Cassel et al., eds., *Geriatric Medicine,* 16–27; U.S. Congress, Office of Technology Assessment, *Life-Sustaining Technologies and the Elderly* (Washington, D.C.: U.S. Government Printing Office, 1987); and the OTA report, *Losing A Million Minds.*

20. In the study by Lo, McLeod, and Saika, 80 percent of patients over sixty-five stated they would decline tube feeding if they became demented, and only 42 percent of younger patients gave this response ("Patient Attitudes to Discussing Life-Sustaining Treatment,"

1614). In another study, one limited to elderly patients (mean age of 73.4 years), 61 percent responded that they would refuse tube feeding if they were to develop severe Alzheimer's disease. See Thomas E. Finucane et al., "Planning with Elderly Outpatients for Contingencies of Severe Illness: A Survey and Clinical Trial," *Journal of General Medicine* 3 (July–August 1988): 322–25.

21. For a discussion of the legal status of nonstatutory instruction directives, see Meisel, *The Right to Die* and *1992 Cumulative Supplement*. Even if their legal status is unclear, from the perspective of shared decision-making, instruction directives can provide important guidance.

22. Both documents are reproduced in Weir, *Abating Treatment*, 427–29. As indicated above, the Society for Right to Die and Concern for Dying have merged into Choice In Dying. The Choice In Dying Living Will is more restrictive than either of the earlier documents. Like most statutory living wills, unless people give instructions to the contrary, it goes into effect only when patients are near death or permanently unconscious.

23. Linda L. Emanuel and Ezekiel J. Emanuel, "The Medical Directive: A New Comprehensive Advance Care Document," *Journal of the American Medical Association* 261 (June 9, 1989): 3288–93. For an expanded version of this advance instruction directive, see Linda Emanuel, "The Health Care Directive: Learning How to Draft Advance Care Documents," *Journal of the American Geriatrics Society* 39, no. 12 (December 1991): 1221–28.

24. Allen E. Buchanan and Dan W. Brock, *Deciding for Others: The Ethics of Surrogate Decision Making* (New York: Cambridge University Press, 1989), 103–7. Buchanan and Brock conclude that "in principle there is a special limitation on the moral authority of advance directives" (108). However, they do *not* support the terminal condition or permanent unconsciousness requirement. Moreover, for policy reasons, they are wary of paternalistic restrictions on people's ability to direct their future medical care by means of advance directives: "Even if a paternalistic limitation on the authority of a small class of advance directives is justifiable in principle, efforts to restrict the limitation to *just those cases in which it is appropriate* may fail. If this occurs, then most of the value of advance directives as a means of exercising individual self-determination would be lost" (111).

25. For a critique of living wills that list specific medical interventions to be forgone, see Allan S. Brett, "Limitations of Listing Specific Medical Interventions in Advance Directives," *Journal of the American Medical Association* 266, no. 6 (August 14, 1991): 825–28.

26. See Buchanan and Brock, *Deciding for Others*, 99–100.

27. Lynn claims that the "standard form living will" has "little justification" unless it is used as "a trigger for further communication." Joanne Lynn, "Why I Don't Have a Living Will," *Law, Medicine & Health Care* 19, nos. 1–2 (Spring and Summer 1991): 102. Studies have consistently shown that patients generally, and elderly patients in particular, want to discuss health care preferences and goals with physicians. See Lo, McLeod, and Saika, "Patient Attitudes to Discussing Life-Sustaining Treatment;" Finucane et al., "Planning with Elderly Outpatients for Contingencies of Severe Illness;" Robert H. Shmerling et al., "Discussing Cardiopulmonary Resuscitation: A Study of Elderly Outpatients," *Journal of General Medicine* 3 (July–August 1988): 317–21; Elizabeth R. Gamble, Penelope J. McDonald, and Peter R. Lichstein, "Knowledge, Attitudes, and Behavior of Elderly Persons Regarding Living Wills," *Archives of Internal Medicine* 151 (February 1991): 277–80; and Ronald S. Schonwetter et al., "Educating the Elderly: Cardiopulmonary Resuscitation Decisions before and after Intervention," *Journal of the American Geriatrics Society* 39, no. 4 (April 1991): 372–77. Unfortunately, however, these studies also indicate that only a small percentage of patients have had advance discussions about life-sustaining treatment with their physicians.

28. See Brett, "Limitations of Listing Specific Medical Interventions in Advance Directives."

29. For a discussion of difficulties in interpreting living wills and the importance of patient-physician communication to clarify patients' intentions, see Stuart J. Eisendrath and Albert R. Jonsen, "The Living Will: Help or Hindrance?" *Journal of the American Medical Association* 249, no. 15 (April 15, 1983): 2054–58. See also Ashwini Sehgal et al., "How Strictly Do Dialysis Patients Want Their Advance Directives Followed?" *Journal of the American Medical Association* 267, no. 1 (January 1, 1992): 59–63. In the revised "Health Care Directive" referred to above, Linda Emanuel adds items relating to patients' *goals*. This information can help prevent unwarranted literal readings and can facilitate interpretations that capture the patient's intent and goals.

30. See Rebecca Dresser, "Life, Death, and Incompetent Patients: Conceptual Infirmities and Hidden Values in the Law," *Arizona Law Review* 28 (1986): 373–405; Rebecca Dresser and John A. Robertson, "Quality of Life and Nontreatment Decisions for Incompetent Patients: A Critique of the Orthodox Approach," *Law, Medicine, & Health Care* 17 (1989): 234–44; and John A. Robertson, "Second Thoughts on Living Wills," *Hastings Center Report* 21, no. 6 (November–December 1991): 6–9.

31. Dresser challenges the moral authority of advance directives by arguing that whenever there is a conflict between the advance directive of a patient who lacks decision-making capacity and the patient's contemporaneous best interests, the latter should prevail. See Dresser, "Life, Death, and Incompetent Patients." For critiques of Dresser, see Nancy Rhoden, "Litigating Life and Death," *Harvard Law Review* 102 (1988): 375–446; and Buchanan and Brock, *Deciding for Others,* chapter 3. Dresser responds to Rhoden in "Relitigating Life and Death," *Ohio State Law Journal* 51 (1990): 425–37.

32. Buchanan and Brock, *Deciding for Others,* 105–6. See also Dresser, "Life, Death, and Incompetent Patients."

33. The argument also challenges the moral authority of *contemporaneous* refusals. If humans are adaptable and changes in their capacities are often correlated with changes in what will give them pleasure and enjoyment, then people may not be the best judges of their own best interests when they are confronted with a choice between almost certain death and a medical intervention that will keep them alive but in a significantly altered condition. Examples of such choices include (1) deciding whether to accept or refuse an amputation; (2) deciding whether to accept or refuse treatment for severe, disabling and disfiguring burns; and (3) deciding whether to accept or refuse ventilator support after becoming a quadriplegic due to an accident. However, even if it is doubtful that patients who are confronted with such choices are the best judges of their own interests, their *autonomy* interests need to be considered. Dresser argues that patients with severe mental impairment do not possess autonomy interests. Her position will be examined below.

34. Ronald Dworkin draws a helpful distinction between a person's "experiential" and "evaluative" interests. The former relate to "the felt quality" of a person's future experiences, and the latter relate to "the overall value or worth" of a person's life. Ronald Dworkin, "Philosophical Issues in Senile Dementia," a contract paper written for the OTA report, *Losing a Million Minds.* A short excerpt from Dworkin's paper was published as "Autonomy and the Demented Self," *Milbank Quarterly* 64, suppl. 2 (1986): 4–15. Dworkin draws another useful distinction between "evidentiary" and "integrity" views of autonomy. According to the evidentiary view, respect for autonomy is based on the assumption that people are the best judges of their own interests. According to the integrity view, the value of autonomy "lies in the scheme of responsibility it creates: autonomy makes each of us responsible for shaping his own life according to some coherent and distinctive sense of character,

conviction, and interest" ("Autonomy and the Demented Self," 8). The fourth asymmetry between contemporaneous and advance treatment refusals poses a challenge to the moral authority of advance directives from the perspective of the evidentiary, but not the integrity, view of autonomy.

35. For a discussion of dignity in relation to senile dementia, see Dworkin, "Philosophical Issues in Senile Dementia."

36. See Rhoden, "Litigating Life and Death," 415–16.

37. Dresser, "Life, Death, and Incompetent Patients" and "Relitigating Life and Death."

38. Dresser, "Life, Death, and Incompetent Patients," 390 and 389.

39. See Rhoden, "Litigating Life and Death," 378ff.

40. Dresser, citing Parfit, also challenges the moral authority of advance directives by questioning whether a patient before and after losing decision-making capacity is *the same person.* See "Life, Death, and Incompetent Patients," 379ff.; and Derek Parfit, *Reasons and Persons* (New York: Oxford University Press, 1986). For an effective critique of Dresser's position, see Buchanan and Brock, *Deciding for Others,* chapter 3. Rhoden also criticizes Dresser's position.

If the person whose name is Germaine Wicclair is not the same person as my mother, then in the absence of social conventions to the contrary, it would be appropriate for me to stop visiting her, paying her nursing home bills, referring to her as my son's "grandma," and so forth. If a philosophically defensible criterion of personhood has these implications, then, to paraphrase Pascal, the heart may have reasons that reason cannot understand.

41. There are other possible justifications for a decision to withhold treatment when a consideration of a patient's current experiential interests alone cannot justify such a decision. For example, it might be claimed that ventilator support is appropriate only if my mother is expected to regain her "distinctly human capacities," such as the capacity to interact with others. See John D. Arras, "Toward an Ethic of Ambiguity." *Hastings Center Report* 14, no. 2 (April 1984): 25–33. Rhoden adopts a similar standard. See "Litigating Life and Death," 437. My mother's living will suggests that she also accepted this standard. However, there is an important difference between saying "it is justified to withhold treatment because of my mother's dignity interests documented in her living will," and "it is justified to withhold treatment because treatment will fail to accomplish any reasonable medical objective."

42. In some cases, the intelligent use of living wills can mean that they should be used in conjunction with the substituted judgment standard. This standard will be discussed below.

43. For a discussion of durable powers of attorney and statutory medical powers of attorney, see Meisel, *The Right to Die* and *1992 Cumulative Supplement.*

44. This information is from a June 23, 1992, Choice In Dying fact sheet entitled "State Law Governing Durable Power of Attorney/Health Care Agents/Proxy Appointments."

45. For a comparison of the advantages and disadvantages of instruction and proxy directives, see Meisel, *The Right to Die;* and Lawrence J. Schneiderman and John D. Arras, "Counseling Patients to Counsel Physicians on Future Care in the Event of Patient Incompetence," *Annals of Internal Medicine* 102, no. 5 (May 1985): 693–98.

46. For two studies that conclude that there are significant differences between elderly patients' treatment preferences and the decisions others would make on their behalf, see Nancy R. Zweibel and Christine K. Cassel, "Treatment Choices at the End of Life: A Comparison of Decisions by Older Patients and Their Physician-Selected proxies" *The Gerontologist* 29, no. 5 (1989): 615–21; and Uhlmann, Pearlman, and Cain, "Physicians' and Spouses' Predictions of Elderly Patients' Resuscitation Preferences." This issue will be discussed in the section on substituted judgment.

47. See Meisel, *The Right to Die,* 321–22.

48. For a report on several such studies, see Zweibel and Cassel, "Treatment Choices at the End of Life." According to the studies which they cite, from 4 percent to 17.5 percent of respondents had executed living wills. See also John La Puma, David Orentlicher, and Robert J. Moss, "Advance Directives on Admission: Clinical Implications and Analysis of the Patient Self-Determination Act of 1990," *Journal of the American Medical Association* 266, no. 3 (July 17, 1991): 402. Emanuel et al. report that although "57 percent of the patients [in the study] wanted a document specifying future care, only 7 percent had one" ("Advance Directives for Medical Care—A Case for Greater Use," 891). In a study of ambulatory elderly persons in a rural county in North Carolina, whereas 86 percent only wanted basic medical care or comfort care in the event of a terminal illness, none of the seventy-five persons questioned had executed a living will. See Gamble, McDonald, and Lichstein, "Knowledge, Attitudes, and Behavior of Elderly Persons Regarding Living Wills." In another study of noninstitutionalized elderly persons, High reports that only 17.5 percent executed a formal living will. Dallas M. High, "All in the Family: Extended Autonomy and Expectations in Surrogate Health Care Decision-Making," *The Gerontologist* 28, suppl. (1988): 46–51. Gamble, McDonald, and Lichstein identify one possible source of a reticence to execute living wills: "concerns about signing any legal document that [people] believe may limit their freedom and expose them to legal and societal forces that are beyond their control" (280).

49. Omnibus Budget Reconciliation Act of 1990. Pub. L. No. 101–508, Sections 4206 and 4751 (codified at 42 U.S.C. Sections 1395cc and 1396a. For a summary of the PSDA, see Meisel, *1992 Cumulative Supplement No. 2,* 210–213. One of the goals of the PSDA is to encourage people to execute advance directives. See Wolf et al., "Sources of Concern About the Patient Self-Determination Act," *New England Journal of Medicine* 325, no. 23 (December 5, 1991): 1666. See also Rouse et al., "Practicing the PSDA," special supplement, *Hastings Center Report* 21, no. 5 (September–October 1991): S1–S16. However, Sehgal and colleagues report that "few subjects in our study executed advance directives, even after spending 30 minutes discussing them with a sympathetic interviewer" ("How Strictly Do Dialysis Patients Want Their Advance Directives Followed?" 63). By contrast, in a study of 39 nursing home residents, it was reported that although only 18 percent executed an advance directive previously, 63 percent signed the Florida living will during the study. See Eric L. Diamond et al., "Decision-Making Ability and Advance Directive Preferences in Nursing Home Patients and Proxies," *The Gerontologist* 29, no. 5 (1989): 622–26. A national study conducted in November 1991 found that "up to 24 percent of Americans now have living wills." *Choice In Dying News* 1, no. 1 (Spring 1992): 2. *Choice In Dying News* touted this figure as a "dramatic increase," which it attributed in part to passage of the PSDA.

50. The substituted judgment standard is widely recognized in law and medical ethics. For a discussion of the legal doctrine of substituted judgment, see Meisel, *The Right to Die.* For a discussion of substituted judgment from the perspective of medical ethics, see the President's Commission reports, *Making Health Care Decisions* and *Deciding to Forego Life-Sustaining Treatment;* and Buchanan and Brock, *Deciding for Others.* To satisfy the "fully informed" condition, it is necessary to imagine that the patient is aware of the fact that she lacks decision-making capacity. See *Deciding for Others,* 94.

51. Buchanan and Brock distinguish between "acts of will" and "expressions of preference," and they claim that "a properly executed advance directive" is "a *performance,* an act of will," and "not merely evidence of an individual's preference" (*Deciding for Others,* 116). They claim that the moral authority of acts of will is greater than that of expressions of preference.

52. See the President's Commission reports, *Making Health Care Decisions* and *Deciding to Forego Life-Sustaining Treatment;* and Buchanan and Brock, *Deciding for Others.* One reason for recognizing the authority of family members to serve as surrogates is they are best qualified to serve in that capacity. An additional reason is derived from the value of the family as a social unit.

53. Legal guardians may also be qualified surrogates for the purposes of substituted judgment.

54. See Lo, McLeod, and Saika, "Patient Attitudes to Discussing Life-Sustaining Treatment;" Zweibel and Cassel, "Treatment Choices at the End of Life;" Finucane et al., "Planning with Elderly Outpatients for Contingencies of Severe Illness;" Uhlmann, Pearlman, and Cain, "Physicians' and Spouses' Predictions of Elderly Patients' Resuscitation Preferences;" Emanuel et al., "Advance Directives for Medical Care—A Case for Greater Use;" and Allison B. Seckler et al., "Substituted Judgment: How Accurate are Proxy Predictions?" *Annals of Internal Medicine* 115, no. 2 (July 1991): 92–98.

55. Buchanan and Brock provide five helpful rules of thumb for assessing the evidential basis of substituted judgment. See *Deciding for Others,* 120–21.

56. "Physicians' and Spouses' Predictions of Elderly Patients' Resuscitation Preferences," M119.

57. Seckler et al., "Substituted Judgment: How Accurate are Proxy Predictions?"

58. "Treatment Choices at the End of Life." Zweibel and Cassel presented vignettes to designated proxies on ventilation, resuscitation, chemotherapy, amputation, and tube feeding. After each of the five vignettes, the proxy-subjects were asked two questions: (1) "If this were (Patient), what would you tell the doctor to do?" (2) "If this were you, what would you want your child to tell the doctor to do?" Responses to the first and second questions were very similar, and much closer than the answers to the first question and the patients' responses. Zweibel and Cassel state that the first question "was intentionally worded in an effort to reflect our view of how most physicians not trained in biomedical ethics usually approach families to make decisions for incapacitated patients" (616). Since proxy-subjects were not specifically asked to decide as patients themselves would have, it is unclear whether this study warrants conclusions about the *ability* of proxies to make reliable substituted judgments. A study by Tomlinson et al. suggests that Zweibel and Cassel's results would have been significantly different if they had specifically asked surrogates to make substituted judgments. See Tom Tomlinson et al., "An Empirical Study of Proxy Consent for Elderly Persons," *The Gerontologist* 30, no. 1 (1990): 54–64.

59. See Amy Horowitz, Barbara M. Silverstone, and Joann P. Reinhardt, "A Conceptual and Empirical Exploration of Personal Autonomy Issues Within Family Caregiving Relationships," *The Gerontologist* 31, no. 1 (1991): 23–31.

60. See High, "All in the Family;" and Dallas M. High and Howard B. Turner, "Surrogate Decision-Making: The Elderly's Familial Expectations," *Theoretical Medicine* 8, no. 3 (October 1987): 303–20.

61. See the President's Commission reports, *Making Health Care Decisions* and *Deciding to Forego Life-Sustaining Treatment;* and Buchanan and Brock, *Deciding for Others.*

62. Conditions (a) and (b) are adapted from Buchanan and Brock, *Deciding for Others,* 146–47.

63. For a defense of family discretion, see Rhoden, "Litigating Life and Death;" and John D. Arras, "The Severely Demented, Minimally Functional Patient: An Ethical Analysis," *Journal of the American Geriatrics Society* 36, no. 10 (October 1988): 938–944.

64. For a discussion of the legal status of the best interests standard, see Meisel, *The*

Right to Die and *1992 Cumulative Supplement*. For a discussion of the best interests standard from the perspective of medical ethics, see the President's Commission reports, *Making Health Care Decisions* and *Deciding to Forego Life-Sustaining Treatment;* and Buchanan and Brock, *Deciding for Others*. The Supreme Court decision in the Nancy Cruzan case suggests that the legal status of the best interests standard is not so firm as its status in medical ethics. *Cruzan v. Director, Missouri Department of Health,* 110 S.Ct. 2841 (1990). For a discussion of the *Cruzan* decision and its implications, see Meisel, *1992 Cumulative Supplement;* Robert A. Pearlman, "Clinical Fallout from the Supreme Court Decision on Nancy Cruzan: Chernobyl or Three Mile Island?" *Journal of the American Geriatrics Society* 39, no. 1 (January 1991): 92–97; Jacqueline J. Glover and Joanne Lynn, "After Cruzan—the Work to be Done," *Journal of the American Geriatrics Society* 39, no. 4 (April 1991): 423–24; and Larry Gostin and Robert F. Weir, "Life and Death Choices after *Cruzan:* Case Law and Standards of Professional Conduct," *Milbank Quarterly* 69, no. 1 (1991): 143–73.

65. For an analysis of the concept of patient interests, see Daniel Wikler, "Patient Interests: Clinical Implications of Philosophical Distinctions," *Journal of the American Geriatrics Society* 36, no. 10 (October 1988): 951–58.

66. See the President's Commission reports, *Making Health Care Decisions* and *Deciding to Forego Life-Sustaining Treatment;* and the OTA report, *Life-Sustaining Technologies and the Elderly*.

67. See the President's Commission reports, *Making Health Care Decisions* and *Deciding to Forego Life-Sustaining Treatment*.

68. Arras presents a stricter standard: "the burdens of a patient's life with the proposed treatment would *clearly and markedly* outweigh whatever benefits she might derive from continued life" ("The Severely Demented, Minimally Functional Patient," 941; emphasis added). This standard is derived from the first prong of the two-pronged "pure objective test" formulated by the Supreme Court of New Jersey in *Conroy:* "the net burdens of the patient's life with the treatment should clearly and markedly outweigh the benefits that the patient derives from life." The Court added the following second prong: "Further, the recurring, unavoidable and severe pain of the patient's life with the treatment should be such that the effect of administering life-sustaining treatment would be inhumane." The court also formulated a "limited-objective test," which states: "life-sustaining treatment may be withheld or withdrawn . . . when there is some trustworthy evidence that the patient would have refused the treatment, and the decision-maker is satisfied that it is clear that the burdens of the patient's continued life with the treatment outweigh the benefits of that life for him." The court formulated a third test, the "subjective standard," which states: "life-sustaining treatment may be withheld or withdrawn from an incompetent patient when it is clear that the particular patient would have refused the treatment under the circumstances involved." *In re Conroy,* 98 N.J. 321, 486 A.2d 1209 (1985).

69. See Buchanan and Brock, *Deciding for Others,* 126–32; and Arras, "The Severely Demented, Minimally Functional Patient," 939–40.

70. Arras (940) and Buchanan and Brock (126) suggest that the best interests standard *requires* life-sustaining treatment when there is no expected benefit or harm to patients (for example, PVS patients). However, since providing treatment in such circumstances is not expected to promote the patient's interests better than forgoing treatment, this conclusion appears to assume that the best interests standard requires life-sustaining treatment unless forgoing treatment can be justified by that standard. As I have stated the best interests standard, it does not justify forgoing or providing life-extending treatment that is not expected to benefit or harm patients.

71. See Ronald E. Cranford, "The Persistent Vegetative State: The Medical Reality

(Getting the Facts Straight)," *Hastings Center Report* 18, no. 1 (February–March 1988): 27–32.

72. Several studies report that most people do not want aggressive life-extending treatment if they were to become permanently unconscious. See, for example, Emanuel et al., "Advance Directives for Medical Care—a Case for Greater Use;" and Marion Danis et al., "A Prospective Study of Advance Directives for Life-Sustaining Care," *New England Journal of Medicine* 324, no. 13 (March 28, 1991): 882–88.

73. See the OTA report, *Losing a Million Minds* and Arras, "The Severely Demented, Minimally Functional Patient."

74. See Dresser, "Life, Death, and Incompetent Patients."

75. These three reasons were cited as reasons for allowing members of a functional family to serve as surrogates when decisions are made by applying the substituted judgment standard.

76. See Horowitz, Silverstone, and Reinhardt, "A Conceptual and Empirical Exploration of Personal Autonomy Issues Within Family Caregiving Relationships."

77. This condition is similar to one proposed in relation to family exercise of substituted judgment.

78. Mark Yarborough, "Continued Treatment of the Fatally Ill for the Benefit of Others," *Journal of the American Geriatrics Society* 36, no. 1 (January 1988): 63–64. Although Yarborough claims that it can be *morally* permissible to treat patients who are beyond help medically for the benefit of family members, he holds that the practice would constitute *bad medicine*. The obligation to practice good medicine, he concludes, overrides a concern for the well-being of family members. Yarborough also claims that economic considerations present "a practical barrier to justifying unnecessary treatment" (66).

79. Paternalism is discussed in Chapter 4.

80. Yarborough recognizes this problem. He asks, "can the physician judge that greater benefit [for the family member] is achieved by a protracted dying?" (66).

81. Ethical issues associated with forgoing nutrition and hydration are discussed in Chapter 1.

82. Wash. Rev. Code Ann. 70.122.010 to 70.122.905 (June 7, 1979), reprinted in *Deciding to Forego Life-Sustaining Treatment*, 382–87; and Wash. Rev. Code Ann. 70.122.010 to 70.122.905 (supp., 1989), reprinted in Society for the Right to Die, *1991 Refusal of Treatment Legislation*, WA-1–WA-5.

83. See the study by Emanuel et al. cited above, "Advance Directives for Medical Care—A Case for Greater Use." Whereas 9 percent of the respondents said they would want artificial nutrition if they had dementia and a terminal illness, the response was only 2 percent higher for dementia with no other life-threatening illness.

84. Some living will laws specifically exclude artificial nutrition and hydration from the scope of "life-sustaining treatment." However, recent living will legislation in some states stipulates that life-sustaining treatment includes artificial nutrition and hydration. The Washington Natural Death Act is silent on this issue. See Society for the Right to Die, *1991 Refusal of Treatment Legislation*.

85. It is doubtful that this information would be sufficient to trigger the *Conroy* "limited objective" test. See *In re Conroy* 98 N.J. 321, 486 A.2d 1209 (1985); and Meisel, *The Right to Die*.

86. See Emanuel et al., "Advance Directives for Medical Care;" Eric L. Diamond et al., "Decision-Making Ability and Advance Directive Preferences in Nursing Home Patients and Proxies;" Uhlmann, Pearlman, and Cain, "Physicians' and Spouses' Predictions of Elderly Patients' Resuscitation Preferences;" Lo, McLeod, and Saika, "Patient Attitudes to Discuss-

ing Life-Sustaining Treatment;'' Schonwetter et al., ''Educating the Elderly: Cardiopulmonary Resuscitation Decisions before and after Intervention;'' Finucane et al., ''Planning with Elderly Outpatients for Contingencies of Severe Illness;'' and Shmerling et al., ''Discussing Cardiopulmonary Resuscitation.''

87. In the study by Emanuel et al., when asked whether they would want artificial nutrition if they were in a coma with a small chance of full recovery, 20 percent of the respondents said they would want it, 60 percent said they would not want it, 12 percent said they would want a trial, and 8 percent were undecided. See ''Advance Directives for Medical Care,'' 893.

88. On July 1, 1991, a Hennepin County, Minnesota probate court judge ruled that the husband of Helga Wanglie, an 86-year-old ventilator-dependent patient in a PVS, was competent to serve as her surrogate for medical decisions. Oliver Wanglie's competency to serve as his wife's surrogate was in question because he insisted, against the advice of physicians, that Mrs. Wanglie continue to receive ventilator support. See *In re The Conservatorship of Helga M. Wanglie,* State of Minnesota, County of Hennepin, District Court—Probate Court Division, Fourth Judicial District, File No. PX-91-283. Helga Wanglie died about a week after the probate court decision. For a discussion of the Wanglie case, see Alexander Morgan Capron, ''In Re Helga Wanglie,'' *Hastings Center Report* 21, no. 5 (September–October 1991): 26–28.

CHAPTER 3

Age-Rationing, Ageism, and Justice

There is growing concern over the constantly increasing cost of health care in the United States. The amount spent on health care in 1989 reached $604.1 billion, an 11.1 percent increase from the previous year.[1] According to a Commerce Department estimate, $817 billion was spent on health care in 1991, an increase of about 11 percent from 1990.[2] Official forecasts indicate that the percentage of the gross national product (GNP) spent on health care will rise to 15 percent by the year 2000.[3]

The prospect of increasing health care costs has led to claims that health care rationing is unavoidable and that the question is no longer *whether* health care will be rationed, but rather *how* it will or should be rationed.[4] There are a wide variety of rationing principles and schemes.[5] However, in view of the growing cost of health care for the elderly, rationing by *age* appears to offer a tempting means of substantially reducing spending on health care.[6]

As I will use the term, "age-rationing" implies that elderly patients are denied access to potentially beneficial health care services to which younger patients are not denied access. Rationing should be distinguished from cost-containment measures that merely result in withholding medical services that are of no expected benefit to patients.[7] Accordingly, age-rationing occurs only when elderly patients are denied access to medical services that are of *expected benefit* to them.[8] Brock distinguishes between "strong" and "weak" age-rationing. Under the former, the elderly have "*no* entitlement to social resources for the provision of [specified medical services]."[9] By contrast, under weak age-rationing, "*greater weight* [is given] to the claims on social resources for [specified medical services]" of patients below a certain age.[10] However, if it is to be an effective means of cost-containment, even weak age-rationing will result in denying potentially beneficial medical services to elderly patients. Moreover, as Churchill observes, when "most people talk about age-rationing, . . . they typically favor . . . having an age cut-off for access to some services."[11]

A form of age-rationing is practiced by physicians who participate in the British National Health Service.[12] Long-term dialysis is generally not offered to patients over sixty-five, and access to other life-extending measures by elderly patients is also restricted.[13] Since the British National Health Service offers free health care for everyone, and since there is no comparable national health care system in the United States, it is questionable whether age-rationing British-style is suitable for health care delivery American-style. However, several studies suggest that age is already used as a criterion to exclude elderly patients from certain medical services in the United States, and age-rationing proposals tailored to U.S. conditions have been advanced.[14] A proposal by Daniel Callahan to eliminate public funding of life-extending treatment for elderly patients has received considerable attention.[15] Such a policy would only deny life-sustaining treatment to elderly persons who were not willing and/or able to pay.[16] In this respect the policy Callahan recommends is a form of rationing by price. However, insofar as some of the medical services that would be accessible to poor younger patients would not be accessible to poor older patients, Callahan is also endorsing age-rationing.

Age-rationing under the British National Health Service is limited to dialysis and other life-extending measures. Proposals for age-rationing also tend to single out scarce and/or costly *life-extending* technologies, distinguishing them from goods and services that are relatively inexpensive and widely available (for example, antibiotics), measures to enhance quality of life (for example, hip replacement surgery and various personal care and social support services), and measures to reduce pain or suffering (for example, painkillers and comfort care).[17] The focus on life-extending technology is undoubtedly associated with the belief that a substantial amount of money is spent ("wasted") on costly medical technology to (temporarily) sustain the lives of elderly patients who are near death.[18]

However, Scitovsky reports that spending on hospital and physician services during the last year of life is significantly less for patients 80 years and older than for patients 65 to 79. Her study indicates that it is spending on supportive care (nursing homes and home health services), and not hospital and physician services, that is higher in the last year of life for patients age 80 and older than for patients aged 65 to 79.[19] Accordingly, it is unclear that age-rationing of life-extending technology alone would result in a significant reduction in health care spending for the elderly.[20] Nevertheless, since proposals for age-rationing tend to be limited to life-extending treatment and to exclude long-term or supportive care, for the purposes of this discussion it will be assumed that age-rationing is to apply exclusively to such treatment, and the term "age-rationing" will be used as a shorthand expression for "age-rationing of scarce and/or costly life-extending measures."

Justifications of Age-Rationing

Since age-rationing implies that elderly patients are denied access to potentially beneficial life-extending medical care to which younger patients are not denied access, and since life-extending treatment can literally mean the difference between life and death, it seems as though age-rationing requires the elderly to make significant sacrifices that are not required of the non-elderly. In addition, insofar as age-rationing increases access to life-sustaining measures by younger patients, the young appear to be the primary beneficiaries of the sacrifices of the old, and the young appear to benefit at the expense of the old. In addition to placing the burden of rationing exclusively on the shoulders of the elderly, age-rationing also appears to allocate health care on the basis of a criterion, age, that is no more relevant than sex or race. These observations support the impression that age-rationing reflects ageism or age bias and is unjust. To determine whether these negative characterizations of age-rationing are warranted, it is necessary to examine the primary arguments that purport to defend the practice. First, however, we need to ascertain when it is appropriate to use the characterizations, "ageism" and "age bias."

Ageism and Age Bias

Policies, practices, actions, beliefs, arguments, and so forth are ageist, or express ageism, if they are based on false or unfounded universal or statistical generalizations that attribute negative characteristics to the elderly or old age. Examples of false universal generalizations include the following: "all elderly people are forgetful," "all elderly people are ill-tempered," "all elderly people suffer from depression," "mental impairment is endemic to old age." The statistical generalizations associated with ageist policies are often imprecise, such as, "most elderly people have no interest in, and cannot enjoy, sex." As Butler puts it: "Ageism can be seen as a process of systematic stereotyping of and discrimination against people because they are old, just as racism and sexism accomplish this with skin color and gender. Old people are categorized as senile, rigid in thought and manner, old-fashioned in morality and skills."[21]

Transforming true statistical generalizations into false universal generalizations is another form of stereotyping. Examples of this form include transforming the proposition, "the chances of developing a serious illness increase in old age" into "sickness is endemic to old age"; and transforming "the chances of mental impairment increase in old age" into "all elderly people are mentally impaired." This form of ageism should be distinguished from another form of discrimination based on true statistical generalizations. Let us suppose that a nursing home aide correctly believes that 80 percent of nursing home residents over eighty-five are x (for example, moderately to severely demented). Since it would take considerable time and effort to ascertain on a case-by-case basis which residents are, and which are not, x, the aide decides for reasons of efficiency to treat all residents over eighty-five as if they were x. In so doing, the aide treats residents over eighty-five as members of the class, "nursing home residents over the age of eighty-five" rather than as individuals. The aide's decision is not based on any false generalizations and does not appear to express ageism, but it does seem to reflect a form of (statistical) discrimination.[22]

A belief that elderly people are inferior in ethical status and a corresponding devaluation of the elderly need not be based on false or unconfirmed (empirical) generalizations about elderly people or old age. Nevertheless, such attitudes are expressions of ageism. However, for the purposes of assessing defenses of age-rationing, the foregoing characterization of ageism will suffice.

Unlike ageism, age bias may, but need not, be based on ageist beliefs and attitudes.[23] Classifications, criteria, allocations, and so forth will be said to reflect age bias only if they are incompatible with a standard of justice. Accordingly, the claim that age-rationing reflects age bias because it benefits the young at the exprense of the old is to be understood as implying that benefiting the young at the expense of the old is unjust. Similarly, the claim that age-rationing reflects age bias because it denies equal access to life-extending measures by old and young is to be understood as implying that it is unjust to deny such equal access.

The use of criteria and classifications that are not "age-neutral" may, but need not, constitute age bias. For example, the policies of denying the vote to four-year-olds and requiring driving tests when people over the age of seventy-five renew their drivers' licenses involve criteria that are not age-neutral, but it does not follow that both policies reflect age bias. To determine whether either of the policies constitutes age bias, it is necessary to decide whether either violates standards of justice. For the reasons stated above, it seems reasonable to conclude *provisionally* that age-rationing is unfair to the elderly and reflects age bias. However, no firm conclusion is warranted until arguments to the contrary have been considered.[24]

The No Benefit Argument

One defense of denying access to scarce and/or costly life-extending technology by the elderly is based on the claim that elderly patients will not derive any significant benefit from such measures. Since age-*rationing* implies denying or restricting access to a potentially *beneficial* medical service, this claim amounts to a denial that withholding life-extending measures from elderly patients constitutes rationing. The argument is as follows. Sickness, ill health, and impaired functioning are endemic to old age. Due to their poor overall health, elderly patients are not medically suitable candidates for life-sustaining measures.[25] Moreover, even if those measures were to succeed, the quality of elderly patients' lives, due to continuing ill health and impaired functioning, will remain very poor. Since life is hardly enjoyable in a constant state of ill health and impaired functioning, extended life under such circumstances is not a substantial benefit. Thus, if elderly patients fail to receive life-extending measures, they are not deprived of any substantial benefit, and denying access to scarce and/or costly life-extending technology by the elderly is neither discriminatory nor unjust.

This line of argument is ageist. It is based on false universal generalizations, such as "all elderly persons are sickly," "no elderly persons are medically suitable candidates for specific life-extending measures," and "all elderly persons are impaired." To be sure, the chances of experiencing ill health and impaired functioning do increase as people age, and it may therefore be appropriate to examine elderly patients more carefully for the existence of conditions that might make them medically unsuitable candidates for specific life-extending technologies (for example, dialysis or transplants).[26] However, many elderly people are medically suitable candidates for a wide range of life-sustaining measures, and many older people enjoy good health and unimpaired functioning.[27] It is ageist to assume the contrary. Moreover, many conditions that are more likely to occur in old age are treatable. Great strides have been made, for example, in treating osteoarthritis with the aid of total joint arthroplasties (joint replacements), and coronary arteriosclerosis can be treated by means of drugs and coronary bypass surgery.[28]

To be sure, there may be cases in which it is plausible to claim that life-extending treatment is of no expected benefit to elderly patients because the chances of success are extremely low and/or because expected outcomes are very poor. Such a claim seems plausible, for example, in relation to dialysis for a comatose 75-year-old patient with untreatable brain cancer and widespread metastases. But it does not follow that dialysis is *never* of any expected benefit to 75-year-old patients. For example, it is implausible to claim that dialysis is of no expected benefit to an otherwise healthy 75-year-old patient who develops end-stage renal failure. Moreover, the *age* of the patient is of no significance in the example of the comatose patient with untreatable brain cancer and widespread metastases. The expected benefit of dialysis would not be significantly greater for a 35-year-old patient with that medical condition than for a 75-year-old patient with the same medical condition. It would be ageist to hold otherwise.

The Lower Chances of Benefit Argument

It is ageist to defend age-rationing by claiming that since the elderly are condemned to ill health and impaired functioning, age-rationing of life-extending care denies them no significant benefits. However, it can be admitted that although elderly patients may benefit from life-extending care, the *chances* of benefiting from those measures are lower for older patients than for younger patients.[29] The defense of age-rationing is as follows. It is false to claim that *all* elderly people are sick and disabled, but there is a grain of truth to this common stereotype, namely, the chances of being sick and disabled increase as people age. Since life is hardly enjoyable in a constant state of ill health and impaired functioning, extended life under such circumstances is not a substantial benefit. Thus, the chances of benefiting from life-extending measures decrease as people age. Moreover, since elderly patients are less likely to be medically suitable for surgery and other medical interventions, the chances of success (and benefit) are lower for older patients than for younger patients. Consequently, if life-extending measures are withheld from elderly patients, the chances of denying a significant benefit are less than they would be if those measures were withheld from younger patients. Therefore, age-rationing is not unjust and it does not reflect ageism or age bias.

If the probability claims underlying the foregoing argument are false or unfounded, then it is no less ageist than the first (no benefit) argument. However, for the sake of analysis, let us assume that the following claim is warranted: the probability that people over the age of seventy will experience a significant benefit from life-extending measure M is x, and the probability that people under the age of seventy will experience a significant benefit from life-extending measure M is $x + y$. Moreover, let us assume that the difference between x and $x + y$ is significant and that a similar conclusion applies to all scarce and/or costly life-extending measures. These assumptions protect the lower chances of benefit argument against charges of ageism, but they do not provide the basis for a convincing defense of age-rationing against the charge of age bias.

If, as the lower chances of benefit argument assumes, the objective is to increase the likelihood of benefit, there are more reliable indicators of likelihood of benefit than age. A patient's overall health status is generally a more reliable indicator of medical suitability than age alone.[30] For instance, although frail elderly cancer patients may not be able to withstand chemotherapy so well as younger patients whose overall health is good, younger patients who are in poor health may not respond so well to chemotherapy as older patients with no health problems other than cancer. Similarly, a patient's current general health status is generally a more reliable indicator of whether she is likely to experience health problems than is age alone. The chances, say, that a 50-year-old with high blood pressure, a high cholesterol level, and artheriosclerosis will suffer a heart attack or a stroke in five years are probably higher than those of a 74-year-old person with normal blood pressure and cholesterol levels and with no prior history of cardiovascular disease. From the perspective of likelihood of benefit, then, overall health status is a more appropriate criterion for relevant *groups* or *classes* than age. Consequently, even if the use of age instead of general health status does not express ageist attitudes (for example, a devaluation of the elderly), it does reflect age bias.

This conclusion can be confirmed by considering the principle of equality, an important standard of justice. It is incompatible with that principle to treat people the same when they are different in relevant respects, and to treat people differently when they are not different in a relevant respect. Accordingly, since general health status is a relevant characteristic from the perspective of likelihood of success, if the aim is to select patients with the best chances of success, it is incompatible with the principle of equality, and unfair, to deny life-extending measures to *elderly* patients, regardless of their general health status, and to make such measures available to *younger* patients, regardless of their general health status. Consequently, the impression that age-rationing reflects age bias is reinforced if it is defended by claiming that the chances of denying a significant benefit are less when life-extending measures are withheld from elderly patients than when those measures are withheld from younger patients.[31]

The Greater Benefit Argument

Another defense of age-rationing holds that *more benefits* can be expected when life-extending measures are received by younger patients. Accordingly, it is said that age-rationing serves to *maximize* benefits from life-extending measures. Three specific claims along these general lines should be distinguished. First, since younger persons are more productive than elderly persons, age-rationing constitutes an efficient means of allocating resources and will promote overall social welfare.[32] Second, with respect specifically to *experimental* medical procedures, drugs, and the like, the ends of scientific research are best served by excluding elderly patients. Third, since younger patients can be expected to benefit more, and at a lower cost, age-rationing promotes the goals of maximum overall benefit and cost-effectiveness.[33]

To begin with the first claim, if it is based on the assumption that elderly persons are unproductive, it is ageist, since people sometimes remain productive up to and beyond eighty. However, suppose the claim is based on the following assumption: as people age, it is increasingly likely that they will become unproductive, or that their productivity will decrease significantly. Even if this assumption were true for some standard of productivity or other, age may be a poor indicator of productivity compared to general health status, employment history and current employment status, and so forth.[34] If so, then an objection similar to one discussed in relation to the lower chances of benefit argument applies. Insofar as general health status, or some other characteristic, is a more appropriate criterion for relevant *groups* or *classes* than age, then even if the use of age does not express ageist attitudes, it does reflect age bias. Consequently, the impression that age-rationing reflects age bias is reinforced if it is defended by claiming that younger persons are more likely to be (more) productive than elderly persons.

A similar analysis applies to the second claim. If it is based on the assumption that disease and poor overall health are endemic to old age, it has an ageist basis. It might not have an ageist basis if it were based on assumptions such as the following: (1) younger subjects are likely to live longer, so their use increases the chances of being able to study long-term responses and effects; or (2) younger patients who require life-extending measures are more likely to respond favorably to therapies and to tolerate side effects of drugs than elderly patients who require those measures. However, even if these assumptions were true, overall health status still may be a better general indicator of suitability to serve as an experimental subject than age. Insofar as general health status, or some other characteristic, is a more appropriate criterion for relevant *groups* or *classes* than age, then even if the use of age does not express ageist attitudes, it does reflect age bias. Consequently, the impression that age-rationing reflects age bias is reinforced if it is defended by claiming that younger persons are more likely to be suitable subjects for medical research than elderly persons.

However, for the sake of analysis, let us assume that age is a sufficiently reliable indicator of productivity (the first claim), and of suitability to serve as an experimental subject (the second claim) to counter the charge that its use as an indicator of either reflects age bias. A defense of age-rationing on either basis still would fail to counter the impression that age-rationing reflects age bias.

With respect to the first claim, elderly persons who would fail to receive treatment, and who would die because of age-rationing, would bear the burdens, but they would not enjoy any of the benefits derived from the increased productivity that is said to result from reserving life-extending measures for younger people. According to this rationale, then, age-rationing benefits the young by placing burdens on the old, which reinforces the impression that it is unfair and an expression of age bias.

The second claim, the claim that the ends of research are often best served by utilizing younger patients as subjects, fails to address an important reason for thinking that age-rationing of (experimental) life-extending measures expresses age bias. The reason is that the *distribution* of the benefits of experimental life-extending measures, a distribution that favors the young over the old, is unfair, and the foregoing defense of limiting potentially beneficial research to younger patients is silent on this important issue.[35] Thus, the impression remains that excluding the elderly reflects age bias because it (unfairly) denies them access to an important potential benefit to which younger patients have access.

These observations suggest that it is important to distinguish two questions: (1) Does age-rationing reflect age bias? and (2) Does age-rationing promote an important goal? If, say, the enslavement of a racial minority, or the practice of assigning positions on the basis of race or sex, were to maximize the GNP, it would not follow that those practices do not reflect race or sex bias. Similarly, if age-rationing were to serve an important collective goal (for example, increased productivity or more effective medical research), it would not follow that the practice does not reflect age bias.

To move on to the third claim, the claim that age-rationing serves the ends of maximum overall benefit and cost-effectiveness because younger patients can be expected to benefit more, and at a lower cost, if that claim is based on the assumption that poor health and poor quality of life are endemic to old age, then the claim has an ageist basis. However, let us suppose that the claim is based on the following assumptions. (1) Older patients probably will not live so long after receiving treatment as will younger patients. For example, all other things being equal, if a heart is given to a 40-year-old patient, it is likely to extend life longer than if it is transplanted into a 63-year-old patient. (2) The probability of a successful outcome is generally greater in younger patients than it is in older patients. (3) The likelihood of poor health and poor quality of life increases with age. (4) Since elderly patients are more likely to experience complications, and since the period of recovery for them is likely to be longer, certain procedures are likely to cost more for them than for younger patients.

Even if the fourth assumption were true, it can still be claimed that it is unfair to deny certain classes of people (say, the elderly or the handicapped) access to a benefit simply because it would cost more to provide them with access to that benefit than to other classes of people (the nonelderly or the nonhandicapped). Justice can require greater expenditures. Moreover, even if the first three assumptions were true, expected patient benefit can depend on a variety of factors other than a patient's age, including a patient's outlook on life and whether she has close personal relationships with others and satisfying jobs or other interests. Consequently, it is doubtful that age per se is the best indicator of expected patient benefit. Even if "benefit" is construed more narrowly as "medical utility" (additional years of more or less healthy or disease-free life or quality-adjusted life years), or more narrowly still as simply additional years of life, age may be a less reliable indicator of expected patient benefit than the patient's overall health status.[36] Accordingly, although the use of age as an indicator of expected patient benefit may not reflect ageism, its use as such an indicator hardly counters the impression that age-rationing reflects age bias.

Moreover, even if age were a reliable indicator of expected patient benefit, a defense of age-rationing on the grounds that it allocates scarce health care resources to patients who will benefit most fails to show that it is not unjust. To see why, suppose I have two sons, David and Danny, who want to go to summer camp. I can afford to send only one of them to camp, and the one who does not get to go will have to get a job. My two sons and I agree that David will benefit more from the camp. Although Danny enjoys group activities, David enjoys them more. It will be a learning experience for both, and both will have fun, but David is likely to learn more, to have more fun, and so forth. Suppose that Danny's expected benefit from camp is B and David's expected benefit is $B + b$, where $B + b$ is substantially greater than B. I decide to send David to camp because he will benefit more. Danny concedes that David will benefit more and that it would be cost-effective to send his brother to camp, but he still can protest that he has not been treated fairly. It is plausible for Danny to claim that although David would benefit more, he (Danny) should be given a *fair opportunity* to receive the benefits that he could derive from attending camp. To select David solely on the basis that he would benefit more, Danny might plausibly claim, denies him (Danny) a fair opportunity to go to camp. Moreover, Danny might point out that if the greater benefit criterion were to be used in subsequent years, he might never get an opportunity to go to camp.

Like Danny, a 65-year-old candidate for a heart transplant can concede that a 35-year-old candidate will benefit more, and still plausibly claim that it is unfair to be given no chance to benefit at all.[37] Even if older patients do not benefit so much as younger patients from certain procedures, as long as significant benefits are possible, they can still insist on being given a fair opportunity to receive those benefits. Moreover, elderly patients can claim that they are not given such an opportunity when access to health care is limited to younger patients on the grounds that the latter will benefit more. Accordingly, even if age-rationing allocates life-extending measures to patients who will benefit most, it does not follow that age-rationing is not unjust. Consequently, the claim that younger patients can be expected to benefit more fails to counter the impression that systematically denying access to the potential benefits of life-extending measures by the elderly is unjust and reflects age bias.

With appropriate changes, this analysis of the greater benefit argument applies as well to the lower chances of benefit argument. To return to the example of Danny and David, suppose there is a .7 chance that David will benefit from going to camp, and only a .3 chance that Danny will benefit. From Danny's perspective, a .3 chance of benefiting is better than no chance at all (the alternative to camp is working). Accordingly, Danny can claim that if David is selected because the likelihood of benefit is greater, he (Danny) will not have had a fair opportunity to enjoy the potential benefits of going to camp. Similarly even if it is true, say, that the chances of benefiting from life-extending measures are lower for elderly patients, it still can be claimed that age-rationing denies elderly patients a fair opportunity to receive a potential benefit and therefore reflects age bias.

Equal Opportunity Arguments

In defense of age-rationing, and in response to the claim that it denies the elderly a fair opportunity to receive life-extending care, it can be argued that the principle of equal opportunity supports age-based limits on life-extending medical treatment. There are two versions of this claim. One asserts that critically ill elderly patients have had a greater opportunity for well-being over their lifetimes than critically ill younger patients, and age-based limits are said to be supported by the principle of equal opportunity.[38] The second defends age-based limits on life-extending medical care on the grounds that "there should be, insofar as possible, an equal opportunity to live to the same age as others."[39]

There are several problems with each claim. To begin with the first claim, it is not clear how we are to ascertain whether one person has had greater opportunity for well-being than another. Suppose Harry and Harriet are both 30 years old. Both have been healthy most of their lives in the sense that both have been free of pain and have been able to function normally. In this specific respect, both have had an equal opportunity for well-being. But Harry would not have been able to function normally or to enjoy a pain-free life had he not received costly medication since the age of five. By contrast, Harriet has had no serious illness. What is the standard for determining whether Harry has had a greater opportunity for well-being than Harriet: the amount of health care resources consumed or the years of good health (that is, capacity to function normally and absence of pain)? Whatever the answer, there would be no simple correlation between age and opportunity for well-being. Chronically ill young children may have consumed more medical resources in a year or two than some 75-year-olds have consumed in their entire lives.[40] And a 67-year-old patient who has lived in institutions most of his life due to poor health has enjoyed less good health over his entire life than a critically ill 25-year-old who never was seriously ill before. If good health were adopted as a standard of opportunity for well-being, the principle of equal opportunity would generate a "black hole" effect: people who have been unhealthy most of their lives would have the strongest claim on (more) health care resources, and people who have been healthy most of their lives would have the weakest claim on health care resources.

Opportunity for well-being is not limited to good health and/or health care. Suppose, say, Harry has received costly medication for twenty-five years, but he was an abused child, grew up in poverty, and was thrown out of the house by his parents when he was eighteen. By contrast, Harriet had wealthy and caring parents who sent her to college. How is it to be determined whether Harry or Harriet has had the greater overall opportunity for well-being? Whatever the answer, if other factors are added to years of good health and/or amount of medical resources consumed, it is even less likely that there will be a correlation between age and opportunity for well-being.[41]

Finally, it is not clear that denying life-extending medical care to elderly patients can be justified by stating that they have had a greater opportunity for well-being than younger patients. Unless it is assumed that there is a lifetime cap on opportunity for well-being—a questionable assumption—it is not clear why the fact that elderly patients have had a greater opportunity for well-being than younger patients should provide a good reason for concluding that it is just to systematically withhold potentially beneficial life-extending medical care to younger patients.[42]

There are also several problems associated with the second equal opportunity defense of age-rationing. To begin with, how are we to determine whether one person has had an equal opportunity to live to the same age as others? If we are to consider various factors that can affect a person's longevity (for example, socioeconomic status, type of work, health habits, environmental conditions, genetic factors), then there is no correlation between a person's age and her opportunity to live as long as others. However, even if we are to consider only medical services, there is still no correlation between age and a person's opportunity to live to the same age as others. Suppose Ms. A. is seventy-nine, is in good health, and has never been hospitalized. Ms. B. is seventy-eight and has end-stage kidney disease. Until recently, she was in good health and was never hospitalized. However, Ms.

B. will die within a few weeks if she fails to receive dialysis or a kidney transplant. Mr. C. is 26 and has had three liver transplants. Without a fourth transplant, he will die in a few weeks. Despite the fact that Mr. C. is only twenty-six, if consumption of medical services is the exclusive standard, then he has had a greater opportunity to live as long as Ms. A. than has 78-year-old Ms. B.

Perhaps the idea is that Mr. C. has a greater claim to medical services than Ms. B. because he has lived considerably less than she. However, it is not clear why the mere fact that Ms. B. has lived much longer than Mr. C. provides a good reason for concluding that it is just to withhold potentially beneficial life-extending medical care from her and give another transplant (or other life-extending measures) to Mr. C. If Ms. B. and Mr. C. were guests at a party, and she had three pieces of cake to his one, then it might be fair to give the last piece of cake to Mr. C. It seems plausible to claim that Ms. B. should be satisfied with three pieces of cake and that she has already had (more than) her fair share of cake. If Ms. B. continues to demand that the last piece of cake should be given to her rather than to Mr. C., she is subject to the charge of being greedy and unfair.

Ms. B. should be satisfied with three pieces of cake, but should she be satisfied with having lived seventy-eight years? It may be greedy or unfair for Ms. B. to demand that she have an equal opportunity to get the last piece of cake, but can the same be said of her if she desires to live longer and wants the same opportunity as Mr. C. and other younger patients to get life-extending medical care? Callahan offers a "natural life span" argument in support of age-rationing that suggests an affirmative answer to these questions; that argument will be examined in the following section.[43]

The Natural Life-Span Argument

In *Setting Limits: Medical Goals in an Aging Society,* Callahan proposes a communitarian basis for a public policy of denying life-extending medical treatment to people who have reached a natural life span. Specifically, he believes that only a public or community-based conception of the "meaning of aging" and "the nature of a good life for the elderly" will legitimize such a policy (32, 220). Thus, the policy of denying life-extending health care to elderly persons who have achieved a natural life span is to be based on "a general and socially established ideal of old age" (135). As several commentators have observed, there is currently no social consensus about the meaning of aging and the social significance of the elderly, and such a consensus is not to be expected in a pluralistic society such as the United States.[44] More important, as those same commentators have pointed out, efforts to forge such a consensus may threaten other important values, such as freedom and autonomy. However, Callahan presents arguments in support of age-rationing that are independent of controversial claims about the meaning of aging and the social significance of the elderly.[45]

Callahan defends age-rationing by arguing that after reaching a natural life span, people should be satisfied with having lived as long as they have and should not desire or receive life-extending medical care. He defines a "natural life span" as "one in which life's possibilities have on the whole been achieved and after which death may be understood as a sad, but nonetheless relatively acceptable event."[46] According to Callahan, the end of a natural life span ordinarily occurs when people are in their early seventies, but can sometimes "extend through the late 70s to early 80s" (148). People should be satisfied with living out a natural life span, and it is inappropriate for those who have done so to desire or receive life-extending medical care. According to Callahan, "medicine should be used not for further extension of the life of the aged, but only for the full achievement of a natural and fitting life span and thereafter for the relief of suffering" (53).

Since the notion that elderly people have lived a natural life span may well have popular appeal, and since it eliminates doubts about the fairness of age-rationing, it merits careful attention. A natural life span is said to be one in which "life's possibilities have on the whole been achieved," but what, precisely, does that mean?[47] It would be relatively uncontroversial to claim that a person's life possibilities have been achieved if (1) the person is dying (death is imminent and unpreventable), or (2) the person is severely impaired physically and/or mentally and the condition is irreversible (for example, a patient in a persistent vegetative state). Fortunately, however, conditions like these do not strike all people at the age of seventy-five or even eighty; and unfortunately, they can occur at any age. Consequently, these conditions cannot be used to explain the *age*-related notion of a natural life span.

So what does it mean to say that a person's "life possibilities have on the whole been achieved?" Callahan's response is as follows: "I mean something very simple: that most of those opportunities which life affords people will have been achieved by that point" (66). He cites the following opportunities: "work, love, the procreating and raising of a family, life with others, the pursuit of moral and other ideals, the experience of beauty, travel, and knowledge" (66). According to Callahan, "by old age—and here I mean even by the age of 65—most of us will have had a chance to experience those goods; and will certainly experience them by our late 70s or early 80s" (66–67). Thus, to say that a person's life possibilities have been achieved is a statement about the person's *past* opportunities and experiences, and not a statement about the person's incapacity to have and pursue interests in the future. People can have and pursue a wide range of interests well after the age of eighty-five. Callahan admits that in such cases "life's possibilities will never be exhausted; death at *any* time, at age 90, or 100, or 110, will frustrate those further possibilities, which are endless and likely never to be satisfied for one who has remained lively and inquiring'' (67). Nevertheless, he claims, by "old age" most people "already have had *ample time* to know the pleasures of such things" (67; emphasis added). According to Callahan, then, there is a specifiable number (or range) of years of *ample time* to be alive, in the sense that (most) people should be satisfied with a life of that length and should no longer desire life-prolonging medical care. I shall refer to this as the "ample time" thesis.

The ample time thesis is far from obvious. Why, say, should an 85-year-old who has interests and the capacity to pursue those interests be satisfied with eighty-five years of life? Why should such a person not desire life-extending care if it will enable her to pursue her interests and enjoy life for several more years?[48] It is one thing to say that due to scarce resources, all of our legitimate desires cannot be satisfied and we must therefore establish priorities and make hard choices. But the ample time thesis is not based on a scarcity premise.[49] Rather, it is based on the view that the desire for life-extending medical care past a certain age is not a legitimate desire. Is this position defensible?

One argument in support of the ample time thesis is based on the assumption that beyond a certain age, people generally do not develop completely new interests (that is, interests that are different in kind from interests they had and/or pursued when they were younger). Callahan admits that elderly people *sometimes* develop new interests in old age. He cites as examples, "people who take up jogging at 75 and compete in marathons at 80" and people who, like Grandma Moses and his own mother, "discover a whole new set of interests and talents in their later years" (67). But, Callahan claims, cases such as these are rare, and people *generally* do not take on significantly new life projects after the age of seventy-five.[50] If, as Callahan claims, Grandma Moses and his mother are exceptions to the rule, and people generally do not develop and/or pursue completely new interests beyond the age of seventy-five or eighty, then for most people beyond that age life is *more of the same:* more reading, more time with children and grandchildren, more golf, more travel, more bridge, more gardening, and so forth. When people reach such a stage, Callahan appears to suggest, they should be satisfied with the amount of time they have lived, and they should not desire to have their lives extended medically.

One problem with this defense of the ample time thesis is that a similar line of reasoning may well apply to (much) younger people. It may be unlikely that people will begin to pursue and/or develop completely new interests after the age of seventy-five, but for many people it is hardly less likely that this will occur after the age of sixty, fifty, or even forty. Thus, if the ample time thesis is defended in the foregoing manner, it is arbitrary and perhaps ageist to conclude that only people over seventy-five have had "ample time" to experience life's opportunities, and should neither desire nor receive life-extending medical care.

There is another problem with the foregoing defense of the ample time thesis. It is not clear why people cannot legitimately desire more time to live even if it is "only" to pursue old or familiar interests. Suppose, say, that a 75-year-old retired stockbroker has a continuing interest in financial matters, and that he has the capacity to pursue that interest. It is hardly plausible to say that since he has not developed any new interests and is unlikely to do so any time in the future, he should be satisfied with having lived seventy-five years and should not receive or desire life-extending medical care that would enable him to pursue his (old) interests.

There is a second basis for the ample time thesis, namely, what Callahan takes to be the common—and proper—reaction to the death of elderly people (71–76). Callahan's account can be summarized as follows. Although the death of an elderly person may be the occasion for sadness and a sense of loss, it is generally not the occasion for "bitterness," "sharp regret," or an "acute feeling of loss." Such feelings are more common and more appropriate in response to the death of younger people.[51] In contrast to the death of younger people, the death of elderly persons is generally not perceived as an "evil." That is, when elderly persons die, death is generally not perceived as an event that results in the loss of significant potential or as a sign of the "absurdity and irrationality of life itself" (73). By contrast, these perceptions are common responses to the death of younger people. In short, whereas it is both common and proper to view the deaths of older people as "tolerable" or "acceptable" events, these attitudes are neither common nor appropriate in response to the deaths of younger persons.

It may well be correct to claim that the deaths of older and younger people tend to elicit significantly different responses. For example, regardless of how one were to rank them as composers, the deaths of Mozart and Mendelssohn before reaching the age of forty are more likely to be perceived as tragic events than the death of Haydn at the age of seventy-nine. As another example, consider first Claude Pepper, a congressman and champion of the elderly, who died of cancer at the age of eighty-eight, and then John F. Kennedy who died at forty-six. Even people who think that Congressman Pepper was the equal of President Kennedy, and who view Kennedy's death at the age of forty-six as a tragic event, are unlikely to characterize Pepper's death at the age of eighty-eight as such.[52] A similar observation applies to relatives and friends. Whereas the death of an 84-year-old parent or grandparent may well prompt feelings of sadness, the death of a 10-year-old child or 30-year-old friend is more likely to give rise to grief, shock, outrage, and anger. These different responses are associated in part with the belief that the death of someone who is younger than fifty is a *premature* death, and the death of someone who is over seventy-five or eighty is not.

However, even if it is conceded that the foregoing responses are both typical and proper, it does not follow that seventy-five or eighty years are "ample time" in the sense that it is generally inappropriate for people who are older to receive or desire life-extending medical care. When it is thought that the death of someone over eighty does not warrant the sense of loss, grief, despair, or outrage that is warranted by the death of someone under thirty, it is probably assumed that the former's "time had come" in the sense that the person over eighty died of "natural causes" (for example, a heart attack, stroke, or untreatable cancer) and that the person's death was not preventable. Suppose that contrary to fact, Congressman Pepper had been healthy and was shot and killed by a mugger. It would be appropriate to respond to his murder with no less (moral) outrage than to the murder of John F. Kennedy or any other (innocent) person, and it would be no less ethically wrong for Congressman Pepper to have been killed at the age of 88 than at the age of 40.[53] Thus, it is misleading for Callahan to contrast the death of his paternal grandmother, who died in her early eighties with the death of Anne Frank. Whereas he characterizes Anne Frank's death as an "evil," he does not think that this label applies to his grandmother's death because he does not feel sad that she died and because her own children did not remain "sad for long that she was no longer alive" (72). If Callahan's grandmother had died in a Nazi concentration camp, it would be appropriate to view her death as no less of an outrage ("evil") than the death of Anne Frank, despite the differences in their ages.

It is therefore important to distinguish between instances of unpreventable death from natural causes, on the one hand, and instances of unjustified killing, on the other hand. However, it is no less important to distinguish between instances of unpreventable death from natural causes and instances of *preventable* death. Let us assume that Congressman Pepper's death from stomach cancer at the age of eighty-eight is properly understood, in Callahan's words, "as a sad, but nonetheless relatively acceptable event." But suppose that contrary to fact, Pepper was otherwise healthy and died because he was refused dialysis for treatable kidney failure on the grounds that he was "too old" to receive dialysis. Insofar as Pepper's death would have been preventable and dialysis would have benefited him and enabled him to live several more satisfying and productive years, it is far from obvious that his death from kidney failure would have been an equally "acceptable event." It is also far from obvious that it would have been inappropriate for Pepper to have desired and to have received life-extending dialysis.

Similar observations apply to *anyone* over the age of seventy-five or eighty. Thus, even if it is the case generally that unpreventable death from natural causes of people over seventy-five or eighty is properly understood as an "acceptable event," it does not follow that it is generally acceptable to withhold life-extending medical care from people over seventy-five or eighty.[54] It also does not follow that it is generally improper for people over seventy-five or eighty to desire life-extending care that would enable them to continue to pursue their interests. Therefore, Callahan's notion of a natural life span and the related "ample time" thesis fail to provide a basis for a persuasive defense of age-rationing.

The Prudential Life-Span Argument[55]

From the perspective of a particular point in time, such as the present, it is natural to question the justice of age-rationing, as the practice appears to benefit one class of persons (the nonelderly) at the expense of another class of persons (the elderly). Accordingly, age-rationing appears to give rise to serious interpersonal and intergenerational questions of justice. But Daniels proposes an alternative perspective, that of a *life span*.[56] Over a normal life span, age-rationing would not favor anyone. People who benefit from, and are not subject to, age-rationing when they are young will be subject to age-rationing when they are old. Viewed from the perspective of a normal life span, then, everyone is treated equally, and it is incorrect to state that age-rationing favors one class of people (the nonelderly) at the expense of another class of people (the elderly). Accordingly, policies that favor certain age groups are unlike policies that favor certain racial groups or men or women. Over the course of a normal life span, a person is both young and old. But, with the possible exception of sex change operations, people are male or female and black or white *for life*. Consequently, rationing by race or sex would favor men/women or whites/blacks over their entire lifetimes, and it would work to the serious disadvantage of members of the disfavored groups over their entire lifetimes.

Since it is possible to treat everyone unjustly at one or more stages of life, the insight that age-rationing treats people equally over a life span does not suffice to show that the practice is not unjust.[57] Consider, for example, the following policies: permitting the death penalty for certain crimes committed by minors, compulsory military service at age eighteen, and mandatory retirement and unpaid public service at age sixty-five. Over the course of a normal life span, these policies would apply to everyone, but it does not follow that they are just. A more extreme illustration of this point is provided by a science fiction movie, *Logan's Run*, in which everyone was killed at the age of thirty. The policy resulted in the death of *everyone* who lived to be thirty, but it does not follow that the policy was just. Accordingly, even if, say, a policy of denying people over the age of sixty-five access to long-term dialysis were to affect *everyone* who reaches the age of sixty-five, it does not follow that the practice is just.[58] To hold otherwise would imply that the most egregious injustices would be compatible with the requirements of justice as long as *everyone,* or everyone under or over a certain age, were subject to the same treatment. Whereas a policy that affects everyone similarly over the course of their lives might satisfy a purely formal standard of justice, substantive requirements or justice also need to be considered.

It would not suffice to add a consent condition. If, say, young and old alike were to consent to a policy of denying dialysis and certain other costly life-extending measures to persons over sixty-five, it still would not follow that the policy is just.[59] There are a variety of factors and pressures, including a lack of reasonable alternatives, duress, and passivity, that can help to generate consent for unjust policies and practices.[60] In addition, ageist attitudes can have an important distorting impact. Suppose young and middle-aged people believe that aging results in significantly diminished capacities and social worth and that the elderly are properly to be regarded as "second-class" citizens. As a result of these ageist attitudes, the young and middle-aged fear growing old and are resigned to the fact that they too will have the status of second-class citizenship when they are old.[61] In such circumstances, even if young and old alike voluntarily consent to age-rationing, it clearly does not follow that age-rationing is just.

This conclusion can be confirmed by considering the following point. In relation to the Holocaust, it is sometimes thought that Nazis could have been made to see the injustice of humiliating, torturing, and killing Jews if they had been asked: "Would *you* want to be treated like that?" Nazis, it is assumed, would have said, "Of course not!" But this analysis overlooks the following possibility. Insofar as they accepted racist doctrines about Jews, *consistent* Nazis might have responded: "If I had the misfortune of being such a despicable creature, I would deserve no better treatment." Even if Nazis actually would have responded in this way, it obviously would not follow that Jews were treated justly by the Nazis. Moreover, whereas it is doubtful that a Nazi would have held on to his racist beliefs if, say, he were to have discovered at the age of sixty-five that he was a Jew, some people may continue to accept ageist beliefs as they grow older. Thus, consent to age-rationing by elderly persons may be influenced by ageist beliefs that were acquired when they were young, and consent to age-rationing based on ageist beliefs has no more justificatory force than the response of a "consistent Nazi."

To justify age-rationing, Daniels substitutes *hypothetical* consent for actual consent. His defense of age-rationing rests on the following claim:

Under certain resource and knowledge constraints, and with the proviso that their choices are to be constrained by the principle of fair equality of opportunity (the basic principle of justice in relation to health care), "prudent deliberators" will favor a health care allocation scheme that includes age-rationing. Consequently, according to Daniels, a just health care system can include age-rationing, and age-rationing need neither express ageism nor reflect age bias.

Daniels imposes two knowledge constraints on prudent deliberators. First, they have no knowledge of their age; that is, as they consider alternative allocation schemes, they do not know whether they are young, middle-aged, or old. Second, they have no knowledge of their specific life plans or conceptions of the good; that is, they cannot use their personal preferences and values to assess alternative allocation plans. The first constraint, ignorance of age, reflects the objective of showing that what appears to be an *interpersonal* problem of allocating health care goods and services among the young and the old is analyzable as a problem of budgeting those resources *over a normal life span.*[62] It is to be expected, say, that there would be significant differences in the allocation schemes preferred by 70-year-olds and 25-year-olds. Accordingly, if prudent deliberators knew their age, the problem of allocation would take on an interpersonal dimension, pitting the claims and interests of the young against the claims and interests of the old. However, if prudent deliberators are ignorant of their age, it is appropriate for them to adopt a life-span perspective, thereby avoiding interpersonal conflicts among the young and the old.

Daniels holds that the second knowledge constraint, ignorance of life plans or conceptions of the good, is associated with a requirement of prudence. People's life plans or conceptions of the good can and do change during their lives. Prudence, he holds, requires that we keep our options open and not make choices now that will foreclose our ability to pursue different projects and goals in the future.[63] The stipulation that deliberators remain ignorant of their current life plans ensures that they will heed this supposed requirement of prudence and will not select a lifelong allocation of health care resources that could significantly restrict their capacity to pursue and enjoy alternative plans of life in the future.

Although prudent deliberators lack knowledge of their specific conceptions of the good, it is assumed that they recognize the value of health care. According to Daniels, health care helps to maintain and restore normal ("species-typical") functioning. Since impaired functioning diminishes opportunity (that is, the range of life plans that are open to an individual), health care helps to protect and promote opportunity; therein lies its primary value and ethical significance.[64] Thus, although prudent deliberators are ignorant of their specific life plans, they understand that health care helps to maximize the range of such plans open to them, a desirable goal in view of their ignorance of their specific conception of the good.

An important resource constraint that underlies Daniels's analysis is a moderate scarcity condition. His argument for age-rationing assumes the following specific resource constraint: "Providing very expensive or very scarce life-extending services to those who have reached normal lifespan can be accomplished only by reducing access by the young to those resources."[65] Corresponding to this specific resource constraint, prudent deliberators are presented with a choice between two allocation schemes. One, scheme A, employs rationing by age:

> No one over age 70 or 75—taken to represent normal lifespan—is eligible to receive any of several high-cost, life-extending technologies such as dialysis, transplant surgery, or extensive by-pass surgery. Because age-rationing reduces utilization of each technology, there are resources available for developing them all, though under this scenario that development will be only for the young. (87)

The other, scheme L,

> rejects age-rationing and allocates life-extending technology solely by medical need. As a result, it can either develop just one such major technology, say dialysis, making it available to anyone who needs it, or it can develop several technologies, but then ration them by lottery. (87)

If prudent deliberators were to choose scheme A over scheme L, since age-rationing frees up medical resources for people who have not yet reached a normal life span, they would secure a greater likelihood of living a normal life span. However, compared to scheme L, there would be a lower chance of living beyond a normal life span if they were to attain it. Conversely, if deliberators were to choose scheme L over scheme A, they would have a greater chance of living beyond a normal life span if they were to attain it. However, compared to scheme A, their chances of living a normal life span would be lower.

Daniels justifies age-rationing by claiming that prudent deliberators who were ignorant of their age and conceptions of the good would choose scheme A over scheme L. He defends this claim by considering two decision rules that prudent deliberators might use. One, the "maximin" rule, instructs us to "maximize the minimum," that is, to select the option that has the best possible (or least undesirable) worst outcome. This rule is said to be appropriate when it is infeasible to assign probabilities to possible outcomes and/or when the worst possible outcome is extremely undesirable. Daniels claims that even someone who believes that the most meaningful and satisfying stage of life is old age ("Golden Age") would agree that it is worse to die young than to die just short of Golden Age. Accordingly, he concludes, if prudent deliberators were to use the maximum rule, they would identify death at a young age as the worst possible outcome and would avoid it by selecting scheme A over scheme L.

Daniels considers a second decision rule, one that he refers to as the *standard rule*. This rule instructs us to maximize expected benefits, that is, the product of the value and (estimated) probability of outcomes. Daniels considers two standards of value in relation to this rule. One is number of years. He argues that even if scheme A is not the obvious winner on the basis of quantity alone, the case in its favor is strengthened considerably by observing that the increased likelihood of disability and disease warrant discounting the value of years past the normal life span. As an alternative to number of years, Daniels considers the standard rule from the perspective of a "Golden Age life plan," according to which old age is the most meaningful and valuable stage of life. From the perspective of this view, scheme L appears to be preferable to scheme A. However, since they do not know their particular life plans, prudent deliberators would not know whether theirs was a Golden Age plan. According to Daniels, they "would estimate it to be more likely that they will have typical plans than Golden Age plans," and they would select scheme A over scheme L "because they want to increase their chances that they live through the middle stages of their lives: That is what will most ensure success of their probable plan of life" (90).

One might question whether, under the resource and knowledge constraints specified by Daniels, scheme A is the clear winner over scheme L from the perspective of prudence. Consider a person who believes that Golden Age is extremely valuable and that an important function of earlier stages of life is to prepare for Golden Age. If death at fifty-five and death at sixty-eight both would prevent such a person from enjoying Golden Age, it is not clear that the former is substantially worse than the latter. Even if the probability of having a Golden Age life plan is known to be low compared to other plans, if the value of Golden Age to some is known to be high, there may be no one clear choice from the perspective of prudence.

At a more fundamental theoretical level, one might question the *ethical* significance of *hypothetical* choices. That is, even if it is reasonable to conclude that prudent deliberators would opt for age-rationing in a hypothetical choice situation, it might be questioned whether this thought experiment justifies the practice of age-rationing in the real world. Pursuing these questions would take us too far afield, so I will focus on another point, one more germane to the specific issue of age-rationing: Even if Daniels's reasoning for scheme A over scheme L is sound and even if hypothetical choices can justify actual practices, the argument sketched above provides a very limited and qualified basis for concluding that age-rationing is compatible with justice; indeed, Daniels himself warns against construing his prudential life-span account as a general and unqualified defense of age-rationing. The limitations and qualifications include the following.

First, the scope of Daniels's prudential life span account is limited to institutions that allocate health care over a lifetime (institutions that constitute a health care system). Thus, his defense of age-rationing would not apply to piecemeal age-rationing by particular physicians or hospitals (96). Accordingly, if a physician has a personal policy of not offering and/or recommending against long-term dialysis for patients over sixty-five, she cannot use Daniels's prudential life-span account to justify that policy.

Second, Daniels's argument for scheme A can be used to justify an age-rationing scheme only if that scheme utilizes resources saved by age-rationing to provide life-extending medical care to younger patients. A common rationale for rationing of health care is to reduce its total cost, but Daniels's argument for scheme A cannot be used to justify an age-rationing scheme that functions primarily as a cost-saving device rather than as a device to allocate scarce medical resources prudently over people's lifetimes. Accordingly, Daniels's argument cannot be used to justify, say, a policy of excluding certain expensive life-extending measures from Medicare coverage unless the savings were to be used to increase access to those measures, and/or other health care resoures, by people when they are young.

There may be other reasons favoring age-rationing from a prudential life span perspective. One that Daniels suggests is to free up resources to provide more personal care and social support services for impaired elderly persons. Such services can significantly enhance opportunity and quality of life. However, it is one thing to say that some or even most people would be willing to trade diminished access to life-extending measures late in life for increased access to personal care and social support services, and it is quite another thing to say that prudent deliberators deprived of knowledge of their conceptions of the good would agree to such a trade off. Whether such a trade-off is prudent would seem to depend in part on one's preferences, interests, and values (conception of the good). Reasonable people may disagree about whether such a trade-off is prudent, and there may be no "neutral" perspective from which it can be demonstrated to be *the* prudent choice. For example, although it may be plausible to claim in support of scheme A over scheme L that death at an early age is the "worst possible outcome," reasonable people might differ over whether it is worse to live as a disabled elderly person who is denied access to personal care and social support services or to die because one was denied access to life-extending care; and reasonable people might disagree about whether an increased risk of not having access to personal care and social support services is worth the increased chance of living longer. Consequently, it is doubtful that a case for the trade-off can be made by utilizing Daniels' model of prudent choice.

In the absence of a prudential life-span argument for such a trade-off, it might be advisable to give individuals an opportunity to select from alternative benefit packages. For example, instead of instituting a general denial of Medicare benefits for certain life-extending procedures in order to facilitate a significant increase in assistance for impaired elderly persons, individuals could be offered a choice of alternate Medicare benefit packages. If the choice were made at the time of qualification for Medicare benefits, this proposal would not be subject to Daniels's objection that a selection of benefit packages by *"young adults . . .* would *bias* the plans toward the interests and preferences of young adults" (55; emphasis altered). However, the proposal has a second, undesirable, implication: to protect the integrity and financial solvency of the system, life-extending medical treatment would have to be denied to elderly patients who change their minds at a later date.

Third, Daniels's argument for scheme A rests on a specific assumption about scarcity: "Providing very expensive or very scarce life-extending services to those who have reached normal lifespan can be accomplished *only by* reducing access by the young to those resources" (86; emphasis added). From this resource constraint, it follows that if life-extending measures are not rationed by age, then some form of rationing that will reduce the availability of the same measures to the young is unavoidable. Accordingly, it is appropriate to present deliberators with a choice between scheme A, which utilizes age-rationing, and scheme L, which reduces the availability of (some) life-extending measures to younger patients. In the United States and other developed nations, however, reducing the young's access to life-extending measures is *not* the only means of assuring access to those measures by elderly patients who are likely to benefit. There is no lack of alternatives, from increasing revenues and expenditures and/or instituting cost-containment measures that do not require rationing, to decreasing spending on defense, farm subsidies, transportation, housing, education, the arts, and so forth.[66] In view of these alternatives, age-rationing of life-extending measures cannot be justified simply by showing that prudent deliberators would prefer scheme A to scheme L. Rather, it would have to be shown that they would prefer scheme A to scheme L *and* other feasible alternatives. Since the choice between scheme A and various alternatives requires a ranking of competing goals and priorities, it is a value-dependent choice. It is therefore difficult to see how a case for the selection of scheme A over a feasible set of alternatives can be made by utilizing Daniels's model of prudent choice.

Fourth, there is an important *ethical* constraint on Daniels's prudential life span justification of age-rationing. He presents prudent deliberators with a limited problem: to decide how lifetime fair shares of health care should be allocated over a life span. The lifetime fair shares that they are to allocate over a life span are derived from principles of justice that govern *interper-sonal* distributions, and not from considerations of prudence.[67] Daniels's language suggests that we think of the allocation of lifetime fair shares over a life span as the second step of a two-stage sequence.[68] In the first stage, principles of distributive justice are applied to determine lifetime fair shares of health care, "the overall budget that prudent deliberators must allocate over the lifespan" (53). Judgments about lifetime fair shares of health care are based in part on the principle of fair equality of opportunity: "Fair shares of health care resources . . . are the entitlements an individual should have, given one's health status and given a health-care system designed so that it protects fair equality of opportunity."[69] The result of the first stage serves as a frame for the second stage, when prudent deliberators are to determine how lifetime fair shares are to be allocated over a life span.

In view of the manner in which Daniels frames the problem of choice, when prudent deliberators are given the task of selecting between scheme A and scheme L, it is to be assumed that the corresponding lifetime shares of health care satisfy the principle of fair equality of opportunity. If this condition were not satisfied, then it could not be said that scheme A, the age-rationing scheme, is compatible with the requirements of justice. Suppose, say, that prudent deliberators select A over L. If the background scarcity condition reflects the fact that access to health care goods and services fails to satisfy the principle of fair equality of opportunity, then despite the choice of A, age-rationing is still not just.

Whether or not one agrees with Daniels that the primary principle of justice for health care is the principle of fair equality of opportunity, the general point is that age-rationing schemes are just only if they are part of an overall system of health care that is just. Suppose that a prudential life-span argument can be generated to support a particular age-rationing scheme R. If the scarcity that gives rise to a comparison of R and alternative rationing schemes is attributable to the existence of an unjust health care system, then the prudential life-span argument for R would fail to show that R is just. That argument may show that R does not reflect *age bias,* but there are other forms of injustice. If, say, the British National Health Service fails to provide sufficient resources to satisfy requirements of justice, then even if a prudential life-span argument can be used to defend the practice of denying dialysis to patients over sixty-five against the charge of *age bias,* it does not follow that the practice is just. As another example, let us suppose that a prudential life-span account can be used to support a proposal to eliminate Medicare coverage for certain life-extending measures and to use the funds saved to pay for nursing home care and assistance for impaired elderly persons living at home. It can be concluded that this age-rationing scheme is just only if the scarcity constraints that make the proposed trade-off a prudent choice do not indicate that inadequate resources are provided to satisfy requirements of justice. Indeed, it can be concluded on the basis of the prudential life-span account that the age-rationing scheme does not reflect age bias only if the total amount available to meet the health care needs of the elderly represents a prudent allocation of health care resources over a life span. Moreover, insofar as the wealthy could buy life-extending care not covered by Medicare, it can be concluded that the age-rationing scheme is just only if it is compatible with justice to allow access to health care to be determined in part by one's ability to pay. Thus, even if the proposed elimination of Medicare coverage for life-extending measures does not reflect age bias, it is still important to consider whether it reflects bias against the *poor elderly*.

Fifth, even if an age-rationing scheme were to function within the context of a just health care system, there is a "start-up" problem during the first generation. When elderly patients are denied access to life-sustaining measures as a result of a newly implemented age-rationing program, it cannot be said that *they* benefited from the scheme when they were younger. It is only current and successive generations of younger people who will benefit from age-rationing. A similar problem arises whenever new life-extending technology becomes available.[70] Daniels recognizes that elderly patients might complain that a particular life-extending technology that is only available to younger patients was not available to them when they were young because it was unknown at the time. He responds by pointing out that at "some point in its life, each cohort will be denied the best available life-extending technologies, but at all other points in its life it will have a better chance of receiving them" (129). Daniels's response does not address the objection that the first generation of elderly patients under a newly implemented age-rationing scheme will only experience the *burdens* of age-rationing over a life span.

At most, then, Daniels succeeds in presenting a very limited and qualified defense of age-rationing. Accordingly, even if it is possible to construct a theoretical model to justify age-rationing, we should not allow ourselves to become less vigilant in scrutinizing actual or proposed age-rationing schemes for age bias and injustice.

Case Study: Age and Aggressive Treatment for Breast Cancer

It has been claimed that some forms of age-rationing already are practiced in the United States.[71] One frequently cited example of rationing by age in public policy is the system of Medicare "diagnosis related groups" (DRGs), a scheme of fees according to diagnostic categories which replaced fee-for-services payment.[72] The focus of a recent study by Greenfield et al. is on the practices of individual physicians.[73] Significant differences were reported in the treatment received by elderly and younger breast cancer patients. According to the authors, among younger and older breast cancer patients who displayed no significant differences from a medical perspective, a significantly higher percentage of the younger patients received aggressive treatment when it was medically indicated. The authors claim that their study establishes age bias in the treatment of breast cancer, a claim that merits careful examination. It is no less important to consider whether their study documents a form of age-rationing. The study is summarized in the following case description.

Case Description

A retrospective review was performed of the medical records of 374 breast cancer patients in seven Southern California hospitals. The records examined were of patients age fifty and older. Patients were divided into two age groups: patients seventy and older ("elderly patients"), and patients aged fifty to sixty-nine. No significant differences between these two age groups were found in two respects: stage of cancer when first examined by a physician and diagnostic procedures employed. The first point suggests that elderly patients in the study had not delayed seeking medical assistance longer than the patients in the younger age group. And the second point indicates that a patient's age played no significant role in determining whether mammograms, bone and liver scans, and other diagnostic tests were performed. The study did, however, reveal a significant difference in medical treatment received by patients in the two age groups: "In patients aged 70 years and older, 67.4 percent received treatment deemed appropriate vs 83.4 percent in the 50- to 69-year-old age category" (2768).

For the foregoing comparison, no distinction was made among stages of cancer, and no allowance was made for the overall health status of patients. However, it was found that both of these factors were significant. Whereas 84 percent of stage I and II patients received "appropriate" treatment (treatment in accordance with generally accepted clinical standards), only 34 percent of stage III and IV patients received that level of treatment. To measure overall health status, the investigators used a three point (0-2) "comorbidity index." The index took into account diseases (for example, asthma, bronchitis, and emphysema) and functional status. The latter "is composed of signs and symptoms from 11 system categories . . . [including] circulation, respiration, neurological, mental status, urinary, feeding, ambulation, transfer, vision, hearing, and speech" (2767). The study found that whereas 81.3 percent of the patients who were assigned comorbidity indices of 0 or 1 received "appropriate" treatment, only 58.9 percent of patients with indices of 2 received such treatment.[74]

The standard of "appropriate treatment" that was used for the study was keyed to the stage of cancer: For example, "appropriate treatment for patients with stage I and II disease was defined as the performance of either a radical or modified radical mastectomy, or local excision, axillary dissection, and radiation therapy" (2767). This standard of appropriate treatment for stage I and II breast cancer includes no variable for overall health status. The authors recognize, however, that overall health status is a relevant consideration in determining how aggressively to treat breast cancer. They admit that poor health or functioning can interfere with a patient's ability to withstand surgery, radiation, and chemotherapy. The authors of the study also concede that the standard of treatment for stages III and IV "is more controversial" than it is for stages I and II (2769). Consequently, they recognize the need to control for health status and stage of illness, and they did so by comparing the treatment received by patients in the two age groups who were in stages I and II and whose comorbid indices were 0 or 1. The authors of the study observe that appropriate treatment for the 242 patients in this subgroup was essential because those patients had "the best prognosis for both the cancer and other coexisting conditions" (2769). Nevertheless the investigators found that whereas 96 percent of the patients in the younger age group received appropriate treatment, only 83 percent of the patients seventy and older received such treatment. The authors state their conclusion as follows: "We conclude that physicians may manage patients with this highly treatable disease [stage I and II breast cancer] according to chronological age without regard for physiological condition and that this age bias may result in a less favorable prognosis than could be achieved using currently recommended therapy" (2766).

Case Analysis

The information presented in the foregoing case description appears to establish a connection between patient age and aggressiveness of treatment, but does it document age bias, ageism, and/or age-rationing? To answer these questions, it is necessary to explore the specific nature of the connection between patient age and aggressiveness of care. Did the age of patients have a direct impact on whether they received aggressive treatment, and if so, what was the basis of its impact? Unfortunately, the study provides insufficient data to answer this and other crucial questions, but we can consider several possibilities and their respective implications.

One possibility is the following: Some physicians may have relied on age as an indicator of medical suitability for aggressive therapy, and they may have done so because they believed that age is no less reliable as such an indicator than a patient's overall health status. That is, some physicians may have (falsely) believed that there is no significant difference between age and a health-related index, such as the "comorbidity index" referred to in the study by Greenfield et al.

To be sure, it would be naive to think that there are no general physiological differences between, say, persons who are twenty and persons who are eighty that are likely to affect recovery from surgery, postoperative prognosis, ability to tolerate chemotherapy, and so forth; and physicians should be sensitive to conditions correlated with age that can significantly affect outcomes. The point is simply that it is unsound clinical practice to decide whether a patient is a medically suitable candidate for aggressive treatment on the basis of age alone. Judgments about medical suitability that are based exclusively on age are unreliable. So, too, are clinical judgments for 80-year-olds that are based exclusively on data pertaining to healthy 20-year-olds.

If a physician relies on age as an indicator of medical suitability because she believes that age is no less reliable as a relevant indicator than specific medical criteria, decisions to withhold aggressive treatment from elderly patients probably have an ageist basis. This characterization appears to apply to a British physician who defended the practice of not referring patients with chronic renal failure for dialysis if they are older than fifty-five by stating that "everyone over fifty-five . . . is 'a bit crumbly' and therefore not really a suitable candidate for therapy."[75] Physicians who treat elderly patients less aggressively as a result of ageist beliefs may be practicing bad medicine, but insofar as they sincerely believe that they are withholding aggressive treatment on medical grounds, it is misleading to characterize their differential treatment of elderly patients as "age-rationing." Physicians who sincerely believe that aggressive cancer therapy is not medically indicated for patients over sixty-nine may withhold treatment in conformity with a policy of rationing by age (for example, a Medicare rule that would deny payment for chemotherapy and radiation therapy for cancer patients over sixty-nine), but their decisions to withhold such treatment are not decisions to ration by age.

Another possibility is that some physicians may have relied on age as an indicator of medical suitability for aggressive therapy even though they recognized that age generally is (much) less reliable as an indicator of medical suitability than a patient's overall health status. Insofar as the difference in treatment received by older and younger patients had the foregoing basis, that difference reflects age bias. If a decision to use a less reliable indicator such as age was motivated, say, by considerations of time and convenience, then there was (unintentional) age bias without ageism. Physicians who, to the detriment of their patients' health, allow considerations of time and convenience to supersede medical considerations may be practicing bad medicine, but it does not follow that they are rationing medical care by age.

Yet a third possibility is that some physicians may have taken patient age into account, but not as an indicator of medical suitability for aggressive treatment. That is, some physicians may have believed that aggressive treatment is not appropriate for elderly patients, and this belief may *not* have represented a (sound or unsound) *clinical* judgment. Instead it may have been based on either of the following reasons: (1) elderly patients, even those who are otherwise relatively healthy, are near the end of life (do not have much longer to live); or (2) elderly patients already have lived a full life. Strictly speaking, since there is no mention of resource scarcity in (1) or (2), if physicians withheld aggressive care for reasons such as these, it does *not* follow that they were *rationing* aggressive therapy by age. By contrast, if a decision to withhold aggressive treatment was based on either of the following lines of reasoning, it *does* follow that it was a decision to *ration* aggressive care by age: (1*) It is not feasible to give aggressive care to everyone who might derive some benefit. In such conditions of scarcity, aggressive therapy should go to patients who will benefit most. Since younger patients whose overall health is good can be expected to live longer than older patients whose overall health is also good, the former will benefit more than the latter. Consequently, it is inappropriate to treat older patients aggressively. (2*) It is not feasible to give aggressive care to everyone who might derive some benefit. In such conditions of scarcity, aggressive therapy is inappropriate for elderly patients because they have lived a full life and younger patients have not.

(1*) is a form of the greater benefit argument, and (2*) is a form of the natural life-span argument, arguments that were discussed and criticized previously in this chapter. There is no need to repeat those criticisms here, but there is an additional point that merits attention. Quite apart from the question of whether (1*) or (2*) provides the basis for a successful defense of age-rationing against charges of ageism and age bias, it would be disturbing if individual physicians currently were withholding treatment for either of those reasons. There has been little public debate concerning the merits of withholding medical care from elderly patients for such reasons, and there is hardly a consensus on the propriety of doing so within society at large or within the medical profession. Physicians have considerable expertise and power, but it is beyond the scope of the expertise and proper authority of individual physicians, acting on their own, to make policy, especially on controversial nonclinical matters.

Economic reasons are another category of nonclinical reasons that might have prompted physicians to attach significance to the age of patients. In the study by Greenfield et al., patients classified as "elderly" were seventy and older. Thus, it is likely that a significantly larger percentage of elderly patients were Medicare patients, than were the "younger" patients (patients aged fifty to sixty-nine). Did DRGs and other cost-containment measures act as disincentives to offering aggressive treatment to Medicare patients?[76] If such economic disincentives prompted the decision to withhold aggressive care, physicians were (intentionally or unintentionally) carrying out a (deliberate or unintended) form of rationing by age.

The prudential life-span account, the most promising strategy for defending age-rationing against the charges of age bias and injustice, cannot be used to defend such a form of age-rationing. For one thing, the primary function of DRGs and other similar measures is to reduce health care costs and not to allocate scarce (health care) resources more prudently over a life span. Since advocates of such measures often deny that any health care needs will be unmet as a result of cost containment, it is not to be expected that those measures will represent prudential life-span solutions to conditions of scarcity. Second, unlike a physician in the British National Health Service who withholds dialysis from patients over sixty-five, a U.S. physician who withholds aggressive care from elderly patients in response to cost-containment measures cannot offer the following rationale: "I am promoting a more reasonable allocation of scarce health care resources over a life span, for example, less for acute care near the end of life, more for acute care earlier in life, more for prevention throughout life, and more for personal care and social support services for the frail elderly."[77] If aggressive treatment is withheld in response to DRGs and other cost-containment measures in the United States, it is primarily to protect the financial interests of physicians and/or hospitals, and it is doubtful that one can count on an "invisible hand" to mesh those interests with prudential life-span considerations. Consequently, if physicians were prompted to ration aggressive treatment by age as a result of Medicare cost-containment measures, the prudential life-span account cannot be used to defend their action against charges of age bias and/or injustice.

Finally, the possibility that some elderly patients *refused* aggressive treatment should not be overlooked. Some physicians may have failed to offer aggressive treatment as an option to patients, and others may have recommended against it. However, it is also possible for patients to refuse treatment when it is recommended and/or offered by physicians. Accordingly, in some cases physicians may have accepted Greenfield et al.'s standard of "appropriate" care and recommended and/or offered aggressive treatment, but patients nevertheless may have refused aggressive care. Whereas the authors' standard of "appropriate" care for breast cancer is a *clinical* one, patients can have interests other than extending life in the most effective manner. Patients can have other ends (such as staying at home with family until one dies), and for patients the end (lengthened life) may not always justify the means (disfigurement, nausea, repeated hospitalization, and so forth). The possibility cannot be overlooked that (clinically) "appropriate" therapy was rejected more often by elderly patients than by patients in the younger age group, and that this phenomenon cannot be attributed to decisions or negative recommendations of physicians. If so, then the fact that elderly patients received aggressive treatment less frequently is not attributable to age-rationing by physicians.

However, an elderly patient's refusal of aggressive therapy may reflect ageism. For one thing, even if a physician presents an accurate and unbiased explanation of a patient's condition, prognosis, available treatment options, and so forth, the patient can be subject to the subtle, and sometimes not so subtle, influence of family and friends. Consider the effect, for example, when an adult son asks his elderly mother, who is considering whether to have a radical mastectomy, "Do you really want to be disfigured and sick to your stomach for the rest of your life?" Pressure from friends and family members against aggressive therapy can be motivated by a number of concerns, from genuine compassion, at one extreme, to greed and a desire to collect an inheritance sooner rather than later, at the other extreme. But ageism is another possible factor, as when it is thought that "grandmother's time has come" when she develops breast cancer at the age of eighty even though she is active, and her health and functional status are otherwise generally good.

Misconceptions about aging and old age that are accepted by older people themselves can also influence their decisions to forgo aggressive treatment. Grandmother herself, for example, might think that her time has come because she accepts the ageist views of society and her family. This is not to suggest that there are no good, nonageist reasons for an elderly patient to decide against aggressive treatment. The point is simply that it would be mistaken to think that ageism can affect elderly patients' decisions to forgo aggressive treatment only *indirectly* through the influence of family, friends, and physicians. Since it is desirable that treatment decisions not be influenced by ageist beliefs and attitudes, it is important not to overlook the possibility that elderly patients may not favor aggressive therapy because they themselves accept ageist views.

Notes

1. *Washington Post,* December 21, 1990, p. A3.
2. *New York Times,* January 12, 1992, p. A18.

3. *Health Care Financing Review* 8 (1987): 1ff.

4. See Larry R. Churchill, *Rationing Health Care in America: Perceptions and Principles of Justice* (Notre Dame: University of Notre Dame Press, 1987). Churchill maintains that health care is already being rationed in the United States. See also Henry Aaron and William B. Schwartz, "Rationing Health Care: The Choice Before Us," *Science* 247 (January 26, 1990): 418–22. Aaron and Schwartz cite prospective payment Diagnostic Related Groups (DRGs) and the Oregon Medicaid program as two instances of health care rationing. Baruch Brody is more cautious. He claims that "at least some Americans will not get at least some of the care from which they could benefit" and argues that rationing is "a morally appropriate policy" because "it is better to base the decision as to who gets which forms of care upon a deliberate rationing plan." Baruch A. Brody, "Physicians and Rationing," *Texas Medicine* 87, no. 2 (February 1991): 87. For a dissenting view see Arnold S. Relman, "Is Rationing Inevitable?" *New England Journal of Medicine* 322, no. 25 (June 21, 1990): 1809–10; and Arnold S. Relman, "The Trouble With Rationing," *New England Journal of Medicine* 323, no. 13 (September 27, 1990): 911–13.

Cost containment is only one possible motivation for rationing. Another is a concern about limited or inequitable access to health care. Rationing can be proposed as a means to increase access to (some) health care services without requiring a corresponding increase in overall health care spending. An example is the rationing plan in the Oregon Basic Health Services Act of 1989, which was designed in part to provide access to "basic" health care for uninsured Oregonians. See Harvey D. Klevit et al., "Prioritization of Health Care Services: A Progress Report by the Oregon Health Services Commission," *Archives of Internal Medicine* 151 (May 1991): 912–16.

5. Churchill lists eighteen ways to ration health care originally identified by John Wax. See Larry R. Churchill, "Should We Ration Health Care by Age?" *Journal of the American Geriatric Society* 36, no. 7 (July 1988): 644.

6. As one critic of age-rationing put it: "Because the elderly require a disproportionately large amount of medical resources, the greatest potential savings lie in excluding them from treatment." John F. Kilner, *Ethical Criteria in Patient Selection: Who Lives? Who Dies?* (New Haven: Yale University Press, 1990), 79. By contrast, Schwartz and Aaron argue that limiting health care expenditures for the elderly will not do much to contain overall health care costs. See William B. Schwartz and Henry J. Aaron, "A Tough Choice on Health Care Costs," in Paul Homer and Martha Holstein, eds., *A Good Old Age? The Paradox of Setting Limits* (New York: Simon and Schuster, 1990), 87–90. Binstock and Post link age-rationing of health care to "scapegoating" of the elderly. Robert H. Binstock and Stephen G. Post, "Old Age and the Rationing of Health Care," in Robert H. Binstock and Stephen G. Post, eds., *Too Old for Health Care? Controversies in Medicine, Law, Economics, and Ethics* (Baltimore: Johns Hopkins University Press, 1991), 1–12.

7. Schaffner identifies withholding care that is expected to *benefit* the patient as part of the "core sense" of rationing. Kenneth F. Schaffner, "Health Care Rationing: Major Forms and Alternatives" (manuscript). Schaffner distinguishes between rationing by market mechanisms (rationing by price) and rationing in the sense of denying a good or benefit to people who can afford to purchase them. Schaffner refers to the latter as the "core sense" of rationing. See also Aaron and Schwartz, "Rationing Health Care."

8. See Nancy S. Jecker and Robert A. Pearlman, "Ethical Constraints on Rationing Medical Care by Age," *Journal of the American Geriatrics Society* 37, no. 11 (November 1989): 1069.

9. Dan W. Brock, "Justice, Health Care, and the Elderly," *Philosophy & Public Affairs* 18, no. 3 (Summer 1989): 308.

10. Brock, "Justice, Health Care, and the Elderly," 305; emphasis added.

11. Churchill, "Should We Ration Health Care by Age?" 645.

12. See Henry J. Aaron and William B. Schwartz, *The Painful Prescription: Rationing Hospital Care* (Washington, D.C.: Brookings Institution, 1984).

13. Aaron and Schwartz observe that there is no official age-rationing policy under the British National Health Service. According to the authors, when physicians fail to offer dialysis and other life-extending measures to elderly patients, they are unlikely to characterize their action as either "rationing" or "age-rationing." Poor overall health status is a more likely rationale for failing to offer treatment to patients over a certain age. Nevertheless, Aaron and Schwartz construe the practice of denying or restricting the elderly access to certain life-extending measures as rationing in response to budgetary constraints.

14. Kilner cites several studies that report that age is used as a criterion for excluding patients from certain medical services. See Kilner, *Who Lives? Who Dies?* 77–79.

15. Daniel Callahan, *Setting Limits: Medical Goals in an Aging Society* (New York: Simon and Schuster, 1987). Several critical responses to Callahan's book, as well as his response, are reprinted in Homer and Holstein, *A Good Old Age?*

16. As Brock observes, Callahan "does not support what can be called *very strong age rationing,* which would prohibit persons even from using their own resources to purchase [life-extending] care" ("Justice, Health Care, and the Elderly," 308). However, Callahan calls for an attitude change on the part of the medical profession and the general public, including the elderly, which would involve accepting the view that after a "natural life span" (roughly between seventy-five and eighty-five years), life-extending medical care is no longer appropriate. Callahan's position will be discussed in greater detail below.

17. A notable exception is Battin, who assumes that rationing would include palliative and comfort measures. See Margaret P. Battin, "Age Rationing and the Just Distribution of Health Care: Is There a Duty to Die?" in Timothy M. Smeeding, ed., *Should Medical Care Be Rationed by Age?* (Totowa, N.J.: Rowman & Littlefield, 1987), 69–94. Determining whether medical interventions are "life-prolonging" or "life-improving" in particular cases is not so obvious and unproblematical as Callahan and other advocates of age cutoffs for the former but not the latter appear to assume. See Christine K. Cassel, "The Limits of *Setting Limits*" and Terrie Wetle and Richard W. Besdine, "Letting Individuals Decide" in Homer and Holstein, eds., *A Good Old Age?* 196–206 and 55–57.

18. Scitovsky refers to "a widespread belief that excessive amounts of high-cost technology care is expended on patients, mainly elderly ones, whose prognosis is poor and who will die despite the intensive care they get." Anne A. Scitovsky, "Medical Care in the Last Twelve Months of Life: The Relation between Age, Functional Status, and Medical Care Expenditures," *Milbank Quarterly* 66, no. 4 (1988): 640.

19. Of the 365 decedents in the study, it was reported that for the last year of life "expenses for hospital services for the group aged 80 and over were about 50 percent and for physician services about 46 percent of the expenses of those aged 65 to 79 years, and 54 percent and 30 percent, respectively, of the expenses of those under 65 years of age. In other words, the oldest group received very much less of the relatively intensive type of care exemplified by hospital services and to a lesser extent by physician services, but obtained largely supportive care in the form of nursing home and home health care services." The proportion of medical expenditures devoted to hospital and physician services was substantially less for the 80-year-old and older group than for the 65- to 79-year-old group; and the proportion of medical expenditures that went to supportive care was considerably greater for the former group than the latter group. Even *total* medical expenses were less for older patients: "the total expenses of the oldest age group were about 80 percent of those of the

younger age groups." Scitovsky, "Medical Care in the Last Twelve Months of Life," 648.
Another important finding was that patients with poor functional status received primarily
supportive care during the last year of life. See also Muriel R. Gillick, "Limiting Medical
Care: Physicians' Beliefs, Physicians' Behavior," *Journal of the American Geriatrics Society*
36, no. 8 (August 1988): 747–52; and Dennis W., Jahnigen and Robert H. Binstock, "Economic and Clinical Realities: Health Care for Elderly People," in Binstock and Post, *Too Old
for Health Care?* 13–43.

20. Scitovsky concludes that "limiting the use of high-cost technology by a formal
program of rationing may not be required." Scitovsky, "Medical Care in the Last Twelve
Months of Life," 657. As noted above, Schwartz and Aaron ("A Tough Choice on Health
Care Costs") argue that limiting health care expenditures for the elderly will not do much to
contain health care costs. Callahan admits that his proposal to deny life-sustaining measures to
anyone beyond a "natural life span," but to provide supportive and long-term care, would
increase costs, at least in the short term. See "Why We Must Set Limits" in Homer and
Holstein, eds., *A Good Old Age?* 34.

21. Robert N. Butler, *Why Survive? Being Old in America* (New York: Harper and Row,
1975), 12. Butler is generally credited with having first coined the term "ageism" as a
correlate to racism and sexism. See Robert N. Butler, "Age-Ism: Another Form of Bigotry,"
The Gerontologist 9 (1969): 243–46.

22. The aide's decision may also reflect age bias, a concept that will be discussed below.
For a discussion of the notion of "statistical discrimination," see Lester C. Thurow, "A
Theory of Groups and Economic Redistribution," *Philosophy & Public Affairs* 9, no. 1 (Fall
1979): 25–41.

23. In both *Why Survive?* and "Age-Ism: Another Form of Bigotry," Butler does not
draw a clear distinction between ageism and age bias.

24. For a critical examination of several arguments in support of age-rationing, see John
F. Kilner, "Age as a Basis for Allocating Lifesaving Medical Resources: An Ethical Analy-
sis," *Journal of Health Politics, Policy and Law* 13, no. 3 (Fall 1988): 405–23; John F.
Kilner, "Age Criteria in Medicine: Are the Medical Justifications Ethical?" *Archives of
Internal Medicine* 149 (October 1989): 2343–46; and Kilner, *Who Lives? Who Dies?* chapter
7. See also Nancy S. Jecker and Robert A. Pearlman, "Ethical Constraints on Rationing
Medical Care by Age," *Journal of the American Geriatrics Society* 37, no. 11 (November
1989): 1067–75.

25. Aaron and Schwartz cite a British physician who defended the practice of not offering
long-term dialysis to patients over fifty-five by stating that "everyone over fifty-five . . . is
'a bit crumbly' and therefore not really a suitable candidate for therapy" (*The Painful
Prescription,* 35). This physician is offering a *medical* justification. In effect, he is denying
that he *rations* dialysis by age.

26. Kilner endorses the use of age as a "symptom" or "rule of thumb" in relation to
medical assessments of patients. He states that age "may serve as a tool the physician uses in
applying a medical criterion, not as a criterion in its own right" ("Age as a Basis for
Allocating Lifesaving Medical Resources," 416–17). See also Robert F. Weir, *Abating Treatment With Critically Ill Patients: Ethical and Legal Limits to the Medical Prolongation of Life*
(New York: Oxford University Press, 1989), 383.

27. For an analysis of how life-sustaining measures can benefit elderly patients, see
Roger W. Evans, "Advanced Medical Technology and Elderly People," in Binstock and
Post, *Too Old for Health Care?* 44–74. The Hastings Center *Guidelines on the Termination of
Life-Sustaining Treatment and the Care of the Dying* (Briarcliff Manor, N.Y.: Hastings
Center, 1987) cautions that "age is at best a crude and imprecise factor to use in assessing a

given patient's prognosis and the benefits and burdens of a given treatment'' (136). An OTA report states that ''[c]hronological age per se is a poor criterion on which to base individual medical decisions'' U.S. Congress, Office of Technology Assessment, *Life-Sustaining Technologies and the Elderly* (Washington, D.C.: U.S. Government Printing Office, July 1987), 23. However, both the Hastings Center *Guidelines* and the OTA report state that age may be a legitimate criterion from the perspective of policy and general resource utilization and allocation decisions. See also Weir, *Abating Treatment,* 380–81.

28. See Lawrence A. Pottenger, ''Orthopedic Problems'' and Nanette K. Wenger, ''Cardiovascular Disease,'' in Christine K. Cassel et al., eds., *Geriatric Medicine,* 2d ed. (New York: Springer-Verlag, 1990), 212–27 and 152–63.

29. As Kilner puts it, ''[k]nowing that elderly patients are less likely to benefit from certain treatments than are younger patients, some physicians support age criteria on these grounds'' (''Age Criteria in Medicine,'' 2344).

30. This point is reiterated in many of the essays in Cassel et al., eds., *Geriatric Medicine.* In ''Economic and Clinical Realities,'' Jahnigen and Binstock maintain that an elderly person's clinical conditions(s) and functional status are much more important predictors of the success or failure of a wide range of medical interventions than the person's age.

31. As noted below, an objection to the greater benefit argument, the next argument to be considered, also applies to the lower chances of benefit argument.

32. In *Who Lives? Who Dies?* and ''Age as a Basis for Allocating Lifesaving Medical Resources,'' Kilner classifies arguments for and against age-rationing as either ''productivity oriented'' or ''person oriented.'' The former is a *goal*-oriented argument. I am using productivity in a narrower sense. Productivity is one goal or good, but there are others, for example, happiness and health.

33. Smeeding claims that ''health care procedures are likely to cost more for the elderly than for other groups simply because of the generally lower health status of the elderly, while the benefits are liable to be lower because the expected improvement in quantity (years) and quality of life is lower than for other groups.'' Timothy M. Smeeding, ''Artificial Organs, Transplants and Long-Term Care for the Elderly: What's Covered? Who Pays?'' in Smeeding, ed., *Should Medical Care Be Rationed by Age?,* 143. For a discussion of various ways in which cost-benefit and cost-effectiveness analyses in relation to health care work to the disadvantage of the elderly, see Jerry Avorn, ''Benefit and Cost Analysis in Geriatric Care: Turning Age Discrimination into Health Policy,'' *New England Journal of Medicine* 310, no. 20 (May 17, 1984): 1294–1301.

34. Kilner appears to concede too much when he states that a policy of denying life-extending treatment to the elderly ''will indeed insure a better return on the investment of health care resources'' (*Who Lives? Who Dies?,* 82). Moreover, the productivity of elderly persons may be inhibited by social barriers rather than ''natural limitations'' associated with aging. See Jecker and Pearlman, ''Ethical Constraints on Rationing Medical Care by Age,'' 1070.

35. The distinction between research with therapeutic potential (''therapeutic research'') and research without therapeutic potential (''nontherapeutic research'') is discussed in Chapter 5.

36. As noted above, in ''Economic and Clinical Realities,'' Jahnigen and Binstock maintain that an elderly person's clinical condition(s) and functional status are much more important predictors of the success or failure of a wide range of medical interventions than the person's age. For a critique of quality-adjusted life years as a standard for allocating medical care to newborns and the elderly, see Helga Kuhse and Peter Singer, ''Age and the Allocation of Medical Resources,'' *Journal of Medicine and Philosophy* 13 (1988): 101–16.

37. It might be objected that the example of Danny and David is not analogous to the example of the two candidates for a heart transplant because the principle of equal opportunity supports giving priority to the younger patient. This line of argument will be considered below.

38. See Robert M. Veatch, "Justice and the Economics of Terminal Illness," *Hastings Center Report* 18, no. 4 (September 1988): 34–40. Veatch proposes to give "persons priority in inverse proportion to their age" (39). Although Veatch speaks of giving priority to younger patients, his argument is meant to support "age-based limits on all health care" (39).

39. Robert M. Veatch, "Justice and Valuing Lives" in Robert M. Veatch, ed., *Life Span: Values and Life-Extending Technologies* (New York: Harper and Row, 1979), 218.

40. See Kilner, "Age as a Basis for Allocating Lifesaving Medical Resources," 409; Jecker and Pearlman, "Ethical Constraints on Rationing Medical Care by Age," 1072; and Norman Daniels, *Am I My Parents' Keeper? An Essay on Justice Between the Young and the Old* (New York: Oxford University Press, 1988), 92–93. See also Kuhse and Singer, "Age and the Allocation of Medical Resources."

41. Kilner fails to distinguish between the two equal opportunity arguments (equal opportunity for lifetime well-being and equal opportunity to live to the same age as others). He also fails to distinguish between equal *opportunity* for lifetime well-being and equal lifetime well-being. Thus, he criticizes the claim that age-rationing gives people "an equal opportunity to live a long time" by stating that "other factors, such as one's socioeconomic or spiritual condition, have much more to do with one's lifetime experience of well-being than age does" ("Age as a Basis for Allocating Lifesaving Medical Resources," 409). There is no correlation between actual well-being and opportunity for well-being. On the one hand, people can have considerable opportunity for well-being (good health, intelligence, favorable socioeconomic conditions) and can have miserable lives because they failed to take advantage of the opportunity they had. On the other hand, people with limited opportunity for well-being can make the most of the little opportunity they have and can have better lives than those who have had considerably more. In any event, there is no correlation between age and either aggregate individual well-being or aggregate individual opportunity for well-being. For a discussion of the aggregate individual well-being argument ("the argument for over-a-lifetime well-being"), see the OTA report, *Life-Sustaining Technologies and the Elderly*, 157–58.

42. Additional reasons for this conclusion, including Daniels's "prudential lifespan" argument, will be discussed below.

43. Callahan, *Setting Limits*. Page references in parentheses will be to this book.

44. See Brock, "Justice, Health Care, and the Elderly;" and Nancy S. Jecker, "Disenfranchising the Elderly from Life-Extending Medical Care," *Public Affairs Quarterly* 2, no. 3 (July 1988): 51–68. Excerpts of both articles are reprinted in Homer and Holstein, *A Good Old Age?* For a defense of a communitarian approach to health care allocation policy, see Larry R. Churchill, "Getting from 'I' to 'We'" in *A Good Old Age?* and Churchill, *Rationing Health Care in America*. The work of the Oregon Health Services Commission appears to suggest that even in a pluralistic society, agreement on some health care priorities may be attainable. See Klevit et al., "Prioritization of Health Care Services."

45. It is doubtful that Callahan's general conception of the meaning of aging and the social significance of the elderly entails the conclusion that no one over seventy-five or eighty-five should receive or desire life-extending treatment, much less the specific age-rationing policies which he recommends. Thus, additional arguments are required.

46. *Setting Limits,* 66. Before he offers his definition of a natural life span, Callahan states that the notion of a "tolerable death" is "the basis for a correlative idea of a natural life

span'' (66). Callahan defines a "tolerable death" as "the individual event of death at that stage in a life span when (a) one's life possibilities have on the whole been accomplished; (b) one's moral obligations to those for whom one has had responsibility have been discharged; and (c) one's death will not seem to others an offense to sense or sensibility, or tempt others to despair and rage at the finitude of human existence" (66). Callahan's subsequent definition of a natural life span ("one in which life's possibilities have on the whole been achieved and after which death may be understood as a sad, but nonetheless relatively acceptable event") includes only the first and third conditions of a tolerable death. Adding the second condition to Callahan's definition of a natural life span would have no significant impact on the plausibility of his argument, and there is therefore no need to consider that additional condition here.

47. Callahan states that the phrase "on the whole" signals a generalization with acknowledged exceptions. He admits that "little imagination is required to find an exception to any of my generalizations about old age" (67).

48. See the essays by Jecker, Singer, Cassel, and Holstein in Homer and Holstein, eds., *A Good Old Age?*

49. Callahan states that "even with relatively ample resources, there will be better ways in the future to spend our money than on indefinitely extending the life of the elderly. That is neither a wise social goal nor one that the aged themselves should want, however compellingly it will attract them" (*Setting Limits,* 53). In this passage, Callahan refers to the goal of *indefinitely* extending the lives of the elderly, a goal he associates with the "modernization of aging" (26ff.). The latter includes a tendency to deny death and the process and effects of aging. However, it is one thing to criticize a failure to accept death and aging and quite another thing to criticize a desire for medical care that will enable people to live and pursue interests past the age of seventy-five or eighty-five.

50. There is some tension between this position and Callahan's view that elderly persons have a unique social function: "that of providing the young with an image of the pursuit of a life of meaning" (46). The claim that the elderly have a unique social function seems to cast doubt on the view that they have already achieved their "life possibilities."

51. Leaving aside capital punishment and other considerations of retribution and/or revenge, the death of innocent younger people is not always an occasion for profound grief or outrage. For example, when Karen Quinlan and Nancy Cruzan died after surviving for several years in persistent vegetative states, grief or anguish were probably not appropriate. Those feelings were more appropriate when they first suffered permanent loss of consciousness.

52. Kennedy's death was particularly shocking because it was the result of an assassination. However, the profound sense of loss that many felt at his *premature* death probably would not have been significantly less had he died suddenly as a result of a heart attack or a car accident.

53. A similar point applies to the law. Citing a doctoral dissertation by Nora K. Bell, Kilner observes that murderers "are not generally punished less for killing 65-year-olds than for killing 25-year-olds" ("Age as a Basis for Allocating Lifesaving Medical Resources," 409).

54. In *Setting Limits,* Callahan was unwilling to accept all of the implications of his natural life-span theory. Thus, he held that for "physically vigorous" elderly persons, "all levels of care [including life-extending measures] appear appropriate, at least through the first round of illness and disease, and even for those who have lived a natural life span if there is a solid prospect of a few (say, four or five) more years of good life" (184). Callahan's only stated reason for making an exception in such cases hardly qualifies as a *justification* and appears to undermine his notion of a natural life span: "I make an exception . . . because I do not think anyone would find it tolerable to allow the healthy person to be denied lifesaving

care'' (184). Subsequently, Callahan indicates that it was a mistake to allow any exceptions to his position. In an "Afterword" in *A Good Old Age?* he states that "to be consistent in the use of age as a standard, no exceptions should be made, particularly exceptions based on the conditions of an individual patient; the whole point of a categorical standard is to avoid having to make judgments of that kind" (311–12). The price for consistency on this point is the implausible implication that no matter how healthy people are, and no matter how much they still enjoy living, if they are past a certain age, it is improper for them to receive, or even want or desire, life-extending treatment for a reversible condition. See Brock, "Justice, Health Care, and the Elderly," and Jecker, "Disenfranchising the Elderly from Life-Extending Medical Care," in *A Good Old Age?* (149–50 and 148ff.).

55. A prudential life-span argument is presented by Daniels in *Am I My Parents' Keeper?*

56. Daniels, *Am I My Parents' Keeper?* For earlier formulations of the life-span account of intergenerational justice, see Norman Daniels, "Am I My Parents's Keeper?" *Midwest Studies in Philosophy* 7 (1982): 517–40; and Norman Daniels, "Justice between Age Groups: Am I My Parents' Keeper?" *Milbank Memorial Fund Quarterly / Health and Society* 61, no. 3 (1983): 489–522.

57. Daniels does *not* draw the conclusion that once age-rationing is viewed as a system that functions over a lifetime, there is no longer any need to examine it from the perspective of justice. His justification of age-rationing is based on the claim that it can be understood as a prudent allocation of a "fair share" of health care resources over a life span. His prudential life-span defense of age-rationing will be examined below.

58. Insofar as people can purchase medical care, age-rationing under the British National Health Service does not affect everyone equally. This aspect of the British system gives rise to another important question of justice, as does Callahan's proposal for not expending public funds on life-extending treatment for the elderly.

59. As noted above, in *The Painful Prescription,* Aaron and Schwartz report that when British National Health Service physicians did not offer long-term dialysis to elderly patients, they generally did not tell patients that the latter were "too old." Accordingly, the acquiescence of British patients was not informed consent to age-rationing.

60. Kilner states that age is a "convenient" criterion because "it can be applied with little resistance from the elderly, who as individuals (even if not collectively) can be relatively unassertive" ("Age as a Basis for Allocating Lifesaving Medical Resources," 406).

61. Butler suggests that ageism is associated with a fear of growing old on the part of the young and middle aged: "Age-ism reflects a deep seated uneasiness on the part of the young and middle-aged—a personal revulsion to and distaste for growing old, disease, disability, and fear of powerlessness, 'uselessness,' and death" ("Age-ism: Another Form of Bigotry," 243). If Butler is right, then one might well expect some people to continue accepting these negative views as they themselves age and to have negative self-images of themselves as elderly persons. One is reminded of the phenomenon of the oppressed adopting the views of their oppressors.

62. The knowledge constraints that Daniels imposes are similar to those associated with Rawls's "veil of ignorance." See John Rawls, *A Theory of Justice* (Cambridge: Harvard University Press, 1971). However, Daniels denies that Rawlsian assumptions are required to justify the constraints he imposes on the knowledge of prudent deliberators: "My use of Rawlsian devices [for example, knowledge constraints] does not depend on an appeal to his robust Kantian account of the nature of persons or to his claims that the choice situation is procedurally fair to such persons" (*Am I My Parents' Keeper?* 62). See also Norman Daniels, "The Biomedical Model and Just Health Care: Reply to Jecker," *Journal of Medicine and Philosophy* 14 (1989): 680 n.1.

63. Parfit challenges this conception of prudence and what he refers to as the *requirement of equal concern* (for temporally different parts of one's life). See Derek Parfit, *Reasons and Persons* (New York: Oxford University Press, 1986). Daniels responds in an appendix, "Problems with Prudence" (*Am I My Parents' Keeper?* 157–76).

64. Brock holds that this conception of the value of health care is too narrow. Health care is also important as a means of eliminating, reducing, or preventing pain and otherwise improving quality of life in respects that are independent of opportunity. ("Justice, Health Care, and the Elderly, 305). See also Allen E. Buchanan, "The Right to a Decent Minimum of Health Care," *Philosophy & Public Affairs* 13, no. 1 (Winter 1984): 63.

65. *Am I My Parents' Keeper?* 87. Page references in parentheses will be to this book.

66. For suggestions on how to reduce the cost of medical care in the United States without rationing see Arnold S. Relman, "Reforming the Health Care System," *New England Journal of Medicine* 323, no. 14 (October 4, 1990): 991–92.

67. Daniels speaks of "framing" the "age-group problem," that is, the problem of allocation over a life span:

> We may appeal to prudence to solve the age-group problem only if we *frame* that problem. We must constrain prudential reasoning about the age-group problem by assuming that other principles of distributive justice already govern interpersonal distributions. These principles of justice define the overall budget that prudent deliberators must allocate over the lifespan. . . . In our restricted or framed problem, the problem of justice between age groups, we are to suppose that hypothetical deliberators already know what inequalities in lifetime expectations are acceptable. That is, they already know what counts as a fair share, and they must decide a further question: How *should* that lifetime expectation of enjoying a certain level of primary goods be distributed over each stage of life so that lifetime well-being is maximized? (*Am I My Parents' Keeper?* 53 and 61–62)

"Primary goods" are supposed to be of value to people, no matter what their specific conceptions of life plans or the good. Opportunity is a primary good, and health care promotes opportunity by maintaining and restoring normal functioning.

68. Although Daniels's language may suggest a two-stage sequence, it is probably misleading to conceptualize his prudential life-span account as the second step in a two-stage sequence. Surely, an appropriate question to consider when setting a lifetime fair share of health care is whether an allocation that would make age-rationing a "prudent choice" is compatible with the requirements of fair equality of opportunity. Thus, it seems more appropriate to think of a complex one-stage procedure, whereby applying the principle of fair equality of opportunity requires prudential considerations of the sort that Daniels discusses.

69. *Am I My Parents' Keeper?* 73. Daniels offers the following account of the relation between health care and the principle of fair equality of opportunity. Health care helps "to prevent or cure diseases and disabilities, which are deviations from species-typical functional organization ('normal functioning' for short)" (69). Normal functioning is related to opportunity. Specifically, in the absence of normal functioning an individual's opportunity range will be less extensive than the society's "normal opportunity range" (that is, "the array of life plans reasonable persons in it are likely to construct for themselves"). Since the principle of fair equality of opportunity requires equal opportunity "for persons with similar skills and talents" (70), that principle requires efforts to prevent or cure diseases and disabilities that are deviations from normal functioning and that prevent an individual from enjoying the extent of the society's normal opportunity range that corresponds to her skills and talents. Accordingly, the "moral function" of a health care system is "to help guarantee fair equality of opportunity" (71).

70. See Kilner, "Age as a Basis for Allocating Lifesaving Medical Resources," 411–12.

71. As noted above, Kilner cites several studies that report that age is used as a criterion for excluding patients from certain medical services. See Kilner, *Who Lives? Who Dies?* 77–79.

72. See Daniels, *Am I My Parents' Keeper?* 140; and Aaron and Schwartz, "Rationing Health Care," 421.

73. Sheldon Greenfield et al., "Patterns of Care Related to Age of Breast Cancer Patients," *Journal of the American Medical Association* 257, no. 20 (May 22–29, 1987): 2766–70. Page references in parentheses are to this article.

74. The authors of the study combined the 0 and 1 levels "because physicians would not likely change management strategies based on a small difference between the absence of disease and very mild controlled disease" (2769).

75. Aaron and Schwartz, *The Painful Prescription,* 35.

76. I am assuming that a significant percentage of younger patients were not uninsured. A study by Weissman and Epstein suggests that there are significant differences in the care received by insured and uninsured hospital patients. Medicare patients were not included in their study, but the authors do report a difference in the number of procedures received by Medicaid and privately insured patients. See Joel Weissman and Arnold M. Epstein, "Case Mix and Resource Utilization by Uninsured Hospital Patients in the Boston Metropolitan Area," *Journal of the American Medical Association* 261, no. 24 (June 23–30, 1989): 3572–76.

77. Daniels identifies several important differences from a prudential life-span perspective between rationing under the British National Health Service and cost containment in the United States. See *Am I My Parents' Keeper?* 140–48.

CHAPTER 4

Paternalism and the Elderly

One of life's cruel ironies is the possibility of ending it much as one began: unable to care for oneself, unable to understand and process information, and unable to make important decisions. Another irony is the possibility of a reversal in the roles of parent and child. Elderly persons who protected their young children by not allowing them to make decisions for themselves may have their opportunity to make decisions substantially curtailed by protective adult children; and elderly persons who shielded their young children from potentially disturbing or upsetting information may be treated in similar ways by grown children. In these and countless other ways, elderly persons may be treated paternalistically by adult children and other younger relatives.

Family members are hardly the only source of paternalism toward the elderly. Elderly persons are subject to paternalistic treatment by a wide range of providers of medical, personal, and social services, including physicians, nurses, nursing home aides, and social workers.[1] Physicians sometimes withhold information to "protect" elderly patients; nursing home residents are subject to significant restrictions and constraints said to be "for their own good;" and, as Monk and Abramson indicate "social workers, no matter how well meaning, often slip into overprotectiveness and paternalistic interventions."[2]

As Halper has observed, "the stratum of the adult population that is most often the object of paternalistic endeavors is the aged."[3] Since people who either are, or are thought to be, cognitively impaired are more likely to be treated paternalistically, it is to be expected that elderly persons are prime targets for paternalistic treatment. On the one hand, due to a variety of conditions that are more frequent in old age, including stroke, arteriosclerosis, and Alzheimer's disease, older adults are more likely to suffer some form of cognitive impairment than younger adults.[4] On the other hand, popular stereotypes encourage a presumption that elderly persons are mentally impaired or "senile."[5] For their part, the current generation of the elderly may be especially inclined to expect and accept paternalistic treatment by physicians and other professionals.[6]

It is important to examine paternalism toward the elderly from an ethical perspective. First, however, it is necessary to examine the nature of paternalism.

The Nature of Paternalism

In one respect, paternalism is probably a little like pornography: people tend to think that they know it when they see it, but its *definition* is elusive. Although it is relatively easy to recognize examples of paternalistic behavior toward the elderly, it is more difficult to specify the identifying characteristics of such behavior.

One characteristic is clear: One person (A) behaves paternalistically toward another person (S) only when A acts *for the sake of S;* that is, to promote S's welfare, well-being, good, or interests.[7] Suppose, say, that despite his 75-year-old father's protests, Jim manages his father's finances. If Jim's reason for doing so is to protect *his* future inheritance and not to protect his father's interests, Jim is not acting paternalistically. As another example, consider the case of an elderly nursing home resident who is kept in a wheelchair by restraints in order to prevent her from walking and falling. Insofar as it is done to protect the *nursing home,* the woman's confinement to the wheelchair is not an instance of paternalism. Paternalism, then, is a type of benevolence.[8]

Even though benevolence, or acting for the sake of someone else, is a necessary condition of paternalism, it is not sufficient. That is, paternalism does not occur whenever a person acts to promote someone else's welfare. For example, I do not act paternalistically toward my 65-year-old neighbor who is incapacitated by severe rheumatoid arthritis when I shovel snow from his sidewalk in order to help him.[9] What distinguishes paternalistic benevolent acts from nonpaternalistic ones?

It is sometimes said that paternalism occurs only when people interfere with the liberty of action of those whom they are trying to help or protect.[10] The corresponding condition (the *liberty of action condition* or C_{LA}) can be formulated as follows:

A behaves paternalistically toward S only if A interferes with S's liberty of action.

Insofar as it is implausible to claim that I interfered with my neighbor's liberty of action when I shoveled his sidewalk, C_{LA} appears to support the conclusion that I was not acting paternalistically toward him.[11] Thus, C_{LA} generates the correct conclusion in this case. Nevertheless, since it is possible to act paternalistically toward people without interfering with their liberty of action, C_{LA} will not do as a general condition of paternalism.

Consider withholding information from people for their own good, a paradigm instance of paternalism. Suppose, say, that a physician deliberately refrains from telling a 76-year-old patient that he has inoperable prostate cancer that has metastasized to other organs. The physician withholds the information from the patient because she fears that he will become severely depressed if he is told. This is a clear instance of paternalism, but the physician does not appear to be interfering with the patient's freedom of action. To be sure, he may not do some of the things that he would have done if he had been told that he is dying (for example, attempt a reconciliation with his estranged daughter, update his will, contact friends and relatives he has not seen for several years, and so forth). But since he remains free to do all of these things, it is doubtful that the physician has interfered with the patient's freedom of action.[12]

But, then, what does distinguish paternalism from other forms of benevolence? A variety of answers have been given to this question; the simplest including "a refusal to accept or to acquiesce in another person's wishes, choices, and actions,"[13] an "overriding of a person's wishes or intentional actions,"[14] or "a violation of a person's autonomy."[15] Other efforts to characterize paternalistic benevolence are much more complex. For example, Gert and Culver offer an analysis with no fewer than five conditions.[16] A comprehensive review and evaluation of these and other analyses of paternalism would require another entire chapter, if not a whole book. However, since VanDeVeer offers a cogent critique of the leading definitions of paternalism and an analysis designed to avoid the pitfalls that he identifies, his definition provides a suitable point of departure.[17]

VanDeVeer offers a complex triconditional analysis of paternalism (paternalistic behavior), or to be more precise, of the expression: "A's doing or omitting some act X to, or toward, S is paternalistic behavior." However, for our purposes, it will suffice to consider a simplified version of the condition that is supposed to distinguish *paternalistic* benevolence from benevolence generally:[18]

A believes that doing X is contrary to S's concurrent preferences (S's actual preferences at the time A decides to do X).[19]

If this condition (the *believed to be contrary to preferences condition* or C_{BCP}) is accepted, withholding information can be classified as paternalism even when C_{LA} is not satisfied. Recall the physician who did not tell her patient that he has inoperable prostate cancer because she feared that he would become severely depressed if he knew. According to C_{BCP}, the physician acted paternalistically if she believed that withholding the diagnosis was contrary to the patient's actual wishes at the time.

Insofar as C_{BCP} is satisfied if and only if the physician *believed* that it was contrary to the patient's actual wishes at the time to withhold the diagnosis, that condition is *subjective*. A corresponding *objective* criterion (the *actually contrary to preferences condition* or C_{ACP}) would be satisfied if and only if it was *actually* contrary to the patient's concurrent preferences to withhold the diagnosis. C_{ACP} is clearly unacceptable. Suppose, say, the physician believed that the patient wanted to know his diagnosis, but she withheld the information anyway in order to protect him. If the patient's actual preferences are unknown, or if he did not want to know that he had terminal cancer, C_{ACP} is not satisfied. However, insofar as the physician *believed* that she was acting contrary to the wishes of the patient, it seems counterintuitive to conclude that she did not act paternalistically. Thus, it seems that C_{BCP} is preferable to C_{ACP}. However, it does not follow that C_{BCP} is acceptable. The following two scenarios suggest that it is not.

Scenario 1.   When the physician decided not to tell her patient that he had inoperable prostate cancer, she failed even to consider whether withholding information was compatible with the patient's actual wishes. Her decision to withhold the information was based exclusively on her desire to protect the patient. When asked whether withholding information was compatible with the patient's own wishes, she responds: "I don't really know. Frankly, though, I don't think it matters, for my primary responsibility was to protect the patient, and it was for this reason that I decided not to tell him that he has inoperable prostate cancer."

Scenario 2.   The physician believed that the patient did not want to know that he had inoperable prostate cancer. When asked to state her basis for this belief, the physician responds: "Since it would have been very upsetting to the patient to learn that he had a terminal illness, I concluded that he did not want to know."

In both scenario 1 and scenario 2, the physician did not believe that she was acting contrary to the patient's concurrent preferences. According to C_{BCP}, then, the physician did not act paternalistically in either instance. This conclusion is problematic for two reasons. First, like the physician in both scenario 1 and scenario 2, most physicians who withhold information from patients probably do not believe that they are acting contrary to patients' wishes. Consequently, whereas withholding information for the good of patients is commonly regarded as a paradigm case of "medical paternalism," to adopt C_{BCP} would significantly limit the instances in which this practice could be characterized as paternalism.[20] Second, it seems counterintuitive to hold that the physician did not act paternalistically in either of the two scenarios. With respect to scenario 1, insofar as the physician failed even to consider whether withholding information was compatible with the patient's concurrent preferences because her desire to promote the patient's well-being led her to discount the importance of his actual wishes, it seems appropriate to characterize her action as paternalistic. With respect to scenario 2, insofar as the physician believed that there was no need to ascertain the patient's actual wishes directly because she thought she could infer his preferences from her own assumptions, it also seems appropriate to characterize her action as paternalistic.[21] Thus, scenarios 1 and 2 suggest that C_{BCP} is too narrow.

C_{BCP} is too narrow in relation to determining whether withholding information is paternalistic behavior. It also excludes instances of other common forms of paternalism toward the elderly. Physicians, nurses, nursing home aides, social workers, and family members sometimes make decisions on behalf of elderly persons concerning food, clothing, daily activities, living arrangements, finances, medical care, and so forth without soliciting the elderly persons' input or seriously considering their actual wishes. A 45-year-old son, say, who makes decisions concerning his 74-year-old mother's finances, living arrangements, and health care, and who does so to promote her well-being, might do so without first soliciting her approval or ascertaining and considering her preferences. Insofar as his mother can refuse to acquiesce, and the son uses no undue pressure or influence (for example, intimidation or threats) to secure her assent and/or compliance, he is not interfering with her liberty of action. Moreover, if the son does not believe that he is acting contrary to his mother's preferences—as is likely if he fails to even consider her wishes—then according to C_{BCP}, he does not act paternalistically toward his mother. However, it is unwarranted to conclude that the son's behavior is not paternalistic. Even though C_{BCP} is not satisfied, it is appropriate to characterize the son's behavior as paternalistic in each of the following three scenarios.

Scenario 3. Like the physician in scenario 1, the son fails to consider whether his actions on behalf of his mother are compatible with her concurrent preferences because his primary objective is to advance her long-term interests, and he concludes that her actual wishes at the time are therefore of no importance.

Scenario 4. The son decides not to consider his mother's actual wishes because he believes her preferences are generally unreliable, unstable, uninformed, distorted, and/or incoherent.

Scenario 5. Although the son fails to solicit his mother's opinions or to take any other direct steps to ascertain her concurrent preferences, like the physician in scenario 2, he nevertheless believes that his decisions reflect his mother's actual wishes. This belief is based on his assumption that he can infer his mother's preferences from considerations of her welfare and that independent (direct) evidence of her actual wishes is unnecessary.

It can be said that the physician in scenarios 1 and 2 and the son in scenarios 3–5 *disregarded* the concurrent preferences of the person on whose behalf they acted. It also can be said that someone disregards the preferences of the person on whose behalf she is acting if she knowingly acts in a manner contrary to the other person's preferences. Accordingly, when someone (A) does X with the aim of promoting someone else's (S's) well-being, A *disregards* S's concurrent preferences if any of the following conditions is satisfied:

1. A believes that doing X is contrary to S's concurrent preferences.
2. A fails to consider whether doing X is contrary to S's concurrent preferences because A's objective is to advance S's interests, and A concludes that S's actual wishes are therefore of no importance.
3. A believes that it is unnecessary to consider whether doing X is contrary to S's concurrent preferences because A believes that S's preferences are generally unreliable, unstable, uninformed, distorted, and/or incoherent.
4. A believes that doing X is compatible with S's concurrent preferences, but that belief is based on inferences derived from assumptions concerning means to protect or promote A's well-being, and A discounts the importance of independent (direct) evidence of S's concurrent preferences.

The notion of disregarding a person's concurrent preferences can be used to formulate a more satisfactory account of paternalism. For C_{BCP}, let us substitute the following condition (the *disregarding preferences condition* or C_{DP}):

When A decides to do X, A disregards S's concurrent preferences.

Since paternalism is a type of benevolence, benevolent acts that satisfy C_{DP} are paternalistic. Accordingly, it can be said that A acts paternalistically toward S if:

A does X with the aim of promoting S's well-being, and in deciding to do X, A disregards S's concurrent preferences.

This analysis appears to capture the idea that when A treats S paternalistically, A acts as if A were S's parent and S were A's (young) child.[22] When attempting to promote the well-being of children, parents often disregard their preferences. For example, children's preferences are disregarded when parents: impose restrictions on where, when, and with what and whom children may play; restrict the television programs, films, magazines, and books their children may view or read; and require their children to eat certain foods, get their shots, do their homework, go to Sunday school, and go to bed at a specified hour. Accordingly, insofar as it is a mark of paternalism toward elderly adults that their preferences are disregarded when others attempt to promote their good, paternalism toward the elderly is fundamentally similar to the parent-child relationship.

Soft and Hard Paternalism

Soft paternalism is the view that paternalistic behavior in relation to a decision or action (the "targeted" decision or action) is ethically justified only if the decision or action is substantially nonautonomous.[23] The condition that the targeted decision or action is substantially nonautonomous will be referred to as the "soft paternalism condition." Hard paternalism can be characterized negatively as a rejection of soft paternalism. Stated positively, hard paternalism is the view that paternalistic behavior is sometimes justifiable when the targeted decision or action is substantially autonomous (that is, when the soft paternalism condition is not satisfied).[24]

Soft paternalism is sometimes referred to as "weak" or "limited" or "restricted" paternalism, and hard paternalism is sometimes referred to as "strong" or "extended" paternalism.[25] There are also different formulations of the soft paternalism condition. One states that the targeted decision or action is substantially *nonvoluntary*.[26] Another states that the targeted person "suffers from some defect, encumbrance, or limitation in decision-making or acting."[27] Any statement of the soft paternalism condition that applies only to decisions or actions may be too narrow. If one wants to know, say, whether withholding potentially upsetting information from a 72-year-old nursing home resident would satisfy the soft paternalism condition, the answer may not depend on whether an identifiable decision or action is substantially nonautonomous. Accordingly, if there is a relevant "defect, encumbrance, or limitation," it may not be in "decision-making or acting." Rather, it may have more to do with the person's character and emotional or psychological stability, and there may be no identifiable decision or action to target for paternalistic intervention. A more comprehensive statement of the soft paternalism condition might be that the targeted person has a relevant and substantial cognitive, psychological, or emotional impairment, limitation, or deficit. However, for the purposes of this discussion, it will suffice to consider the condition that a targeted decision or action is substantially nonautonomous.

The primary difference between soft and hard paternalism is that the former accepts, and the latter rejects, the principle that substantially autonomous decisions and actions are immune from paternalistic behavior.[28] Accordingly, when decisions and actions that are substantially autonomous expose an elderly person to a significant risk of harm, hard paternalism appears to require judgments of value, or a weighing of conflicting values (such as autonomy and well-being), on a case-by-case basis. By contrast, soft paternalism appears to reflect the general judgment that autonomy has priority over well-being and to eliminate thereby the need to make judgments of value, or weigh conflicting values, on a case-by-case basis. From the perspective of soft paternalism, if a decision or action is substantially autonomous, it is immune from paternalistic behavior, and there appears to be no need to weigh respect for autonomy and beneficence.[29]

However, it would be mistaken to think that the soft paternalist's insistence that substantially autonomous decisions and actions are immune from paternalistic behavior eliminates the need to make judgments of value, or to weigh conflicting values, on a case-by-case basis. Such a view might be plausible if people and their decisions and actions were either *fully* autonomous (the uncoerced and fully informed decisions and actions of mature, cognitively unimpaired, and emotionally stable adults) or *fully* non-autonomous (the decisions and actions of infants, young children, and profoundly retarded or severely demented adults). Then, it always would be clear whether an elderly person and/or her actions and decisions were autonomous, and the only issue remaining would be whether paternalistic behavior is justified in relation to any of her autonomous decisions and actions. However, "fully autonomous" and "fully nonautonomous" simply serve to mark off two extremes on a continuum, and the decisions and actions of many cognitively impaired elderly persons fall somewhere between. Accordingly, soft paternalists need to determine where and how to draw the boundaries of *substantially* autonomous and nonautonomous decisions and actions. Depending on where and how these boundaries are drawn, say, a mildly demented elderly person's decision to remain at home rather than move into a nursing home might be considered substantially autonomous and immune from paternalistic intervention, or substantially nonautonomous. The soft paternalist's judgment that a decision or choice is substantially autonomous represents the *conclusion* that it is immune from paternalistic intervention, and a justification of this conclusion may require a complex and controversial weighing of competing values.

Theories of soft paternalism typically employ a variable standard to determine when actions and choices are *substantially* autonomous. According to Feinberg, for example, autonomy (voluntariness) should be treated "as a 'variable concept,' determined by higher and lower cutoff points depending on the nature of the circumstances, the interests at stake, and the moral or legal purpose to be served."[30] Setting the appropriate level of autonomy in a particular case can require considering and weighing different values. Feinberg holds that when the purpose is to identify choices and actions that are "voluntary [autonomous] enough" to be immune from paternalistic behavior, one relevant consideration is the risk: "The more risky the conduct the greater the degree of voluntariness [autonomy] required."[31] In effect, when the risk is high, less weight is assigned to an individual's opportunity to choose for herself, and more weight is assigned to that person's well-being or good.[32] Thus, whereas hard paternalists weigh conflicting values to determine whether paternalistic interventions with substantially autonomous decisions and actions are justified, soft paternalists weigh conflicting values to determine whether choices or actions are substantially autonomous and immune from paternalistic behavior.[33]

The following case will help to illustrate this point.[34] Ms. J. is a 72-year-old widow who lives with her son Peter and his wife Selma. Ms. J. had suffered some memory loss and exhibits other signs of mild dementia. She enjoys long walks by herself, but Peter is concerned about his mother's safety and tries to persuade her to stop. He is unsuccessful, and contemplates taking steps to prevent her from walking alone. As a soft paternalist, however, Peter will not intervene against his mother's wishes if her conduct is substantially autonomous. What criterion should he use to determine whether his mother's decision to continue walking alone is substantially autonomous?

According to the variable standard analysis, if, in view of Ms. J.s mental status, her decision is neither fully autonomous nor fully nonautonomous, Peter should consider his mother's cognitive capacities *and* the seriousness of the risk to her.[35] The more dangerous Peter perceives his mother's walking alone to be to her, the less importance he should assign to her opportunity to decide for herself, and the stronger should be his standard of substantial autonomy. Accordingly, if she faces serious danger (say, a high probability of being hit by a car, mugged, or dying of hypothermia), he might appropriately conclude that her decision is substantially nonautonomous. On the other hand, if the probability and gravity of harm are both relatively low, Peter might appropriately decide that his mother's decision is substantially autonomous and immune from paternalism.

Uncertainty or disagreement about the justifiability of paternalistic behavior in specific cases can, but need not, involve uncertainty or disagreement about the legitimacy of hard paternalism. When the legitimacy of hard paternalism is at issue, it is clear that the uncertainty or disagreement is in part about conflicting values (here, autonomy and well-being). However, the uncertainty or disagreement may also be in part about conflicting values when the legitimacy of hard paternalism is not at issue.

Suppose, say, that after considering his mother's cognitive capacities and the probability and seriousness of the harm to her, Peter remains uncertain about the justifiability of overriding her preferences for her own good. To be sure, Peter might have no doubt that his mother's conduct is substantially autonomous, and his uncertainty may simply reflect his ambivalence about restricting a (substantially) autonomous decision for his mother's own good. However, Peter's uncertainty might have a different basis. He might reject hard paternalism (that is, he is convinced that substantially autonomous decisions and actions are immune from paternalistic behavior), but he might have difficulty deciding whether his mother's decision is substantially autonomous. Let us consider some possible sources of Peter's uncertainty.[36]

First, the severity and extent of his mother's cognitive impairment. For illustrative purposes, suppose decisions can be assigned a score of 0 to 20, where 0 is fully nonautonomous and 20 fully autonomous. Peter concludes that in view of the probability and gravity of harm to his mother, her decision would have to be rated at least 12 to qualify as substantially autonomous. However, Peter is uncertain whether his mother's cognitive impairment is sufficiently severe and extensive to warrant placing her below this threshold.

Second, the probability and gravity of harm to Ms. J. Supposse that both autonomy and risk of harm can be rated on scales of 0 to 20. After considering his mother's cognitive capacities, Peter assigns an autonomy score of 12 to her decision. However, he does not know whether to rate the risk of harm to her as 3, 4, or 5. If he were to rate it as 5, let us suppose, the appropriate threshold of substantial autonomy would be 14, and his mother's decision would not be substantially autonomous. On the other hand, if he were to rate the risk of harm as 3, the threshold would be 11, and his mother's decision would be substantially autonomous and immune from paternalism.

Third, the relative weight or importance of Ms. J.'s opportunity to decide for herself and her well-being. Suppose Peter assigns an autonomy rating of 12 to his mother's decision and rates the risk of harm to her as 4. However he does not know how much weight or importance to assign to her opportunity to decide for herself and to her well-being. Depending on how much weight or importance he assigns each, the appropriate threshold of substantial autonomy would be 11 or 13. If the importance Peter assigns to his mother's opportunity to decide for herself is sufficient to tip the balance toward the lower threshold, his mother's decision would be substantially autonomous and immune from paternalistic intervention. However, if the importance he assigns to his mother's well-being tips the balance toward the higher threshold, his mother's decision would not be substantially autonomous. In this case, then, to determine whether his mother's decision is substantially autonomous, Peter first has to weigh conflicting values (his mother's opportunity to decide for herself and her well-being). Thus, it is mistaken to think that only hard paternalists have to weigh conflicting values.

Next, let us consider a disagreement between Peter and Selma, his wife. Peter considers his mother's cognitive capacities and the probability and seriousness of the harm to her and concludes that her decision is substantially autonomous and immune from paternalistic intervention. After considering the same factors, Selma concludes that paternalistic intervention *is* warranted. The disagreement between Selma and Peter is subject to two mutually exclusive interpretations. First, although Peter and Selma agree that Ms. J.'s conduct is (substantially) autonomous, Selma accepts, and Peter rejects, hard paternalism. According to this interpretation, their disagreement is in part clearly about values: whereas Selma believes that beneficence outweighs respect for autonomy in the circumstances, Peter assigns priority to respect for autonomy. Second, both Peter and Selma reject hard paternalism. Whereas Peter concludes that his mother's decision is substantially autonomous, Selma reaches the opposite conclusion. It is not as obvious in the case of this interpretation that the disagreement between Peter and Selma is in part about values (here, a disagreement about the relative importance of Ms. J.'s opportunity to decide for herself and her well-being). However, it could be.

If, as the second interpretation postulates, Peter and Selma disagree about whether Ms. J.'s decision is substantially autonomous, their disagreement could have any of the following bases. First, Peter and Selma accept the same standard of substantial autonomy, but they disagree about the extent and seriousness of Ms. J.'s cognitive impairment. Second, Peter and Selma agree in their assessment of the extent and seriousness of Ms. J.'s cognitive impairment, but they differ in their assessment of the probability and/or gravity of harm to Ms. J. Third, Peter and Selma agree in their assessment of Ms. J.'s cognitive abilities and the risk of harm to her, but they disagree about the relative weight or importance of Ms. J.'s opportunity to decide for herself and her good. Compared to Selma, Peter assigns more weight to his mother's opportunity to choose for herself because: (a) Peter assigns more value to Ms. J.'s opportunity to make this particular decision for herself, and/or (b) Peter assigns more weight generally to autonomy. In this case, both Peter and Selma reject hard paternalism, and they therefore agree that when decisions or actions are substantially autonomous, respect for autonomy overrides beneficence. Nevertheless, differing value judgments (here, a difference in the relative weights each assigns to Ms. J.'s opportunity to decide for herself and her well-being) underlie their disagreement about whether Ms. J.'s decision is substantially autonomous.

This discussion supports two conclusions. First, the rejection of hard paternalism does not guarantee that decisions and actions that are immune from paternalistic behavior can be identified without having to make value judgments, or weigh conflicting values, on a case-by-case basis. Second, uncertainty or disagreement about the justifiability of paternalistic behavior in specific cases can, but need not, involve uncertainty or disagreement about the legitimacy of hard paternalism. This discussion also suggests that when it comes to evaluating specific instances of paternalistic behavior toward mildly demented elderly persons, the distinction between hard and soft paternalism may have little practical significance. This point will be explored more fully in the following section.

Paternalism Toward the Elderly: An Ethical Assessment

Value judgments similar to those made by hard paternalists to decide whether paternalistic behavior is justified in a particular case may be required when soft paternalists decide whether a particular decision or action is substantially autonomous. This observation is especially pertinent in relation to mentally impaired elderly persons, and in particular to those who are only mildly demented or otherwise cognitively impaired. In this wide range between fully autonomous and fully nonautonomous, the distinction between hard and soft paternalism can have little, if any, bearing on whether paternalistic behavior is justified.

To be sure, soft paternalists will insist that paternalistic intervention is unjustified whenever the targeted choice or action is substantially autonomous, and hard paternalists will disagree. However, when it comes to deciding whether contemplated paternalistic behavior toward an elderly person is justified, the same factors are relevant and should be considered and weighed. The importance of the following questions cuts across the distinction between soft and hard paternalism. (1) Will the contemplated paternalistic behavior protect the elderly person from harm? (2) Are there reasons for not disregarding the elderly person's preferences? (3) Does the elderly person have a relevant cognitive, psychological, or emotional deficit? (4) Is the targeted decision or action more or less "in character" or "out of character?" (5) Is the contemplated paternalistic intervention guided by the elderly person's own enduring values and settled preferences? (6) Does the contemplated paternalistic behavior involve means that are morally suspect or prima facie wrong? Answers to each of these questions have an important bearing on an ethical assessment of paternalistic behavior. Accordingly, determining whether paternalistic behavior is justified in a particular case requires careful consideration of context-dependent factors and is not reducible to a choice between competing abstract values and principles such as autonomy and beneficence.

Will the Contemplated Paternalistic Behavior Protect the Elderly Person from Harm?

By definition, a general objective of paternalistic behavior toward someone is to promote that person's good or well-being. This objective provides the primary justifying reason for paternalistic behavior.[37] The case for paternalistic behavior toward an elderly person is strongest when it protects that person from harm (the "expected harm").[38] The strength of harm prevention as a justifying reason is a function of the level of the expected harm (its probability and seriousness and whether it is irreversible) and the probability that the paternalistic intervention will prevent it. If the level of the expected harm and the probability that the paternalistic intervention will prevent it are high, harm prevention is a strong justifying reason. On the other hand, if the level of the expected harm and the probability that the paternalistic intervention will prevent it are low, harm prevention is a weak justifying reason.

People's interests can vary, and assessments of harm can be controversial. However, there are certain general interests, such as an interest in health and an absence of pain, which can provide a more or less objective and noncontroversial basis for concluding that an elderly person is exposed to a risk of an identifiable and more or less serious harm.[39] Consider two decisions by Mr. J., a 78-year-old widower who lives alone and who recently developed angina: (1) a decision to watch the World Series on television at home rather than participate in group activities at a nearby senior citizens' center, and (2) a decision to run in a 5K (five-kilometer) race. No matter what Mr. J.'s other interests may be, it is reasonable to assume that he has an interest in health, and running in a 5K race will expose him to a high probability of serious harm. From the perspective of harm prevention, insofar as his decision to run in the race will make him worse off, there is a strong reason for paternalistically interfering with the second decision.[40] By contrast, although Mr. J.'s mental and physical abilities might atrophy further if he were to regularly stay home and watch television, the probability and seriousness of harm from the first decision are very low. Consequently, from the perspective of harm prevention, there is only a (very) weak reason for paternalistically interfering with that decision.

From the perspectives of both soft and hard paternalism, the level of expected harm to Mr. J. from each of the two decisions has a bearing on whether paternalistic intervention is justified. From the perspective of soft paternalism, the level of expected harm has a bearing on the strength of the standard for determining whether the choice is substantially autonomous. The low level of expected harm from the first decision supports a weak standard; and the high level of expected harm from the second decision supports a stronger standard. The high level of expected harm from the second decision can support the conclusion that paternalistic behavior is justified, but only if it supports a strong standard for determining whether the decision is substantially autonomous, and the appropriate standard supports the conclusion that the second decision is not substantially autonomous.

The level of expected harm from the two decisions is no less important from the perspective of hard paternalism. However, the primary question is not whether the level of expected harm in either case supports the conclusion that the decision is substantially nonautonomous. Since hard paternalists reject the assumption that decisions and actions are immune from paternalistic intervention if they are substantially autonomous, there is no need to consider risk in the context of determining whether a decision or action reaches the threshold of substantial autonomy.[41] For hard paternalists, the question is whether the level of the expected harm from either decision is high enough to provide a sufficiently strong justifying reason; that is, one that warrants the conclusion that paternalistic behavior is justified, all things considered.

Even when it is beyond question that an elderly person is at high risk of a serious harm that paternalistic intervention could prevent, it does not follow that forgoing paternalistic intervention will leave the person *worse off*. It is arguable that if forgoing paternalistic intervention will not leave the person worse off, harm prevention cannot be cited as a justifying reason for paternalistic intervention. Consider three cases:

Case 1. Ms. A., a 73-year-old woman, refuses hip replacement surgery that is expected to significantly improve her mobility and quality of life. Without the surgery, she will suffer pain and discomfort that will only be partially controllable with medication, and her condition will deteriorate to the point where she will be confined to a wheelchair. However, there is a painful recovery period of several weeks; and, in view of Ms. A.'s medical history, there is a significant risk that hip replacement surgery will result in serious mental and/or physical impairment or even death. Thus, it is not clear whether Ms. A.'s decision to forgo surgery will leave her worse off. It seems reasonable to hold that whether she will be worse off depends in part on her preferences and values.

Case 2. Ms. B., a 73-year-old widow, subjects herself to a substantial risk of being robbed and beaten when she walks in Bloomfield, a community with a high crime rate. No matter what her other interests may be, Ms. B. has an intererst in bodily integrity and keeping her money. However, Ms. B. has lived in Bloomfield her entire life, and the freedom of walking in that community is so important to her that she values it more than her security. In view of her priorities (which reflect her values and preferences), it is doubtful that a decision to walk in Bloomfield would leave her worse off. Accordingly, it does not seem appropriate to cite harm prevention as a justifying reason for paternalistically interfering with that decision.

Case 3. Like Ms. B., Ms. C. is a 73-year-old widow. Ms. C. does not live in Bloomfield, but walking in that high crime area is necessary for her community service work, and she is willing to risk her security for the good of others. In view of her priorities, walking in Bloomfield may leave Ms. C. worse off from the perspective of her *self*-interest, but not from the perspective of her *overall* interests.[42] Accordingly, it does not seem appropriate to cite harm prevention as a justifying reason for paternalistically interfering with that decision.

As these three cases indicate, determining whether harm prevention can be cited as a justifying reason for paternalistic intervention is not simply a matter of identifying a (serious) harm that the intervention will prevent. Even when a generally recognized interest, such as health, is involved, to determine whether harm prevention can be cited as a justifying reason for a paternalistic intervention, it may be necessary to consider the elderly person's other interests and her values and preferences. Accordingly, an elderly person's interests and her values and preferences can significantly limit the primary justifying reason for paternalistic intervention.[43]

Are There Reasons for Not Disregarding the Elderly Person's Preferences?

It has been established that someone (A) acts paternalistically toward another person (S) if A does X with the aim of promoting S's well-being, and in deciding to do X, A disregards S's concurrent preferences. Accordingly, if there is a general reason to respect, and not disregard, the preferences of elderly persons when attempting to promote their good, then there is a general reason against paternalistic behavior toward them. A general reason of this type, appears to be derivable from the principle of respect for autonomy.[44] Provided the targeted decision or action is sufficiently autonomous to fall within the scope of respect for autonomy, it is incompatible with that principle for A to do X with the aim of promoting S's well-being, and in deciding to do X, to disregard S's concurrent preferences. To confirm this judgment, let us consider four ways in which A can disregard S's concurrent preferences while attempting to promote S's well-being.[45]

With one possible exception, if A does X to promote S's well-being, and A believes that doing X is contrary to S's actual wishes, A fails to respect S's autonomy. If A were truly to respect S's autonomy, then when A seeks to promote S's well-being, A would be guided by S's preferences, and not by A's (conflicting) inferences concerning means to promote S's well-being. If, say, Mr. P.'s wife and adult children believe that he would want to be told that he has terminal cancer, then it is incompatible with respect for his autonomy to fail to tell him because they believe that telling him would be detrimental to his well-being.

There is one possible exception to the general rule that when A does X to promote S's well-being, and A believes that doing X is contrary to S's concurrent preferences, A fails to respect S's autonomy. If S gave his *prior consent* to A's doing X, and S knows that A's doing X is likely to be contrary to his preferences at a later time, then if A does X contrary to S's concurrent preferences at a later time, it is arguable that A does not fail to respect S's autonomy. A typical example along these lines is when people fear that due to "weakness of will," they will act in ways that are contrary to their own better judgment (imprudently according to their current assessment of what is in their own best interests). For example, fearing that he will succumb to temptation, a 71-year-old man who has been advised to stop drinking liquor for health reasons, asks family members and friends to confiscate any liquor that they might find in his house. He instructs them to do so even if he protests at the time. When, in accordance with the man's prior wishes, family members or friends confiscate liquor over the man's protests, it is arguable that their action is not incompatible with respect for his autonomy. This conclusion can be supported by either citing the man's *prior consent* or claiming that insofar as he lacks the disposition to *act* in accordance with his own conception of his best interests, his action is not sufficiently autonomous to fall within the scope of the principle of respect for autonomy.

Let us consider next the category of paternalism in which A fails to consider whether doing X is contrary to S's concurrent preferences because A's objective is to advance S's interests, and A concludes that S's actual wishes are therefore of no importance. In such cases, A's paternalistic behavior is incompatible with the principle of respect for autonomy. To comply with that principle, A would have to consider S's actual wishes. Suppose, say, a social worker believes that it is in the best interests of an elderly widow who is living alone to hire someone to do housekeeping and cooking. Convinced that he is acting to promote his client's good and that there is therefore no need to consider her actual wishes, the social worker secures someone's services without first consulting with his client. The social worker has failed to comply with the principle of respect for autonomy.

A third category of paternalism occurs when A believes that it is unnecessary to consider whether doing X is contrary to S's concurrent preferences because A believes that S's preferences are generally unreliable, unstable, uninformed, distorted, and/or incoherent. In such cases, A holds in effect that the principle of respect for autonomy is inapplicable because S is not sufficiently autonomous. However, if S or the specific targeted decision or action is sufficiently autonomous, then whatever S's overall mental status, A's paternalistic behavior is incompatible with respect for autonomy.

Suppose, for example, that Ms. N., an 85-year-old mildly demented woman, lives with her daughter, Ms. O. Ms. O. is devoted to her mother and constantly tries to make her life comfortable and pleasant. To this end, Ms. O. plans her mother's life down to the smallest detail. However, Ms. O. fails to consider Ms. N.'s preferences and wishes because she believes that her mother is "senile." Ms. O.'s belief that her mother is senile is a blanket judgment; that is, Ms. O. thinks that since her mother is senile, there is no need to assess her cognitive capacities in relation to specific decisions such as whether to have her gall bladder removed, whether to drive a car, what to wear, what to eat, which television programs to watch, and when to go to bed. By labeling Ms. N. as "senile," and failing to assess her mother's ability to make specific decisions, Ms. O. runs the risk of sometimes treating her mother in a manner incompatible with respect for autonomy.

Finally, let us consider cases in which A believes that doing X is compatible with S's concurrent preferences, but that belief is based on inferences derived from assumptions concerning means to protect or promote A's well-being, and A discounts the importance of independent (direct) evidence of S's concurrent preferences. There is little difference between this category of paternalism and the second category; that is, cases in which people fail even to consider whether actions on behalf of others are contrary to their concurrent preferences.

To confirm this conclusion, let us return to the example of the social worker who arranged to have someone do cooking and housekeeping for an elderly widow. Insofar as the social worker acted on behalf of his client without even considering her actual wishes, he failed to comply with the principle of respect for autonomy. It is hard to see why the conclusion should be any different if it is added that the social worker assumed that since he was acting to promote his client's good, his action was compatible with her wishes. To comply with the principle of respect for autonomy, the social worker would have to make a reasonable effort to ascertain the widow's *actual wishes*. This condition is not satisfied if the social worker's only grounds for judgments about his client's actual wishes are inferences derived from assumptions about means to protect or promote her well-being.

There may be circumstances in which it is infeasible to ascertain a person's concurrent preferences before acting to promote his or her well-being. For example, if I were to see an elderly man begin to walk in the path of a speeding car, I probably would not have time to ask him whether he *wants* me to pull him out of the way. In these circumstances, it is reasonable to assume that intervention on the man's behalf is in his best interests, and he would have assented had there been time to ask him. Accordingly, it is implausible to hold that if I were to pull the man to safety without first securing his permission, I would fail to respect his autonomy. To be sure, the man may have been attempting suicide. But in the absence of evidence to the contrary, it is reasonable to assume that he was not deliberately walking into the path of the car to end his life. By contrast, it is not uncommon for elderly people who are living alone to resist the kind of assistance that the social worker wanted to arrange. Consequently, it is not reasonable to assume that the widow would welcome help with cooking and cleaning, and the social worker fails to respect his client's autonomy if he acts on the assumption that hiring a housekeeper reflects her actual wishes because it will make her life easier and more comfortable.

From the perspective of the principle of respect for autonomy, then, when the targeted decision or action is sufficiently autonomous to fall within the principle's scope, paternalistic behavior in relation to elderly persons is prima facie wrong; that is, wrong unless there is an overriding justifying reason.[46] This general autonomy-based reason against paternalism applies to all instances of paternalistic behavior (provided the targeted decision or action is sufficiently autonomous). However, its strength varies with the importance of the specific autonomy interest at issue.

Some preferences and choices express a person's core values and convictions, for example, a 71-year-old man's considered decision to enter a hospice program rather than to receive chemotherapy and ICU (intensive care unit) care for a prostate cancer with metastases to the liver and colon; and a 73-year-old widow's considered decision to continue to live in her own house rather than move in with her son or into a nursing home. Each of these decisions expresses something important about the person and who he or she is.

Other preferences and choices are more or less peripheral, for example, a nursing home resident's preference for bingo over arts and crafts and her preference for colored sheets over white sheets. Between these two extremes, there is a wide range of preferences and decisions.[47] As an elderly person's preferences and choices approach the "core value" end of the continuum, the strength of the autonomy-based reason against paternalism increases. Conversely, as an elderly person's preferences and choices approach the other end of the continuum, the strength of the autonomy-based reason against paternalism decreases. A possible exception to this generalization occurs when an elderly person's opportunities to make choices that involve core values are significantly restricted due to mental impairment and/or living conditions (such as conditions in a nursing home). In such circumstances, "mundane" preferences, such as a preference for bingo over arts and crafts and a preference for colored sheets over white sheets, can take on added significance because they enable elderly persons to make *some* choices and exercise *some* conrol over their lives.[48]

Respect for autonomy is an important consideration in relation to paternalistic behavior toward the elderly. However, focusing on respect for autonomy as a basis for not disregarding a person's preferences poses a dilemma in relation to a sizable group of elderly persons: those who are cognitively impaired. On the one hand, the scope of the discussion can be limited to decisions and actions that are sufficiently autonomous to fall within the scope of the principle of respect for autonomy, and the relevance of these discussions for cognitively impaired elderly persons is questionable.[49] On the other hand, whenever it is concluded that paternalistic intervention with a cognitively impaired elderly person's decision or action is unwarranted, it can be stipulated that the targeted decision or action is "sufficiently autonomous." In this case, the notion of sufficient autonomy fails to function as an independent standard, and there is a danger that the concept will be unduly weakened.

One way to avoid the second horn of this dilemma is to recognize that respect for autonomy is not the only reason that can be given for respecting the preferences of cognitively impaired elderly persons.[50] First, disregarding the preferences of cognitively impaired elderly persons can result in increased mental impairment and diminished autonomy.[51] If parents are overprotective and fail to give older children increased opportunities to make decisions for themselves, the children may remain immature and may fail to develop the capacity to make prudent choices for themselves. Similarly, if family members, physicians, nurses, nursing home aides, and social workers are overprotective and fail to give cognitively impaired elderly persons an opportunity to affect decisions concerning their lives, their (remaining) cognitive abilities may further atrophy.

Second, even if decisions and actions lack sufficient autonomy to fall within the scope of the principle of respect for autonomy, choosing and doing what they prefer to do can be a source of satisfaction and meaning for cognitively impaired elderly persons. Conversely, ignoring or overriding the preferences of cognitively impaired elderly persons can be a source of frustration to them and can contribute to boredom and depression.[52]

Suppose, say, that Ms. V. insists on selecting her own clothing. Whenever Ms. V.'s daughter-in-law takes her shopping, Ms. V. selects colors, designs, and sizes that seem inappropriate to her daughter-in-law. Ms. V. has Alzheimer's disease and is incapable of deliberating about the benefits and burdens of her clothing selections. Nevertheless, from the perspective of her well-being it might be better to allow her to form and act on her own preferences. It might turn out, say, that although Ms. V. would not be much bothered by the poor fit or the negative opinions and ridicule of others (her daughter-in-law's primary concerns), she would be very upset by attempts to prevent her from selecting her own clothes. Further, exercising her preferences in general, and selecting her own clothes in particular, may give her pleasure and satisfaction, and her opportunities to exercise her preferences may be significantly restricted due to her cognitive impairment. Consequently, without insisting on the fiction that Ms. V. has the capacity to deliberate and to weigh the advantages and disadvantages of selecting her own clothing, there is still a reason to respect her preferences for clothing.[53]

Caplan makes a compelling case for allowing "competent, cognitively intact" nursing home residents to make choices concerning "everyday" matters, such as what to eat, when to bathe, use of the telephone, selection of roommates, what to wear, when and where one can walk, and when to go to sleep and get up.[54] Control over such "everyday" matters, Caplan rightly observes, can contribute significantly to a nursing home resident's quality of life. Consequently, he argues, it is important not to focus exclusively on decisions concerning life and death. However, when discussing such everyday matters in relation to elderly persons in and outside of nursing homes, it is equally important not to focus exclusively on people who are competent and cognitively intact. For there can be strong reasons against ignoring or overriding the preferences of elderly persons concerning everyday matters even when they are moderately to severely demented.

Does the Elderly Person Have a Relevant Cognitive, Psychological, or Emotional Deficit?

It is common to distinguish between paternalistic behavior toward infants and young children, on the one hand, and adults, on the other hand. On the one hand, paternalism toward infants and young children (such as making decisions for them, closely supervising their activities, and shielding them from potentially upsetting information) is considered appropriate and even a mark of responsible parenting. On the other hand, unless adults are demented, profoundly retarded, or emotionally or psychologically unstable, paternalism toward them is commonly viewed as morally suspect. There are two reasons for thinking that paternalistic behavior toward infants and young children generally is less objectionable than paternalism toward adults. First, since infants and young children generally lack the reasoning ability, judgment, maturity, foresight, self-control, and emotional stability to direct their own lives, autonomy-based objections do not apply, or apply less forcefully, to them. Second, due to their lack of cognitive and emotional development, it seems plausible to hold that paternalistic behavior is essential for the well-being of infants and young children.

If we think of infants and autonomous adults as two endpoints on a continuum, then paternalism becomes harder to justify as the level of autonomy increases and approaches the autonomous adult end of the continuum, and becomes easier to justify as the level of autonomy decreases and approaches the infant end of the continuum. Accordingly, all other things being equal, it is harder to justify paternalism in relation to a mildly demented elderly person than it is in relation to a severely demented elderly person; and it is harder to justify paternalism in relation to a mentally intact elderly person than it is in relation to a mildly demented elderly person.[55]

Suppose that Mr. R., a wealthy 72-year-old retired corporate executive, lives with his son. Mr. R. is planning to marry a 28-year-old woman, Ms. Q., whom he has known for only two months. Mr. R.'s son tried to talk his father out of this decision but failed. To determine whether paternalistic intervention with Mr. R.'s decision is justified, it is essential to assess his mental capacities (here, his ability to comprehend and appreciate the risks associated with his planned marriage and to understand his son's arguments). Whether paternalistic intervention with Mr. R.'s decision is justified depends in part on the extent to which such capacities are limited. There are two bases for this conclusion: (1) the strength of the autonomy-based objection to paternalistic intervention with Mr. R.'s decision is in part a function of the degree to which his relevant mental capacities are unimpaired, and (2) the likelihood that Mr. R's decision will make him worse off is in part a function of how mentally impaired he is.

The foregoing analysis is compatible with both hard and soft paternalism. The hard paternalist's position that paternalistic intervention can be justified when decisions and actions are (substantially) autonomous is compatible with the view that it becomes increasingly difficult to justify paternalistic behavior as the level of autonomy increases. A hard paternalist can agree that paternalistic intervention would be difficult to justify if Mr. R. had no significant mental deficits and easier to justify if he were mentally impaired, and still claim that a high probability of substantial and irreversible harm (e.g., there is convincing evidence that Ms. Q. will kill Mr. R. for his money) could justify paternalistic intervention.

In contrast to hard paternalism, soft paternalism seems to require an "all-or-nothing" approach: Mr. R.'s decision to get married either is or is not substantially autonomous; if it is, then no matter how strong the reasons for paternalistic intervention, such intervention is wrong. It might be thought that such an all-or-nothing approach is incompatible with the view that there are various degrees of autonomy and the degree to which Mr. R.'s decision is autonomous is just one of many factors that have a bearing on the justifiability of paternalistic intervention. This conclusion might be warranted if soft paternalism required a *fixed* standard for determining whether Mr. R.'s decision is substantially autonomous. However, insofar as soft paternalists utilize a *variable* standard (one that varies in relation to other morally relevant factors, such as the level of risk), this conclusion is unwarranted. If a variable standard is used to determine whether Mr. R.'s decision to get married is substantially autonomous, then a weighing of other factors is required to determine whether that decision is substantially autonomous, and the following propositions are compatible: (1) it is harder to justify paternalistic intervention as Mr. R.'s decision approaches the higher (autonomous) end of the continuum; and (2) Mr. R.'s decision is immune from paternalistic intervention if it is substantially autonomous.

As children grow older, their cognitive, psychological, and emotional capacities develop and mature, and they become capable of making more and more choices for themselves. The reverse can happen as elderly people grow older. That is, their cognitive, psychological, and emotional capacities may deteriorate, and they may be able to make fewer and fewer choices for themselves. This deterioration can be sudden and total, for example, permanent loss of cognitive function as the result of a massive stroke. However, it can also be gradual and more or less specific, and elderly persons may retain an ability to direct their own lives in some respects and not in others.[56] Accordingly, to have a bearing on the justifiability of a paternalistic intervention in relation to an elderly person, a mental deficit must impair that person in a *relevant respect*. For example, a mental deficit would have a bearing on the justifiability of paternalistically overriding Mr. R.'s decision to marry only if it limits his capacity to make that particular decision. Mental deficits that do not impair his ability to make that decision have no bearing on whether paternalistic intervention with it is warranted.

In some cases, there might be a relevant mental deficit if a decision is made for one reason, but not if it is made for another reason. Suppose, say, Ms. E. is a 75-year-old widow who has been advised by her daughter, a financial analyst, not to invest in company A because it is a very risky investment. Ms. E. rejects her daughter's advice and decides to invest 50 percent of her savings in company A. Due to a stroke, Ms. E.'s mathematical ability is substantially impaired, and she is no longer able to analyze financial data. If her goal is to make a safe and financially sound investment, she has a relevant mental deficit. However, if company A is owned by her husband's former partner, and her goal is to help him, she may not have a relevant mental deficit. She would have a relevant deficit if, say, she were unable to understand that she risks losing a significant part of her savings by investing in company A. However, it cannot be assumed that if Ms. E. is unable to analyze financial data or perform mathematical operations, she also lacks the ability to understand that she risks losing a substantial part of her savings by investing in company A.

Is the Targeted Decision or Action More or Less "In Character" or "Out of Character"?

Decisions of elderly persons, including those who are cognitively impaired, can be "in character" or "out of character." Decisions are in character when they are consistent with core preferences and values that have been reflected in decisions and actions over an extended period of time prior to the onset of mental deterioration. By contrast, decisions are out of character when they are inconsistent with such core preferences and values. People can and do change. However, when a mentally impaired elderly person's choice is out of character, there is more reason to suspect that it is attributable to a defect in the person's mental capacity than when the choice is in character. Accordingly, all other things being equal, it is harder to justify paternalistic intervention in relation to a decision or action when it is in character than when it is out of character.[57] Suppose a mildly demented woman decides to contribute 20 percent of her savings to the local dance council. It would be harder to justify paternalistically overriding her decision if it were known that she loved ballet and regularly went to dance concerts until her mental and physical capacities deteriorated; it would be easier to justify paternalistically overriding her decision if it were known that she had had no previous interest in dance or the arts generally.

The foregoing analysis is compatible with both soft and hard paternalism. From the perspective of soft paternalism, knowing that the woman's decision was in character could make it harder to justify paternalistic intervention by supporting the conclusion that the decision was substantially autonomous; knowing that the woman's decision was out of character could make it easier to justify paternalism by supporting the opposite conclusion. Hard paternalists would not accept this particular account of the function of knowing whether a decision or action is in or out of character. However, they can agree that knowing the woman's decision was in character would make paternalism harder to justify, and knowing her decision was out of character would make paternalism easier to justify.

Is the Contemplated Paternalistic Intervention Guided by the Elderly Person's Own Values and Preferences?

Mentally intact and mildly demented elderly persons may retain (some of) their preferences and values, and these can guide paternalistic behavior. Generally, when A's paternalistic behavior is guided by S's preferences and values: (1) A is more respectful of S's autonomy and shows more respect for S as a person, and (2) A's paternalistic behavior is more likely to be compatible with S's good. Accordingly, the case for paternalistic behavior toward an elderly person is stronger when it is guided by that person's own preferences and values and weaker when it is not (for example, it is guided by the values and preferences of the paternalist).

Suppose Ms. F., a mildly demented 79-year-old woman, still thinks of herself as a Conservative Jew, still values her independence, and continues to have settled preferences about food, clothing, leisure-time activities, and so forth. She is almost blind; although cataract surgery is expected to restore her vision, she refuses it. The case for paternalistically overriding her refusal is strengthened if regained sight will substantially increase her ability to lead a life that, from the perspective of her own values and preferences, is a good life.[58]

Family members may be more familiar with an elderly person's values and preferences than physicians, nurses, social workers, and nursing home aides. Consequently, all other things being equal, the case for paternalism may be stronger when family members act on behalf of their elderly relatives.[59] However, interpersonal communication among family members may be poor, and generational differences between elderly persons and younger relatives can increase the emotional and psychological distance that can separate family members. Accordingly, even when family members sincerely believe that their decisions and actions reflect the values and preferences of an elderly relative, they may not know the elderly person well enough, or so well as they think they do. (Chapter 2 cites several studies that support this assumption.) In addition, decisions and actions on behalf of elderly relatives may actually reflect the interests of family members. Suppose, say, that Ms. F.'s family concludes that regained sight will substantially increase her ability to lead a good life. They may have little, if any, evidence to support this judgment, and/or it may be influenced by a desire to reduce Ms. F.'s dependency and the burden to them.

Severely demented elderly persons may no longer have values and preferences to guide paternalistic behavior. However, they do have histories, and these histories are ethically relevant when contemplating and assessing paternalistic behavior. In this respect, there is an important difference between once mentally intact severely demented elderly persons and young children. For the most part, infants and (very) young children do not yet have histories, and decisions on their behalf are largely future-oriented; that is, guided by a conception of the persons they will/should become. By contrast, severely demented elderly persons can have rich histories and limited futures, and decisions on their behalf may appropriately be in part past-oriented; that is, guided by knowledge of the persons they once were.[60] Suppose Ms. B., an 83-year-old severely demented nursing home resident, experiences a substantial loss of blood from an injury as the result of a fall. She was a lifelong Jehovah's Witness, and she had consistently stated that she never wanted a blood transfusion. This history is part of who Ms. B. is, and should not be ignored when making decisions on her behalf.[61]

Does the Contemplated Paternalistic Behavior Involve Means that are Morally Suspect or prima facie Wrong?

According to some ethical theories, certain actions and practices (for example, killing, coercion, lying, and promise-breaking) are prima facie wrong.[62] That is, they are ethically wrong unless there is an outweighing justifying reason. Paternalistic behavior toward elderly persons can involve a wide range of such prima facie wrong means, for example, coercion, intimidation, lying, deception, and the use of physical constraints. The use of such means, provides a reason against paternalistic behavior and a basis for holding that it is prima facie wrong.[63]

Suppose Mr. J. and Mr. K. are mildly demented nursing home residents. They shared a room for over a year, and became friends. One night an aide forgot to check whether Mr. K.'s bed rails were up, and he fell to the floor. The sound of his falling awoke Mr. J., who rang for help. Mr. K. was unconscious and was taken to the hospital, where he died the following day. Mr. J. asked Ms. L., an aide, to tell him whether Mr. K. was seriously injured and when he would return. Ms. L. knew that Mr. K. had died, but she told Mr. J. that Mr. K.'s injuries were minor. She stated that Mr. K. was temporarily staying with his daughter, and that another person would be moved into the room temporarily until Mr. K. returned.

Consider two reasons for telling Mr. J. that Mr. K.'s injuries were minor: to protect Mr. J. from becoming upset and depressed, and to protect the nursing home and its staff from liability for negligence. If lying is prima facie wrong, then it is prima facie wrong to tell Mr. J. that Mr. K.'s injuries were minor for either of the two reasons. From the perspective of the prima facie obligation not to lie, it is prima facie wrong to protect Mr. J. by telling him that Mr. K.'s injuries were minor because doing so would be an instance of *lying,* and not because doing so would be an instance of paternalistic behavior.

Both soft and hard paternalists can recognize the relevance of such prima facie obligations for an ethical assessment of paternalistic behavior. Accordingly, to determine whether it would have been ethically justified to protect Mr. J. by telling him that Mr. K.'s injuries were only minor, soft and hard paternalists can agree that it is essential to consider the prima facie obligation not to lie. A soft paternalist might reason that the prima facie obligation not to lie supports a weaker standard of substantial autonomy, and that a paternalistic lie would not have been justified because Mr. J. was substantially autonomous.[64] This line of reasoning is not available to a hard paternalist.

However, a hard paternalist might also conclude that a paternalistic lie would have been unjustified, and the prima facie obligation not to lie can also be a decisive consideration. A hard paternalist might conclude, say, that the paternalistic lie would have been wrong because, all things considered, the prima facie obligation not to lie was not outweighed in the circumstances. Thus, although their stated rationales might differ, both soft and hard paternalists might well weigh the same considerations, including the prima facie obligation not to lie, and reach the same conclusion.

There can be significant ethical differences among paternalistic means. For example, it can be claimed that the nonconsensual use of physical constraints or drugs to protect nursing home residents from injury is ethically worse than the practice of removing potentially dangerous possessions (such as scissors, knives, and matches) from residents' rooms against their wishes. In support of this claim, it might be argued that whereas removing potentially dangerous possessions involves a limited interference, physical restraints and drugs impose sweeping and more or less indiscriminate limitations on the freedom of movement and choice of nursing home residents. All other things being equal, when the means are ethically worse, it is harder to justify paternalism.

When A does X for S's good with S's voluntary informed consent, A is not behaving paternalistically toward S because A is not disregarding S's preferences. However, even when A lacks S's consent, A might secure S's *assent,* and the *means* used to secure S's assent can have a bearing on an ethical assessment of A's paternalistic behavior. Suppose, for example, that Ms. D., a 73-year-old diabetic with no apparent mental deficits other than minor memory loss, develops gangrene of the left foot. The attending physician recommends an amputation, but Ms. D. refuses. Efforts by the attending physician and Ms. D.'s family to change her mind and secure her voluntary informed consent are fruitless. Her assent (here, compliance and signature on a consent form) might be secured by a number of means, including (1) holding a gun to her head; (2) threatening to take her cats to the humane society where they would be "put to sleep"; (3) wearing her down; or (4) ignoring her refusal, scheduling surgery, and giving her the form to sign at the last moment.[65] None of these means of gaining Ms. D.'s assent satisfy the requirements of informed consent, but the fourth means is closer to informed consent than the first. (Informed consent is discussed in Chapter 5.) Moreover, securing Ms. D.'s assent by the fourth means is closer to informed consent than the strategy of waiting until she loses consciousness and performing an emergency amputation without her assent. There are two reasons for holding that it becomes less difficult to justify paternalistic behavior as an elder person's assent approaches voluntary informed consent. First, the force of the autonomy-based objection to paternalistic behavior diminishes as assent approaches voluntary informed consent. Second, the likelihood that the paternalistic behavior is compatible with the person's good increases as her assent approaches voluntary informed consent.

Elderly persons who have no serious mental impairment, or who are only mildly demented, can make mistakes due to inadequate information or misinformation, carelessness, denial, fear, and so forth.[66] If persuasion is an effective means of getting an elderly person to recognize and correct a mistake, it is preferable to paternalistic intervention.

Persuasion will not always succeed in relation to mentally intact or mildly demented elderly persons. Moreover, in most, if not all, contexts it is not feasible to help severely demented elderly persons recognize and correct mistakes. However, there may still be alternatives to paternalistic intervention that are preferable from an ethical perspective. Suppose Mr. G., a 73-year-old nursing home resident with Alzheimer's disease, willingly goes to lunch and dinner and feeds himself, but he refuses to go to breakfast. In order to assure that he gets adequate nutrition, he is restrained and taken in a wheelchair to the dining room where he is fed by an aide. Mr. G.'s wife had served him breakfast in bed at home for five years until her death two weeks ago, when Mr. G. moved into the nursing home. If Mr. G. would willingly eat breakfast in his own room, it would be preferable to respect his preferences than to paternalistically disregard them.[67]

Case Study: Paternalism and Adult Protective Services

Adult protective services programs have been characterized as a "system of preventive, supportive, and surrogate services for the elderly living in the community to enable them to maintain independent living and avoid abuse and exploitation."[68] Protective services programs include two components. One is a service component, a coordinated effort to provide a wide range of services that will facilitate continued independent living in the community. These services are coordinated by a caseworker, and include health care, meals, housing, housekeeping, and personal care. A second component involves "authority to provide substitute decision-making."[69] Ironically, although an important aim of protective services programs is to help the elderly avoid institutionalization and to "maintain *independent* living," since recipients of assistance are often believed to be at risk due to impaired mental capacity, they are prime targets for paternalistic intervention. Accordingly, Monk and Abramson hold that for case managers of elderly clients, "the risks of slipping into a paternalistic stance are constant, most specially when dealing with clients who require protective services";[70] and Regan observes that protective services programs "raise again the profound issue of paternalism versus individual liberty.''[71] This important issue is brought to the fore in the following case.

Case Description

It was mid-June when J. Z., who had been an adult protective services caseworker for almost six years, received a call about Ms. T., a widow in her late seventies. The anonymous caller reported that Ms. T.'s husband had died about a year earlier, and that she had lived alone since her husband's death. The caller stated that he was concerned for Ms. T.'s health and safety. He reported that Ms. T.'s diet consisted primarily of potato chips and soda pop, items that she paid a teenager to purchase for her. He stated that Ms. T.'s house was filthy, and that she had worn the same soiled clothes for months. Neighborhood youths had vandalized Ms. T.'s garage, and the caller feared that they might rob Ms. T.

When J. Z. went to Ms. T.'s house to investigate, she discovered that the information supplied by the anonymous caller was accurate. Trash, including empty potato chip bags and soda pop cans, was strewn all over the kitchen, dining room, and living room. There were feces on the floors and furniture, and there was an unmistakable smell of urine. Ms. T. had trouble walking, so J. Z. surmised that it was difficult for her to reach the only bathroom in the house, which was located on the second floor. In addition, Ms. T.'s clothes were torn and filthy.

Since Ms. T. was fixated on the past (she talked mostly about her husband and their life together), it was very difficult for J. Z. to discuss Ms. T.'s current situation with her in much detail. Ms. T. did state that she had no children, that she had no family in the area, and that her only income was her monthly Social Security check.

J. Z. was able to confirm the information that Ms. T. provided. She also was able to locate a niece and nephew. They lived in a city more than five hundred miles away and had lost contact with their aunt several years ago after the death of their father (Ms. T.'s brother). Currently, they shared responsibility for the care of their mother who had Alzheimer's disease. Neither knew Ms. T. well, and neither was willing to assist in her care or in decision-making concerning Ms. T.

When J. Z. questioned Ms. T. about the conditions in which she was living, Ms. T. responded that she saw nothing wrong with her current lifestyle. "I am content," she insisted. In addition, she repeatedly stated that she did not want to be "put away."

After several visits, and considerable persuasion, J. Z. was finally able to get Ms. T. to agree to pay Ms. L., a neighbor, to buy food, and to come several times a week to cook, clean, and help Ms. T. with her personal hygiene. Ms. T. also reluctantly agreed to allow J. Z. to help her with her finances and to help her write checks to pay utility bills.

During subsequent visits to Ms. T.'s house, J. Z. observed a significant improvement in Ms. T.'s personal hygiene and the appearance of her home. It had also become easier for J. Z. to communicate with her client. During one visit, however, J. Z. discovered what appeared to be a serious infection on Ms. T.'s right foot. Since she suspected gangrene, J. Z. urged Ms. T. to go to a doctor immediately. Ms. T. refused to go to a physician, but J. Z. was able to persuade Ms. T. to allow a doctor to examine her at home.

The physician reported that Ms. T.'s foot was gangrenous and should be amputated. She explained that an amputation now might be able to save most of Ms. T.'s leg, but the infection was life-threatening if not treated immediately. Accordingly, the physician recommended that Ms. T. go to the hospital immediately.

Ms. T. refused. "My time has come," she said. "I prefer to die at home on my own terms rather than slowly in a hospital or nursing home."

Ms. T. refused to talk any further to either J. Z. or the physician about leaving her home and going to the hospital. When J. Z. indicated that she would like to have a psychiatric social worker visit Ms. T., she refused: "I'm not crazy. I just want to stay here until I die."

J. Z. is deeply troubled. On the one hand, she feels that hospitalization would be in her client's best interests, and she contemplates seeking court appointment of a guardian to authorize hospitalizing Ms. T. against her wishes. On the other hand, J. Z. is unsure whether it would be ethically warranted to disregard Ms. T.'s expressed wishes.

Case Analysis

An important question for J. Z to consider is whether Ms. T. will be worse off by refusing to go to the hospital. Initially, it may seem there can be no doubt that Ms. T.'s decision will leave her worse off. After all, the expected outcome is that her condition will deteriorate, and she will die. However, Ms. T.'s evaluation of the expected outcome of hospital care should also be considered. If her mental functioning had been intact and she had refused to go to the hospital because the expected outcome was unacceptable to her on quality of life grounds, it would be arguable that her refusal reflects her values and settled preferences and will not make her worse off.

However, there are three reasons for J. Z. to resist drawing this conclusion. First, since Ms. T. cut off the efforts by J. Z. and the physician to explain why she should go to the hospital, it is doubtful that her refusal was an informed one. Second, the expected outcome of hospital care cannot be determined unless Ms. T. receives a thorough medical work-up. She may expect the worst (death in the hospital or physical and mental deterioration that will leave her bedridden and totally dependent on others), but her prognosis may be much less bleak. Third, there are several grounds for suspecting that Ms. T. is mentally impaired. J. Z. initially found Ms. T. "fixated on the past," and she may be suffering from depression as a result of the death of her husband and the subsequent isolation and loneliness. In addition, Ms. T.'s mental capacities may be impaired as a result of poor health (such as malnutrition, gangrene, and other undiagnosed conditions).

Ultimately, it is up to the courts, and not J. Z., to determine whether Ms. T. is legally competent to refuse hospitalization and to care for herself at home. For J. Z., the question is whether to *initiate* legal steps to have Ms. T. removed from her home and hospitalized against her wishes. In making this decision, J. Z. should not try to substitute her judgment for that of physicians or a court. However, to subject Ms. T. to a legal test of her decision-making capacity and her ability to care for herself can have significant ethical costs that J. Z. should not ignore. That process can be upsetting, traumatic, and demeaning. In addition, it might significantly restrict Ms. T.'s freedom; and, to her detriment, it might set into motion institutional forces that are uncontrollable and/or not sufficiently sensitive to her specific needs and interests. Consequently, J. Z. should pursue other alternatives before initiating the process of having a guardian appointed to consent to hospitalization against Ms. T.'s wishes.

One possibility would be for J. Z. to try to set up home visits by a physician and/or a registered nurse. Such home visits would not be a long-term solution, but they might help to calm Ms. T.'s fears and win her trust. Proper nutrition and medication might also help to improve her mental status. Finally, this strategy might help to buy some additional time for J. Z. to try to negotiate an agreement with Ms. T.

To this end, J. Z. should try to ascertain why Ms. T. does not want to go to the hospital. Ms. T. may fear that if she agrees to go to the hospital and has the amputation, she will have to go to a nursing home and will never be able to return to her house. If this is one of Ms. T.'s reasons for refusing to go to the hospital, J. Z. can assure her that she will do what she can to enable Ms. T. to return home after she is released from the hospital. For example, J. Z. might offer to arrange for a visiting nurse and a physical therapist to go to Ms. T.'s home. If Ms. L. is unwilling or unable to provide adequate assistance with shopping, cooking, and cleaning, J. Z. might offer to make other arrangements through social agencies. The possibility of remodeling the house so that Ms. T. can live on the first floor might also be explored. J. Z. can also assure Ms. T. that if and when she can no longer receive adequate care at home, there are alternatives to nursing homes (such as personal care homes and religious or nonsectarian congregate care facilities). Finally if

J. Z. can get Ms. T. to express her specific fears about living in a nursing home, she might be able to calm some of her client's anxieties.

Ms. T. may worry that she will never leave the hospital alive. She may believe that she is going to die one way or the other, and she may prefer to die at home rather than in a hospital. If this is one of Ms. T.'s reasons for refusing to go to the hospital, it is imperative to help her understand that her chances of surviving are substantially better if she has an amputation. Moreover, J. Z. should point out that it is essential for Ms. T. to go to the hospital for tests because her condition may be far less serious than she imagines. J. Z. should communicate to her client that she may have treatable conditions (such as diabetes or hypothyroidism), and that medical treatment might significantly improve her health, enhance her ability to function, and make her feel better.

Ms. T. may fear that once she is hospitalized, she will lose control over her life and medical decision-making. She may worry that if and when her physical and mental health deteriorate, she will be kept alive long past the time that she would want to be. If Ms. T. expresses this fear, she can be assured that she can retain significant control by discussing her wishes and goals with her physicians. Depending on Ms. T.'s mental status, J. Z. might also point out that Ms. T. can execute an advance directive to guide decision-making if she is no longer able to do so.

If J. Z. is unable to ascertain Ms. T.'s concerns and fears and/or negotiate an agreement that will get her to go to the hospital, J. Z. may initiate legal proceedings to have a guardian appointed for Ms. T. Such a step would be appropriate as a last resort if J. Z. suspects that Ms. T.'s decision to "die at home" was influenced by her impaired cognitive capacities. However, such a measure would not be ethically justified if J. Z. was convinced that Ms. T.'s decision reflected her enduring values and preferences and was not attributable to a mental defect or impairment. A more appropriate response under these conditions would be for J. Z. to offer to arrange for the provision of services in Ms. T.'s home to make her as comfortable as possible.

Notes

1. Laws and policies can also be paternalistic. For a discussion of paternalistic policies toward the elderly, see Thomas Halper, "The Double-Edged Sword: Paternalism as a Policy in the Problems of Aging," *Milbank Memorial Fund Quarterly / Health and Society* 58, no. 3 (1980): 472–99.

2. Abraham Monk and Marcia Abramson, "Older People," in Shaker A. Yelaja, ed., *Ethical Issues in Social Work* (Springfield, Ill.: Charles C. Thomas, 1982), 154.

3. Halper, "The Double-Edged Sword," 473.

4. An Office of Technology Assessment report states that whereas only 1 percent of

people between the ages of sixty-five to seventy-four experience severe dementia, 25 percent of people over the age of eighty-four suffer from it. U.S. Congress, Office of Technology Assessment, *Losing a Million Minds: Confronting the Tragedy of Alzheimer's Disease and Other Dementias* (Washington, D.C.: U.S. Government Printing Office, 1987), 7. For a general discussion of aging and cognitive ability, see Marilyn S. Albert, "Cognition and Aging," in William R. Hazzard et al., eds., *Principles of Geriatric Medicine and Gerontology*, 2d ed. (New York: McGraw-Hill, 1990), 913–19.

5. See Mark H. Waymack and George A. Taler, *Medical Ethics and the Elderly: A Case Book* (Chicago: Pluribus, 1988), 29; and Halper, "The Double-Edged Sword," 473.

6. See Christine K. Cassel, "Research in Nursing Homes: Ethical Issues," *Journal of the American Geriatrics Society* 33, no. 11 (November 1985): 795–99.

7. I shall ignore any differences between "S's welfare," "S's well being," "S's good," and "S's interests," and these expressions will be used interchangeably.

8. Feinberg identifies one category as *nonbenevolent paternalism*. As an example of this form of paternalism, he cites rules that treat factory workers like children, but that have the objective of increasing efficiency and profits. According to Feinberg, "[w]hat makes non-benevolent authoritative governance paternalistic is a certain (vague) kind of demeaning spirit implicitly suggested by the phrase 'as if children.' The treatment must seem arbitrary and unnecessary, and expressive of a lack of the trust that is normally due to adults." Joel Feinberg, *The Moral Limits of the Criminal Law*, vol. 3, *Harm to Self* (New York: Oxford University Press, 1986), 5. Feinberg rightly stresses the feature of treating subjects as if they were children, but the benevolence condition is commonly accepted, and I see no good reason to reject the standard understanding of paternalism. Thus, I will assume that paternalism is a type of benevolence.

9. If I know that he does not want my assistance and I disregard his wishes because I think I know what is best for him, then I am treating him paternalistically.

10. In an oft-cited definition, Gerald Dworkin states that paternalism is "interference with a person's liberty of action justified by reasons referring exclusively to the welfare, good, happiness, needs, interests, or values of the person being coerced." Gerald Dworkin, "Paternalism," reprinted in Rolf Sartorius, ed., *Paternalism* (Minneapolis: University of Minnesota Press, 1983), 20. Here paternalism is identified with *coercive* interference with liberty of action. Since coercion is absent in many paradigm instances of paternalistic behavior (such as acting on behalf of others without their knowledge or consent and withholding information for a person's own good), coercion is clearly not an identifying characteristic of paternalism. In a later article Dworkin construes paternalism more broadly as "a violation of a person's autonomy." See Gerald Dworkin, "Paternalism: Some Second Thoughts" in Sartorius, ed., *Paternalism*, 105–11.

11. Since my neighbor was unable to shovel his walk himself, I did not prevent him from doing so. Still, I did prevent him from paying someone to shovel his walk, or from having his grandson do it. Does it follow that I interfered with his liberty of action? The answer depends on how the notion of "interference with liberty of action" is analyzed, a task that is beyond the scope of this study. In any event, it does not follow that I acted *paternalistically* toward my neighbor.

12. Buchanan denies that withholding information constitutes interference with liberty of action: "Withholding information may preclude an *informed* decision, and it may interfere with attempts to reach an informed decision, without thereby interfering with a person's freedom to decide and to act on his decision. Even if I am deprived of information which I must have if I am to make an informed decision, I may still be free to decide and to act." Allen E. Buchanan, "Medical Paternalism," reprinted in Sartorius, ed. *Paternalism*, 62.

However, in the case of the physician who withheld a diagnosis of prostate cancer, an unqualified statement to the effect that the physician did not interfere with the patient's freedom of action would require an analysis of the notion of "interference with freedom of action." As already noted, such an analysis is beyond the scope of this study.

13. James F. Childress, *Who Should Decide? Paternalism in Health Care* (New York: Oxford University Press, 1982), 13.

14. Tom L. Beauchamp and James F. Childress, *Principles of Biomedical Ethics,* 3d ed. (New York: Oxford University Press, 1989), 214.

15. Gerald Dworkin, "Paternalism: Some Second Thoughts," in Sartorius, ed., *Paternalism,* 107. For a critique of the view that autonomy and paternalism are incompatible, see Douglas N. Husak, "Paternalism and Autonomy," *Philosophy & Public Affairs* 10, no. 1 (Winter 1981): 27–46.

16. Bernard Gert and Charles M. Culver, "Paternalistic Behavior," *Philosophy & Public Affairs* 6, no. 1 (Fall 1976): 45–57. In a later book, they provide a somewhat simplified (four-condition) analysis. See Charles M. Culver and Bernard Gert, *Philosophy in Medicine* (New York: Oxford University Press, 1982), 130.

17. Donald VanDeVeer, *Paternalistic Intervention: The Moral Bounds of Benevolence* (Princeton: Princeton University Press, 1986).

18. VanDeVeer, in *Paternalistic Intervention,* formulates the condition as follows: "A believes that his (her) doing (or omitting) X is contrary to S's operative perference, intention, or disposition at the time A does (or omits) X [or when X affects S—or would have affected S if X had been done (or omitted)]" (22). The other two conditions of VanDeVeer's analysis serve to identify benevolent (altruistic) acts. One stipulates that "A deliberately does (or omits) X." The other condition stipulates that "A does (or omits) X with the primary or sole aim of promoting a benefit for S [a benefit which, A believes, would not accrue to S in the absence of A's doing (or omitting) X] or preventing a harm to S [a harm which, A believes, would accrue to S in the absence of A's doing (or omitting) X]" (22).

19. "Doing *X*" is to be understood as shorthand for "doing or deliberately omitting *X.*"

20. VanDeVeer formulates his definition for the stated purpose of including paternalistic omissions; ironically, the example he cites of paternalistic omissions is an instance of *withholding information* from a patient: "If I withhold the information from you (that your spouse has died) to prevent you from experiencing distress when you are about to undergo surgery, it is plausible to describe my behavior as paternalistic" (*Paternalistic Intervention,* 22). In contrast to scenario 1 and scenario 2, in this example it is reasonable to assume that the person who withheld the information believed that the patient wanted to be told. Thus this example appears to satisfy C_{BCP}. The claim about the patient's concurrent preferences in VanDeVeer's example should be distinguished from the claim that since successful surgery was more important from the perspective of the patient's long-term preferences and interests than immediately learning of his wife's death, withholding the news of his wife's death before surgery was compatible with his overall good. The latter claim may support the assertion that the paternalistic act of withholding information was *justified.* It does *not* support the conclusion that withholding information was not paternalistic behavior.

21. As Buchanan observes in "Medical Paternalism," many of the generalizations that are used to defend paternalistic actions are highly speculative and unproven. However, even if it were known that most patients who are told that they have terminal cancer experience substantial emotional trauma, it is important to bear in mind that some who will suffer substantial emotional trauma may still *want* to know the truth. On the other hand, if it were known that most patients do *not* want to be told that they have a terminal illness, then it may not be paternalistic to withhold that information from patients without first ascertaining their

wishes. However, since *some* patients might want to know, physicians who fail to make any effort to ascertain the actual wishes of individual patients would not respect them as persons (individuals).

22. Reflecting the fact that *pater* is Latin for "father," the *American Heritage Dictionary* defines paternalism as the "policy or practice of treating or governing people in a fatherly manner" A paradigm of "fatherly" (more generally, parental) treatment is to be found in the parent-child relationship. For a discussion of the father (parent) metaphor in relation to paternalism, see Childress, *Who Should Decide?* 4ff.

23. If A acts, or contemplates acting, paternalistically toward S with the objective of thwarting a specific decision or action, that decision or action will be referred to as the "targeted decision or action," and S will be referred to as the "targeted person." Elderly persons in persistent vegetative states and severely demented elderly persons lack the capacity to make any substantially autonomous decisions. However, when elderly persons are less impaired cognitively, some of their decisions and actions can be substantially nonautonomous while others can be substantially autonomous. For example, a cognitively impaired elderly person's decision to smoke in bed may be substantially nonautonomous, and her choice of clothing may be substantially autonomous. Moreover, specific choices and actions of elderly persons who have no significant cognitive impairment can be substantially nonautonomous. Consequently, it would be misleading to identify soft paternalism as the view that paternalistic behavior toward a person (S) is justified only if S is substantially nonautonomous.

24. For defenses of hard paternalism, see Beauchamp and Childress, *Principles of Biomedical Ethics,* 3d ed., 219–22; and Clifton B. Perry and William B. Applegate, "Medical Paternalism and Patient Self-determination," *Journal of the American Geriatrics Society* 33, no. 5 (May 1985): 353–59. Although Perry and Applegate claim to support hard (strong) paternalism, some of their alleged instances of "justified hard paternalism" do not appear to be instances of hard paternalism. For example, they claim that even when patients want information, if it is "irrelevant or relevant but unnecessary" from the perspective of a general professional standard, physicians may justifiably withhold it. Leaving aside the question of justification, it is doubtful that a physician acts *paternalistically* when she withholds information because it is "irrelevant or relevant but unnecessary" from the perspective of a general professional standard. As a second example, Perry and Applegate claim that it is justified paternalism when physicians disregard patients' choices that "indicate a distorted view of reality or that are counterproductive to the achievement of their chosen ends" (355). Such behavior on the part of physicians may well be paternalistic, but it is doubtful that the behavior is an instance of *hard* paternalism.

25. Feinberg, in *Harm to Self,* distinguishes between soft and hard paternalism, but in an earlier article ("Legal Paternalism," *Canadian Journal of Philosophy* 1, no. 1 [1971]: 105–24), he used the terms "weak" and "strong" to draw the same distinction. Feinberg attributes this change in terminology to his belief that the former terms have become more common. (*Harm to Self,* 377). However, Beauchamp and Childress still use the terms "weak" and "strong" paternalism (*Principles of Biomedical Ethics,* 218–19). Childress (*Who Should Decide?*) refers to soft paternalism as "limited or restricted" paternalism and hard paternalism as "extended" paternalism.

26. According to Feinberg, soft paternalism is the view that it is legitimate to prevent "self-regarding harmful conduct . . . *when but only when* that conduct is substantially nonvoluntary, or when temporary intervention is necessary to establish whether it is voluntary or not" (*Harm to Self,* 12). Beauchamp and Childress prefer "substantially nonautonomous" to "substantially nonvoluntary," but they take the difference to be essentially terminological (*Principles of Biomedical Ethics,* 218–19).

27. Childress, *Who Should Decide?* 17. A person's decision or action can be substantially nonautonomous or nonvoluntary as a result of coercion or a "defect, encumbrance, or limitation in decision-making or acting."

28. The distinction between soft and hard paternalism is also used to differentiate between two types of paternalistic behavior. Paternalistic behavior is an instance of soft paternalism when the soft paternalism condition is satisfied, and paternalistic behavior is an instance of hard paternalism when the soft paternalism condition is not satisfied. Since a particular instance of paternalistic behavior might satisfy the soft paternalism condition according to one formulation, but not according to another, it is more accurate to state that paternalistic behavior is or is not an instance of soft paternalism in relation to a specified formulation of the soft paternalism condition.

29. See, for example, Beauchamp and Childress, *Principles of Biomedical Ethics,* 219.

30. *Harm to Self,* 117. As noted above, Feinberg refers to "voluntariness" rather than "autonomy" and identifies soft paternalism with the view that substantially voluntary conduct is immune from paternalistic behavior.

31. *Harm to Self,* 118.

32. See Dan Brock, "Paternalism and Autonomy, *Ethics* 98, no. 3 (April 1988): 562.

33. If the judgment that a decision or action is substantially autonomous reflects the conclusion that paternalism is unjustified, then the claim that paternalistic behavior is unjustified if the decision or action is substantially autonomous amounts to a tautology. A similar point was made in Chapter 1 concerning the claim that it is not justified to override a treatment refusal by a patient with decision-making capacity.

34. This is a hypothetical case. For a discussion of an actual case that illustrates many of the issues discussed here, see Steven H. Miles, "Paternalism, Family Duties, and My Aunt Maude," *Journal of the American Medical Association* 259, no. 17 (May 6, 1988): 2582–83.

35. Feinberg lists five conditions of a "perfectly voluntary [fully autonomous] choice": (1) the agent is competent (that is, he is not an animal, an infant, insane, severely retarded, or comatose); (2) the agent does not choose under coercion or duress; (3) the agent does not choose because of more subtle manipulation (such as subliminal suggestion, posthypnotic suggestion, and "sleep-teaching"); (4) the agent does not choose because of ignorance or mistaken belief; and (5) the agent does not choose in circumstances that are temporarily distorting (impetuously, while fatigued, while excessively nervous, under the influence of a powerful passion, under the influence of mind-altering drugs, while in pain, under severe time pressure, or a neurotically compulsive or obsessive choice). These conditions are said to constitute an "impossibly high standard" of a choice that is "deficient in *none* of the ways that are *ever* taken into account for *any* moral or legal purpose in *any* context" (*Harm to Self,* 115).

36. All of these factors may contribute to Peter's uncertainty, but each will be isolated for the purposes of illustration.

37. Feinberg observes that soft paternalists are not committed to preventing people from exercising their preferences whenever their choices and actions are substantially nonautonomous (nonvoluntary): "Persons may act as nonvoluntarily as is imaginable and as frequently as possible, so far as the soft paternalist is concerned, provided no harm is caused thereby" (*Harm to Self,* 118).

38. Feinberg distinguishes between "harm-preventing paternalism" and "benefit-promoting paternalism" (*Harm to Self,* 8). Childress distinguishes between "positive paternalism," which involves the promotion of good, and "negative paternalism," which involves the prevention of evil (harm). He claims that *"ceteris paribus,* negative paternalism is easier to justify than positive paternalism" (*Who Should Decide?* 18). The line between harm

prevention and benefit promotion may not always be clear. Sometimes a paternalistic intervention can be described alternatively as a means to prevent harm or as a means to provide a benefit. For example, suppose a 78-year-old woman has executed a power of attorney that designates her son as her representative or attorney in fact. The woman's son decides that his mother should move to a retirement apartment (congregate care facility), and he sells her house against her wishes. The son's action can be described alternatively as a means to prevent his mother from harm (loneliness, depression, and further mental and physical deterioration), or as a means to benefit her (to promote her mental and physical health and to give her an opportunity to enjoy life more).

39. There is considerable controversy about whether "health" and "disease" are value-neutral concepts. For a defense of value neutrality, see Christopher Boorse, "On the Distinction Between Disease and Illness," *Philosophy and Public Affairs* 5, no. 1 (Fall 1975): 49–68. For a systematic critique of value neutrality, see K. W. M. Fulford, *Moral Theory and Medical Practice* (Cambridge: Cambridge University Press, 1989). Several essays on this issue are collected in Arthur L. Caplan, H. Tristram Engelhardt, Jr., and James J. McCartney, eds., *Concepts of Health and Disease* (Reading, Mass.: Addison-Wesley, 1981).

40. It will be argued below that harm prevention can be cited as a justifying reason for paternalistically interfering with an elderly person's decision only if the decision makes the person *worse off*. Although Mr. J. has an interest in health, whether his decision to run in the race will make him worse off depends on his other interests and his enduring values and settled preferences.

41. The view that the standard for determining whether decisions and actions are substantially autonomous varies with the risk is similar to the view discussed in Chapter 1 that the standard of decision-making capacity varies with the risk. The assumption that decisions should be respected if they are made by patients who possess decision-making capacity underlies the view that risk can play a decisive role in determining whether a patient possesses decision-making capacity. Similarly, an assumption accepted by soft paternalists and rejected by hard paternalists, namely, that decisions and actions are immune from paternalistic intervention if they are substantially autonomous, underlies the view that risk can play a decisive role in determining whether a particular decision or action is substantially autonomous. Since hard paternalists reject this assumption, there is no need for them to consider risk in the context of an all-or-nothing determination about whether a decision or action is substantially autonomous (or whether a patient possesses decision-making capacity).

42. For a discussion of the distinction between a person's self-interests and overall interests, see Richard B. Brandt, "Rationality, Egoism, and Morality," *Journal of Philosophy*, 69 (1972): 681–97.

43. According to Brock, there are two bases for anti-paternalism: a right to self-determination (respect for autonomy), and a preference-based theory of the good for persons. In effect, the latter tends to undermine the harm-prevention rationale for paternalistic intervention. As Brock observes a "preference-based good-promotion" critique of paternalism is based on "a deep skepticism about whether there is an objectively correct view of the good for persons or the good life, objective in the sense that it is not ultimately based for each person on his or her own basic aims and values" ("Paternalism and Autonomy," 561). In the absence of an "objectively correct" account of the good for persons, an individual's own enduring values and settled preferences constitute the primary basis for deciding how to promote the person's well being. According to a "corrected preference" account of the good for persons, if a person's actual preferences satisfy certain procedural criteria, it is reasonable to assume that they reflect her good. For a systematic account of such procedural criteria, see Richard B. Brandt, *A Theory of the Good and the Right* (Oxford: Oxford University Press, 1979).

44. As noted above, there may also be a preference-based good-promotion foundation for a general reason against paternalism.

45. Lest it be thought that the incompatibility of paternalism and autonomy is obvious, Husak, as noted above, argues that they are not incompatible. See Husak, "Paternalism and Autonomy."

46. Kagan prefers "pro tanto" to "prima facie." See Shelly Kagan, *The Limits of Morality* (Oxford: Clarendon Press, 1989). As Kagan explains the difference, "a prima facie reason *appears* to be a reason, but may actually not be a reason at all, or may not have weight in all cases it appears to. In contrast, a pro tanto reason is a genuine reason—with actual weight—but it may not be a *decisive* one in various cases" (17). I shall continue to use the more common term "prima facie" to refer to "genuine" reasons and duties (those with "actual weight").

47. McCullough and Wear distinguish between decisions that involve a person's "basic moral concerns" and "choices or decisions that an individual happens to make at a particular time and in a particular circumstance" that do not involve such basic moral concerns. L. B. McCullough and Stephen Wear, "Respect for Autonomy and Medical Paternalism Reconsidered," *Theoretical Medicine* 6 (1985): 297. As examples of choices that reflect basic moral concerns, the authors cite refusals of transfusions by Jehovah's Witnesses and refusals of life-sustaining treatments.

48. See Arthur L. Caplan, "The Morality of the Mundane: Ethical Issues Arising in the Daily Lives of Nursing Home Residents," in Rosalie A. Kane and Arthur L. Caplan, eds., *Everyday Ethics: Resolving Dilemmas in Nursing Home Life* (New York: Springer 1990), 37–50.

49. See, for example, Caplan, "The Morality of the Mundane." Caplan's essay, and the anthology as a whole, make a significant contribution by examining "everyday" ethical problems in nursing homes. However, the value of the book is diminished somewhat by the restricted attention to "the competent, cognitively intact resident" (39).

50. For a different approach, see Charles W. Lidz, Lynn Fischer, and Robert M. Arnold, *The Erosion of Autonomy in Long-term Care* (New York: Oxford University Press, 1992). The authors develop a conception of autonomy that they apply to the everyday concerns and activities of mildly and moderately demented nursing home residents. See also Bart J. Collopy, "Autonomy in Long Term Care: Some Crucial Distinctions," *The Gerontologist* 28, suppl. (1988): 10–17; George J. Agich, "Reassessing Autonomy in Long-Term Care," *Hastings Center Report* 20, no. 6 (November–December 1990): 12–17; and Bart Collopy, Philip Boyle, and Bruce Jennings, "New Directions in Nursing Home Ethics," *Hastings Center Report* 21, no. 2, (special supplement, March–April 1991). The authors of the latter article recommend a conception of "autonomy within community" for nursing home residents. This conception of autonomy "draws on a notion of moral personhood that is not abstracted from the individual's social context and state of physical and mental capacity" (9).

51. See Feinberg, *Harm to Self,* 24.

52. According to Hofland, relevant psychosocial research supports the conclusion that "lack of control has negative effects on the emotional, physical, and behavioral well-being of nursing home residents." Brian F. Hofland, "Autonomy in Long Term Care: Background Issues and a Programmatic Response," *The Gerontologist* 28, suppl. (1988): 5. One noteworthy study along these lines is Judith Rodin, "Aging and Health: Effects of the Sense of Control," *Science* 233 (September 19, 1986): 1271–76.

53. In Chapter 1, a similar point was made in relation to decision-making capacity. There it was observed that when the treatment preferences of cognitively impaired elderly patients

are not set aside because they correspond to their best interests, there is no need to insist on the fiction that they possess decision-making capacity.

54. Caplan, "The Morality of the Mundane."

55. Diminished autonomy alone does not support paternalistic behavior. If a severely demented person's behavior does not put her at risk of harm, there is no reason for paternalistic intervention.

56. As VanDeVeer rightly observes, even "generally competent persons" ("those who have the capacities to direct their own lives") "may be incompetent to foster their own conception of the good in certain restricted 'areas' of their lives" (*Paternalistic Intervention,* 266). Generally competent persons can process what VanDeVeer refers to as "pockets of incompetence." Conversely, people who are not generally competent can display "pockets of competence."

57. Feinberg warns against a conception of voluntariness (autonomy) that would automatically classify decisions or actions as substantially nonvoluntary (nonautonomous) if they reflect unusual or socially frowned upon character traits (for example, impetuousness or adventurousness). From the perspective of social norms, such actions might seem "unreasonable" or "irrational," but they still can be substantially voluntary or autonomous. In effect, being in character can help to immunize decisions and actions from being characterized as substantially nonvoluntary or nonautonomous. See *Harm to Self,* 106–13. For an examination of the conception of autonomy as "consistency" in the context of long-term care, see Lidz, Fischer, and Arnold, *The Erosion of Autonomy in Long-Term Care.*

58. Ms. F.'s refusal may be contrary to her own good. However, unless she has consistently made contrary choices in similar situations, it cannot be said that her refusal is "out of character."

59. Miles suggests that there is more reason for physicians to refrain from paternalistic interventions than there is for family members to do so. See Miles, "Paternalism, Family Duties, and My Aunt Maude," 2583.

60. See, for example, David C. Thomasma, "Freedom, Dependency, and the Care of the Very Old," *Journal of the American Geriatrics Society* 32, no. 12 (December 1984): 909.

61. This position assumes that Ms. B. as a severely demented 83-year-old is the *same person* as Ms. B. before she became demented. This issue is discussed in Chapter 2.

62. See, for example, W. D. Ross, *The Right and the Good* (Oxford: Clarendon, 1930). Ross identifies several prima facie duties. Insofar as I have a prima facie duty to refrain from doing *X,* it is prima facie wrong for me to do *X.*

63. According to Culver and Gert, paternalism is prima facie wrong because "violating a moral rule" is a defining condition of paternalism (*Philosophy in Medicine,* 130). By contrast, VanDeVeer claims that some instances of paternalism are "innocuous" from a moral perspective. Nevertheless, he observes that "many paternalistic practices happen to involve acts which are presumptively wrong" (*Paternalistic Intervention,* 21). Perry and Applegate hold that since "uninvited interference" is "essential to paternalism," the *"intrinsic act of paternalism* is also possessed of a moral status" ("Medical Paternalism and Patient Self-determination," 353; emphasis added).

64. Soft paternalists might impose a condition that hard paternalists would reject: protecting Mr. J. can justify violating the prima facie obligation not to lie only if he is substantially nonautonomous in a relevant respect.

65. Miles discusses the use of a strategy along the lines of the fourth means. See Miles, "Paternalism, Family Duties, and My Aunt Maude." He suggests that although it may be unacceptable for physicians to pursue this strategy unilaterally, family members may have broader authority to act on behalf of loved ones. The broader authority of the family is in

part attributable to their more extensive knowledge of the elderly person's values and life history.

66. Brock and Wartman identify six possible sources of "irrational choices" by competent patients: "the bias toward the present and near future, the belief that 'it won't happen to me,' the fear of pain or the medical experience, patients' values or wants that make no sense, framing effects, and conflicts between individual and social rationality." Dan W. Brock and Steven A. Wartman, "When Competent Patients Make Irrational Choices," *New England Journal of Medicine* 322, no. 22 (May 31, 1990): 1595. Brock and Wartman distinguish such "irrational" choices, which physicians "may seek to change," from "merely unusual choices that should be respected." However, they argue that "even the irrational choices of a competent patient must be respected if the patient cannot be persuaded to change them" (1595).

67. Considerations of Mr. G.'s good might not justify failing to respect his preferences, but other factors (such as cost and administrative efficiency) might be cited.

68. John J. Regan, "Intervention Through Adult Protective Services Programs," *The Gerontologist* 18, no. 3 (1978): 251. For this "traditional definition" of protective services, Regan cites G. Mathiasen, *Guide to the Development of Protective Services for Older People* (Washington, D.C.: National Council on Aging, 1973).

69. Regan, "Intervention Through Adult Protective Services Programs," 251.

70. Monk and Abramson, "Older People," 144.

71. Regan, "Intervention Through Adult Protective Services Programs," 254.

CHAPTER 5

Research with Elderly Subjects

Physicians, nurses, psychologists, social workers, and other professionals provide services to elderly patients and clients. But members of professions such as these also engage in research with elderly subjects. Physicians use elderly subjects to conduct research on the aging process, diseases and medical conditions, the effects of drugs, and a variety of surgical, therapeutic, diagnostic, and preventive procedures. Psychologists use elderly subjects to conduct research on memory, cognitive abilities, and personality. Social workers and policy planners conduct research with elderly subjects to assess the effectiveness of social programs and service delivery systems. Research in fields such as medicine, psychology, and social work provides a scientific basis for the corresponding professions, and thereby significantly expands the ability of professionals in these fields to provide effective services.

To gain knowledge that will enable professionals to serve *elderly* patients and clients effectively, it is often necessary to conduct research with elderly subjects. For example, to test the safety and effectiveness of drugs in elderly patients, research with elderly subjects is indispensable.[1] Similarly, research with older subjects is needed to evaluate and improve social services for senior citizens.

Research with elderly subjects presents several important ethical issues. Before exploring them, however, it is essential to explain more fully the distinction between research and the service- or practice-related activities of professionals.

Research: A Conceptual Framework

It will be helpful to begin by distinguishing between "practice-oriented" and "research-oriented" activity. This distinction is based on the respective *aims* of each type of activity.[2] A professional's activity is practice-oriented in relation to a *particular* patient or client insofar as the aim is to utilize the professional's expertise for the benefit of the patient or client. On the other hand, a professional's activity is research-oriented insofar as the aim is to generate *generalizable* knowledge.[3]

It may be helpful to apply the distinction between practice- and research-oriented activity to an example. Suppose a psychologist gives an elderly client a questionnaire to fill out. Is this activity practice-oriented or research-oriented? The answer depends on the aim of the activity. Is the aim to gather information that will help treat the client? If so, having the client fill out the questionnaire is a practice-oriented activity. Is the aim to gather information that will promote a better understanding of the cognitive capacities of elderly people? Then giving the questionnaire to the client-subject is research-oriented activity.

Significant differences in observable behavior generally correspond to the difference in aims between practice- and research-oriented activity. If a psychologist has an elderly person fill out a questionnaire in order to gather generalizable knowledge, one would expect this event to be part of a comprehensive pattern of activity, including the distribution of similar questionnaires to a scientifically selected pool of subjects, careful statistical assessment of the data, efforts to publish the results, and so forth. By contrast one would not expect a pattern of activity of this nature if the questionnaire was distributed exclusively to aid the psychologist in treating the particular individual.

Psychologists can, of course, ask clients to fill out questionnaires for more than one purpose. For example, questionnaires might be distributed to gather information that will help psychologists treat the individual clients who fill them out *and* to gather information that will expand generalizable knowledge. Similarly, a physician might seek to enroll a patient in a phase II clinical trial of an experimental drug for Alzheimer's disease in an effort to benefit the patient *and* for the purpose of generating more knowledge about the effectiveness of the drug. In such cases, the professional's activity is partially practice-oriented and partially research-oriented.[4]

Although professionals can engage in activities that are partially practice-oriented and partially research-oriented, there can be a tension between these two activities.[5] The use of experimental drugs illustrates this tension. If a physician is not conducting research on an experimental drug and her use of the drug is exclusively practice-oriented, its use can be tailored to maximize patient benefit. For example, dosages can be adjusted in response to specific patient reactions, its use can be stopped altogether if unwanted side effects are detected, and alternative modes of treatment can be explored. However, modifying medication and therapy in response to the specific reactions of individual patients would thwart the aims of research if a physician were administering an experimental drug as part of a randomized clinical trial (RCT).[6]

A recent study of the relation between depression and mortality among nursing home residents illustrates the tension that can exist between practice-oriented and research-oriented activity.[7] The study showed that over a one-year period there was a significant difference in the mortality rates of residents with depressive disorder and the rates of residents without. Whereas 47.4 percent of residents with depressive disorder died, only 29.8 percent of residents without depression died. It was also reported that nursing home physicians had diagnosed depression in only 14.3 percent of the residents who satisfied the study's criterion for depressive disorder. From the perspective of the practice-oriented aim of benefiting individual residents, a primary goal of diagnosing depression is to communicate the proper diagnosis to residents, family members, and/or nursing home physicians and to facilitate appropriate treatment. By contrast, a research-oriented goal of the study was to determine the effects of depression on nursing home residents.[8] Since effective treatment of depression would thwart a study of its effects, there was considerable tension between these two goals.[9]

The tension between research-oriented and practice-oriented activity is not restricted to the medical profession; it can and does arise in other fields. For example, in a study designed to evaluate the effectiveness of an innovative health and social service program for the frail elderly, participants in the program were compared to a control group that consisted of elderly persons who had "multiple health and psychosocial problems" and who were not served by the program under review.[10] To determine the effectiveness of that program, health assessments of participants in both groups were conducted at regular six-month intervals. Intervention to help subjects who were found to have unmet service needs would have been appropriate from a practice-oriented perspective. However, insofar as such intervention would have compromised the data, it would have thwarted the aims of research.[11]

The term *nonvalidated practices* is commonly used to refer to procedures, drugs, and so forth that are "experimental" in the sense that they have not been proven safe and/or effective.[12] Nonvalidated practices can be utilized in the context of practice-oriented activity.[13] For example, a physician might recommend an experimental drug to a 73-year-old patient with liver cancer because she believes that no other measure offers a reasonable prospect of success. Often, when a nonvalidated practice is utilized in the context of practice-oriented activity, its use is also part of a study designed to evaluate its safety and/or effectiveness.

Nonvalidated practices also can be utilized in the context of activity that is exclusively *research*-oriented. Even when nonvalidated practices are utilized in this context, they can offer the possibility of direct practice-related or "therapeutic" benefits to subjects. Insofar as a procedure or drug has not been validated by scientific research, it is not known beforehand whether its use will be beneficial to subjects. For example, when an RCT is used to compare nonvalidated procedure B to standard procedure A, it is not known whether B is better or worse than A. However, if B is superior to A, then (most) subjects who receive B rather than A will benefit. Similarly, when a double-blind clinical trial is used to compare drug D and placebo P, it is not known whether D is more beneficial or less harmful on balance than P. However, if D is safe and effective, then (most) patient-subjects who receive it will benefit. An appropriate designation for research-oriented activity that offers the possibility that subjects will derive direct practice-related benefits is "research with therapeutic potential."

When nonvalidated practices are utilized in the context of activity that is research-oriented, they may not offer the possibility of direct practice-related or "therapeutic" benefits to subjects. During phase I clinical testing, for example, new drugs that usually have been tested on animals are given to healthy human subjects to determine whether they are safe. Subjects may benefit, for instance, by getting a sense of satisfaction from doing something to help others or by receiving compensation. However, insofar as they are healthy, subjects do not stand to derive any direct practice-related (therapeutic) benefit from the drugs being tested. This type of research is sometimes referred to as "nontherapeutic research." However, the distinction between "nontherapeutic" and "therapeutic" research can generate considerable confusion, and I therefore will not use either term.[14] When subjects do not stand to derive any direct practice-related benefit from research designed to test the safety and/or effectiveness of nonvalidated practices, it will be said that they are taking part in "research without therapeutic potential."

Ethics and Research and Elderly Subjects

General ethical standards for research with human subjects apply to older and younger adults alike.[15] There is no good reason to think that different ethical requirements apply, say, to research with 25–40-year-old subjects and 65–80-year-old subjects. Thus, in contrast to infants and young children, in the case of research with elderly subjects age per se does not appear to call for special ethical standards. Unfortunately, however, one recent study suggests that little attention is paid to ethical standards in published reports of research with elderly subjects.[16]

There are several ethical issues that merit particular attention in relation to research with elderly subjects. An important cluster of such issues is associated with what might well be called the "first principle" of research with human subjects: the principle of informed consent. Although it would be ageist to assume that people lose the capacity to consent when they reach a certain age, some studies suggest that there are changes associated with the aging process that require investigators to exercise particular caution when they seek the informed consent of elderly persons. These reported changes include vision and hearing impairments[17] and diminished memory and comprehension.[18] Accordingly, whereas a recent article on research with older subjects cautions against "ageism or discriminatory stereotyping" and maintains that "using age as a marker for consent issues is not very helpful," it concludes that "when one refers to older people in general and excludes the special concerns of the effects of institutionalization and cognitive impairment, the data suggest that greater attention may need to be paid to the adequacy of the informed consent."[19] In a similar vein, an editorial in the *Journal of the American Geriatrics Society* observed that the "difficult field of informed consent in clinical geriatrics deserves . . . ethical thoroughness. There are factors peculiar to the obtaining of informed consent from geriatric patients."[20] Consequently, although the requirements of informed consent apply to both older and younger adult subjects, it is important to consider the requirements and implications of informed consent specifically in relation to the elderly.

People with severe cognitive impairment lack the capacity to give informed consent, and such cognitive disability is more prevalent among the elderly than among younger adults.[21] Accordingly, a related issue that also merits attention is the recruitment of cognitively impaired elderly persons who are unable to give informed consent. Specifically, it is essential to consider whether surrogate consent for such persons is ethically acceptable, and if so, under what conditions.

Informed Consent

It is probably no exaggeration to refer to informed consent as the "first principle" of research with human subjects.[22] From an ethical perspective, the importance of informed consent is clear. A fundamental goal of the informed consent requirement is to enable prospective subjects to decide for themselves whether to participate, and respect for autonomy requires that they be given an opportunity to do so.[23] Respect for autonomous elderly persons requires that they do not be used as research subjects without their authorization; to seek the informed consent of prospective subjects is to seek their authorization.

Despite the obvious connection between the requirement of informed consent and respect for autonomy, it should not be overlooked that other ethical considerations provide additional support for that requirement. For one thing, although investigators and institutional review boards (IRBs) are obligated to screen proposed research projects for undue risks of harm to subjects, letting prospective subjects decide whether to participate after having had an opportunity to assess expected benefits and harms functions as an additional check against undue risks of harm.[24] In addition, the informed consent requirement may help protect particularly vulnerable classes of the elderly (e.g., noninstitutionalized elderly persons who need assistance with activities of daily living and nursing home residents) and promote a more equitable distribution of the burdens associated with serving as a research subject.

Informed consent is ordinarily analyzed in terms of its constituent elements or components.[25] Five components can be identified: (1) decision-making capacity, (2) disclosure of information, (3) comprehension, (4) voluntariness, and (5) assent.[26] The first four components are prerequisite if the fifth (assent) is to be *informed* consent. According to this analysis, individuals who agree to participate give their informed consent if and only if they are capable of deciding whether or not to participate, they are given adequate information, their comprehension is adequate, and they have voluntarily chosen to participate. Let us now examine each of these four prerequisite components, paying special attention to their implications for research involving elderly subjects.

Decision-Making Capacity

Assent by elderly persons to serve as research subjects satisfies the informed consent requirement only if they have and exercise the capacity to decide whether or not to participate. The concept of decision-making capacity was discussed in Chapter 1. The standard analysis, it will be recalled, lists three requirements: (1) capacity to understand and communicate, (2) capacity to reason and deliberate, and (3) possession of a set of values and goals. The *capacity* to understand is distinct from the *actual understanding* (comprehension) of information disclosed by an investigator. Whereas the capacity to understand is a necessary condition of actual understanding, possession of that capacity does not guarantee that a prospective subject will understand the specific information that an investigator discloses to her on a particular occasion.

Decision-making capacity, it will be recalled, is not an all-or-nothing concept. People who lack the capacity to make some choices may have the capacity to make others. Accordingly, decision-making capacity should be construed as a *task*-related concept. It was observed in Chapter 1 that many commentators also recommend a *risk*-related standard. Several problems associated with the use of a risk-related standard in connection with decisions concerning life-sustaining medical interventions were discussed in Chapter 1, and the arguments presented there need not be repeated here. However, since cognitive impairment is more common among older people, it is important to consider whether low-risk research with elderly subjects warrants the use of a weak standard (one that does not require a capacity to evaluate and weigh expected benefits and harms and to make reasoned choices, and one that therefore can be satisfied by elderly persons with substantial cognitive impairments).

A line of reasoning sometimes used to support a weak standard in relation to health care decision-making does not apply to the kind of research closest to medical practice, namely, post–phase I clinical trails with nonvalidated practices. In the context of health care decisions, it will be recalled, proponents of a risk-related standard sometimes claim that it represents an appropriate balance between respect for patient autonomy and concern for patient well-being. Accordingly, a weak standard of decision-making capacity is said to be appropriate when patients assent to treatment and when any associated risks are minor and are clearly outweighed by expected therapeutic benefits to the patient. Drane, it will be recalled, maintains that *"awareness in the sense of orientation or being conscious of the general situation"* is a sufficient condition of decision-making capacity for "those medical decisions that are not dangerous and objectively are in the patient's best interest."[27] When it is known that risks are low and the expected benefit-to-harm ratio is high, it may be reasonable to conclude that a certain treatment option is in a patient's best interests. However, in the case of clinical trials, it generally is not known that risks are low or that the expected benefit-to-harm ratio of a nonvalidated practice is high. When a procedure or drug is the subject, say, of an RCT, it is not known whether it is safe and effective or whether it is more safe and effective than other alternatives. Consequently, with the possible exception of cases in which elderly patients are seriously ill or dying and no alternative therapy or drug offers a reasonable prospect of success, it generally cannot be concluded in advance that participation in a clinical trial is "not dangerous and [is] in the patient's best interest."[28]

Although the risks and benefits of most clinical trials may not be known beforehand, in other categories of research (such as studies limited to observation and/or interviews), the risks are sometimes reasonably expected to be low. In such cases it might be claimed that a weak standard of decision-making capacity strikes a proper balance between respect for autonomy and a concern for the well-being of elderly prospective subjects. To be sure, when the risks are low, a strong standard of decision-making capacity does not seem to be needed to protect subjects from harm; and a prospective subject's desire to avoid an unacceptably high risk of harm is an obvious reason for refusing to serve as a research subject. But there are other reasons, including an objection *in principle* to scientific research generally, or to specific types of research (for example, research without therapeutic potential in nursing homes, research designed to compare the IQs of members of different racial groups, research designed to compare the mathematical abilities of women and men, or research on birth control measures and reproductive technologies). If a weak standard of decision-making capacity were to be used whenever risks are low, there is a danger that elderly prospective subjects' assent will not reflect firmly held values and convictions that they never repudiated or renounced.

Authorization by elderly subjects indicates that conducting research with them is compatible with respect for autonomy, and an elderly person's authorization therefore provides an important ethical justification for conducting research with her. However, if elderly subjects only satisfy a weak standard of decision-making capacity, it is doubtful that it can be said that they *authorize* their use as research subjects when they assent. Suppose, say, that an investigator carefully explains a research project to nursing home residents. She provides information about its aims and expected benefits, she states that it will require subjects to undergo monthly blood tests for a period of a year, and she carefully explains the minor health risks, discomforts, and inconveniences. If some residents satisfy a weak standard of decision-making capacity, but lack the capacity to make a reasoned choice, then even if they assent, or fail to dissent, it seems odd to say that they *authorized* their participation.

Lack of valid authorization is particularly problematical in relation to research without therapeutic potential. If elderly subjects have not authorized their participation, it can be charged that research without therapeutic potential is unethical because investigators inappropriately use those subjects as means to promote generalizable knowledge and fail to respect them as persons. This charge may be unwarranted if research is limited to observation or assessment of data and there is no intervention with, or manipulation of, subjects; such conditions may be correlated with low risk. However, if significant intervention and/or manipulation occurs and elderly subjects only satisfy a weak standard of decision-making capacity, then even if the risks are low, the charge that subjects were inappropriately used as a means to benefit others cannot be refuted by claiming that they *authorized* their participation.[29] Furthermore, whether or not significant intervention and/or manipulation occurs, when elderly subjects only satisfy a weak standard of decision-making capacity, it is implausible to refute the charge that investigators failed to respect their *privacy* by claiming that the subjects *waived* their privacy claims.[30]

If elderly subjects authorize their participation, and if other relevant ethical requirements are satisfied, then it can be said that subjects share moral responsibility for any burdens and harms which they experience.[31] However, since it is doubtful that the assent of elderly subjects who only satisfy a weak standard of decision-making capacity constitutes valid authorization, it also is doubtful that their assent supports the claim that they share moral responsibility for any burdens and harms which they experience. It is therefore reasonable to conclude that a weak standard of decision-making capacity is generally not appropriate in relation to research with elderly subjects.

Disclosure of Information

The basis for the disclosure of information condition (hereafter to be referred to simply as "the disclosure condition") is straightforward. If elderly prospective subjects are uninformed about the aims, risks, expected benefits, and so forth of a study, their assent surely does not constitute *informed* consent. Except in unusual cases, for example, when subjects for drug trials are themselves knowledgeable physicians, disclosure of relevant information by investigators is a prerequisite of informed consent. But what information is "relevant," and what is the scope of the disclosure condition? At the very least, elderly prospective subjects generally should be informed of known risks and expected benefits.[32] Such knowledge would appear to be a minimum condition of truly informed consent. However, it is not sufficient for investigators to divulge information *known* to them about risks. In addition, they should exercise due care to *identify* risks. Ignorance, if it is a result of negligence, insufficient preliminary investigation, carelessness, and the like, is not an excuse for a failure to communicate information about risks to prospective subjects.

It seems reasonable to claim that investigators have an ethical obligation to make a conscientious effort to uncover unknown potential harms and burdens to subjects. However, it is doubtful that there is a similar obligation with respect to potential benefits to subjects. First, agreeing to serve as a research subject and experiencing unexpected harms and burdens can be worse from the perspective of the individual than not serving as a research subject and missing the corresponding benefits. Second, when there was insufficient disclosure of risks by investigators, subjects can claim to have been inappropriately used as a means to benefit others. However, a similar charge cannot be made when subjects fail to volunteer because there was inadequate disclosure of potential benefits by investigators. Third, whereas it seems plausible to claim that elderly persons have a (negative) right to *refuse* to serve as research subjects, it is doubtful that they have a (positive) right to participate in studies of their choosing. In any event, since expected benefits provide an important inducement to prospective subjects, it is to be expected that investigators will conscientiously identify and disclose potential benefits.

The condition that investigators exercise due care to identify possible harms requires special caution on the part of researchers who plan to utilize elderly subjects. Assessments of risks may presuppose that subjects are young, well-nourished, and healthy, or the data that is used to make such assessments may be based on more or less randomized samples. In either case, it may be necessary to revise these assessments when the use of elderly subjects is contemplated.[33] For one thing, there are physiological differences between older and younger people that can be significant.[34] For example, due to changes associated with aging, there can be significant differences in the way drugs affect younger and older persons.[35] In addition, although it would be ageist to assume that all elderly people are in poor health and take drugs, older people are more likely to have medical problems and to take medication than younger people.[36] One study reports that at a time when people aged sixty-five and older comprised about 11 percent of the population of the United States, they accounted for over 25 percent of drug use.[37] A study of residents of the Philadelphia Geriatric Center found that the "average number of diagnoses per person is 9.6, and the average number of drugs being taken by each person is 9.3."[38] If researchers fail to consider possible differences in the medical circumstances of older and younger prospective subjects, and if they do not tailor their risk assessments to the particular medical circumstances of elderly prospective subjects, there is a danger that they will (unintentionally) disclose unreliable information.

A related consideration pertains to efforts to evaluate the *significance* of risks. Obviously, investigators cannot and need not communicate to prospective subjects all conceivable harms, no matter how unlikely or trivial they might be. Hence, investigators must distinguish between "significant" risks that should be communicated and "insignificant" or "negligible" risks that need not be communicated. From the perspective of the principle of informed consent, the ideal is that the judgments of investigators correspond to the assessments that subjects themselves would make.[39] This ideal may be difficult to realize in practice generally, but there is a special problem in the case of elderly subjects. When dealing with the elderly, investigators should be particularly sensitive to the possibility that risks which seem negligible to younger subjects seem significant to older people. For example, one article warns that since "vision and mobility are inordinately valuable commodities" for aging subjects, "even a *miniscule* [*sic*] risk of vision or mobility impairment may become a material consideration affecting consent and therefore requiring [sic] disclosure to this particular population."[40] Another article observes that "the risk of fasting venipuncture may be minimal, but the potential disruption in the daily routine may create so much anxiety in an older participant that the perceived threat to comfortable living is substantial."[41]

To satisfy the disclosure condition, prospective subjects should have an opportunity to ask questions, and these questions should be answered honestly and forthrightly.[42] If, for the purposes of securing the participation of prospective subjects, investigators withhold requested information or give deceptive answers to questions, they fail to respect the autonomy of prospective subjects and do not respect them as persons. Accordingly, it seems warranted to require truthful, nondeceptive answers to prospective subjects' questions, even if such answers will compromise the usefulness of some individuals as research subjects.[43] The requirement to give prospective subjects an opportunity to ask questions and to answer these questions honestly and forthrightly applies to all human subjects with decision-making capacity, but satisfying it in the case of the elderly can be especially demanding. For example, since elderly subjects may have memory deficits and other cognitive impairments, effective responses to their (repeated) questions may require skill and considerable patience.

In addition to information about potential harms and benefits, several other items have been suggested for inclusion in the disclosure condition. Among these are information about the purpose of the research, research procedures, the selection of subjects, and the identities of the investigators.[44] Respect for autonomy supports many of these additional items. For example, since people might refuse to participate if they knew the objectives or procedures, disclosure of such information expresses respect for the autonomy of prospective subjects.

In some cases, disclosure can compromise research objectives. Some studies of human behavior, for example, may permit only a limited disclosure of objectives and methods, and some studies may be feasible only if investigators deceive subjects.[45] In view of the moral significance of the informed consent condition, investigators should be able to *justify* deception or incomplete disclosure in each case, and IRBs should carefully scrutinize research protocols to determine whether deception or incomplete disclosure is justified. Unfortunately, there is no absolute formula, and there are likely to be cases ("hard cases") about which reasonable people will disagree.

The following conditions and guidelines, however, seem to strike a reasonable balance between respect for prospective research subjects and a concern that valuable research not be unnecessarily thwarted.[46] First, incomplete disclosure or deception is acceptable only if it is not feasible to carry out the proposed research project properly without either. This condition is satisfied, say, when truthful disclosure will distort the data. It is *not* satisfied when incomplete disclosure or deception is required to recruit subjects. Second, incomplete disclosure or deception is acceptable only if it can be reasonably concluded that neither will cause subjects to experience significant and lasting harm. Third, information about expected harms and benefits must be free of deception or incomplete disclosure. Accordingly, if the specific nature of a potential harm is not identified, its probability and seriousness must be disclosed. Fourth, whenever feasible, prospective subjects should be informed that due to the nature of the research project, some details about its aims, methods, and so forth cannot be disclosed in advance. Fifth, whenever appropriate, there should be a "debriefing" session after the study is completed. During this session, the project should be explained in full to subjects, and appropriate measures should be taken to minimize negative reactions.

Special care may be needed to satisfy these general conditions and guidelines when prospective subjects are elderly persons. For example, particular attention may be required to identify special circumstances that can increase an elderly subject's vulnerability to harms, such as depression, loneliness, disorientation, and confusion. Elderly people generally, and especially frail elderly persons and nursing home residents, may have special needs and circumstances that should be considered before as well as after the conclusion of the research. Some of these special needs and circumstances will be discussed more fully in the following section.

Comprehension

No matter how much information is disclosed to elderly prospective subjects, if they do not understand the information, their assent is not informed consent. There are two determinants of comprehension. One has to do with the manner in which investigators present information to prospective subjects. The other relates to the cognitive capacities of prospective research subjects. Among elderly persons who have the capacity to decide whether to participate in a study, there can be a wide variation in relevant cognitive skills and abilities. Consequently, statements and explanations that are intelligible to one elderly person with decision-making capacity may be unintelligible to another.

To satisfy the informed consent requirement, investigators should communicate information to elderly prospective subjects in a manner intelligible to them. Whereas the disclosure condition is satisfied when a sufficient quantity of information is provided, the requirement that the information be understandable to prospective subjects includes an assessment of the quality of the information as communicated. The information as communicated should be clear, coherent, well-organized, audible and/or readable, and so forth. Moreover, since elderly prospective research subjects are unlikely to have the technical training and expertise of investigators, information should be presented in a manner that can be understood by nonprofessionals.

Potential individual differences among prospective subjects should be considered when investigators present information. For example, comprehension may require that investigators tailor their presentation of information to the intelligence, education level, communication ability, and so forth, of prospective subjects. These considerations can have special importance in the case of elderly subjects. A manner of presenting information that is appropriate, say, for younger college students may not be appropriate for certain classes of the elderly. As noted previously, older persons are more likely to have impaired vision and hearing than younger persons, and these diminished capacities can be undetected and undiagnosed or denied. Accordingly, investigators may have to take extra precautions to ensure that older subjects are able to read the consent forms they sign. Similarly, investigators should be sensitive to any hearing difficulties of elderly prospective subjects, and should modify their manner of speaking if needed. In addition, investigators should look out for communication problems that can result from an older person's partial reversion to his or her native language.[47] There may also be important generational differences in attitudes and knowledge that need to be taken into account. For example, in a study of survey research, the following generational difference is noted: "The issue of informed consent is perhaps more important to the current population of elderly than to the next generation of the aged. Many elderly respondents do not understand the implications of their participation or their right to refuse."[48]

Although it would be ageist to assume that elderly subjects generally suffer from memory loss and other mental impairments, as noted above, it appears to be a fact of life that such conditions are more likely to occur as one grows older. In addition, comprehension is in part a function of education level, and elderly adults currently may have lower education and reading levels than younger adults.[49] Accordingly, investigators should exercise special caution to ensure that the information they provide to elderly prospective subjects is presented in a manner that is both understandable and understood. One strategy is to simplify consent forms, but the effectiveness of this measure is unclear. Although at least one study reports that simplifying informed consent materials did not significantly improve comprehension, others report that simplification can have a significant impact on comprehension.[50] Some commentators recommend the use of comprehension tests, but the significance and reliability of such tests is also questionable.[51] A less cumbersome and more effective alternative may be for investigators to ask elderly prospective subjects follow-up questions and, where appropriate, to try to help them acquire a better understanding of pertinent details.

Voluntariness

If the participation of an elderly subject with decision-making capacity is not voluntary, then even if she assents after having been given adequate information that she understands, the informed consent requirement is not satisfied. One obvious way in which participation can be nonvoluntary occurs if subjects who initially agreed to participate, and who subsequently want to withdraw, are not permitted to do so. This situation can be prevented easily by giving subjects an opportunity to withdraw at any time, a standard research norm.[52]

Coercion is another obvious violation of the voluntariness condition.[53] For example, if an elderly person living alone agrees to participate in a research project involving home health care only after being threatened with involuntary commitment, her participation is secured by means of coercion, and her assent is not voluntary. Investigators who secure the participation of subjects by means of coercion fail to respect them as persons and violate the principle of respect for autonomy. Coercion also can increase the likelihood of harm and injury. Coercion is clearly incompatible with informed consent, but there are other types of pressure that can compromise informed consent, such as duress and manipulation.[54]

Although many elderly people are independent and healthy, many others rely on social services, require medical care, and/or reside in nursing homes. Research with elderly persons in these three categories can be valuable as well as efficient and convenient.[55] However, such persons are also particularly vulnerable, and they may be subject to various pressures. Since there is an increased danger that the assent of elderly persons in each of the three categories will not satisfy the voluntariness condition, their recruitment for research warrants particular attention.

Elderly Social Services Recipients

If elderly social services recipients are induced to serve as subjects by threatening to withdraw services or benefits to which they are entitled, their participation is not voluntary. Such blatant coercion is easily avoidable. However, there are more subtle pressures that are also problematical from the perspective of informed consent. Even if there is no stated threat to withdraw services, when elderly social services recipients are asked to participate in research projects, they may believe that their benefits will be cut off or reduced if they refuse. One study reported that among the elderly, those who were home care users were more likely to agree to be interviewed than those who were not home care users.[56] Many factors might help explain this difference. However, it is significant that despite having been informed that university investigators were conducting the study, it was reported that "many home care users thought that the interviewer represented the government, particularly home care."[57] Consequently, the possibility cannot be overlooked that home care users may have feared loss of services if they refused to participate.

Investigators do not intend to threaten elderly prospective subjects who mistakenly assume that their benefits will be cut off if they do not agree to participate. Nevertheless, the pressure that those elderly persons experience is troubling from the perspective of informed consent. Although persons who agree to participate under such conditions are not deliberately manipulated by investigators, the pressure that they experience can compromise the voluntariness of their assent if it induces them to assent when they otherwise would have refused to participate.

One way to reduce the risk that voluntariness will be compromised in this way would be to exclude elderly persons who are social services recipients from the pool of eligible research subjects. However, even if it were limited to research without therapeutic potential, such a broad constraint is unwarranted. Among other things, it would prevent valuable research designed to evaluate and increase the effectiveness of social programs that serve the elderly. Moreover, it is not clear that such an extreme measure is required to safeguard voluntariness adequately.

Alternative means available to investigators include (1) giving prospective subjects oral and written assurances that refusal to participate in a research project will not jeopardize their benefits, and (2) refraining from participating in the process of obtaining informed consent for research studies from their own clients.[58] The risk that assent will not be voluntary might be reduced even more if elderly persons who are clients of an investigator were excluded from the pool of eligible subjects for studies by that investigator. However, this additional safeguard might significantly hamper research by some investigators while offering little additional protection to elderly prospective subjects. Without relevant empirical data, it is unclear whether this additional safeguard is warranted.

If it appears that despite reasonable safeguards, elderly social services recipients believe that a refusal to take part in a study will result in a loss of benefits, it might be advisable to exclude them unless the research at issue has therapeutic potential and/or no significant harms or burdens to subjects are foreseen. Whereas the mere inconvenience of responding to a list of questions does not constitute a significant burden or harm, invasions of privacy, emotional distress, and physical injury do. It may not be easy to determine whether elderly social services recipients believe that a refusal to participate in a research project will result in a reduction in benefits. However, as a first step, investigators can carefully question prospective subjects on the matter. More scrutiny is needed when elderly social services recipients are approached by investigators or their representatives than when they volunteer in response, say, to announcements in newspapers and newsletters, on bulletin boards, and at meetings. There may be no perfect way to determine when to exclude elderly recipients of social services from the pool of eligible research subjects, but the aim should be clear: to avoid taking advantage of people's dependency to secure their participation in burdensome or potentially harmful research that they otherwise would have shunned and that they have a right to refuse.[59]

Elderly Patients

If elderly patients are induced to serve as subjects by threats to lower the quality of medical care, their participation is not voluntary. Although such blatant coercion is easily avoidable, there are less obvious pressures that are also problematical from the perspective of informed consent. Even though investigators may not intend to penalize elderly patients if they do not agree to serve as research subjects, patients may assent because they believe that the quality of their health care will deteriorate if they refuse. Moreover, physician-investigators can command considerable power and authority that can compromise the voluntariness of assent as a result of undue influence. There may be some important generational differences in this regard, and the current generation of elderly patients may be more prone to undue influence than subsequent generations will be.[60] Whether it is because of fear or undue influence, the end result can be that elderly patients who agree to participate in research have not given their (voluntary) informed consent.

Investigators can reduce the risk that voluntariness will be compromised in these ways by (1) giving oral and written assurances that refusal to participate in a study will not influence the quality of health care, and (2) refraining from participating in the process of obtaining informed consent for research from their own patients.[61] However, these precautions may be inadequate. Suppose, say, that an investigator asks an elderly hospital patient to serve as a research subject, and he agrees. The investigator assures the patient that a refusal would in no way affect the quality of his health care. Nevertheless, the patient might assent only because he believes that a refusal will have a negative impact on the quality of his health care. Even when investigators are not physicians or members of a patient's health care team, patients may still believe that a refusal to participate in research will have a negative effect on the quality of their care. Accordingly, a rule similar to one suggested in relation to social services recipients may be warranted in relation to research without therapeutic potential: if it appears that despite reasonable safeguards, elderly patients believe that a refusal to participate in research without therapeutic potential will result in a deterioration in their health care, it may be advisable to exclude them unless no significant harms or burdens are foreseen. A similar rule is not appropriate in relation to research with therapeutic potential because it would deny elderly patients a chance to receive significant health-related benefits.

Physician-investigators could further reduce the risk that assent will fail to be voluntary by excluding their own patients from studies. However, when medical research has therapeutic potential, this measure may be counterproductive. If physicians were to recommend, say, that patients go to other doctors to participate in phase II clinical trials, patients might feel abandoned, or they might be deterred from volunteering by an understandable reluctance to change physicians. Nevertheless, physician-investigators should attempt to identify and eliminate threats to voluntariness that stem from their dual roles as practitioner and researcher. They might, say, recommend a consultation with another physician. This safeguard seems to strike a reasonable compromise between a general rule against conducting research with a physician's own patients, on the one hand, and no measures to protect voluntariness, on the other hand.

Voluntariness can also be compromised if participation in a study provides access to health care that otherwise would be beyond the financial means of elderly subjects. Depending on the circumstances, voluntariness can be compromised, say, by offers to pay transportation costs and to provide medication, physical examinations, follow-up treatment, and home medical care.[62] An elderly patient's assent to serve as a research subject is given under duress and is not voluntary if (1) there is a level of medical care (for example, a "decent minimum") that ought to be accessible to people, regardless of their ability to pay; (2) the patient agrees to serve as a research subject because it will give her access to medical care that is beyond her financial means; and (3) the medical care referred to in (2) is within the scope of the level of care referred to in (1), and is generally accessible to people with financial means.[63]

Elderly Nursing Home Residents

Unfortunately, residents in some nursing homes are subject to abuse and/or neglect, and in such settings there is reason to suspect that coercion and duress will play a significant role in securing residents' participation in research. In such settings, assent by elderly residents who have the capacity to decide whether to serve as a research subject is unlikely to be voluntary.

Investigators can reduce the risk that assent will fail to be voluntary by conducting research without therapeutic potential in a nursing home only if they are confident that its residents are not regularly abused or neglected.[64] There are two reasons for not taking a similar position in relation to research with therapeutic potential. First, there may be less reason to suspect that coercion or duress had a significant impact on assent in relation to research with therapeutic potential.[65] Second, from the perspective of residents' well-being, in view of the potential health-related benefits from research with therapeutic potential, there may be more reason to risk coercion or duress.

Even in nursing homes where residents generally are treated with respect and concern, there are several factors that can compromise the voluntariness of consent. For one thing, despite clear and honest disclaimers to the contrary, residents might believe that their treatment by staff will decline if they refuse to cooperate.[66] Second, residents can be unduly influenced by nursing home staff. This can occur when staff encourage or recommend participation, or even when residents simply believe that staff members approve and agree to participate as a means of pleasing caregivers.[67] Recommending participation to prospective subjects ordinarily does not constitute undue influence. But there are special circumstances that need to be kept in mind in the case of older nursing home residents. One is their dependency, which can foster an overdeferential attitude toward staff. This can be reinforced by a tendency among some older persons to defer to the judgment of physicians and other health care professionals.[68] Consequently, nursing home staff can (unintentionally) exercise undue influence on residents who are asked to participate in research. In addition, residents may experience a variety of pressures from other residents, and such pressures can also compromise the voluntariness of consent.[69]

In view of these considerations, it might seem that investigators should cease conducting research without therapeutic potential in nursing homes. However, it is also necessary to consider the case *for* conducting such studies. One argument is that such research has considerable value.[70] To discontinue such research, it is claimed, would deprive various disciplines of important scientific knowledge, knowledge that can lead to significant improvements in the lives of older and younger people. A second line of argument is that participating in research can be a valuable experience for nursing home residents.[71] It can give them a sense of satisfaction, a sense of meaning and purpose, and a sense that they are making a significant contribution to others. In addition, participation in research can help reduce boredom and loneliness.

Ironically, the second set of reasons points out another problem with research in nursing homes from the perspective of the voluntariness condition. Unfortunately, a certain amount of boredom and loneliness are inescapable facts of life for many residents in nursing homes. But such feelings can also arise because a nursing home fails to provide adequate opportunities for stimulation, interaction with others, decision-making, activity, and so on. If the conditions in a particular nursing home fall below an ethically acceptable standard, a decision to participate in research without therapeutic potential because it will reduce boredom and loneliness is made under duress.[72] Consequently, participation in research without therapeutic potential in such cases would fail to satisfy the voluntariness condition. In such cases a concern for the well-being of residents should prompt measures to improve conditions in the nursing home. Such efforts, not research without therapeutic potential, would reflect genuine respect and concern for nursing home residents.[73]

In view of the potential benefits to subjects and to others, it appears unwarranted to conclude that investigators should cease conducting research without therapeutic potential in nursing homes. However, investigators and IRBs should carefully scrutinize protocols to determine whether the expected benefits are sufficient to warrant conducting the study in an environment with formidable obstacles to voluntary consent. At the very least, unless the expected indirect or nontherapeutic benefits clearly outweigh expected burdens to subjects, it seems reasonable for investigators to avoid conducting research without therapeutic potential in nursing homes when it is feasible to recruit suitable subjects elsewhere. In view of the difficulty in ascertaining and securing compliance with the voluntariness condition in nursing homes and the vulnerability of nursing home residents, considerations of convenience and efficiency alone cannot justify efforts to recruit subjects for research without therapeutic potential in those settings. Finally, unless risks and burdens are negligible, research without therapeutic potential should not be conducted in nursing homes that fail to provide residents with an environment that meets minimal standards of satisfactory care. This appears to be a reasonable measure to reduce the risk of significant harm from assent given under duress, and it might also serve as a stimulus to nursing home reform.

Surrogate Consent

Elderly persons can lack the capacity to decide whether to serve as research subjects. This situation is not unique to the elderly. All people lack that capacity at the beginning of their lives; some people, for example, the profoundly retarded, will never acquire it; and accidents and illness can deprive people of the capacity to make choices at any age. But as people grow older, there is an increasing chance of significant cognitive impairment as a result of multi-infarct dementia, Alzheimer's disease, and other chronic illnesses.[74]

Cognitively impaired elderly persons are prime candidates for research. For one thing, investigators may deem their conditions, or related medical or social problems, worthy of study. In addition, many cognitively impaired elderly persons spend time in hospitals and/or nursing homes, and such institutions are a convenient source of research subjects. Accordingly, it is imperative to consider the ethics of research with elderly persons who are themselves unable to decide whether to serve as subjects.

A possible ethical rule, which I shall refer to as the "no surrogate consent" rule, would allow no exceptions to the requirement of informed consent. According to this rule, it would be permissible to use elderly subjects for a study only if (1) they have the capacity to consent or refuse, and they consent to participate in the study; or (2) they currently lack the capacity to consent or refuse, but they consented to participate in the study in advance while their cognitive capacities were still intact.[75] The second condition would be satisfied, say, if investigators secure the advance consent of patients with early Alzheimer's disease to participate in a study of the disease after they become severely demented. Surrogates would have only a limited supervisory function in relation to research with cognitively impaired elderly persons who consented in advance. Among other things, surrogates might determine whether unanticipated changes in research procedures and/or the prospective subject's physical condition increased the expected harm beyond the scope of that to which the prospective subject consented in advance.[76]

Cognitively impaired elderly persons are exceptionally vulnerable. The no surrogate consent rule appears to prevent utilizing such vulnerable persons as research subjects when doing so would be incompatible with respect for persons. When participation is based on contemporaneous or advance consent, it is implausible to claim that the subject is inappropriately used as a means to benefit others. However, there are several problems with the no surrogate consent rule.

First, it disregards the pre-dementia preferences and wishes of cognitively impaired elderly persons unless they formally consented in advance to take part in a particular study. People whose consent for a particular study is not secured in advance may nevertheless want, or be willing, to participate in certain types of research if and when they become cognitively impaired. Just as people can want, or be willing, to have their bodies used for medical research after they die, so, too, people can want, or be willing, to serve as a research subject after they become cognitively impaired. For example, when their decision-making capacity was still intact, elderly persons with multi-infarct dementia might have been willing to participate in studies of dementia if they were to become cognitively impaired. Even when there was no explicit prior expression of a willingness to serve as a research subject, family members and friends may know a person well enough to conclude reasonably that she would have consented to participate in a study if she had had the capacity to make that decision. Accordingly, the no surrogate consent rule appears to thwart respect for autonomy by substantially limiting the scope of the pre-dementia preferences and wishes of cognitively impaired elderly persons which may be given effect.

Second, although the no surrogate consent rule would protect cognitively impaired elderly persons from harm due to participation in research, it would also significantly restrict their access to possible benefits. For example, it would exclude demented elderly persons from clinical trials of drugs or medical procedures that offer the possibility of substantial direct or therapeutic benefits unless those drugs and procedures were known prior to the onset of dementia. Subjects also can benefit from participation in research without therapeutic potential, and the no surrogate consent rule would also substantially restrict access to such benefits by elderly persons who lack decision-making capacity.

Finally, the no surrogate consent rule may significantly curtail valuable research. For one thing, advance *informed* consent is feasible only in certain types of situations; for example, when a person has a degenerative disease that is known to result in dementia, and when the nature of the proposed study is known in advance. Second, advance consent is not a common phenomenon. To be sure, the situation might change if more investigators were to seek prior consent from elderly persons with degenerative diseases, such as Alzheimer's, which will produce cognitive deterioration. However, at the present time, advance consent is unlikely to legitimize a substantial amount of research with cognitively impaired elderly subjects.

For all these reasons, it seems desirable to reject the no surrogate consent rule and to permit consent by surrogates. But under what conditions is surrogate consent for research an acceptable substitute for informed consent by subjects themselves? One possible condition, the "substituted judgment" condition, is an analog to the substituted judgment standard for surrogate decision-making in relation to health care (see Chapter 2). It states that surrogate consent for research is acceptable if the surrogate concludes that the prospective subject would have consented if she had had the capacity to do so. Under such circumstances, surrogate consent approximates consent by the subject herself and appears to be compatiable with respect for autonomy and respect for persons. It is then implausible to claim that she is inappropriately used as a means to benefit others.

Unfortunately, however, it is doubtful that enough is known about most elderly persons without decision-making capacity to determine whether they would have agreed to participate in a study if they had had the capacity to decide. It is unlikely that many people have given much serious thought to serving as a research subject, much less to whether they would want to serve as a research subject if they were to become moderately to severely demented. Even if people have considered such questions, they may not have given sufficient attention to drawing a line between research projects in which they are willing to participate (based on the nature of the research and the seriousness of risks), and those in which they are not willing to participate. In addition, even when people have thought about such matters, their wishes may not be known by potential surrogates (e.g., family members or friends).[77] Consequently, surrogates' judgments that elderly prospective subjects would have agreed to participate if they had the capacity to decide for themselves are likely to be highly speculative.[78] Accordingly, there is a danger that surrogates will give their consent when elderly persons themselves would not have. This possibility is particularly troublesome in relation to research without therapeutic potential. If surrogates consent to such research when elderly persons themselves would not have, it is arguable that subjects are inappropriately used as means to benefit others and are not respected as persons.

One response is to reject the substituted judgment condition. This is the view expressed by the American College of Physicians (ACP) in their 1989 position paper "Cognitively Impaired Subjects." According to the ACP, the only legitimate function of substituted judgments in relation to research is a negative one; namely, to ascertain whether the prospective subject would have *refused* to participate. Surrogate consent for research is unacceptable when a surrogate concludes that a prospective subject would have refused to participate. Otherwise, the ACP recommends that surrogate decision-making in relation to research be based on the best interests standard.[79]

The ACP Position Paper distinguishes between "nontherapeutic research" (research without therapeutic potential) and "therapeutic research" (research with therapeutic potential), and proposes a different standard for each (844–45). First, surrogates "should not consent to nontherapeutic research that presents more than a minimal risk of harm or discomfort." The recommended standard for "minimal risk" is the same as in Department of Health and Human Services (DHHS) regulations: risks "not greater, considering probability and magnitude, than those ordinarily encountered in daily life or during the performance of routine physical or psychological examinations or tests" (845). Strictly speaking, the ACP-proposed standard for research without therapeutic potential is not a best interests standard. Surrogates are not instructed to consent to research without therapeutic potential only if participation is expected to be in the prospective subject's best interests. Rather, they are instructed to consent only if the risk of harm or discomfort is not greater than minimal. Consequently, the standard proposed by the ACP is weaker than a best interests standard and sets a threshold on acceptable risk of harm or discomfort. Second, surrogates "may consent to therapeutic research if participation is in the incompetent person's best inter-est, that is, if the net additional risk caused by participation is small, and there is scientific evidence that participation is reasonably likely to offer benefits over standard treatment or no treatment, if none exists."[80]

These proposed guidelines may protect cognitively impaired elderly per-sons from unjustified harm as a consequence of serving as a research subject. However, by rejecting the substituted judgment condition, these guidelines may also fail to give sufficient weight to the earlier wishes, preferences, and values of cognitively impaired elderly persons. The following guidelines protect cognitively impaired elderly persons without completely abandoning the substituted judgment condition:

1. For research with therapeutic potential, surrogates should be instructed that they may consent under only two conditions. They may consent if (a) considering the nature of the proposed study, the potential benefits and harms to subjects, and what is known about the cognitively impaired person, they can reasonably conclude that the person would have con-sented, or (b) they do not believe that the cognitively impaired person would have refused to participate, and considering the potential direct or therapeutic benefits and potential harms, they can reasonably conclude that participation is a sensible choice from the perspective of the person's well-being.

2. For research without therapeutic potential, surrogates should be in-structed that they may consent under only two conditions. They may consent if (a) considering the nature of the proposed study, the potential benefits and harms to subjects, and what is known about the cognitively impaired person, they can reasonably conclude that the person would have consented, or (b) they do not believe that the cognitively impaired person would have refused to participate, and they can reasonably con-clude that the risk of harm or discomfort to the person is minimal.

3. Surrogate consent on the basis of 1(a) or 2(a) is acceptable only when surrogates can demonstrate that it is reasonable to conclude that cog-nitively impaired persons would have consented if they had had the capacity to decide.

4. Whenever feasible, if surrogate consent is based on 1(a) or 2(a), the reasoning of surrogates should be scrutinized by persons who do not have a vested interest in recruiting subjects.

5. When surrogate consent is based on 1(a) or 2(a), as the seriousness of possible harm or discomfort to the cognitively impaired person increases, the strength of the evidence supporting the conclusion that the person would have consented should also increase.

6. Surrogate consent for research without therapeutic potential is acceptable only if cognitively impaired subjects themselves cooperate.

7. Whenever feasible, instructions to be given to surrogates and criteria for determining whether surrogate consent for a proposed study is acceptable should be subject to IRB review.

Conditions 1(b) and 2(b) are similar to standards for research with and without therapeutic potential, respectively, in the ACP guidelines. Conditions 1(a) and 2(a) permit surrogate consent, but speculative judgments are discouraged by requiring explicit instructions and criteria to be given to surrogates.[81] The risk of speculative judgments and the associated risk that surrogates will consent when cognitively impaired persons themselves would not have consented are further reduced by the third guideline.

In the case of research with therapeutic potential (such as post–phase I clinical trials), it is not known whether the benefits of participation will outweigh the burdens to patient-subjects, but a choice to participate can nevertheless be reasonable from the perspective of their well-being. To determine whether participation is a reasonable choice from the perspective of a cognitively impaired elderly patient's well-being, it is appropriate to consider such factors as the patient's condition, the potential benefits to the patient, the potential harms to the patient, and available alternatives. When considering potential harms and benefits, it is important to consider whether cognitive impairment will prevent subjects from understanding what is being done with and to them. The burdens of research may be greater when subjects fail to understand its nature than when they possess such understanding. Respect for autonomy requires that insofar as it is feasible, the standard of benefit and harm should be that of elderly patients themselves. When not enough is known about the patient, it is appropriate to adopt a "reasonable person" perspective (see Chapter 2).

There is a stipulation in conditions 1(b) and 2(b) that surrogates should consent only if they do not believe that a cognitively impaired person would have refused to participate. I shall refer to this stipulation as the "refusal proviso." Although the appropriateness of the refusal proviso is clear, its application can be problematical. For one thing, there is a danger that previously voiced objections to life-sustaining medical interventions will be interpreted too broadly. Suppose, say, that Mr. L., who is 73-years-old, decided several years ago after witnessing the death of his wife from cancer that he would not want "heroic means" employed to prolong his life if he were to become terminally ill. He executed a living will and discussed his wishes with members of his family (see Chapter 2 for a discussion of advance directives). Subsequently, Mr. L.'s cognitive status deteriorated, and he moved into a nursing home. If Mr. L. has a type of cancer that is currently incurable, then his previously expressed objection to "heroic means" appears to support a decision to make comfort, and not life-prolongation, the primary treatment goal. But his stated desire to forgo "heroic means" does not warrant the conclusion that it would be contrary to his wishes to enroll him in a clinical trial of an experimental drug that offers a possibility of remission and that was unknown when he executed his living will.

Surrogates should also be wary of collapsing the refusal proviso into a consideration of expected harms and benefits. Although it is generally reasonable to assume that people want to avoid mental and physical harm, it cannot be assumed that wanting to avoid such harm to oneself is the only reason that a person can have for refusing to become a research subject. As observed previously, people might object *in principle* to scientific research generally or to specific types of research. In addition, as one study of nursing home residents suggests, when people refuse to serve as a research subject they might do so in part because they do not want "to be used as guinea pigs."[82] Accordingly, the refusal proviso requires more from surrogates than risk/benefit calculations.

When consent is based on condition 2(b), surrogates might find it helpful to consider whether they would volunteer. An affirmative answer to this question should not be taken as either a necessary or a sufficient condition of acceptable surrogate consent based on 2(b). However, the question may furnish valuable guidance to surrogates, and a negative answer should give rise to serious doubts about the propriety of granting permission to participate in studies without therapeutic potential when the wishes and preferences of cognitively impaired persons are unknown.

The interest investigators have in recruiting subjects may introduce a bias in favor of accepting surrogate consent. The aim of the fourth guideline is to prevent such potential conflicts of interest. To satisfy this guideline in the case, say, of research in nursing homes, nurses or specially designated ombudspersons might review the reasoning of surrogates.

The fifth guideline sets a sliding-scale standard of evidence for determining whether a cognitively impaired elderly person would have consented. For example, for a study with no therapeutic potential, more supporting evidence concerning a cognitively impaired person's willingness to participate seems warranted when subjects are to undergo lumbar punctures than when they are to undergo venipunctures.[83] A sliding-scale standard in this context strikes an appropriate balance between the aim of respecting the prior wishes and preferences of cognitively impaired elderly persons, on the one hand, and the aim of protecting such vulnerable persons, on the other hand.

The sixth guideline prohibits forcing uncooperative cognitively impaired elderly persons to (continue to) participate when research has no therapeutic potential. This guideline stems from two considerations. First, a failure to cooperate may signal that participation is more burdensome than surrogates anticipated. For elderly persons who cannot understand what investigators are doing and why they are doing it, "harmless" interventions can be traumatic or disagreeable. Second, a lack of cooperation indicates a lack of assent, and this in turn suggests that participation is contrary to the person's preferences. It is arguable that even in the case of cognitively impaired elderly persons, it is contrary to respect for persons to disregard such preferences when research has no therapeutic potential.

In view of the vulnerability of cognitively impaired elderly persons, and the risk that they will be improperly used to benefit others, it may be warranted to add the following constraint (C_1): when research has no therapeutic potential, surrogate consent for cognitively impaired elderly persons is acceptable only when it is not feasible to conduct the research with subjects who have the capacity to decide whether to participate. C_1 implies that when there is no therapeutic potential, considerations of convenience or efficiency alone do not justify conducting a study with cognitively impaired elderly subjects if it could be conducted with subjects who are not cognitively impaired.[84] C_1 might also be supported by considerations of fairness: since cognitively impaired elderly persons are vulnerable and relatively disadvantaged, it seems unfair to impose additional burdens on them if those burdens could be borne by less vulnerable and disadvantaged persons.

It is unwarranted to impose a similar constraint on research with therapeutic potential. First, in view of the potential benefits to subjects, their vulnerability and concerns about unfairness seem to be less of an issue. Second, in contrast to research without therapeutic potential, when research has therapeutic potential, it is immune from the charge that subjects are being used exclusively as means for the good of others.

Although the risk of harm or discomfort is minimal, it nevertheless might be charged that cognitively impaired elderly persons are inappropriately used as means for the benefit of others when surrogate consent for studies without therapeutic potential is based on condition 2(b) (that is, surrogates do not believe that a cognitively impaired person would have refused to participate, and they reasonably conclude that the risk of harm or discomfort to the cognitively impaired person is minimal). One response to this charge is to emphasize the potential benefits to subjects even when research has no therapeutic potential. It might be claimed, say, that even when research has no therapeutic potential, if the risk of harm or discomfort is minimal, the benefits to subjects may well outweigh the burdens. However, this response suggests an additional constraint on surrogate consent (C_2): surrogate consent for research without therapeutic potential that is based on condition 2(b) is acceptable only if surrogates can reasonably conclude that subjects will derive (indirect or nontherapeutic) benefits that outweigh any expected burdens.

There is a second possible response to the charge that cognitively impaired elderly persons are inappropriately used as means for the benefit of others when surrogate consent for research without therapeutic potential is based on condition 2(b). It might be claimed that there is an *ethical obligation* to participate in potentially valuable research that requires little, if any, sacrifice. This is a controversial assertion, but it might be defended by citing the principles of beneficence and/or justice.[85] Beneficence can be evoked to support an obligation to participate in research with substantial potential benefits to others, provided there is little, if any, significant sacrifice to subjects. Justice can be cited to support a similar conclusion; it might be argued that insofar as most people benefit from research, those who refuse to serve as research subjects are "free riders" who fail to do their "fair share."

Even if there were an ethical obligation to participate in minimal risk research without therapeutic potential, its import would be limited. For one thing, like an obligation to give to charity, it would be an "imperfect" or open-ended obligation. Even if I have an obligation to give to charity, it is still up to me to decide when, how much, and to which charity I will contribute. Similarly, even if I have an obligation to serve as a research subject, it is still up to me to decide when to volunteer and for which specific studies. Thus, even if it is assumed that there is an obligation to participate in potentially valuable research that requires little, if any, sacrifice, it would not follow that people have an obligation to participate in any particular study. People with decision-making capacity could permissibly decide whether or not to volunteer for any particular study. Since cognitively impaired elderly persons whose participation is based on condition 2(b) did not have the same opportunity to decide whether to volunteer as subjects with decision-making capacity had, the equity of surrogate consent based on that condition might be questioned.

In addition, if surrogate consent on the basis of condition 2(b) is justified by an appeal to an obligation to participate in minimal risk research without therapeutic potential, then it would seem that surrogates should consider whether cognitively impaired elderly persons participated in studies in the past. Suppose Ms. X., a cognitively impaired 78–year-old woman, volunteered for and participated in several studies while she was still cognitively intact. Mr. Y., a cognitively impaired 78-year-old man, has never participated in a research study. All other things being equal, it is more plausible to cite an obligation to participate in minimal risk research without therapeutic potential to justify surrogate consent based on condition 2(b) in the case of Mr. Y. than in the case of Ms. X.

Case Study: Research in a Nursing Home

Since nursing homes provide a convenient and readily available source of research subjects, and since most nursing home residents are elderly persons, it is appropriate to examine a case involving research in such facilities. The following case description is based on a research project and follow-up study conducted with nursing home residents.

Case Description

Two nursing homes, one Protestant and the other Jewish, were selected to conduct a "prospective study of morbidity from the long-term use of urinary catheters."[86] The study compared residents who required long-term use of catheters to those who did not. All subjects were sixty-five or older, and they were not expected to benefit directly from participation (that is, the study lacked therapeutic potential). The following were among the procedures employed: daily measurements of temperature, weekly urine tests, and blood tests and abdominal X-rays at the beginning and end of the study.

The consent of prospective subjects was sought if "the opinion of the investigators, the nursing staff, or both was that the patient was able to understand and respond to normal conversation, comprehend the description of the study, and weigh its risks and benefits" (1125). Surrogate consent was sought for residents who were determined to lack decision-making capacity according to this standard. Surrogates were those persons who, according to nursing home records, were responsible for residents. One surrogate was a resident's lawyer, but all of the others were family members. Of the 41 residents whose consent was sought, 21 agreed to participate. Of the 168 surrogates who were contacted, 90 gave their permission.

More than six months after they were originally contacted by investigators, surrogates were again approached. The purpose of the follow-up study was "to examine the bases on which the proxies made their decisions, to identify characteristics that distinguished proxies who refused consent from those who gave consent, and to determine the reasons for refusal" (1125). Among the follow-up study's more significant findings were the following. First, of the surrogates who said that the person whom they were representing would not consent to participate if he or she had been capable of deciding, 31 percent (seventeen out of fifty-five) gave their permission. Second, of the surrogates who said that they themselves would not agree to participate, 21 percent (six out of twenty-eight) gave their permission.

Case Analysis

The studies summarized in the foregoing case description provide an opportunity for an examination of several important ethical issues. They also serve to highlight some practical issues associated with the guidelines discussed above.

In the original study, the method that was used to determine decision-making capacity was more or less informal and impressionistic: "we relied essentially on the common sense of the investigators and nursing staff in deciding whether the patient could understand, reason, and make an informed decision to participate in the project" (1126). In defense of not formulating more exact criteria of decision-making capacity, the investigators claim that the research placed subjects at "minimal risk." They also refer to "the reasonable suggestion that the level of risk inherent in the study should determine the definition of mental competence used in determining who can give consent: a higher risk would require more stringent criteria for competence" (1127–28).

Citing low risk to defend a less stringent and more or less impressionistic criterion of decision-making capacity might be convincing if the primary function of informed consent were to prevent undue harm to research subjects. However, informed consent has other important functions. One of these is to ensure that people have *authorized* their use as research subjects. The assent of elderly nursing home residents who lack decision-making capacity is not valid authorization; and when there is no valid authorization for research without therapeutic potential, it can be charged that subjects are inappropriately used as a means to benefit others and are not respected as persons. Accordingly, even when potential harms are low, the use of a less stringent and more or less impressionistic criterion of decision-making capacity is not without potential ethical pitfalls, especially in settings like nursing homes, where the mental status of many prospective subjects is likely to be questionable and where there are likely to be "borderline" cases.

Even if potential harms and burdens are not an issue, prospective subjects can refuse to participate in studies for a number of other reasons. For example, someone might refuse to serve as a subject for research of the sort conducted in the original study because of her opposition in principle to research without therapeutic potential in nursing homes. When criteria of decision-making capacity are less stringent and/or more or less impressionistic, such non-risk-related reasons for refusing to serve as a subject might be disregarded, and it is incompatible with respect for autonomy to do so. Suppose, say, that unknown to investigators and nursing home staff, for a period of more than ten years before she moved into the nursing home, a resident had crusaded against conducting research without therapeutic potential in nursing homes. Due to memory loss and an overall decline in her mental status, the woman fails to voice any objection to the proposed research. If the research had been high risk, it would have been concluded that she lacked decision-making capacity. However, since the research is considered minimal risk, she is judged to have the capacity to consent. She assents, and she serves as a research subject. In this case, it is arguable that her use as a research subject is not compatible with respect for autonomy or respect for persons.

Let us return to the claim that the original study involved "minimal risk." It may well be that the study posed no serious health risk to subjects. But what about invasion of privacy, discomfort, anxiety, and other perceived burdens?[87] When answering this question, possible differences between alert younger persons and alert or cognitively impaired older persons should not be neglected. For example, whereas drawing blood and giving urine samples may cause no discomfort to younger subjects, they can be more difficult and unpleasant for elderly subjects, and/or these procedures may be perceived as more burdensome by the elderly. These and other procedures can be even more unpleasant and traumatic if elderly subjects are cognitively impaired and do not understand what is happening to them. If surrogates fail to recognize that "minimal risk" may be compatible with burdens that are not negligible in relation to cognitively impaired elderly subjects, then it is doubtful that their consent is either truly informed or sufficiently respectful of the persons they represent.

The investigators are rightly troubled by their discovery that of the fifty-five surrogates who said that the person they represented would not have consented if he or she had the capacity to decide, seventeen (31 percent) consented anyway. The use of those seventeen subjects appears to be incompatible with respect for autonomy and respect for persons, and the authors suggest a procedure to prevent such occurrences: investigators should explicitly ask surrogates whether they think that the person whom they are representing would consent if he or she had the capacity to decide. If the answer is no, even if a surrogate is inclined to give permission, the person in question should not be enlisted as a research subject. This seems to be a reasonable suggestion. In view of the importance of the ethical values of respect for autonomy and respect for persons, it seems warranted to risk the loss of some research subjects for the sake of those values.

The follow-up study does not examine the implications of the finding that six out of twenty-eight (21 percent) of the surrogates who said that they themselves would not participate nevertheless gave their permission. It is also not indicated whether any of these six surrogates stated that the person whom they were representing would consent if he or she had the capacity to decide. However, it might be advisable to ask explicitly surrogates whether they would participate. Although a negative answer need not automatically disqualify a prospective subject, the question may help surrogates make more cautious and thoughtful decisions.

Neither the consenting surrogates who said that the person whom they represented would not consent, nor the consenting surrogates who said that they themselves would not have consented were asked *why* they nevertheless consented. There are several possible reasons, but one is particularly worrisome.[88] Some surrogates may have consented because they feared negative repercussions, for example, a deterioration in relations with nursing home staff and/or a deterioration in quality of care. Surrogate consent for such reasons would have been given under duress, which is no less ethically troublesome in relation to surrogates than it is in relation to prospective subjects.

Explicitly asking surrogates to make "substituted judgments" and to consider whether they would have volunteered may help to bring surrogate consent more in line with respect for autonomy, respect for persons, and nonmaleficence. However, the studies pose a more fundamental question: Was it warranted to conduct the research with cognitively impaired elderly nursing home residents who could not decide whether to participate? The stated objective of the first protocol was to study morbidity associated with the long-term use of urinary catheters. Since there is an obvious connection between a study of this kind and quality of health care, its potential value is significant. In view of the research objective, there appears to have been no feasible alternative to conducting the study with patients in nursing homes, hospitals, and the like. Elderly subjects may have been needed to ensure that the results hold for older people. But would it have been infeasible, or merely less convenient or efficient, to conduct the research only with subjects who had the capacity to consent or refuse? If it was the latter (for example, limiting the study to cognitively intact subjects would have required conducting the research in other long-term and/or acute care settings), then surrogate consent should not have been sought for elderly cognitively impaired nursing home residents. Problems such as those uncovered by the follow-up study would have been avoided, and the research would have been more in line with respect for autonomy and respect for persons. Even when potential harms and burdens are low, the stakes can be too high ethically to utilize surrogate consent out of considerations of convenience or efficiency.[89]

Notes

1. See Robert E. Vestal, "Clinical Pharmacology," in William R. Hazzard et al., eds., *Principles of Geriatric Medicine and Gerontology,* 2d ed. (New York: McGraw-Hill, 1990), 201–11; Jerry Avorn and Jerry Gurwitz, "Principles of Pharmacology," in Christine K. Cassel et al., eds., *Geriatric Medicine,* 2d ed. (New York: Springer-Verlag, 1990), 66–77; T. Franklin Williams, "Drugs and the Elderly," *Drug Information Journal* 19 (1985): 397–400; and Vijaya L. Melnick, "Special Considerations in Geriatric Research: Ethical and Legal Issues," *Drug Information Journal* 19 (1985): 475–82.

2. The National Commission for the Protection of Human Subjects of Biomedical and

Behavioral Research (U.S. National Commission) drew this distinction between "practice" and "research," and this distinction was subsequently incorporated into federal regulations. See United States National Commission for the Protection of Human Subjects of Biomedical and Behavioral Research, *The Belmont Report* (Washington, D.C.: U.S. Government Printing Office, 1978); and Robert J. Levine, *Ethics and Regulation of Clinical Research*, 2d ed. (New Haven: Yale University Press, 1988), 3.

3. Levine identifies a third category, "practice for the benefit of others" (*Ethics and Regulation of Clinical Research*, 7). Examples include quarantine, psychosurgery to prevent violent behavior, removing organs for transplant, and the use of psychoactive drugs to modify the behavior of "disruptive" patients.

4. The National Commission observed of research and practice that "both often occur together" (*Belmont Report*, 2). However, the National Commission stipulated that the term "practice" applies only to "interventions that are designed *solely* to enhance the well-being of an individual patient or client" (2; emphasis added). Levine accepts a similar restriction (*Ethics and Regulation of Clinical Research*, 3). According to this usage, then, any activity that is partially research-oriented, even if it also is partially practice-oriented, is classifiable as *research* and is governed by the norms of research.

5. See Michael Weintraub, "Ethical Concerns and Guidelines in Research in Geriatric Pharmacology and Therapeutics: Individualization, Not Codification," *Journal of the American Geriatrics Society* 32, no. 1 (January 1984): 44–48; Christine K. Cassel, "Ethical Issues in the Conduct of Research in Long Term Care," *The Gerontologist* 28, suppl. (1988): 90–96; and Robert J. Levine, "Clarifying the Concepts of Research Ethics," *Hastings Center Report* 9, no. 3 (June 1979): 21–26.

6. For a review of ethical issues associated with RCTs, see Levine, *Ethics and Regulation of Clinical Research*, 185–212. See also Charles Fried, *Medical Experimentation: Personal Integrity and Social Policy* (New York: American Elsevier, 1974).

7. Barry W. Rovner et al., "Depression and Mortality in Nursing Homes," *Journal of the American Medical Association* 265, no. 8 (February 27, 1991): 993–96.

8. Rovner et al. state their objective as follows: "To determine the prevalence rates of major depressive disorder and of depressive symptoms and their relationship to mortality in nursing homes" (993).

9. The investigators were criticized for not disclosing the diagnosis of depression to residents, family members, or nursing home physicians, and for continuing the study for a year when the correlation between depression and mortality appeared to have been established much earlier. See Greg A. Sachs, Jill Rhymes, and Christine K. Cassel, "Research Ethics: Depression and Mortality in Nursing Homes," *Journal of the American Medical Association* 266, no. 2 (July 10, 1991): Letters, 215. Two of the investigators (Rovner and German) replied by claiming that although residents and families were offered the option of having the diagnosis of depression disclosed to nursing home physicians, they failed to request it. Rovner and German also claimed that the relationship between depression and mortality was "not one of the primary questions of the study; the data linking the two were not explored until 2 years after the study's completion. Because this association had not previously been demonstrated and we were unaware of it during the study, we did not intervene" (216). If the link between depression and mortality was first explored two years *after* the data had been collected, the wording of the first sentence of the study's abstract is unfortunate: "To determine the prevalence rates of major depressive disorder and of depressive symptoms and their relationship to mortality in nursing homes, research psychiatrists examined 454 consecutive new admissions and followed them up longitudinally for 1 year" ("Depression and Mortality in Nursing Homes," 993). Moreover, even if the link between depression and increased mortality was

unknown, there are sufficient harms and burdens associated with depression (known before the study began) to warrant vigorous diagnostic and treatment efforts. In addition, it is troubling that Rovner and German offer the following explanation of the reluctance of residents and their families to request disclosure of examination results to nursing home physicians: "many patients and families were concerned that information from the examination could adversely affect care in the nursing home" (216). This statement suggests that disclosure might have been requested if patients and families could and did receive reassurance that depressed residents would be offered *better care.*

10. Cathleen L. Yordi et al., "Research and the Frail Elderly: Ethical and Methodological Issues in Controlled Social Experiments," *The Gerontologist* 22, no. 1 (1982): 73.

11. Yordi et al. distinguish between "emergency (life-threatening)" and "nonemergency (life-enhancing)" service needs, and between "expressed" and "unexpressed" needs. They recommend that investigators intervene in the case of expressed and unexpressed emergency needs. Limited intervention is advised for expressed nonemergency needs and discouraged in the case of unexpressed nonemergency needs ("Research and the Frail Elderly," 73–75).

12. Levine holds that this term is the "best designation" for preventive, diagnostic, and therapeutic measures when their safety or efficacy lacks a "suitable validation" (*Ethics and Regulation of Clinical Research,* 4). As Levine observes, the Food and Drug Administration (FDA) uses the term "investigational" to refer to experimental drugs and medical devices (that is, those that the FDA has not approved for marketing). For a discussion of the National Commission's analysis of the concept of nonvalidated practices, see Levine, "Clarifying the Concepts of Research Ethics."

13. In the *Belmont Report,* this type of activity is explicitly distinguished from research: "When a clinician departs in a significant way from standard or accepted practice, the innovation does not, in and of itself, constitute research. The fact that a procedure is 'experimental,' in the sense of new, untested or different, does not automatically place it in the category of research" (3). In an earlier report, the National Commission referred to "therapeutic research," which it defined as research "designed to improve the health condition of the research subject by prophylactic, diagnostic or treatment methods that depart from standard medical practice but hold out a reasonable expectation of success." The National Commission for the Protection of Human Subjects of Biomedical and Behavioral Research, *Research on the Fetus: Report and Recommendations* (Washington, D.C.: U.S. Government Printing Office, 1975), 6. Since research, by definition, is not designed to improve the health condition of individual patient-subjects, it is misleading to speak of "therapeutic *research.*" An activity that appears to fit the commission's characterization of "therapeutic research" is the *practice*-oriented use of nonvalidated practices. Although it is misleading to speak of "therapeutic *research,*" some research-oriented activity can be said to have "therapeutic potential," a point that will be discussed shortly.

14. Problems with the notion of "therapeutic research" were discussed above. In its 1975 report, *Research on the Fetus,* the National Commission defined "nontherapeutic" (medical) research as "research not designed to improve the health condition of the . . . subject" (6). As noted above, in the *Belmont Report,* research is defined as "an activity designed to test a hypothesis, permit conclusions to be drawn, and thereby to develop or contribute to generalizable knowledge" (3). By definition, then, research is not designed to improve the health condition of subjects, and all *research* is "nontherapeutic." However, not all activity that is exclusively research-oriented is without therapeutic potential. Thus, it is useful to distinguish between research *with,* and research *without,* therapeutic potential. The *Belmont Report* does not make use of the distinction between therapeutic and nontherapeutic research. Levine

considers both terms "unacceptable terminology" (*Ethics and Regulation of Clinical Research*, 8).

15. Greg A. Sachs and Christine K. Cassel, "Biomedical Research Involving Older Human Subjects," *Law, Medicine & Health Care* 18, no. 3 (Fall 1990): 234–43. For a general discussion of ethical requirements for research with human subjects, see Levine, *Ethics and Regulation of Clinical Research*.

16. Laura Weiss Lane, Christine K. Cassel, and Woodward Bennett, "Ethical Aspects of Research Involving Elderly Subjects: Are We Doing More than We Say?" *Journal of Clinical Ethics* 1, no. 4 (Winter 1990): 278–85.

17. Janet M. Kaye, Powell Lawton, and Donald Kaye, "Attitudes of Elderly People About Clinical Research on Aging," *The Gerontologist* 30, no. 1 (1990): 100; Anne Wilder Zimmer et al., "Conducting Clinical Research in Geriatric Populations," *Annals of Internal Medicine* 103, no. 2 (August 1985): 281; and Sachs and Cassel, "Biomedical Research Involving Older Human Subjects," 236. For a general discussion of vision and hearing problems in the elderly, see L. F. Rich, "Ophthalmology," and Ernest Mhoon, "Otology," in Cassel et al., eds., *Geriatric Medicine*, 394–419.

18. Harvey A. Taub, Marilyn T. Baker, and Joseph F. Sturr, "Informed Consent for Research: Effects of Readability, Patient Age, and Education," *Journal of the American Geriatrics Society* 34, no. 8 (August 1986): 601–6; Barbara Stanley et al., "The Elderly Patient and Informed Consent," *Journal of the American Medical Association* 252, no. 10 (September 14, 1984): 1302–6; and Harvey A. Taub, "Informed Consent, Memory, and Age," *The Gerontologist* 20, no. 6 (1980): 686–90. Taub, Baker, and Sturr report that "comprehension varies directly with education and inversely with age;" and they conclude that "the difficulty of ensuring informed consent appears to increase with age and may be a critical problem for elderly patients with low education levels" (604). For a general discussion of cognitive function and aging, see Marilyn S. Albert, "Cognition and Aging," in Hazzard et al., eds., *Principles of Geriatric Medicine and Gerontology*, 913–25.

19. Sachs and Cassel, "Biomedical Research Involving Older Human Subjects," 242.

20. Richard M. Ratzan, "Informed Consent in Clinical Geriatrics," *Journal of the American Geriatrics Society* 32, no. 3 (March 1984): 176. See also Zimmer et al., "Conducting Clinical Research in Geriatric Populations."

21. Sachs and Cassel, "Biomedical Research Involving Older Human Subjects," 236. As noted in Chapter 2, according to an Office of Technology Assessment (OTA) report, 5 to 7 percent of persons over 65, and 25 percent of those over 84, suffer from severe dementia. U.S. Congress, Office of Technology Assessment, *Losing a Million Minds: Confronting the Tragedy of Alzheimer's Disease and Other Dementias* (Washington, D.C.: U.S. Government Printing Office, April 1987), 15–16.

22. For a historical analysis of informed consent, see Ruth R. Faden and Tom L. Beauchamp, *A History and Theory of Informed Consent* (New York: Oxford University Press, 1986).

23. According to the *Belmont Report*, "the moral requirement that informed consent be obtained is derived primarily from the principle of respect for persons" (15). Respect for persons is one of the "basic ethical principles" cited in the *Belmont Report*. This principle "incorporates at least two basic ethical convictions: first, that individuals should be treated as autonomous agents, and second, that persons with diminished autonomy are entitled to protection" (4).

24. For a discussion of standards for evaluating expected harms and benefits and the functions of IRBs, see Levine, *Ethics and Regulation of Clinical Research*, chapters 3 and 14, respectively.

25. Beauchamp and Childress observe that the "most common approach to the definition of *informed consent* in the literature on the subject has been to specify the elements of the concept." Tom L. Beauchamp and James F. Childress, *Principles of Biomedical Ethics,* 3d ed. (New York: Oxford University Press, 1989), 78. A noteworthy exception to this approach is offered in Faden and Beauchamp, *A History and Theory of Informed Consent.* Although Faden and Beauchamp admit that "there may be more consensus on this analysis of informed consent into its elements than on any other topic in the literature on informed consent" (275), they nevertheless reject this (standard) approach. Their analysis of informed consent is based on the concept of autonomous action, which in turn is analyzed in terms of three conditions: intentionality, understanding, and lack of control by others (noncontrol). Informed consent is given if a person with substantial understanding and in substantial absence of control by others intentionally authorizes his or her use as a research subject (278).

Although their discussion of informed consent is perceptive and illuminating, Faden and Beauchamp overstate the difference between their analysis and the standard approach. For one thing, two of their conditions, (substantial) understanding and (substantial) lack of control by others, correspond to two "components" of informed consent: comprehension and voluntariness. Second, the difference between the standard approach and Faden and Beauchamp's approach on the issue of disclosure of information is attributable largely to a difference of perspectives: whereas the former adopts the perspective of *investigators* who seek informed consent, Faden and Beauchamp adopt the perspective of *subjects* who give or withhold consent. Since information from investigators is not always needed to satisfy the comprehension condition (for example, when a subject for a drug trial is a knowledgeable physician), Faden and Beauchamp are technically correct in stating that disclosure of information is not a necessary condition of informed consent. However, such cases are unusual, and even when prospective subjects claim to know all relevant information prior to any disclosure, prudence would seem to suggest that investigators verify such claims by carefully questioning prospective subjects on relevant details. Consequently, even if disclosure of information is not a necessary condition of informed consent from the perspective of subjects, from the perspective of investigators who seek the informed consent of prospective subjects, its importance is undeniable. Third, although Faden and Beauchamp do not list decision-making capacity as a separate condition, if subjects lack the capacity to decide whether or not to participate, then their assent is not informed consent. Consequently, it is unnecessary to cite decision-making capacity as a separate condition only if autonomous authorization presupposes a corresponding condition. Fourth, although Faden and Beauchamp may be correct when they observe that accepted norms of informed consent reflect a compromise among respect for autonomy, other ethical principles, policy considerations, and the like, they overstate the difference between the standard view and their analysis on this score. Faden and Beauchamp reject the idea that informed consent requires *fully* autonomous decisions: "To chain informed consent to *fully* or *completely* autonomous decisionmaking . . . strips informed consent of any meaningful place in the practical world, where people's actions are rarely, if ever, fully autonomous" (240). It suffices that decisions to participate are "substantially" autonomous, based on "substantial" understanding and noncontrol. The notion of substantially autonomous decisions is offered as a practical concept, and its criteria are to be fixed "in light of specific goals" (241). But this move opens the door to a wide range of ethical considerations in addition to respect for autonomy. Other ethical principles, and perhaps even policy considerations, would seem to be relevant in drawing the lines between control and understanding that are, and are not, "substantial."

26. Beauchamp and Childress list the elements as disclosure, understanding, voluntariness, competence, and consent (78).

27. James F. Drane, "Competency to Give an Informed Consent: A Model for Making Clinical Assessments," *Journal of the American Medical Association* 252, no. 7 (August 17, 1984): 926.

28. In Chapter 1, it was observed that it may not be desirable always to initiate formal steps to determine whether cognitively impaired elderly patients have the capacity to make health care decisions for themselves and to appoint surrogates for those who lack the requisite capacity. However, this conclusion does not apply to the practice-oriented use of nonvalidated practices. In such cases, the measures at issue are not "standard" medical practice, there are generally significant risks, and there may be preferable options from the patient's perspective. Moreover, experimental measures may be recommended in part to facilitate research, and not only because it is believed that they offer a significant prospect of benefit to patients.

29. The claim that investigators inappropriately use elderly subjects as a means to benefit others and fail to respect them as persons can be defeated by showing that subjects (1) have *authorized* their participation, or (2) have an *ethical obligation* to participate. The second response will be considered below in the section on surrogate consent.

30. For a discussion of privacy in relation to research, see Levine, *Ethics and Regulation of Clinical Research,* chapter 7.

31. It does not follow that they should receive no compensation for significant injuries. For a defense of compensation, see James F. Childress, "Compensating Injured Research Subjects: The Moral Argument," *Hastings Center Report* 6, no. 6 (December 1976): 21–27; and Levine, *Ethics and Regulation of Clinical Research,* chapter 6.

32. Harms, burdens, and the like are negative, undesirable states of affairs, and benefits are positive and desirable states of affairs. To say that risks are associated with research, implies the *possibility* of harms occurring. To say that risks are high (low) implies that the probability of experiencing a harm is high (low), and/or that the harm is serious (minor). Thus, the proper contrast with benefits is harms and not risks. Risk/benefit assessments call for comparisons of probabilities and magnitudes of identifiable harms and benefits. See the *Belmont Report,* 15; and Levine, *Ethics and Regulation of Clinical Research,* 37–38.

33. See Richard M. Ratzan, " 'Being Old Makes You Different': The Ethics of Research with Elderly Subjects," *Hastings Center Report* 10, no. 5 (October 1980): 32–42; Mark E. Williams and Sheldon M. Retchin, "Clinical Geriatric Research: Still in Adolescence," *Journal of the American Geriatrics Society* 32, no. 11 (November 1984): 851–57; and Lawrence E. Klein, "Adverse Drug Reactions in the Elderly," *Drug Information Journal* 19 (1985): 469–73.

34. Julie Ann Bell, Franklin E. May, and Ronald B. Stewart, "Clinical Research in the Elderly: Ethical and Methodological Considerations," *Drug Intelligence and Clinical Pharmacy* 21 (December 1987): 1002–7. Several physiological effects of aging are discussed in Cassel et al., eds., *Geriatric Medicine;* and Hazzard et al., eds., *Principles of Geriatric Medicine and Gerontology.*

35. Vestal, "Clinical Pharmacology"; and Avorn and Gurwitz, "Principles of Pharmacology."

36. Cassel and Brody, "Demography, Epidemiology, and Aging"; and Vestal,"Clinical Pharmacology."

37. Judith K. Jones, "Adverse Drug Reaction: Considerations in Geriatric Drug Research," *Drug Information Journal* 19 (1985): 459. See also Zimmer et al., "Conducting Clinical Research in Geriatric Populations."

38. Cited in Zimmer et al., "Conducting Clinical Research in Geriatric Populations," 282. An example of a 73-year-old woman is given. She had eighteen diagnoses: diabetes mellitus, hypertension, coronary artery disease, cerebral arteriosclerosis, ischemic colitis,

diverticulitis, peptic ulcer, hiatus hernia, hemorrhoids, schizophrenia, organic brain syndrome, depression, paranoid trends, bipolar affective illness, post-cholecystectomy, post-hysterectomy, anemia, and arthritis. She was taking seventeen drugs: NPH Iletin, regular insulin, ibuprofen, hydrochlorothiazide, methyldopa, potassium chloride, Maalox, Darvocet, acetaminophen, thyroxine, cimetidine, Metamucil, Peri-Colace, lithium, fluphenazine, imipramine, methylphenidate.

39. See Faden and Beauchamp, *A History and Theory of Informed Consent*. Levine observes that the "standard that is applied most commonly [in the context of medical practice] is the 'reasonable person' or 'prudent patient' test" (*Ethics and Regulation of Clinical Research*, 104). Since this standard does not require physicians to tailor disclosure to the specific interests and goals of individual patients, it falls considerably short of the ideal. Levine proposes a standard in relation to research that is closer to the ideal: "the minimum amount of information that should be imparted by the investigator to each and every prospective subject should be determined by the reasonable person standard. Then, in the course of the consent negotiations, the investigator should attempt to learn from each prospective subject what *more* he or she would like to know" (105). Veatch also rejects a pure reasonable person standard: "If there is any reason to believe that the particular patient or subject wants more information than the reasonable citizen, then the patient or subject's own standard of certainty must apply. This is sometimes referred to as the 'subjective standard.'" Robert Veatch, *The Patient as Partner: A Theory of Human-Experimentation Ethics* (Bloomington: Indiana University Press, 1987), 52.

40. Sandra Berkowitz, "Informed Consent, Research, and the Elderly," *The Gerontologist* 18, no. 3 (1978): 240. See also Ratzan, "'Being Old Makes You Different,'" 34.

41. Williams and Retchin, "Clinical Geriatric Research," 854. Another study reports the "surprising" finding that venipuncture associated with research was "not threatening" to residents in a teaching nursing home. Pamela B. Hoffman et al., "Obtaining Informed Consent in the Teaching Nursing Home," *Journal of the American Geriatrics Society* 31, no. 9 (September 1983): 567. The authors offer the following explanation: "most subjects in a teaching nursing home experience venipuncture on a regular basis, as part of their compulsive [compulsory?] monitoring by the medical staff." This explanation raises serious questions about voluntary informed consent in such settings.

42. See Levine, *Ethics and Regulation of Clinical Research;* and M. J. Denham, "The Ethics of Research in the Elderly," *Age and Ageing* 13 (1984): 324.

43. See United States National Commission for the Protection of Human Subjects of Biomedical and Behavioral Research (U.S. National Commission), *Report and Recommendations: Institutional Review Boards* (Washington, D.C.: U.S. Government Printing Office, 1978), 27.

44. See the *Belmont Report;* and Levine, *Ethics and Regulation of Clinical Research*.

45. Two well-known examples are Milgram's study of obedience and Zimbardo's mock-prison study. Each is discussed in Faden and Beauchamp, *A History and Theory of Informed Consent* (174–76 and 178–79, respectively).

46. See U.S. National Commission, *Report and Recommendations: Institutional Review Boards;* and Levine, *Ethics and Regulation of Clinical Research*.

47. Berkowitz, "Informed Consent, Research, and the Elderly."

48. Laurel A. Strain and Neena L. Chappell, "Problems and Strategies: Ethical Concerns in Survey Research with the Elderly," *The Gerontologist* 22, no. 6 (1982): 528.

49. Taub, Baker, and Sturr, "Informed Consent for Research;" and Zimmer et al., "Conducting Clinical Research in Geriatric Populations."

50. Taub, Baker, and Sturr report that "the simplification of informed consent materials

by reducing the number of syllables per word and words per sentence, may not, by itself, be sufficient to improve comprehension" ("Informed Consent for Research," 605). The opposite conclusion was reached by Alexander J. Tymchuk, Joseph G. Ouslander, and Nancy Rader, "Informing the Elderly: A Comparison of Four Methods," *Journal of the American Geriatrics Society* 34, no. 11 (November 1986): 818–22. In the latter study, an improvement in comprehension was detected only after subjects (residents of the board and care section of a long-term care facility) with "severe cognitive limitations" were excluded. Thus, the results of the two studies may be compatible. See also Alexander J. Tymchuk, Joseph G. Ouslander, Bita Rahbar, and Jaime Fitten, "Medical Decision-Making Among Elderly People in Long Term Care," *The Gerontologist* 28, suppl. (1988): 59–63. This study compared three methods of presenting information: standard, simplified, and storybook formats. The authors report that comprehension was "significantly better" for the simplified and storybook formats.

51. For a defense of testing, see Harvey A. Taub and Marilyn T. Baker, "A Reevaluation of Informed Consent in the Elderly: A Method for Improving Comprehension Through Direct Testing," *Clinical Research* 32, no. 1 (February 1984): 17–21. See also Taub, Baker, and Sturr, "Informed Consent for Research." Faden and Beauchamp question the effectiveness of testing (*A History and Theory of Informed Consent*, 326–29).

52. See Levine, *Ethics and Regulation of Clinical Research*, 112–17.

53. Although it is generally agreed that coercion is incompatible with informed consent, there is significant disagreement about its analysis. Whereas some writers have proposed an objective test for coercion, others favor a subjective test. Gert offers an objective test. He states that coercion "is the result of a threat of evil which provides an unreasonable incentive," and an incentive is unreasonable "if it would be unreasonable to expect any rational man in that situation not to act on it." Bernard Gert, "Coercion and Freedom," in J. Roland Pennock and John W. Chapman, eds., *Nomos IV: Coercion* (New York: Aldine, 1972), 32 and 34. By contrast, in *A History and Theory of Informed Consent*, Faden and Beauchamp propose a subjective criterion, according to which the test is whether *the person threatened* is unable to resist. Another area of disagreement has to do with whether coercion is an empirical or (partly) normative concept. Insofar as Gert as well as Faden and Beauchamp explicate coercion in terms of threats and the capacity to resist them, they seem to view coercion as an empirical concept. For a defense of a normative explication of the concept, see Alan Wertheimer, *Coercion* (Princeton: Princeton University Press, 1987).

54. In *A History and Theory of Informed Consent*, Faden and Beauchamp offer a three-fold typology of means of influencing others: coercion, manipulation, and persuasion. Coercion is incompatible with informed consent, and persuasion is compatible with informed consent. Some forms of manipulation are, and others are not, compatible with informed consent. Some threats are coercive, and some threats are manipulative. The major difference between threats that are coercive and threats that are manipulative has to do with the extent to which the recipient of the threat is able to resist complying. Coercion is involved if the recipient of the threat "is unable to resist acting to avoid it" (339). If the agent is able to resist but does not, and the threat is difficult to resist, it constitutes manipulation that is incompatible with informed consent. If the threat is not difficult to resist, then even if manipulation is involved, it is compatible with informed consent. Offers can also be manipulative and incompatible with informed consent, provided they are not welcome, and they are difficult to resist. Since a detailed analysis of Faden and Beauchamp's account of coercion and manipulation is beyond the scope of this study, the following brief observations will have to suffice. First, it is not clear how to determine when a threat of harm is so sereve that a particular person is *unable* to resist acting to avoid it. Second, it is not clear how to distinguish cases of coercion from

(mere) manipulation where the person could, but did not, resist acting to avoid the threatened harm. Third, the "irresistibility" test for coercion appears to be too strong. Suppose, for example, that a mugger stops Snyder on the street, points a gun at him, and says, "Your money or your life." Snyder, let us suppose, is something of a daredevil, and therefore is *capable* of risking his life and attempting to resist. However, he hands over his wallet because he decides that it is not worth risking his life for five dollars. According to Faden and Beauchamp, we could not say that Snyder was coerced, but it seems perfectly proper to say just that. Fourth, offers to participate in research may be "welcome" to prospective subjects and nevertheless compromise informed consent. For example, a poor elderly person who cannot continue to live alone without home care might welcome the offer of in-home services in exchange for her participation in a research project. However, if it is unknown to her, but known by the investigator who makes the offer, that she is entitled to free in-home services with no strings attached, then even though she welcomed the offer, it seems plausible to question the validity of her authorization on the grounds that she was subject to undue pressure.

55. As Cassel observes: nursing home residents and other institutionalized populations "are extremely convenient research subjects because so many persons can be seen, examined, tested, evaluated, etc., in a single location." Christine K. Cassel, "Informed Consent for Research in Geriatrics: History and Concepts," *Journal of the American Geriatrics Society* 35, no. 6 (June 1987): 543. See also Cassel, "Ethical Issues in the Conduct of Research in Long Term Care"; and Christine K. Cassel, "Research in Nursing Homes: Ethical Issues," *Journal of the American Geriatrics Society* 33, no. 11 (November 1985): 795–99. Cassel also points out that nursing homes are a convenient source of subjects for research because residents are a "captive audience."

56. Strain and Chappell, "Problems and Strategies."

57. Strain and Chappell, "Problems and Strategies," 527.

58. This constraint also reduces actual and perceived conflicts of interest. For a discussion of a similar constraint in relation to physicians and patients, see Weintraub, "Ethical Concerns and Guidelines in Research in Geriatric Pharmacology and Therapeutics."

59. Insofar as elderly persons who qualify for certain social services and benefits have an unconditional entitlement to them, it cannot be claimed that receiving those services and benefits imposes the special obligation on recipients to participate in research related to social programs from which they benefit.

60. See Cassel, "Research in Nursing Homes."

61. See Weintraub, "Ethical Concerns and Guidelines in Research in Geriatric Pharmacology and Therapeutics."

62. Diana Axelsen and Roy A. Wiggins, "An Application of Moral Guidelines in Human Clinical Trials to a Study of a Benzodiazepine Compound as a Hypnotic Agent among the Elderly," *Clinical Research* 25, no. 1 (January 1977): 1–7.

63. For a similar normative analysis of duress in the context of medical research, see Benjamin Freedman, "A Moral Theory of Consent," *Hastings Center Report* 5, no. 4 (August 1975): 32–39. For a defense of the view that the criteria for duress are in part normative, see Wertheimer, *Coercion.*

64. Cassel suggests that it is preferable to conduct research in long-term care settings in which "relatively good quality of care can be anticipated." Cassel, "Ethical Issues in the Conduct of Research in Long Term Care," 95. This suggestion stems from a concern about quality of care rather than undue pressure, such as coercion and duress.

65. Several studies report that elderly persons are more likely to agree to participate in research if they believe that they will benefit. See Kaye, Lawton, and Kaye, "Attitudes of

Elderly People about Clinical Research on Aging"; Jiska Cohen-Mansfield et al., "Informed Consent for Research in a Nursing Home: Processes and Issues," *The Gerontologist* 28, no. 3 (1988): 355–59; Lewis A. Lipsitz, Frances C. Pluchino, and Susan M. Wright, "Biomedical Research in the Nursing Home: Methodological Issues and Subject Recruitment Results," *Journal of the American Geriatrics Society* 35, no. 7 (July 1987): 629–34; Hoffman et al., "Obtaining Informed Consent in the Teaching Nursing Home"; and Marcia A. Leader and Elizabeth Neuwirth, "Clinical Research and the Noninstitutional Elderly: A Model for Subject Recruitment," *Journal of the American Geriatrics Society* 26, no. 1 (January 1978): 27–31.

66. Sachs and Cassel, "Biomedical Research Involving Older Human Subjects"; Cassel, "Ethical Issues in the Conduct of Research in Long Term Care"; and Hoffman et al., "Obtaining Informed Consent in the Teaching Nursing Home."

67. See Cassel, "Ethical Issues in the Conduct of Research in Long Term Care"; and Hoffman et al., "Obtaining Informed Consent in the Teaching Nursing Home."

68. See Cassel, "Research in Nursing Homes."

69. See Cassel, "Ethical Issues in the Conduct of Research in Long Term Care."

70. Cassel, "Informed Consent for Research in Geriatrics"; Cassel, "Ethical Issues in the Conduct of Research in Long Term Care"; Cassel, "Research in Nursing Homes"; and Lipsitz, Pluchino, and Wright, "Biomedical Research in the Nursing Home."

71. Sachs and Cassel, "Biomedical Research Involving Older Human Subjects"; Cassel, "Ethical Issues in the Conduct of Research in Long Term Care"; Cassel, "Informed Consent for Research in Geriatrics"; and Cassel, "Research in Nursing Homes."

72. Like the earlier claim about access to health care as an inducement, this claim assumes that the criteria for duress are in part normative. For a discussion of ethical standards for nursing homes, see Bart Collopy, Philip Boyle, and Bruce Jennings, "New Directions in Nursing Home Ethics," *Hastings Center Report* 21, no. 2, special supplement (March–April 1991): 1–16.

73. For a similar view with respect to the well-known studies of hepatitis in children at Willowbrook, see Veatch, *The Patient as Partner,* chapter 10. See also Sachs and Cassel, "Biomedical Research Involving Older Human Subjects."

74. Sachs and Cassel, "Biomedical Research Involving Older Human Subjects," 236. See also the OTA report, *Losing a Million Minds;* and Jeffrey L. Cummings and Lissy F. Jarvik, "Dementia," in Cassel et al., eds., *Geriatric Medicine,* 428–48.

75. For a discussion and defense of advance consent for research, see American College of Physicians, "Cognitively Impaired Subjects" (position paper), *Annals of Internal Medicine* 111, no. 10 (November 15, 1989): "Position 1," 844.

76. American College of Physicians, "Cognitively Impaired Subjects," 844. The American College of Physicians (ACP) recommends an "advance directive mechanism analogous to a durable power of attorney for health care presently used in treatment decision making and governed by state laws, which would allow for the designation of a proxy to carry out the intent of the directive" (844).

77. Ideally, surrogates should be people who know the prospective subject and who will act on behalf of his or her interests. Generally, family members and friends are most likely to satisfy this requirement. See Chapter 2 for a more detailed discussion of this issue.

78. ACP, "Cognitively Impaired Subjects," 845. Subsequent page references are to this text. See Chapter 2 for a similar point about potential surrogates' judgments concerning health care preferences.

79. For a different view, see Veatch, *The Patient as Partner.*

80. The ACP position paper calls for the creation of a national review body "to evaluate and make a final determination on research protocols involving incompetent persons that may

not otherwise be allowed under the guidelines set forth here, such as nontherapeutic research which poses more than a minimal risk of harm or discomfort to cognitively impaired subjects'' (846). Cassel proposes a policy that prohibits research with persons who lack decision-making capacity if (1) the study lacks ''direct benefit to the subject'' (therapeutic potential) and ''the risks are greater than minimal,'' or (2) ''the risks are significant, and the subject does not stand to benefit from the studies.'' See Cassel, ''Ethical Issues in the Conduct of Research in Long Term Care,'' 95.

81. For a study that reveals some of the problems that can arise when surrogates are not given such explicit guidelines, see John W. Warren et al., ''Informed Consent by Proxy: An Issue in Research with Elderly Patients,'' *New England Journal of Medicine* 315, no. 18 (October 30, 1986): 1124–28.

82. Cohen-Mansfield et al., ''Informed Consent for Research in a Nursing Home,'' 357.

83. One study of surrogate consent for research reports that nine of eleven surrogates of demented nursing home residents consented to venipunctue but refused lumbar puncture. See Hoffman et al., ''Obtaining Informed Consent in the Teaching Nursing Home.''

84. Veatch divides subjects into two classes: Group I subjects (those who possess decision-making capacity) and Group II subjects (those for whom the capacity to consent is ''problematic''). He proposes the following rule in relation to Group II subjects: ''Generally, since we should not treat people as a means without their consent, we should conduct research on patients in this group only when research on Group I patients is impossible (and I mean impossible, not merely inconvenient)'' (*The Patient as Partner*, 56). Veatch imposes an additional condition: research with Group II subjects is said to be permissible only ''in cases when the class of Group II subjects as a whole could be benefited'' (56). It is doubtful that this additional condition can be justified by appealing to the principle that ''we should not treat people as a means without their consent.'' As an alternative, considerations of justice might be introduced. It might be claimed, say, that since cognitively impaired persons are disadvantaged and vulnerable, it is fair to impose the burdens of research on one member of the class only if other members will benefit. This claim is far from obvious.

85. Veatch cites ''obligations to the common welfare'' (*The Patient as Partner*, 57). The claim that there is an obligation to participate in rsearch with expected social benefits is sometimes used to defend research without therapeutic potential in the case of children. See Richard A. McCormick, ''Proxy Consent in the Experimentation Situation,'' *Perspectives in Biology and Medicine* 18, no. 2 (Autumn 1974): 2–20.

86. John W. Warren et al., ''Informed Consent By Proxy: An Issue in Research with Elderly Patients,'' *New England Journal of Medicine* 315, no. 18 (October 30, 1986): 1124. Subsequent page citations are to this article.

87. One study reports that most nursing home residents who refused to participate in a ''nonrisk'' study did so because they viewed the research as an invasion of privacy. The same study reports that ''residents had reached a point of wanting to be left alone, feeling too tired and worn out to participate in anything.'' Cohen-Mansfield et al., ''Informed Consent for Research in a Nursing Home,'' 357.

88. The investigators cite two possible reasons: ''a perception by the proxy that such a decision [consent] would be in the best interests of the patient or that, given the minimal risk, the patient should participate because of the possible benefit to others'' (1127). They do not consider the possibility that surrogates feared negative repercussions if they refused.

89. I do not mean to question the motives or integrity of Warren and his fellow investigators. Their follow-up study displays a sensitivity to several important ethical concerns, and nothing they say suggests that the choice of subjects was dictated by considerations of convenience or efficiency.

CHAPTER 6

Caring for Frail Elderly Parents: The Obligations of Adult Children

It would be ageist to assume that all elderly people are unhealthy and suffer significant mental and physical disabilities. Even the "oldest-old" (people older than eighty-five) can enjoy good health, and they can retain an ability to function without assistance from others.[1] Nevertheless, as people grow older, there is an increased likelihood of ill health, mental and physical impairment, and diminished functional capacity.[2] Such functional impairments can be more or less serious, including significant loss of memory and cognitive function; impaired mobility; inability to drive, to cook, to do house cleaning, to wash clothes, to dress oneself, to bathe or go to the toilet without assistance, or to manage one's finances. Depending on the extent and seriousness of such impairments, the assistance that elderly people require can range from occasional transportation services to long-term care.

In view of the steadily increasing number of elderly persons who will require assistance, several important questions of public policy need to be addressed. Do impaired elderly persons have an ethical entitlement to certain services; and if so, which services? How should the costs and other burdens of providing assistance to frail elderly persons be distributed? How much public funding should go to assistance for impaired elderly persons versus assistance for needy younger people? Increasing attention has been given to such public policy questions.[3] As important as such policy questions are, however, attention should also be given to difficult *personal* choices about the care of impaired elderly family members.

Several studies challenge the "myth of abandonment"; that is, the belief that family members today are less willing to care for impaired elderly persons than they were in the past.[4] One estimate is that families supply 80 percent of the long-term care that is given to partially disabled elderly persons.[5] It appears that many adult children bear considerable burdens to assist frail elderly parents, and a disposition to do so may be a characteristic of a virtuous son or daughter. However even if (some) adult children are willing to make substantial sacrifices for aging parents, it still is important to ask whether adult children have an ethical *obligation* to assist frail elderly parents when such sacrifices are required.

Beneficence and Dependence

One possible basis of an obligation to assist frail elderly parents is a general duty to help others. However, even if such a general obligation of beneficence is recognized, its boundaries are in part a function of the amount of sacrifice or risk involved.[6] Elderly parents who are mentally and/or physically impaired may need assistance that would require considerable sacrifices on the part of adult children. Caring for a frail elderly parent in one's home can be extremely disruptive, stressful, and demanding of time and energy. Significant changes in life-style may be required, leaving little or no time for leisure activities. Moreover, considerable time and energy also can be spent caring for institutionalized elderly parents.[7] Finally, in view of the cost of nursing and personal care in and outside of institutions, paying for such services can require considerable sacrifices on the part of adult children. It is doubtful that a general duty of beneficence requires people to make such substantial sacrifices.

One response is to claim that parents and children alike have *special obligations* that can require substantial sacrifices. Adult children, it might be claimed, have special "filial obligations" that require sacrifices for parents beyond the demands of a general duty of beneficence. However, Callahan pursues another strategy.[8] Without appealing directly to special filial obligations, he attempts to show that adult children have an ethical obligation to make substantial sacrifices to care for their frail elderly parents. Callahan's argument is based on the alleged *dependence* of frail elderly parents on their adult children. He refers to "the neediness and the vulnerability of those elderly who require (or at least desperately want) family care," and he compares the "special dependence" of young children on their parents to the dependence of frail elderly parents on their adult children.[9]

The claim that impaired elderly parents are dependent on their adult children is ambiguous and can be understood in either of two ways. First, it is unlikely that anyone else is willing to make the sacrifices that are required to meet the needs of impaired elderly persons. Second, the specific needs of frail elderly parents can best be met by their children. To begin with the first interpretation of dependence, it is unfortunately true that many functionally impaired elderly people, especially those who have no spouse or whose spouse is also impaired, have no one else to whom they can turn for assistance except their adult children. If their children fail to help, no one else may be willing to do so, and considerable suffering and loss of savings and other assets can result. However, the mere fact that others are unwilling to make substantial sacrifices for impaired elderly persons does not suffice to obligate adult children to do so. To be sure, the thought that their parents will not receive the assistance that they so desperately need may motivate caring children to make substantial sacrifices for their parents. But it is one thing to say that others' unwillingness to help can *motivate* children to come to the aid of their aging parents, and quite another thing to say that others' unwillingness to help *obligates* children to assist frail elderly parents in the absence of special (filial) obligations.

If there is no general duty requiring individuals to make substantial sacrifices for others in need, then when people are unwilling to make substantial sacrifices for frail elderly persons whom they do not know, they are not shirking their duty. But it would be implausible to hold that the unwillingness of one category of persons (strangers) to do something that they have no duty to do obligates another category of persons (adult children) to do the same thing. Consider the following situation. Max and nine other people are standing in front of a burning house. The fire department has been called, but has not arrived. Screams can be heard, and neighbors state that two young children are trapped inside. A rescue effort would be extremely risky, and the other nine people are unwilling to go inside the house. So it is up to Max. If he does not try to save the children, they are certain to die. It does not follow, however, that Max has an obligation to attempt a rescue. If the risk of injury is so high that none of the nine is obligated to attempt a rescue, then even though the children are certain to die if Max fails to act, the fact that the others are unwilling to enter the house does not obligate Max to do so.

On the other hand, if the risk is minimal, then the obligation to attempt a rescue does not fall exclusively on Max. If, after the others refuse, Max also fails to enter the house, it would be wrong to place the blame on him, and him alone. Max would not bear any more moral culpability than any of the other nine people. If, after the other nine people refuse, Max also refuses to attempt a low-risk rescue, then *everyone* would be in the situation he was in when he made his decision: believing that if he or she fails to act, the children are certain to die. If the unwillingness of others to rescue the children does not obligate Max to do so, it is hard to see why the mere fact that others are unwilling to assist impaired elderly persons would obligate the latter's children to do so. To be sure, if Max were the children's father, it might be thought that he would be obligated to take greater risks than strangers. At this point, however, the point is simply, special obligations aside, the mere fact that others are unwilling to make sacrifices that are supererogatory (beyond the call of duty) from the perspective of a general duty of beneficence cannot obligate adult children to make such sacrifices for impaired elderly parents.

Let us now consider the view that the specific needs of impaired elderly parents can best be met by their children. Callahan advances the following claim: "Someone other than the child could, of course, provide care. But an important aspect of the vulnerability of ill or disabled elderly *family* members is that they may want, and surely sometimes need, the kind of intimate, familial care that only someone close to them, an integral part of their life and history, can provide. Caretakers are not utterly interchangeable."[10] As Callahan acknowledges, it is implausible to claim that services for frail elderly persons can be provided effectively only by their children. If children are unable or unwilling to provide transportation, to perform household chores, to offer personal or nursing care, or if impaired elderly persons have no children to perform such services, others can get the job done. The point, then, cannot be that no one except children can take frail elderly persons shopping, cook and clean for them, bathe and dress them, administer medication, supervise their activities, and so forth. Rather, the claim seems to be that although such functions can be performed by others, they will take on special meaning to elderly persons when they are performed by children instead of strangers. For example, although a stranger and a child both can help someone get clean, the process of getting help with bathing will be less alienating and easier to accept if the assistance is provided by a child. The general point, then, is that when such services are performed by paid workers, they are impersonal and they lack the meaning that is present when they are performed by a friend or loved one.

There are a number of problems with this claim. First, for the claim to have any plausibility, it has to be assumed that there is an ongoing, close relationship between parent and child. If the emotional ties between parents and their adult children are weak or nonexistent, then it might make little difference whether services are provided by a child or by someone who is paid to do so.[11] Second, even if there are strong affectional bonds between elderly parents and their adult children, the relationship can become quite strained in the process of caring for frail parents. Children can become resentful, and their resentment and anger can get in the way of affection and intimacy, and even effective care. In addition, although some elderly people may welcome the assistance of their children when they lose their capacity to care for themselves, others may be reluctant to allow their children to assume substantial burdens on their behalf.[12] The guilt that can result from feeling that one is a burden on children can lead to friction and hostility, and it can have a serious impact on the quality of the relationship. In such circumstances, enlisting the services of paid professionals can help protect the parent-child relationship. Third, in cases of severe mental impairment (such as dementia due to stroke or Alzheimer's desease), circumstances that can place the heaviest demands on caregivers, elderly persons may no longer recognize or respond to children and other relatives. At best, then, interpersonal and emotional advantages can be expected when children rather than paid professionals provide services in *some,* but not all, cases.

Moreover, even if it is true that services provided by paid professionals are more impersonal than care provided by children, it is not clear why there cannot be a division of labor between the provision of services, on the one hand, and personal relationships and the provision of emotional support, on the other hand. Surely, adult children can maintain a warm and supportive relationship with their impaired parents without dressing and bathing them, doing household chores, and so forth. If adult children demonstrate their care and concern in other ways, it is unclear why it should matter so much whether they are the ones who provide the services that their frail parents need.

More important, even if it is true that the benefits to frail elderly parents are substantially greater when services are provided by their own children, it still does not follow that children have an ethical obligation to provide those services. Although there may be a general duty of beneficence that requires people to help others, as it is ordinarily construed, people are not required to disregard their own interests completely. People may appropriately consider, among other things, the degree of sacrifice that is required from them as well as the amount of expected benefit to others.[13] With respect to the latter, in relation to frail elderly parents it is not a matter of life or death, or competent care versus incompetent care. Rather, the claimed benefit is "personal" as opposed to "impersonal" care. A general duty of beneficence would not require substantial sacrifices, especially not for a benefit of this order, and caring for frail parents can require considerable sacrifices. Consequently, in the absence of a *special obligation* to make sacrifices for parents that one is not obligated to make for others generally, the alleged *dependence* of frail elderly parents on their adult children fails to generate an obligation to provide services to one's frail elderly parents.

Filial Obligations

A general obligation of beneficence does not require sacrifices of the magnitude typically associated with helping seriously impaired elderly people. From the perspective of a general duty to help others, such sacrifices ordinarily are above and beyond the call of duty. However, it is commonly thought that there are *special obligations,* "filial obligations," that require *more* of children. Accordingly, it is important to inquire into the nature of such obligations and to ask whether they provide the basis for a special duty to care for impaired elderly parents. Three accounts of filial obligations will be examined: (1) traditionalism, (2) the view that friendship and love between parents and children generate special obligations, and (3) the view that parental sacrifices generate special obligations.[14]

Traditionalism

Moral life, it is sometimes claimed, is distorted if we think of the people with whom we interact as nothing more than abstract and interchangeable "agents," and if we think of ethics as a set of general and impartial principles that should regulate our interactions with such agents.[15] People occupy various roles that define and are defined by social practices and institutions, and the corresponding social conventions provide the basis for various rights and obligations. "Parent" and "child" are social roles, and the conventional expectations associated with these roles in a particular society give rise to specific rights and obligations. According to the traditionalist account, then, conventional expectations and the corresponding social practices provide the basis for specific filial obligations. If there is a conventional expectation in a certain society, say, that adult children care for their frail elderly parents, then even though the demands may far surpass general duties of beneficence, adult children have the corresponding obligations. In effect, then, the task of identifying the obligations of adult children toward their aging parents is more the responsibility of sociologists and anthropologists than of moral philosophers.

Insofar as it is commonly acknowledged that husbands, wives, parents, children, friends, and so forth have specific duties of beneficence that require more of them than of strangers, there appears to be a grain of plausibility in the traditionalist position. Nevertheless, there are several problems with its account of filial obligations. For one thing, although there may be more or less homogeneous societies with clear and unambiguous social conventions concerning the duties of adult children, it is doubtful that the United States is such a society. Although most Americans might agree that adult children have an obligation to do more for elderly parents than is required from other people generally, there is unlikely to be substantial agreement concerning the scope and strength of the special obligations of adult children. As one proponent of the traditionalist view admits, filial obligations are "essentially underdetermined."[16] Consequently, theoretical questions aside, the traditionalist approach cannot provide much practical guidance for determining the extent to which adult children in the United States today are ethically responsible for the care of frail elderly parents.

A second problem with the traditionalist analysis is its implicit dismissal of the question, Is there an ethical justification for expecting adult children to care for frail elderly parents? In effect, the traditionalist replaces this question with the following question: "Are there conventional expectations in a particular society that adult children care for frail elderly parents?" There is an important difference between the two questions, a difference obscured by the traditionalist analysis. This point is illustrated by the following example. In a certain society, let us suppose, there is a social expectation that frail elderly people will be cared for by their daughters or daughters-in-law. It seems reasonable to ask whether there is an ethical justification for assigning the care of the frail elderly to their daughters or daughters-in-law, and to classify the practice as a "mere social convention" if there is none.

The traditionalist account undermines efforts to distinguish between practices that are mere conventions and practices that have an ethical basis. On the traditionalist account, if frail elderly persons are cared for by their daughters or daughters-in-law in a particular society, that practice is construed as a "basic fact" that resists further ethical analysis. But it is important to determine whether social expectations governing the care of the frail elderly do or do not have an ethical justification. It is one thing to conclude after careful analysis that particular social expectations have the status of basic facts because they cannot be ethically justified, and quite another thing to assume in advance that all such expectations have the status of basic, unanalyzable facts.

An additional problem with the traditionalist analysis is its implication for the evaluation of social practices. As a consideration of human history suggests, social roles can be oppressive, and too much can be demanded of people. However, the opposite can also occur: too little can be required of people in contributing to the well-being of others. Accordingly, it seems imperative to evaluate social practices and conventions from an ethical perspective.[17] For example, if wives are expected to care for the aging parents of their husbands in a particular society, it is reasonable to ask whether this practice places an undue burden on daughters-in-law. And if there is a well-established practice of adult children abandoning frail elderly parents in another society, it is reasonable to ask whether adult children are doing too little. Such important questions appear to be precluded by the traditionalist view that social conventions are "basic facts" and are not subject to systematic ethical analysis.[18]

The traditionalist account also tends to disregard an ethically significant asymmetry between the roles of parent and child: Whereas the role of parent is often a *voluntary* role (that is, voluntarily assumed), the role of child is *not* a voluntary role. Insofar as people knowingly and voluntarily assume the role of parent, burdens and responsibilities associated with the corresponding conventional norms are less problematical from an ethical perspective than burdens and responsibilities conventionally associated with the role of child, a role that is not assumed voluntarily.

Friendship and Love

It is sometimes claimed that the parent-child relationship is one of friendship, and that friendship gives rise to special obligations. An analysis along these lines is offered by English, who claims generally that "what children ought to do for their parents (and parents for children) depends upon . . . the extent to which there is an ongoing friendship between them."[19] Specifically, with respect to the obligations of adult children, English claims that the "duties of grown children are those of *friends* and result from love between them and their parents."[20] According to English, whatever duties grown children have toward their parents are duties of friendship, and if adult children and their parents are not friends, the former have no obligation toward the latter beyond their "general duty to help those in need."[21]

One rather obvious problem with this analysis is its characterization of the relationship between children and their parents as one of "friendship." In view of the limited emotional and intellectual development of infants and young children, it is unlikely that they can have or be friends. As children grow older and develop emotionally and intellectually, it is still doubtful that their relationship to parents is one of friendship. The child's struggle for independence against a background of parental supervision, discipline, and authority is hardly the stuff out of which friendships are made. Indeed, from the perspective of the emotional and intellectual development of children, it is questionable whether parents should always aim to be their children's "friends."

More important, it is doubtful that the relationship between *adult* children and their parents generally satisfies the criteria of friendship.[22] To be sure, sometimes adult children share common interests with parents, discuss important matters with them, seek advice from and offer advice to them, enjoy their company, and so forth. In such circumstances, it may be warranted to say that parents and children are friends, and they may well think of themselves as friends. However, it can also occur that adult children and parents share few common interests, rarely discuss personal matters, tend to get on each other's nerves, and so forth. In such circumstances, there may still be a perceived "special relationship" between adult children and their parents, but it is implausible to characterize it as "friendship." Memories, both general (for example, the sense that one's parents were there when needed and that they provided care, comfort, and support) and specific (for example, memories pertaining to special moments), can tie adult children to parents who are not currently (and never were) friends, and the emotional pull of these memories can be as strong as the ties of friendship. An extreme example is offered by the case of elderly parents who suffer from Alzheimer's disease or other forms of dementia. Although severe mental deterioration can more or less rule out meaningful communication with such elderly parents, adult children can nonetheless feel a strong emotional bond to them. Thus, the ''special'' quality of the relationship between adult children and their parents may have little to do with the existence of friendship, and may be based more on (memories of) the past than on the present.

Since it is doubtful that adult children and their parents are generally friends, the friendship analysis fails to provide a sufficiently broad characterization of the ''special'' nature of the relationship between adult children and their parents. Love appears to offer a broader and more promising approach than friendship. Even when adult children and their parents are not friends, they often feel connected by ties of love, and there is likely to be a correlation between feelings of love and feelings of obligation. Whether or not they are friends, adult children who feel connected to their frail elderly parents by ties of love are likely to believe that they have an obligation to help care for them; and adult children who do not love their frail elderly parents are unlikely to be friends with them and are less likely to believe that they have a special obligation to care for frail elderly parents. Such *beliefs* neither prove the love account of filial obligations, nor do they disprove the friendship account of filial obligations. However, they do suggest that the love account is more intuitively plausible than the friendship account. Accordingly, let us consider the claim that *love* generates special obligations on the part of adult children.

This claim is ambiguous. It could mean either that love is *one* possible source, among others, of filial obligations; or it could mean that love is the *exclusive* source of filial obligations.[23] On the second interpretation, the claim is questionable. In the case of the obligations of parents toward their young children, it is clearly unwarranted to state that parents who do not love their children have no obligations toward them. On the contrary, it is precisely when the bonds of love prove somewhat weak that it becomes increasingly important to remind parents of their *obligations*. Similarly, it might be claimed that when adult children do not love their parents, it is particularly important to remind them of their *obligations* toward their parents. Thus, although ties of love may provide one basis for filial obligations, other possible bases have to be considered before it can be concluded that adult children who do not love their frail elderly parents have no special obligation to help them.

Although love may provide a basis for special filial obligations, it does not follow that people have an ethical obligation to do everything that they are willing to do for loved ones. Parents have donated kidneys for their ailing children, and adult children have put their own lives on hold to care for impaired parents. Indeed, members of the so-called "sandwich" generation may simultaneously be making sacrifices for aging parents *and* young children. However, it is one thing to observe that people are willing to make substantial sacrifices for loved ones, and quite another thing to say that there is an ethical obligation to do so. To be sure, the willingness to make sacrifices for loved ones may be associated with a belief that one ought to do so, and this belief may well be associated with a normative standard. But not all normative standards are ethical standards. The normative standard in the case of beliefs about what people should do for loved ones is likely to be associated in part with a conception of love, an ideal that presents a picture of what love ought to be, how people who love each other should interact, and so forth. In addition to this general normative standard concerning loved ones, there are likely to be specific norms associated with specific categories of loved ones (norms defining a loving or good parent, spouse, child, and so forth). Although a failure to conform to such ideal standards can give rise to substantial feelings of inadequacy, disappointment, and guilt, such a failure need not constitute an ethical wrong. Indeed, it is to be expected that the demands of such ideal standards will often exceed the demands of ethical duty. It is to be expected, for example, that being a loving son requires considerably more than being a son who fulfills his ethical obligations toward his parents. Consequently, it is unwarranted to assume that all "demands of love" are also *ethical* demands.

Moreover, ethical considerations aside, it is doubtful that there is an unambiguous and clearly defined set of standards concerning what people should do for loved ones. For example, whereas most people would quickly dismiss the suggestion that they have an obligation based on the general duty of beneficence to donate a kidney to a stranger, most parents could not easily decide whether they ought to make such a sacrifice for a child *out of love*. Similarly, although most people would unhesitatingly reject the suggestion that they have an obligation based on the general duty of beneficence to disrupt their lives to care for severely impaired elderly people whom they do not know, it is unlikely that many adult children can easily decide whether *love* requires such a sacrifice for parents. It is doubtful that people's conceptions of love are clearly defined enough to permit a definitive and unambiguous resolution of such practical issues. It is much more likely that when people are confronted with such difficult personal choices, they will be confused and torn. Moreover, even though there is likely to be some agreement among people in the same (more or less homogeneous) culture, love is a highly personal notion and significant variations in people's conceptions of love and its requirements are to be anticipated.

Parental Sacrifices

It is sometimes thought that a duty to make substantial sacrifices for frail elderly parents is included within the scope of special filial obligations based on considerations of justice. On this view, past parental sacrifices generate filial obligations. The reasoning for this account of filial obligations can be summarized as follows. Parents provide care and support for their children while they are young. Providing proper care and support, even when children are generally healthy and parents are not poor, normally requires considerable sacrifices on the part of parents. By bearing significant burdens for the sake of the welfare and proper development of children, parents give special consideration to the interests of their children and often put the interests of children above their own. In view of the special consideration that parents gave their children when the latter were young and dependent, justice requires that grown children give special consideration to their parents when the parents become old and dependent. According to this account, then, parental sacrifices generate filial obligations that require adult children to do (much) more for their parents than is required by a general duty of beneficence.

The parental sacrifice account of filial obligations appears to provide a theoretical basis for a special obligation to assist impaired elderly parents, and it probably reflects the thoughts and feelings of many adult children who have aging parents. I trust I am not alone in feeling that I owe my parents something for all they did for me. Moreover, it is probably common for feelings of obligation toward elderly parents to be strongest among children who think that their parents made significant sacrifices for them. Conversely, it is probably common for feelings of obligation toward elderly parents to be weakest among children who believe that their parents were overselfish. At the extreme, adults who were abandoned, neglected, or abused by their parents are not likely to feel any obligation to care for impaired elderly parents. These feelings appear to reflect the view that we are indebted to our parents for their sacrifices, and that our obligations toward them are in part a function of what they have done for us.

Objections

Despite its apparent intuitive appeal, however, considerable skepticism has been expressed concerning the claim that parental sacrifices generate substantial filial obligations. It is therefore necessary to consider the principal objections to the parental sacrifice account: (1) an objection based on the claim that parental sacrifices are generally unrequested, (2) an objection based on the claim that many parental sacrifices are motivated by love, (3) an objection derived from the claim that parents have a duty to make substantial sacrifices on behalf of their children, and (4) an objection to the effect that the language of ''owing'' is out of place in the parent-child relationship.[24]

PARENTAL SACRIFICES ARE GENERALLY UNREQUESTED

One objection to the parental sacrifice analysis of filial obligations is based on the claim that most parental sacrifices are unrequested. It is assumed that adult children owe nothing to parents for sacrifices that were not requested, and it is concluded that most parental sacrifices fail to generate any filial obligations.[25]

It seems correct to claim that most parental sacrifices are unrequested. Obviously, children did not request to be born, and infants and very young children cannot make requests. Moreover, even when children are older, parental sacrifices on their behalf are generally not made in response to specific requests. For example, saving for a child's college education is generally not prompted by a direct request from the child. Apparently, then, most parental sacrifices were not made in response to explicit requests. But does it follow that parental sacrifices do not generate any special filial obligations?

To explore this question, let us consider the case of twin sisters, Mindy and Sarah. Their parents, let us suppose, made substantial sacrifices for several years so that both sisters could get expensive violin lessons from prominent teachers. The choice to have Mindy and Sarah take violin lessons was made by their parents when the sisters were two years old. At the time, neither sister expressed an interest in violin lessons. Indeed, Mindy and Sarah were not even asked whether they wanted lessons. Whereas Mindy never explicitly asked her parents to continue the lessons, she enjoyed them immensely. She practiced diligently, and became a child prodigy. She is now fifteen and wants to pursue a career as a concert violinist. She realizes that without her parents' sacrifices, she would not have had the opportunity to realize this wish. For her part, Sarah always resented being forced to take violin lessons. She communicated her feelings to her parents, but they continued to insist that she take lessons. Her parents defended their action by observing: ''One day you will thank us for forcing you to take lessons, Sarah.''

Suppose Mindy and Sarah were to claim that since they never requested violin lessons, they owe their parents nothing for the sacrifices that were required to provide those lessons. Sarah does appear to have plausible grounds for claiming that she owes her parents nothing, but not because she never requested the lessons. Rather, the decisive considerations are that Sarah repeatedly and sincerely stated that she did not want lessons, that she continues to resent her parents for forcing her to take lessons, and that expensive violin lessons were not essential to her welfare or proper development. To turn to Mindy, she cannot plausibly support her claim that she owes her parents nothing by pointing out that she never requested lessons. Since she wanted and valued lessons, it would be disingenuous if she were to assert, "Since I never asked for lessons, I don't owe my parents anything for providing them." Moreover, if Sarah were to one day appreciate the fact that her parents forced her to take violin lessons, it would be disingenuous if she were to claim that she owes her parents nothing because she did not ask for those lessons. Thus, if people (concurrently or retrospectively) value goods or services (for example, violin lessons, food, shelter, education, and proper care) provided by their parents, the mere fact that they did not request those benefits when they were young does not suffice to show that they owe nothing to their parents. Since most people do acknowledge the value of having received food, shelter, education, and proper care, it would be implausible for them to claim that they owe their parents nothing for providing those benefits because they never asked for them when they were young. Moreover, if the provision of certain goods and services is known (or reasonably believed) to be essential for the health, well-being, and proper development of children, then whether or not adult children acknowledge their value, it is implausible for them to claim that they do not owe their parents anything for providing those goods and services because they never requested them.

MANY PARENTAL SACRIFICES ARE MOTIVATED BY LOVE

A second objection to the parental sacrifice analysis of filial obligations is based on the claim that many parental sacrifices are motivated by love. It is assumed that adult children owe nothing to parents for sacrifices that were motivated by love, and it is concluded that many, if not all, parental sacrifices fail to generate any filial obligations.[26]

Only an extreme cynic would challenge the claim that many parental sacrifices are motivated by love. However, it remains to ask whether it is possible to defeat the claim that parental sacrifices generate special filial obligations by simply pointing out that the sacrifices at issue were motivated by love. The following example suggests a negative answer to this question. A ten-year-old says to his father, "Dad, please drive me to the soccer game." The boy's father is an avid baseball fan and is watching the World Series on television. Nevertheless, he decides that his son is more important than the World Series. With the observation, "I wouldn't do this for anyone else," the father agrees to drive his son to the soccer game. A few weeks later, the father asks his son to take out the garbage. When the son refuses, the father reminds him of the time that he gave up watching the World Series to drive the son to a soccer game. The son responds as follows: "When you agreed to drive me to the game you obviously did it out of love. Consequently, I don't owe you anything.'' The son's response, in addition to being impudent, does not suffice to refute the claim that he owes it to his father to take out the garbage.

A similar conclusion is supported by the example of Mindy and Sarah, the sisters whose parents made substantial sacifices to provide violin lessons. Suppose Mindy, the sister who valued the lessons, claims that she owes her parents nothing for giving her violin lessons. It would be implausble for her to support this claim by pointing out that her parents were motivated by their love for her. Both examples suggest the same general point: claims to the effect that parental sacrifices generate obligations on the part of children cannot be defeated by pointing out that those sacrifices were motivated by love.

PARENTAL SACRIFICES AND PARENTAL DUTIES

Another common objection to the parental sacrifice account of filial obligations is based on the claim that parents have a *duty* to make sacrifices for their children. It is said that since parents have a duty to provide for the care, development, education, and so forth, of their children, adults owe nothing to their parents for having provided the requisite goods and services.[27] On this view, then, adult children owe nothing to parents for having discharged their parental responsibilities because parents were *only doing their duty*. Parental sacrifices that went beyond the call of duty may generate special filial obligations, but most of the sacrifices that are ordinarily associated with caring for and raising children are said to be within the scope of parental duties and therefore do not generate special obligations.[28]

One problem with this strategy is that it is not clear how many of the sacrifices that parents make for their children fall within the boundaries of "parental duties." What, exactly, are parents obligated to do for their children? It seems reasonable to state that parents are obligated to provide some minimal level of nutrition, care, protection, support, supervision, education, and so forth. But where are the boundaries of the corresponding "minimal levels" to be drawn? When parents spend time and money to provide children with foods that go beyond basic nutritional needs, are they merely doing their duty, or are they being generous? Does the duty to provide clothing for one's children require anything more than the provision of "functional" clothing; that is, relatively inexpensive and plain clothing that will give children adequate protection from the elements? Do parents have an obligation to take an active role in the education of their children by participating in the school PTA, reading to children, taking them to museums, cultural events, and the like? Or are these activities above and beyond the call of parental duty? Do parents have an obligation to save for college education so that their children do not have to attend a less desirable college and work while going to school? Or do such sacrifices indicate a level of concern and generosity that goes beyond the requirements of duty? At the very least, these questions suggest that it is not always obvious where to draw the line between parental sacrifices that fall within the scope of duty and parental sacrifices that go beyond the requirements of duty. Consequently, when it is said that children owe parents nothing for sacrifices that the latter had a duty to make, the force of the statement is not clear. Depending on where the line is drawn between the requirements of duty and supererogatory sacrifices or generosity, it may turn out that the statement fails to present a significant challenge to the view that parental sacrifices generate substantial filial obligations.

Furthermore, even if, as seems unlikely, most of the sacrifices that parents make to provide their children with nutrition, care, protection, support, supervision, education, and so forth are required by duty, it would still be implausible to claim that children owe their parents nothing because they were only doing their duty. For one thing, it is doubtful that people are never owed anything for doing their duty. *Imperfect* duties of beneficence constitute an apparent counterexample. Consider the alleged duty to give to charity. This claimed duty is "imperfect" insofar as it fails to establish corresponding rights or entitlements on the part of charitable organizations or needy individuals. That is, charitable organizations or needy individuals cannot cite an imperfect duty to give to charity as a basis for a corresponding right or entitlement to specific sums of money from individual persons. If there is an imperfect duty of beneficence to give to charity, then I may have a duty to give *some* money to *some* charitable organization(s) at *some* time or other, but it is more or less up to me to decide how much, which one(s), and when. Now, suppose I acknowledge a duty to give to charity, and I decide to discharge that duty by donating $250 to a local food bank. It is implausible to claim that since I was only doing what (I thought) I was obligated to do, the food bank and any individuals who were helped by my contribution owe me nothing. At the very least, it would seem, I am owed *gratitude,* a duty that will be examined below.

It is arguable that in certain circumstances, people can also be owed gratitude for discharging duties of beneficence that are not imperfect duties.[29] It is arguable, for instance, that even if someone is entitled to my assistance, there are circumstances in which the person whom I help can incur a duty of gratitude toward me. However, it is not necessary to pursue this point now. Even if people are never owed anything for discharging *general* duties (for example, general duties of beneficence, nonmaleficence, and justice), the duties of parents are not general duties. Rather, they are special, role-related duties that require parents to bear burdens and make sacrifices that go (far) beyond a general duty of beneficence. Once people have assumed the role of parent, they have these special role-related duties, but it is doubtful that people have a duty to *assume* that role. Considering people exclusively as occupants of the role of parent, it may be unobjectionable to say that people who care for their children are "doing their duty." But insofar as people are under no obligation to assume that social role, it is misleading to say that people are *"only* doing their duty" when they fulfill their responsibilities as parents. Since my parents did not have a duty to have me and to become my parents, for example, it is misleading to say that they were *"only* doing their duty" when they fulfilled their parental responsibilities. Consequently, it is unwarranted to say that I owe my parents nothing for the burdens they bore and the sacrifices they made on my behalf because they were "only doing their duty."[30]

The situation of people who have assumed the role of parents can be compared to that of people who have made promises. Once the promise has been made, it can be said that when people honor their promises they are "doing their duty." But insofar as they had no duty to make a particular promise, it is misleading to say that they are *"only* doing their duty." Suppose, say, that upon graduating, Ms. P., a former student of mine, promises to endow a chair in ethics in the philosophy department if and when she makes a million dollars. Ten years after graduating, she has made a million dollars, and true to her word, she arranges to have an endowed chair in ethics established. Even if it is assumed that Ms. P. had an obligation to keep her promise, it would be misleading to say that she was *"only* doing her duty" ("merely keeping her promise"). Accordingly, members of the philosophy department could not plausibly claim: "We owe Ms. P. nothing for endowing a chair in ethics because she was only doing her duty."

When it is said that nothing is owed to a benefactor because she was "only doing her duty," the implication might be that the person's only *motivation* or *reason* for acting was to fulfill an obligation. Accordingly, it might be said that insofar as parents' sacrifices for children were motivated by a desire to do their duty (or by their sense of obligation), parents were only doing their duty and are owed nothing for such sacrifices. However, it is generally not plausible to claim that people are owed nothing for "only doing their duty" in this sense. Suppose, say, I discover that Ms. P. endowed a chair in ethics only because she felt obligated to keep the promise she made ten years earlier. This information would not justify a failure to show her any gratitude. If it is implausible to hold generally that people are owed nothing for benefiting others out of a sense of duty, it is unclear why there should be an exception for parents and parental sacrifices.[31] In any event many parental sacrifices—even those required by duty—are motivated by feelings of love and affection and a desire to promote the happiness and well-being of children. Thus, it is misleading to hold that parents generally are "only doing their duty'' if this claim implies that parental sacrifices are ordinarily made exclusively out of a sense of duty.

THE LANGUAGE OF ''OWING'' IS INAPPROPRIATE

There is an additional objection to the parental sacrifice account of filial obligations that merits consideration. According to that account, filial obligations are duties that are *owed* to parents for past sacrifices. However, it is sometimes said that since the parent-child relationship is characterized by love and friendship, the language of ''owing,'' and the related notions of ''debts'' and ''indebtedness'' are out of place in the context of that relationship.[32]

To be sure, insofar as the language of ''owing'' is associated with the practice of systematically keeping track of debts owed by and to others, that language does appear to be out of place between friends. It is inappropriate for friends to keep a balance sheet of debits and credits to make sure, say, that one friend's dinner invitations, favors, acts of kindness, presents, sacrifices, and so forth are matched by the other's. Moreover, one need not accept the view that parents and children are friends to agree that there is something very unsavory about the idea of parents and children treating each other as creditors and debtors and constantly keeping a balance sheet to ascertain what one owes the other. People who love each other and care for each other would not be prone to keep track systematically of what they owe each other. Indeed if a parent and a child, a married couple, or two people who claimed to be friends always keep track of what each owes the other, observers could justifiably conclude that genuine friendship and/or love is absent.

If one could not consistently accept the parental sacrifice account of filial obligations without also holding that it is proper for parents and children to constantly treat each other as creditors and debtors, that account would be unacceptable. However, to speak of duties owed by adult children to parents for past sacrifices does not imply that parents and children should treat each and every sacrifice as a credit or debit, nor does it imply that they should keep a running balance sheet to make sure that each ''sacrifice debit'' is offset by a corresponding ''sacrifice credit.'' To be sure, if one party to the relationship constantly gives, and the other constantly receives without giving anything, there is reason to suspect that the relationship is exploitative. But justice does not require strict equality between friends or between parents and children.

To talk of duties owed to parents for past sacrifices also does not imply that when adult children help impaired parents they are and/or should be motivated by a (reluctant) desire to pay back a debt rather than by feelings of love and affection. It might be helpful to consider a similar point about parental duties. To assert, say, that parents have a duty to care for sick children does not imply that when parents care for their sick children, they are and/or should be motivated by a (reluctant) desire to do their duty. The assertion that parents have a duty to care for sick children implies nothing about the motivation of parents. It is desirable for parents to care for sick children out of love, but it is nevertheless important to identify the requirements of duty. Similarly, it is desirable for adult children to help their parents out of love and affection, but it is nevertheless important to know what, if anything, adult children owe parents for past sacrifices. Thus, talk of duties owed by adult children to elderly parents neither implies begrudging assistance in order to pay back a debt, nor does it rule out wholehearted assistance out of love and affection.

There is another reason that is sometimes given for rejecting the language of "owing," and the related notions of "debts" and "indebtedness." It is argued that if it is true to say that adult children "owe" their parents something for past sacrifices, then there should be a simple and specifiable relationship between what parents did for their children and what adult children owe their parents. In addition, it ought to be possible to specify when adult children have discharged the "debt" that they are said to owe their parents. But neither condition appears to be satisfied.[33] Suppose, for example, that it is claimed that a son owes something to his parents for the sacrifices that were required to send him to a private high school. It is fairly clear that he does *not* owe his parents an equivalent number of years in a nursing home, an equivalent amount of money for their care, or even an equivalent amount of sacrifice. But what *does* he owe his parents, and when will he have discharged his debt to them? There does not appear to be a determinate formula for answering such questions. Consequently, it is claimed, it cannot be held that adult children *owe* parents something for their past sacrifices. In order to assess this line of reasoning, it is necessary to consider a distinction between "duties of indebtedness" and "duties of gratitude."

Duties of Indebtedness and Duties of Gratitude

The distinction between the two categories of duty can be explained as follows.[34]

Duties of indebtedness.   A duty of indebtedness implies a *debt,* and it requires repayment of the debt. The obligation to pay back a loan is a paradigm duty of indebtedness. If Martha lends $500 to Sam interest-free, then he has incurred a debt of $500, and he has a duty to pay back that amount. People can be indebted to others for goods and services, as well as money. But even if money is not involved, it is appropriate to say that Sam owes something to Martha as the repayment of a debt only if the following features of the loan paradigm obtain. First, what Sam owes Martha is roughly equivalent to something that Martha gave to, or did for, Sam (say, she gave him $500 or a bushel of apples, or she cared for his cat for two weeks). Second, it is possible to specify more or less precisely what Sam owes Martha (say, $500, a bushel of apples or the equivalent, caring for Martha's cat for two weeks or a task requiring equal time and/or effort). Third, it is possible to determine when Sam has discharged his debt to Martha (when he repays the $500, when he gives Martha a bushel of apples or the equivalent, or when he cares for Martha's cat for two weeks or performs a task requiring equal time and/or effort).

Duties of gratitude. Gratitude can be expressed in a variety of ways, and gratitude does not require even rough equivalence.[35] In contrast to duties of indebtedness, there are no determinate criteria for specifying the content of duties of gratitude or for determining when such duties have been discharged.[36] If, say, Sam owes a duty of gratitude to Martha because she cared for his cat for two weeks while he was on vacation, he can express his gratitude in a variety of ways. Although it would be unwarranted for Martha to claim that Sam has a duty to repay her by caring for her cat for two weeks, there are no clear criteria for determining whether Sam has shown sufficient gratitude. Would it be sufficient gratitude, say, to bring Martha an inexpensive souvenir, an expensive souvenir, or to help her change a flat tire?

Having distinguished between duties of indebtedness and duties of gratitude, it is now possible to consider the claim that adult children cannot be said to "owe" their parents anything for past sacrifices because (1) there is no simple and specifiable relationship between what parents did for their children and what adult children owe their parents; and (2) it is not possible to specify when alleged "debts" have been "discharged." Let us call this the "indeterminacy claim." In effect, the indeterminacy claim supports the conclusion that duties generated by past parental sacrifices cannot be duties of indebtedness. But the indeterminacy claim fails to support the conclusion that past parental sacrifices do not generate duties of gratitude. Let us assume that parental sacrifices generate duties of gratitude rather than duties of indebtedness. Then even if the indeterminacy claim is accepted (that is, even if it is agreed that there are no determinate criteria for either specifying the content of obligations generated by parental sacrifices or determining when those obligations are discharged), it does not follow that talk of duties owed to parents for past sacrifices is inappropriate.[37]

There is another important difference between duties of indebtedness and duties of gratitude. Although A does not incur a duty of *indebtedness* to repay X to B if A neither requested nor voluntarily accepted X from B, A can incur a duty of *gratitude* to B under those circumstances.[38] Recall the example of Mindy and Sarah, the twin sisters whose parents made substantial sacrifices to provide expensive violin lessons with prominent teachers. If Mindy, the sister who came to appreciate the lessons, had agreed to repay her parents for the cost of lessons at a later date, then she would have incurred a duty of indebtedness to repay her parents. However, she did not enter into such an agreement with her parents. She did not ask her parents to give her lessons, and when she was very young, she even lacked the capacity to accept those lessons voluntarily. Accordingly, Mindy might plausibly deny that she has a duty of indebtedness to pay back her parents. However, in view of her attitude toward the lessons, it is doubtful that she can plausibly claim that she owes her parents no gratitude because she did not request or voluntarily accept the lessons. Accordingly, although it may be correct to assert that parental sacrifices that were neither requested nor voluntarily accepted cannot generate duties of indebtedness, it is not correct to claim that such sacrifices cannot generate duties of gratitude.

It appears, then, that the distinction between duties of gratitude and duties of indebtedness eliminates the need to choose between the horns of the following dilemma: either (1) accept the implausible view that the duties generated by parental sacrifices are similar to the duty to pay back a loan, or (2) reject the common belief that adult children owe their parents *something* for their past sacrifices. If the filial obligations generated by parental sacrifices are thought of as duties of gratitude rather than duties of indebtedness, one can consistently both acknowledge that it is misleading to talk of a duty to pay back debts that are owed to parents for past sacrifices, and deny that adult children owe their parents *nothing* for past sacrifices.[39]

Gratitude and the Care of Impaired Elderly Parents

If it is claimed that parental sacrifices generate duties of gratitude, there is no reason in principle to reject the claim that those sacrifices generate special filial obligations.

Since there are countless ways in which adult children can demonstrate gratitude to frail elderly parents, it may not be warranted to assume that the only appropriate way of showing gratitude to them is to help provide needed assistance. However, given the pressing needs of some impaired elderly parents, it may be inappropriate to express gratitude in other ways (such as by verbal expressions of gratitude or by giving them expensive gifts).[40] Generally, A's (current) needs and interests constitute a relevant factor in determining what B owes A out of gratitude.[41] Feinberg illustrates this point in the following manner: "My benefactor once freely offered me his services when I needed them. There was, on that occasion, nothing for me to do in return but express my deepest gratitude to him. . . . But now circumstances have arisen in which he needs help, and I am in a position to help him. Surely, I *owe* him my services now, and he would be entitled to resent my failure to come through."[42]

Even when it is clear that some form of assistance is the most appropriate means of expressing gratitude to frail elderly parents, it does not follow that adult children have a gratitude-based obligation to make the specific and often substantial sacrifices that can be required. The sacrifices that adult children are obligated to make for parents out of gratitude are in part a function of how much gratitude is owed to parents, but there is no determinate standard for specifying how much gratitude grown children owe parents. To be sure, if parents abandoned a child at birth, we can confidently say that as an adult, the child owes her natural parents no gratitude. We can also say that the amount of gratitude that is owed to parents depends on factors such as the following: how much children benefited from what parents did for them, how much parents sacrificed for children, and the extent to which parents were not motivated by self-interest.[43] Based on factors such as these, we can make rough qualitative judgments, such as the following: "Mr. Brown owes his father very little gratitude." "Mr. Brown owes his mother considerable gratitude." "Ms. Spencer owes her mother a great deal of gratitude." But it is not possible to assign any precise value to the amount of gratitude owed, for example: "Ms. Spencer owes her mother X units of gratitude." Without a reliable (quantitative or qualitative) measure of how much gratitude an adult child owes a parent, it is uncertain whether there is a "match" between gratitude owed and the specific demands of assisting a frail elderly parent. Consequently, it is generally not possible to establish that a particular person has a gratitude-based obligation to assume the specific burdens of providing care for an impaired parent.[44]

The same conclusion is supported by the fact that there is also no determinate standard for measuring how much gratitude adult children show parents. To be sure, it is safe to say that no gratitude is expressed if adult children abandon their impaired elderly parents. It might also be thought that if one means of caring for frail elderly parents is more burdensome than another, more gratitude is displayed by caring for parents in the more burdensome manner. However, it is important to bear in mind that depending on factors such as the adult child's attitude, the amount of time spent with a parent, the quality of care that the parent receives, and the parent's preferences, more gratitude can actually be shown by caring for parents in a less burdensome manner. In any event, even when more or less impressionistic qualitative judgments can be made (for example, caring for an impaired parent at home is normally very burdensome and generally expresses a great deal of gratitude), it is not possible to assign any precise value to the amount of gratitude expressed by a particular mode of assistance (for example: an average of X units of gratitude is expressed for each week that a parent lives with his or her son or daughter).

In addition, the more or less impressionistic qualitative judgments that can be made about amounts of gratitude owed and expressed are unlikely to be of much assistance in choosing between alternative means of assisting frail elderly parents. A typical decision that confronts people who have impaired older parents is whether to care for them at home or to provide for their care in a nursing home. Both means of providing assistance for impaired parents can involve considerable sacrifices. For instance, whereas caring for a parent at home can involve considerable time, nursing home care is very expensive, and there is no obvious standard for comparing the "value" of sacrifices of time and money. Moreover, well-to-do grown children who have a frail elderly parent living with them can literally "buy time" by hiring others to help out, and children can spend considerable time visiting and caring for parents in nursing homes. Thus, either means of assisting impaired elderly parents can demand considerable time and/or money. Accordingly, even if it is possible, say, to decide whether a son owes his father only "a little" gratitude or "a great deal" of gratitude, it is doubtful that there is any general correlation between this difference in amounts of gratitude owed and the difference in gratitude expressed by providing assistance to a parent at home and at a nursing home. On the one hand, if the son owes his father "very little" gratitude, then it is doubtful that he has a gratitude-based obligation to make the kinds of sacrifices associated with either of the two means of assistance. On the other hand, if the son owes his father a "great deal" of gratitude, then either of the two means of assistance can satisfy the son's gratitude-based obligations. If, say, the son decides to place his father in a nursing home, and he pays the bills and visits his father frequently, it is doubtful that he shows "insufficient gratitude" to his father—even if he owes his father a "great deal" of gratitude and even if the father would prefer to live at home with the son. Generally, it is doubtful that specifiable differences in amounts of gratitude will correlate with different means of providing assistance to frail elderly parents.

An additional practical problem is the absence of a clear criterion for determining when adult children have discharged duties of gratitude. Suppose a middle-aged woman has looked after her mother since the mother became a widow ten years ago. The woman has spent time with her mother, provided emotional support, and has taken her shopping, to cultural events, on vacations, and so forth. If the woman owed her mother a great deal of gratitude ten years ago, there are no unambiguous criteria for determining whether she has already discharged her duty of gratitude to her mother, or whether, say, she would owe her mother additional assistance if her mother were to suffer a disabling stroke tomorrow. Moreover, if it is thought that the woman still owes her mother gratitude at the time of the stroke, and the woman decides to have her mother live with her, there is no clear standard for deciding if and when she will have discharged her duty of gratitude to her mother. Would it take one, two, five, or ten years for the duty to be discharged; or would it only be discharged when the mother dies? To what extent does the answer to this question depend on the mother's condition and the corresponding demands placed on the daughter? Is a duty of gratitude discharged sooner, say, if the parent is more impaired? If it is more burdensome, all things considered, to provide assistance to a parent in a child's home than in a nursing home, would it take longer to discharge a duty of gratitude to a parent who lives in a nursing home than to a parent who lives in a child's home? Unfortunately, questions such as these are unanswerable, and not only because of a lack of sufficient information. Rather, due to the indeterminacy of the relevant standards, such questions are unanswerable *in principle*.[45]

Due to the indeterminacy of duties of gratitude, it is generally not possible to identify specific gratitude-based obligations (claiming, for example, that someone has a gratitude-based obligation to care for his frail elderly mother in his home). Consequently, when people fail to make a certain sacrifice for a frail elderly parent, there are generally insufficient grounds for holding that they have failed to discharge a gratitude-based duty. Ironically, however, although the indeterminacy of duties of gratitude tends to remove a basis for attributing moral blame to adult children for failing to make a particular sacrifice, it can also give rise to the feeling that one has not done one's duty. In the absence of clear guidelines for determining when adult children have discharged their duties to frail elderly parents, the former may lack adequate assurance that they have done *enough*. Suppose, say, I recognize that there are insufficient grounds for concluding that I have a gratitude-based obligation to care for my mother in my home. Nevertheless, so long as I do not know whether I have shown a sufficient amount of gratitude to her, I might feel guilty for not caring for her in my home. To counteract unwarranted feelings to the effect that no matter what one does for parents, one has an obligation to do more, it is helpful to keep in mind that uncertainty is unavoidable in many cases, and that inability to demonstrate that one has discharged a duty of gratitude does not warrant the judgment that one has an obligation to do more.

Case Study: Caring for an Impaired Elderly Parent

When elderly parents become too frail to live on ther own, adult children are confronted with extremely difficult choices related to their care. On the one hand, there is the question of what is best for impaired parents. Would they, say, be better off living with their children, or would their needs be better satisfied in an institutional setting, such as a nursing home? On the other hand, there is a consideration of the interests of adult children. Whereas nursing home care is very costly, caring for an impaired elderly parent in one's home can be time-consuming and both physically and emotionally taxing. Weighing these considerations and interests can present difficult ethical dilemmas to adult children. One such dilemma—one variation on an all-too-common theme—is illustrated in the following case description.

Case Description

Sally S. is fifty-eight years old and lives in a medium-sized midwestern city. Her husband Edward died three years ago of cancer. His death was slow and painful. Ms. S. cared for her husband at home for more than a year before his death. Caring for her husband was both emotionally and physically draining, and it took Ms. S. almost a year to regain her physical and emotional strength.

Ms. S. has started to put her life back together again. For both practical and emotional reasons, she decided to sell the house that she shared with her husband for almost forty years, and she bought a small condominium apartment. She has developed a very close and satisfying relationship with Howard L., a 61-year-old widower, and they are seriously considering living together. In addition, Ms. S. has decided to go back to school. When she got married, she quit college to support her husband while he attended law school. Now that her three children are grown and living on their own, she feels that the time is right for her to resume her education.

Just when Ms. S. was beginning to feel good about her life and optimistic about the future, she was notified that her 79-year-old mother, Irma W., suffered a serious stroke. Ms. S.'s mother and father had moved to Florida about fifteen years ago when her father retired. When Ms. S.'s father died eight years ago, her mother decided to stay in the condominium apartment in Florida. Up until the time of the stroke, Ms. W. enjoyed relatively good health. Except for arthritis, her only health problems were anemia and malnutrition, primarily a result of poor eating habits. Ms. S.'s mother seemed to be managing quite well living alone. Although there were no close relatives in the area, she had several friends, mostly widows like herself, who lived in the same condominium complex. Thus, Ms. W. was not lonely, and she remained quite active.

However, after the stroke, Ms. W.'s condition deteriorated substantially. She could not walk, and the most optimistic prognosis was that she would be able to move about somewhat with the aid of a walker. She required assistance with eating, bathing, and going to the toilet, and the physicians who examined her held out little hope of any significant improvement in these areas. Her mental condition also deteriorated markedly. Whereas Ms. W. previously had been a very lively person, she seemed subdued and absent, as if she were in a continual trance or daze. She recognized her daughter and her friends, but other than giving short answers to questions, she was uncommunicative. Here, too, none of the physicians saw much hope for improvement.

It was clear that Ms. S.'s mother could no longer live alone. Dr. B., Ms. W.'s internist since she moved to Florida, advised Ms. S. to place her mother in a nursing home when she was released from the hospital. Her mother's assests would cover the cost of nursing home care for several years. But Ms. S. was convinced that her parents would not have made so many sacrifices to save for the future if they thought that their savings would eventually go to a nursing home. It was clear to her that her parents' willingness to save was motivated by a desire for happiness in their later years and by a desire to promote the welfare of their children and grandchildren. Hence Ms. S. was deeply troubled by the prospect of seeing her parents' assets used up to pay for nursing home care. However, Ms. S. was even more upset by the thought of, as she put it, "abandoning my mother and consigning her to a fate worse than death." She also recalled that her mother had repeatedly stated, "I do not want to wind up in a nursing home," and Ms. S. was reluctant to act against her mother's expressed wishes.

In discussing the situation with Mr. L., Ms. S. expressed her feeling that she had an obligation to care for her mother herself: "Given all that my mother did for me, it would be wrong for me to consign her to a nursing home for the rest of her life. I owe it to her to have her live with me and to take care of her myself."

"I admire your devotion to your mother, Sally," responded Mr. L., "but you have already paid your dues. After all, you took care of Edward and your children. Given all you've done for your family, and how much you suffered during Edward's illness, you have a right to think of yourself now. Think of the strain on our relationship if you were to assume the responsibility of caring for Irma, not to mention the impact on your plans to return to college. Put Irma in a nursing home and get on with your own life before it's too late, Sally."

Ms. S. was troubled by Mr. L.'s statement. On the one hand, she realized that there was a danger that she would allow her own life to slip away from her if she took on the responsibility of caring for her mother. On the other hand, she could not shake the feeling that she owed it to her mother to care for her, no matter what.

Case Analysis

Ms. S. assumes that placing her mother in a nursing home is an unacceptable alternative. As she put it, placing her mother in a nursing home would be tantamount to consigning her to "a fate worse then death." Many people— young and old alike—accept this evaluation of nursing homes, and it is understandable that they do. There have been widely publicized horror stories about abuse of residents (beatings, cruelty, maltreatment, and so forth) and numerous reports of inadequate services, overmedication, and patient neglect. Moreover, there is good reason to dread the boredom, apathy, loneliness, mental and physical deterioration, and loss of dignity that many associate with life in a nursing home. For many people, Hobbes's description of the "state of nature" as a condition in which life is "solitary, poor, nasty, brutish, and short," applies to nursing homes.[46]

To be sure, despite their extravagant cost, nursing homes are a far cry from luxury hotels. But there are significant differences among nursing homes that are obscured by commonly accepted negative generalizations. Thanks in part to widely publicized reports of abuse and neglect, efforts by consumer groups and other organizations, and increased oversight and regulation of the nursing home industry, abuse and neglect are not so widespread as they once were.[47] Accordingly, families can probably find nursing homes in which patients are not abused or neglected and whose staff are not incompetent, cruel, hostile, and/or apathetic. By visiting various facilities, families can compare staffs, services, programs, hygiene, food, physical plants, and so forth, and there are likely to be considerable differences. Thus, it is probably unwarranted for Ms. S. to assume that no matter where she would place her mother, putting her in a nursing home would consign her to a "fate worse than death."

It is also important to keep in mind that the perceived mental and physical conditions of nursing home residents can contribute to the impression that life in nursing homes is unbearable. Even if the physical plant is clean and cheerful, the staff is competent and attentive, and there are regular programs and activities for residents, people without serious mental or physical impairments may feel that the lives of nursing home residents are terrible. It is difficult to know what life is like to people who have lost many of their mental and physical capacities, or how they might be affected by the presence of other severely impaired persons. But one thing is clear: to some people with normal capacities, it is very disturbing to encounter others who are severely impaired and dependent and to think of becoming such a person.

Accordingly, it is important to distinguish between the view that nursing homes are *horrible places to live* and the view that *people with horrible (medical) conditions* live in nursing homes. Not all nursing homes are horrible places, but even with respect to those that are not, it might be thought that due to residents' impairments and dependency, their lives are unbearable. But if disability and dependency are the bases for concluding that residents' lives are terrible, then it follows that their lives will also be terrible if they live with their children. If impairment and dependency make life terrible, then it is true that Ms. W.'s life would be terrible if she were to live in a nursing home. But in this view, her life would also be terrible if she were to live with her daughter.

Ms. W.'s statement that she did not want to "wind up in a nursing home," may have had more to do with the (medical) conditions of nursing home residents than with (physical) conditions in nursing homes. It may prove helpful to compare the following statements: (1) "I never want to wind up in a nursing home"; (2) "I never want to wind up in prison." In the latter case, the statement undoubtedly expresses an aversion to the effects of the institution (prison): loss of freedom, isolation from friends and family, boredom, danger, poor living conditions, and so forth. Thus, the statement focuses on changes in living conditions that follow institutionalization (imprisonment) rather than on changes in the person that precede incarceration (becoming a criminal). By contrast, the first statement in part expresses a fear of changes in the person that precede and occasion institutionalization: dependency and loss of mental and physical capacities. Thus, when Ms. W. stated that she did not want to "wind up in a nursing home," it may not be warranted for her daughter to assume that she intended the following: "If I become dependent on others because of impaired mental and physical functioning, I want to be cared for in a setting other than a nursing home." She may have had no specific thoughts or preferences about *where* and *by whom* care should be provided. Instead, she may have been expressing her aversion to becoming a severely impaired person requiring constant care and supervision. Consequently, it is not warranted for Ms. S. to assume that she would be following her mother's wishes if and only if she were to have her mother live with her.

It may also be unwarranted for Ms. S. to assume that her mother will be much better off if her mother were to live with her. Although it is natural to think that a severely impaired parent's life and the care he or she receives will be far superior in the home of a son or daughter than in a nursing home, this assumption may be unrealistic. For one thing, the parent's mental condition can significantly reduce the gap that is thought to exist between receiving care in a child's home and nursing home care. A parent's mental condition may be so poor that there is little, if any, opportunity for meaningful communication with anyone, including children; and from the perspective of a severely demented parent, there may be little difference between care provided by a child and care provided by a nurse or aide in a nursing home. Thus, Ms. S. may be attributing much more importance to her presence and to her personal involvement with her mother's day-to-day care than is warranted. Depending on the extent of Ms. W.'s mental deterioration, it may also mean little to her to be in the more or less familiar setting of her daughter's house.

Another factor to consider is the quality of the treatment and care that Ms. W. is likely to receive. Ms. S. did care for her husband, but in contrast to nursing home staff, she has had no experience caring for elderly people in her mother's condition, and she lacks special training in the care of impaired elderly persons. Thus, if Ms. S. is troubled by the thought that nursing home staff are undertrained, she should keep her own limitations in mind. In addition to experience and training, personal and psychological factors also need to be considered. It is natural to distinguish the impersonal care that is provided by a nurse or aide to the personal care that is provided by a son or daughter. However, in drawing this contrast, there may be a tendency to idealize the child-parent relationship. "Impersonal care" may be preferable to care provided, say, by a daughter who has felt rejected by her mother, or by a son who has frequently argued with his father. But even in cases where there is a good relationship between parent and child, the pressures of caring for a severely impaired parent can exact a very high emotional toll. Love can be clouded by resentment, compassion can be overshadowed by an overwhelming sense of being "trapped," and so forth, and these feelings can have a negative impact on the quality of the relationship and the quality of care.

An additional factor to consider is the quality of the environment, including stimulation and opportunities for activity. Better nursing homes have special programs and activities designed to keep residents active and involved, and to provide an appropriate environment for severely impaired elderly persons. By contrast, it is all too easy for family members to ignore frail elderly parents living with them and to fail to provide adequate stimulation or to make special efforts to keep them as active as possible. It might be more meaningful to an impaired elderly person, say, to play bingo or to participate in a sing-along in a nursing home than to sit in a child's home being ignored while everyone else goes about their business. For all of these reasons, then, it is unwarranted for Ms. S. to assume that her mother's care and quality of life will be far superior if her mother lives with her. To be sure, "dumping" frail parents in substandard nursing homes is hardly compatible with care and concern. But adult children who carefully select nursing homes, regularly visit parents, and look after their needs and interests, can hardly be accused of "dumping" them.

Nevertheless, even if Ms. S. has made an informed and realistic comparison of nursing home versus home care, she may continue to feel that if she were to place her mother in a nursing home, she would not be doing "enough" for her. People have differing conceptions of what they should do for parents and loved ones and how much they should be willing to sacrifice for them. Whereas Ms. S. might believe that a "good" or "loving" daughter should never place her mother in a nursing home, other people (such as Mr. L. or her children) might disagree, and the disagreement might be attributable to differing conceptions of "good" or "loving" children rather than to differing assessments of the benefits and burdens of in-home versus nursing home care. Since there is unlikely to be a convincing argument showing that one of these differing conceptions is better than all the others, none provides a common standard for making and evaluating decisions concerning the care of impaired elderly parents. Accordingly, if Ms. S. believes that a good daughter should not place her mother in a nursing home, it may not be appropriate to ask whether she is "right" or "wrong"; and if Mr. L. or Ms. S.'s children disagree, it may not be appropriate to ask who is "right."

However, Ms. S. appears to have another reason for thinking that she would not be doing "enough" for her mother if she were to place her in a nursing home. She did state a belief that in view of all that her mother did for her, "I owe it to her to have her live with me and to take care of her." This statement is subject to ethical analysis, and duties of gratitude provide the most plausible ethical basis for claims along these lines. Accordingly, an important question to consider is whether it is plausible to claim that Ms. S. owes her mother a duty of gratitude that will be discharged if and only if Ms. S. cares for her mother in Ms. S.'s home.

Duties of gratitude are far too vague and indeterminate to allow specific judgments about the nature of care that is owed frail elderly parents. To specify what Ms. S. owes her mother out of gratitude, one would have to determine the amount of gratitude that Ms. S. still owes her mother. However, there is no precise measure of gratitude owed. At most, one can make impressionistic qualitative judgments, for example: "Ms. S. owes her mother only a little gratitude." "Ms. S. owes her mother a great deal of gratitude." Moreover, even if Ms. S. owed her mother a great deal of gratitude for all that her mother did for her, she already may have shown a lot of gratitude to her mother. For example, Ms. S. may have provided considerable assistance and emotional support for her mother after her father's death. Would such significant displays of gratitude in the past reduce the amount of gratitude that Ms. S. currently owes her mother; and if so, by how much? There are no determinate answers to such questions.

Would Ms. S. be expressing more gratitude by having her mother live with her than by placing her in a nursing home; and if so, how much more?

Presumably, the degree of sacrifice required would be a significant consideration, but considerable sacrifices can be involved in either case. To be sure, if Ms. S. were to place her mother in a nursing home and effectively abandon her there, she would be displaying an unwillingness to make any major sacrifices for her mother. But the same could not be said if she were to spend a lot of time with her mother, and if she were to take pains to ensure that Ms. W. received proper care in the home.

Let us suppose, however, that more sacrifices would be required of Ms. S. if she were to have her mother live with her than if she were to place her in a nursing home. In determining the amount of gratitude expressed, other factors are relevant. For example, it seems plausible to hold that, other things being equal, when sacrifices are performed reluctantly and grudgingly, they demonstrate less gratitude. Suppose, then, that more sacrifices would be required if Ms. S.'s mother were to live with her, but that these sacrifices would be made reluctantly and grudgingly. Further, suppose that fewer sacrifices would be required if Ms. S. were to place her mother in a nursing home, but that she would make them lovingly and without a trace of resentment. Ms. S's attitude is probably relevant, but its significance compared to the amount of sacrifice is unclear. Lacking a determinate standard, comparing attitudes and amount of sacrifice is a little like comparing apples and oranges.

Another relevant factor in determining how much gratitude Ms. S. displays toward her mother is the impact of her actions on her mother's welfare. Suppose, for example, that Ms. W. would be better off in a nursing home. It would be odd to say that since Ms. S. would have to make more sacrifices if she were to care for her mother at home, she would be expressing more gratitude toward her mother by caring for her at home.

For all these reasons, it is doubtful that considerations of gratitude support the conclusion that Ms. S. owes it to her mother to care for her at home. Suppose, say, that Ms. S. still owes her mother a "great deal" of gratitude. Although having an impaired elderly parent live in one's home can express a great deal of gratitude, considerable gratitude can also be shown to parents who reside in a nursing home. Moreover, even if it is assumed that Ms. S. would be expressing more gratitude if she were to have her mother live with her, it is impossible to specify how much more, or to correlate this difference with a specifiable difference in gratitude owed. Consequently, no matter how much gratitude Ms. S. owes her mother, there appears to be no basis for concluding that Ms. S. would be expressing "insufficient" gratitude to her mother if she were to place her in a nursing home. On the other hand, due to the indeterminacy and open-endedness of duties of gratitude, it may not be possible to assure Ms. S. that she would be expressing "sufficient" gratitude toward her mother if she were to place her in a nursing home.

Notes

1. See Bernice L. Neugarten, "Social and Psychological Characteristics of Older Persons," in Christine K. Cassel et al., eds., *Geriatric Medicine,* 2d ed. (New York: Springer-Verlag, 1990), 28–37.

2. One estimate is that 22.9 percent of elderly persons aged sixty-five and older are "functionally disabled." See Pamela Doty, "Family Care of the Elderly: The Role of the Public Policy," *Milbank Quarterly* 64, no. 1 (1986): 34–75. Data from the 1990 National Health Interview Survey indicate that 37.5 percent of individuals sixty-five and older have some limitations of activity caused by chronic conditions; and 10.2 percent of people sixty-five and older are unable to carry on "major activity" such as work and housekeeping. U.S. Department of Health and Human Services, *Vital and Health Statistics: Current Estimates from the National Health Survey, 1990,* Series 10: Data from the National Health Survey, no. 181 (Hyattsville, Md.: DHHS, Publication No. [PHS] 92-1509, December 1991), 106.

3. A few examples include Norman Daniels, *Am I My Parents' Keeper? An Essay on Justice Between the Young and the Old* (New York: Oxford University Press, 1988); Daniel Callahan, *Setting Limits: Medical Goals in an Aging Society* (New York: Simon and Schuster, 1987); Philip Longman, *Born to Pay: The New Politics of Aging in America* (Boston: Houghton Mifflin, 1987); and Harry R. Moody, "Generational Equity and Social Insurance," *Journal of Medicine and Philosophy* 13 (1988): 31–56.

4. Many studies that challenge the myth of abandonment are cited in Doty, "Family Care of the Elderly." The term "myth of abandonment," is used by Ethel Shanas and Elaine Brody. See Ethel Shanas, "The Family as Support System in Old Age," *The Gerontologist* 19 (1979): 169–74; and Elaine Brody, "Women in the Middle," *The Gerontologist* 21 (1981): 471–80.

5. D. L. Frankfather, M. J. Smith, and F. G. Caro, *Family Care of the Elderly* (Lexington, Mass.: Lexington Books, 1981), 6; cited in Daniels, *Am I My Parents' Keeper,* 25.

6. For a discussion of the general obligation of beneficence, see Tom L. Beauchamp and James F. Childress, *Principles of Biomedical Ethics,* 3d ed. (New York: Oxford University Press, 1989), chapter 5. According to Kagan, "ordinary morality" incorporates "agent-centered options," which reflect the principle that people are not always required to promote the overall good at the expense of their own interests. From the perspective of ordinary morality, helping others when substantial sacrifices would be required is ethically *optional.* For a discussion and critique of this and other features of ordinary morality, see Shelly Kagan, *The Limits of Morality* (Oxford: Clarendon, 1989).

7. See Doty, "Family Care of the Elderly."

8. Callahan, *Setting Limits,* chapter 4.

9. *Setting Limits,* 103 and 93ff. Although Callahan unequivocally claims that adult children have a duty to make sacrifices for frail elderly parents insofar as the latter "require (or at least desperately want) family care," he is much less clear about the nature and extent of the sacrifices that adult children have a duty to make. In a later essay, he suggests that "heroic self-sacrifice" may be needed to meet the needs of frail elderly family members. Such sacrifice, he claims, "is only possible if understood within the context of an entire way of life, and a way of life set ultimately within some scheme of religious or higher meaning." Daniel Callahan, "Families as Caregivers: The Limits of Morality," in Nancy S. Jecker, ed., *Aging and Ethics: Philosophical Problems in Gerontology* (Clifton, N.J.: Humana, 1991), 155–70.

10. Callahan, *Setting Limits,* 100.

11. When he critically examines English's claim that the obligations of adult children toward their parents are based on friendship, Callahan expresses considerable skepticism

about the existence of strong emotional ties between elderly parents and their adult children: "Friendship can certainly exist between parent and child, but it often does not. They may come to have little in common other than their biological relationship" (*Setting Limits,* 90). English's analysis of filial obligations will be examined below.

12. See Doty, "Family Care of the Elderly."

13. See Beauchamp and Childress, *Principles of Biomedical Ethics,* chapter 5.

14. Rule utilitarianism (the view that ethical decisions and judgments are to be based on rules, the following of which maximizes overall utility or good) might provide an additional basis for filial obligations. Assigning special responsibilities for providing assistance to impaired elderly persons to their adult children, it might be claimed, tends to promote the general welfare. This claim is controversial in at least two important respects. First, since it is doubtful that there is sufficient empirical evidence to confirm the claim, it is based on controversial empirical assumptions. Second, rule utilitarianism itself is a controversial ethical theory.

15. See, for example, Alasdair MacIntyre, *After Virtue: A Study in Moral Theory* (Notre Dame: University of Notre Dame Press, 1981). Hoff Sommers uses the specific issue of filial obligations to support her critique of "impartial" ethical principles. Christina Hoff Sommers, "Filial Morality," *Journal of Philosophy* 83, no. 8 (August 1986): 439–56. Hoff Sommers claims that a key element in modern ethical theories, including such divergent theories as utilitarianism and Kantian ethics, is a principle of impartiality. This principle is said to entail a view she refers to as the "equal pull (EP) thesis," according to which the moral domain is "a domain of moral patients exerting uniform pull on all moral agents" (444). Hoff Sommers defends the "thesis of differential pull (DP)," according to which "the ethical pull of a moral patient will always partly depend on how the moral patient is related to the moral agent on whom the pull is exerted . . . [and] the 'how' of relatedness will be determined in part by the social practices and institutions in which the agent and patient play their roles" (445). In contrast to EP, DP "recognizes the crucial role of conventional practice, relationships, and roles in determining the nature and force of moral obligation" (445). Only DP morality, Hoff Sommers claims, can provide an adequate account of filial obligations and other special duties.

Modern ethical theories do not necessarily deny that relationships to others can have ethical significance. For example, if acceptance of a rule that requires adult children to do more for their parents than for strangers would tend to promote the general welfare, then rule utilitarianism provides the basis for special obligations on the part of adult children toward their parents. However, in contrast to DP morality, the rule would be derived from an *impartial* principle: the principle of utility, according to which everyone's interests or preferences are given equal weight when attempting to maximize the general welfare. In the case of DP morality, on the other hand, special concern is associated with particular social conventions, and is not derived from general impartial principles.

16. Hoff Sommers, "Filial Morality," 448. Hoff Sommers speaks generally of "filial obligation." Presumably her observation is meant to apply to the United States in particular.

In *Am I My Parents' Keeper?* Daniels uses the term "traditionalist" in a more specific sense. As he uses the term, a "traditionalist" believes both that we should turn to the past to discover what adult children should do for their aging parents today, and that in the past, it was accepted practice for adult children to care for their aging parents. Daniels claims that "the central element in the Traditionalist vision, the appeal to a Golden Age of family responsibility, is an appeal to a myth rather than a social history we share" (28). He also asserts that "a diversity in current beliefs" concerning the scope of filial obligations is "a fact of our social life" (35).

17. Even if participants cannot transcend all cultural norms, insofar as their culture recognizes general ethical principles, they can utilize those principles to assess particular norms and social practices. If general principles fail to provide a basis for conventional expectations, then there is a danger that too much is demanded of adult children; and if conventional expectations fall short of the requirements of ethical principles, there is reason to conclude that too little is asked of adult children.

18. In this respect, traditionalism appears to entail ethical relativism. Hoff Sommers claims that ethical relativism can be avoided "by adopting a deontological principle (noninterference) which may be deployed in assessing and criticizing the moral legitimacy of the traditional arrangements within which purportedly moral interactions take place" ("Filial Morality," 452–53). This statement suggests that a noninterference principle has the status of an independent standard for assessing various social arrangements. However, the status of that principle as an independent standard is called into question by Hoff Sommers's view that its specific content is determined in part by social practices and conventions. According to Hoff Sommers, "the universal deontological principle [of noninterference] is differentiated and specified by local arrangements that determine what is legitimately expected of the moral agent" (453). To the extent that the legitimate expectations that the noninterference principle protects are a function of "local arrangements," that principle does not serve as an independent standard to assess those arrangements. Suppose, say, that "local arrangements" include slavery. If social practices determine the content of the noninterference principle, then it is hard to see how that principle could be used to challenge the institution of slavery. Whereas slave owners would not be interfering with the "legitimate interests" of slaves, slaves who run away would be interfering with the "legitimate interests" of slave owners. Thus, it would appear to follow that slaves who violate the rules, and not slave owners, would violate the principle of noninterference.

19. Jane English, "What Do Grown Children Owe Their Parents?" in Onora O'Neill and William Ruddick, eds., *Having Children: Philosophical and Legal Reflections on Parenthood* (New York: Oxford University Press, 1979), 354. English's important essay is reprinted in Jecker, ed., *Aging and Ethics.*

20. English, "What Do Grown Children Owe Their Parents?" 351; emphasis added. The complete sentence reads as follows: "The duties of grown children are those of friends and result from love between them and their parents, rather than being things owed in repayment for the parents' earlier sacrifices." In her essay, English defends the view that the *current* relationship of friendship between elderly parent and adult child gives rise to the latter's obligations toward the former, and she criticizes the view that those obligations are based on *past* parental sacrifices. The latter view will be examined below.

Hoff Sommers classifies English as a "sentimentalist." She utilizes Gilligan's distinction between an "ethic of rights" and an "ethic of care" to explicate sentimentalism. As she puts it, sentimentalists object to "the aridity of the 'rights perspective' and are urging moral philosophers to attend to the morality of special relations from a 'care perspective'" ("Filial Morality," 448–49). From the perspective of sentimentalism, according to Hoff Sommers, family relationships are "spontaneous, voluntary, and *duty-free*" (450; emphasis added). English's account does exhibit important features of an "ethic of care." However, since she accepts the view that parents and children have moral obligations, it is mistaken to classify her as a "sentimentalist." As we shall see below, English rejects the "owing" idiom, but she does not reject the language of "obligation" in the context of the parent-child relationship. Sommers also mistakenly classifies Simmons and Blustein, whose views will be discussed below, as sentimentalists.

21. English, "What Do Grown Children Owe Their Parents?" 355.

22. Both Callahan (*Setting Limits,* 90) and Daniels (*Am I My Parents' Keeper?* 32) observe that adult children and their parents are not always friends.

23. English suggests that friendship/love is the *exclusive* source of filial obligations.

24. One or more of these objections can be found in English, "What Do Grown Children Owe Their Parents?"; Callahan, *Setting Limits;* and Daniels, *Am I My Parents' Keeper?*

25. English contrasts duties based on past favors with duties of friendship. She argues that the duties of adult children are duties of (ongoing) friendship, not duties based on favors performed by parents in the past. Favors, according to English, involve requests: "I will call this a *favor:* when A, *at B's request,* bears some burden for B, then B incurs an obligation to reciprocate" ("What Do Grown Children Owe Their Parents?" 352; second emphasis added). Although the "when . . . , then" conditional does not appear to have the structure of a definition, the beginning phrase, "I will call this a *favor,"* suggests that English is offering a definition of a favor and that responding to a request is part of that definition. At another point, English states that "[*u*]*nrequested* sacrifices do not themselves create debts" (354).

26. According to English, "friends are *motivated* by love rather than by the prospect of repayment" ("What Do Grown Children Owe Their Parents? 353; emphasis added). According to Daniels, "much that parents do for children is done because parents unconditionally want good things for their children. They love them and have expectations about how they want their children to grow up. Doing good things for children is one of a parent's projects in life that makes life meaningful—for the parent. Such actions are not mere favors and do not give rise to debts on the part of children" (*Am I My Parents' Keeper?* 31).

27. As Daniels puts it, "if someone has a duty or obligation to provide me with some good, I do not thereby incur an obligation to return the good or its equivalent. . . . We are obliged to reciprocate good favors done for us, not goods owed us" (*Am I My Parents' Keeper?* 30–31). Daniels carefully limits his claim to a narrowly defined duty to *reciprocate* (that is, a duty "to return the good or its equivalent"). To anticipate a distinction to be introduced below, it follows only that discharging parental duties cannot generate duties of *indebtedness.* It does *not* follow that discharging parental duties cannot generate duties of *gratitude.*

Unlike Daniels, Callahan explicitly considers gratitude. According to Callahan: "Gratitude may be due not simply because the parents discharged their obligations toward their children, but because in their manner of doing so they went beyond the demands of mere duty, giving voluntarily of themselves in a way neither required nor ordinarily expected of them. . . . [G]ratitude is ordinarily thought due only when, as noted above, a benefactor has gone beyond ordinary duties" (*Setting Limits,* 90–91). The reference to "ordinary duties" is ambiguous. Are these ordinary duties of *parents,* or are these ordinary duties of *people generally?* The significance of this distinction will be examined below.

28. In the following passage, Callahan appears to adopt such a view: "If the procreation and physical rearing of a child does not automatically entail reciprocal duties toward the parents when they are needy and dependent, it is certainly possible to imagine a sense of obligation arising when parents have done far more for children than would morally be required of them. My own parents, for example, did not drop me when I reached eighteen. They sacrificed a good deal to provide me with a higher education, and in fact provided financial support for my graduate education until I was thirty, topping that off by giving my wife and me a down payment on our first house" (*Setting Limits,* 93). It was said that Callahan *appears* to adopt the view described above, because the qualifiers in the first sentence make it difficult to pin down his position. The passage begins with a conditional ("if"); it refers to a psychological concept ("a *sense* of obligation") rather than to the

existence of an actual duty; the thrust of the qualifier "automatically" is unclear; and we are only told that this sense of obligation is "possible to imagine."

29. Simmons claims that gratitude can be owed to those who discharge duties of benefi-cence: "[T]he most common sorts of cases in which considerations of gratitude are involved are precisely cases where the benefactor has a duty to grant the benefits in question. . . . In helping someone in need, we will normally be doing our duty (although we may of course do more than our duty, or less than our duty): the duty to help those in need. But these seem to be just the sorts of cases in which we think a debt of gratitude is owed to the benefactor." A. John Simmons, *Moral Principles and Political Obligations* (Princeton: Princeton University Press, 1979), 179.

Simmons supports the claim that gratitude can be owed to those who discharge duties of beneficence with the following example: "Suppose that I am driving through the country and come upon an accident victim. I am a medical student and know that if he does not reach a hospital in twenty minutes, he will die. But I also know that the only hospital in the area is twenty miles away over rough back roads. So I drive the victim at sixty miles an hour over rough roads in my brand new Porsche, saving his life and damaging its suspension" (179). Simmons makes three claims about this example: (1) the Porsche owner had a *duty* to save the accident victim and incur damage to his car; (2) the accident victim has an obligation to compensate the Porsche owner for the damage to his car; (3) it is possible to "explain this [the latter] obligation only in terms of gratitude" (180). The first and second claims strike me as plausible, but the third claim does not. Considerations of (compensatory) justice that have nothing to do with gratitude can explain the obligation to compensate the owner of the Porsche. Indeed, it seems odd to claim that paying to have the car fixed is an expression of *gratitude*. Rather, compensating the Porsche owner for the damage to his car seems compara-ble to paying for damages when someone is responsible for an accident. Thus, insofar as the accident victim owes the Porsche owner *gratitude*, the former owes the latter more than compensation for damages to the car.

30. Although Simmons rejects the general view that one cannot generate debts of grati-tude by merely fulfilling one's duties, he claims that the "particular duty-meeting conduct [of parents] does *not* generate an obligation of gratitude on the child" (*Moral Principles and Political Obligations*, 182). Simmons's reasoning is as follows. Duties require specific *ac-tions*. It does not make sense to speak of a duty to have a particular *feeling*. Consequently, whereas the parental duty to care for children includes the provision of certain goods, ser-vices, opportunities, and the like, the duty to care for children "cannot be a duty to love them, to 'care for them' in the full sense, or to provide the goods for children which depend on having such feelings" (183). But, Simmons argues, "when parents do *not* do these things, when they do not provide the benefits of warm and affectionate care which are only possible when the parent *feels* in certain ways, we believe, I think, that *no* gratitude is owed them for the care they give their children" (183). This is not the place to evaluate the claim that it is illegitimate to speak of duties to have certain feelings. Putting this particular issue aside, however, Simmons's argument can be challenged on the following grounds. First, even if it is improper to speak of a direct duty to *have* certain feelings, it can still be legitimate to speak of a parent's duty to *perform actions* that, as Simmons puts it, "are only possible when the parent feels in certain ways." Second, it is far from obvious that the scope of parental duties does not include providing "the benefits of warm and affectionate care." At the very least, the scope of parental duties is considerably more fuzzy in this regard than Simmons appears to assume. Third, it is questionable whether *no* gratitude is owed to parents who made substan-tial sacrifices for their children and who were responsible, but more or less distant and unaffectionate. Other things being equal, *more* gratitude may be owed to parents who were

warm and affectionate, but it is doubtful that warmth and affection are generally recognized necessary conditions of *any* gratitude. Not too long ago, it was thought that fathers were supposed to provide financial support, discipline, and practical guidance, but not warmth and affection. However, it is doubtful that fathers were thought to be owed no gratitude from their children.

31. Berger suggests that parents are owed gratitude by children *only if* their sacrifices were motivated by love and a concern for the well-being of children. Fred Berger, "Gratitude," *Ethics* 85 (1975): 298–309. There may be an additional reason for gratitude, or a reason for additional gratitude, in such circumstances. But, provided parental sacrifices were not made too begrudgingly, it is doubtful that no gratitude is owed to parents who were motivated primarily by a desire to "do their duty." However, Berger may well be right to claim that no gratitude is owed to parents who fulfilled their responsibilities "solely for selfish reasons such as keeping up the family name or social standing" (300).

32. An argument along these lines is presented by English. Although she agrees that "there are many things that children *ought* to do for their parents," she holds that "it is inappropriate and misleading to describe them as things 'owed' " ("What Do Grown Children Owe Their Parents?" 351).

33. In the following passage, English appears to advance an argument along these lines: "The quantity of parental sacrifice is not relevant in determining what duties the grown child has. The medical assistance children ought to offer their ill mothers in old age depends upon the mothers' need, not upon whether they endured a difficult pregnancy, for example. Nor do one's duties to one's parents cease once an equal quantity of sacrifice has been performed, as the phrase, 'discharging a debt' may lead us to think ("What Do Grown Children Owe Their Parents? 354). English is probably correct to claim that the amount of assistance a grown child should give her ill mother is not related to the difficulty of the mother's pregnancy. However, it does not follow that the quantity of parental sacrifice *never* has any bearing on what adult children should do for impaired elderly parents. Suppose, for example, that Ms. S. and Ms. F. are women in their forties who have mothers who are eighty. Ms. S.'s mother's pregnancy was very difficult and Ms. F.'s mother's pregnancy was very easy. Both mothers were responsible parents, but whereas Ms. F.'s mother did the bare minimum for her daughter, Ms. S.'s mother consistently put her daughter's interests and happiness above her own, sacrificing career, material benefits, opportunities for travel, and so forth. Ms. S. can consistently (1) acknowledge that the relative difficulty of her mother's pregnancy does not imply that she owes her mother more than Ms. F. owes her mother, and (2) hold that since her mother did so much more to promote her welfare and happiness than Ms. F.'s mother did to promote Ms. F.'s welfare and happiness, she owes her mother more than Ms. F. owes her mother. Thus the observation that there is no connection between the difficulty of a pregnancy and the content and strength of an adult child's duties fails to support the conclusion that the obligations of adult children are totally unrelated to how much parents did for them.

34. For a discussion of the distinction between duties of indebtedness and duties of gratitude, see Jeffrey Blustein, *Parents and Children: The Ethics of the Family* (New York: Oxford University Press, 1982), 175–86. Feinberg prefers the expression "duties of reciprocation" to "duties of gratitude." Joel Feinberg, "Duties, Rights, and Claims," *American Philosophical Quarterly* 3 (1966): 137–44. According to Feinberg, "gratitude, a feeling, is a less appropriate subject for duty than reciprocation, which is, after all, action" (139). However, as we have seen, Daniels assumes that a duty to reciprocate implies "an obligation to return the good or its equivalent," a characteristic of duties of indebtedness. In order to avoid this association, "duties of gratitude" will be used instead of "duties of reciprocation," with

the proviso that the duty requires *actions* (that is, actions that express gratitude), not feelings (that is, feelings of gratitude).

Gratitude may also be construed as a *virtue*. The characteristics of virtuous adult children is a topic that may merit exploration, but the focus of this chapter is on the *duties* of adult children. Accordingly, the question to be pursued here is whether duties of gratitude can be a significant basis of filial obligations that are generated by past parental sacrifices.

35. Simmons argues that an "equal return" requirement in relation to gratitude is "implausible." He claims that "the limits which the value of the benefit received places on the debt generated seem to be very vague indeed" (*Moral Principles and Political Obligations*, 169).

36. Simmons refers to "the 'vagueness' of the content of debts of gratitude" (*Moral Principles and Political Obligations*, 185).

37. English appears to assume that if adult children owe their parents anything for past sacrifices, then the relevant duties are duties of indebtedness. Parental sacrifices could generate duties of indebtedness if they were *favors*, but, English argues, it is generally mistaken to construe parental sacrifices as favors. English fails to consider other possible sources of indebtedness. More important, she fails to consider whether parental sacrifices generate duties of *gratitude*. It is instructive to compare English's claim that "what children ought to do for their parents . . . depends upon . . . their respective needs, abilities, and resources" ("What Do Grown Children Owe Their Parents?" 354) with Simmons's observation that the requirements of gratitude depend on "the needs of the original benefactor and the position of the original beneficiary" (*Moral Principles and Political Obligations*, 168).

38. See Blustein, *Parents and Children*, 180–81 and 183–84.

39. As noted above, Daniels's claim that obligatory parental sacrifices do not generate duties on the part of children is limited to duties of indebtedness. Daniels claims that we do not owe people who benefit us *equivalent* goods or services when they had a duty to benefit us. Accordingly, obligatory parental sacrifices cannot generate duties of *indebtedness*. However, since duties of gratitude do not require strict reciprocity (that is, that the beneficiary "return the good or its equivalent"), even if Daniels is right, it does not follow that adult children owe their parents no gratitude for doing their duty.

40. Berger claims that in view of the nature of parental sacrifices, "verbal expressions" of gratitude to parents are generally insufficient ("Gratitude," 303).

41. This feature of duties of gratitude further distinguishes them from duties of indebtedness. Suppose I give Clark a $2000 interest-free loan that is payable in six months. If I fall on hard times and need more than $2000 when it is time for Clark to repay me, Clark's debt is still only $2000. However, Clark might owe me more than repayment of the loan because he has a duty of *gratitude* in addition to a duty of indebtedness toward me. On the other hand, if Clark were also to fall on hard times, although his debt would not be canceled, it would be less plausible to claim that he has an obligation to help me out of gratitude.

42. Feinberg, "Duties, Rights, and Claims," 139.

43. By contrast, consider the duty of indebtedness that is generated when A gives B a $500 interest-free loan. No matter how much or how little $500 may be worth to B, and no matter how much time and effort it may have taken A to make $500, B owes A a $500 debt. Moreover, even if A loaned the money to B exclusively out of self-interest, B would still owe A a debt of $500. On the other hand, if making the money and/or the loan required a considerable sacrifice on the part of A, if it was very important to B to get the loan, and if A acted out of benevolent motives (such as a desire to help B), then in addition to the $500 debt, B may owe A considerable gratitude.

44. There may also be "counterfactual" or "hypothetical" obligations. For example, although I did not have polio as a child, since my mother would have been willing to make substantial sacrifices to help me if I did, it might be claimed that I should be willing to make substantial sacrifices for her if she were to develop Alzheimer's. If there are such obligations, they cannot plausibly be construed as duties (of gratitude) that are generated by (actual) past parental sacrifices, and they are therefore beyond the scope of this discussion.

45. Daniels holds that filial obligations generally are indeterminate (*Am I My Parents' Keeper?* chapter 2). According to Daniels, there is a "diversity in current beliefs" about the nature and scope of filial obligations, and the indeterminacy to which he refers reflects his skepticism concerning the feasibility of showing that one conception of filial obligations is preferable to the others. However, duties of gratitude are indeterminate in a sense unrelated to an inability to defend one conception of gratitude over competing conceptions. Rather, the *concept* of gratitude is indeterminate in important respects. That is, insofar as they are conceptions of gratitude, *all* such conceptions will display the indeterminacy discussed above. The notions of love and friendship appear to exhibit the type of indeterminacy to which Daniels refers. Since people have significantly different conceptions of love and friendship, there is no common standard for making intersubjective judgments about the requirements of love and friendship. Whereas one conception of love and friendship might provide the basis for one set of obligations and/or virtues, another conception might provide the basis for a significantly different set of obligations and/or virtues, and it is questionable whether a decisive case can be made for *one* conception over all the others.

46. Thomas Hobbes, *Leviathan* (Indianapolis, Ind.: Bobbs-Merrill, 1958), part 1, chapter 13, 107.

47. Reports of abuse and neglect in the 1960s and 1970s prompted increased federal and local regulation of nursing homes. Consistent with its general commitment to de-regulation, in 1981 the Reagan administration proposed to weaken or repeal many of the federal rules pertaining to nursing homes. The administration's plan provoked considerable opposition, and the Department of Health and Human Services asked the National Academy of Sciences for a study of nursing homes. The 1986 academy report was critical of conditions in many nursing homes, and it fueled efforts to strengthen nursing home regulations. In 1987 Congress passed legislation that identified several rights of nursing home residents, set standards for the training of nurse's aides, and spelled out a number of other rather specific requirements and penalties for lack of compliance. See "New Law Protects Rights of Patients in Nursing Homes," *New York Times,* January 15, 1988, p. A1.

Index